SPARROWS OF SENEGAMBIA

To Dave

Best Wishes

SPARROWS OF SENEGAMBIA

A Memoir

CHARLES SAMPSON, PhD

ReadersMagnet, LLC

Sparrows of Senegambia: A Memoir

Published in the United States of America
ISBN Paperback: 978-1-955603-65-2
ISBN Hardback: 978-1-955603-66-9
ISBN eBook: 978-1-955603-64-5

ReadersMagnet, LLC
10620 Treena Street, Suite 230 | San Diego, California, 92131 USA
1.619. 354. 2643 | www.readersmagnet.com

Cover design by Ericka Obando
Interior design by Mary Mae Romero

Contents

Preface vii
Acknowledgements ix
Prologue xi

Chapter I — My genesis lies in the gore of Goree Island 1
Chapter II — Life experiences, work-related travel, and my childhood tapes 39
Chapter III — The US Census, a path to connect my earthly origins 101
Chapter IV — The first generation 114
Chapter V — Tracing the history of the second Sampson generation 133
Chapter VI — The third generation 150
Chapter VII — Family ethos and core values 173
Chapter VIII — Growing up in the "Free State of Jones": ... 195
Chapter IX — The fourth generation: my childhood and my siblings 226
Chapter X — Becoming "Joe College" 261
Chapter XI — Meeting the rest of the Pulley family 301
Chapter XII — Post-baccalaureate life, marriage, and the USAF 307
Chapter XIII — Graduate school and parenthood 318
Chapter XIV — The professoriate, academia, and bureaucratic politics 340

Chapter XV My earthly resurrection:
rising like a phoenix from the ashes 357
Chapter XVI Reconsidering life in the gap 420

Epilogue 453
References. 465

Preface

This memoir connects my birthplace, life, work, educational experiences, and travels in more than a dozen countries on the African continent, places in South America, and several states in the Southern and Midwestern United States, as well as my travels to Europe and Southeast Asia, including Thailand, the Cambodian and Laotian borders, and Indonesia. My 2005 trip to Senegal was the beginning of my knowledge of Senegambia, the historical name of a geographical region in West Africa. The Senegambia region, now no longer recognized by that name, was located where the present-day West African countries of Senegal and the Gambia exist today. My trip to the West African slave port of Goree Island in Senegal opened my eyes to the significance of Senegambia. My life and work experiences caused me to compare my American family to the sparrows; birds that symbolize power in spite of their small size, they represent hard work, diligence, productivity, and persistence. The flight of the sparrow allows it to rise above circumstances of reality, doom, and dismay.

My reflections shape my version of **my** family history, as seen through my interpretation of six generations of American experiences. I believe it is fair to say that I have extensively researched my family background based on oral histories, census documents, and of course, my travels. My hands-on research began with a visit to Eucutta, MS in 1970, then to Ethiopia in 2002, Senegal in 2005, and more than a dozen other African countries. My readings, midnight discussions in my college dormitory room, complemented oral history lessons that emanated from my childhood dinner table. The reflections brought to life the descendants of my paternal great-grandparents, Abe and Carolyn Sampson nee Sanson. I have reconstructed the lessons that were stored on my childhood tapes.

Writing this memoir brought me face-to-face with bygone family trials, tribulations, and triumphs of this American family. A good portion of my understandings have been derived from histories provided in several settings by third generation members, my immediate parents and their siblings. The bulk of these contributions were oral histories. Perhaps most influential in the development of my view resulted from discussions around the dinner table at 115 Melon Street in Laurel, Mississippi during my childhood. These memories are stored in my "childhood tapes," a valuable tool that allows me to travel through the summer forest of my mind and board the cockpit in my time machine. From there, I assess life situations up-close and from afar without regard to the period in which they occurred.

Today, I remain an ardent observer of life in America, and I am given to judge situations and, sometimes, people in a manner that could be more civil. Truth be told, I am one of my harshest critics, but refined introspection makes one wiser.

Acknowledgements

I am indebted to my parents, Plummer and Lurline; my uncles: Milton, Lucius, Abraham, and Hubert C. Marsh (husband of my dad's youngest sister, Annie Laura); my paternal aunts: Lurelia, Iola, and Annie Laura; and my maternal aunt Corrine Alderman, who undoubtedly was my favorite. Fourth-generation contributions came from my siblings: Mazie, Plummer, Jr., James Calvin, Therman, Ezell, and Clarence; fourth generation cousins, LeRoy Sampson, Gerri Samson-Horton, BJ Samson, Kate Buxton, and Annie Nazel Arrington. While growing up in MS, I was fortunate to be supported by devoted public school teachers: Essie Mae Harris, Sammy Malone, Katherine Showers, and Malcolm Black; my childhood church, Friendship Baptist (it was a vibrant church); my neighborhood; and classmates who have remained lifelong friends.

Prologue

Writing my memoir has caused untold self-examination. I grappled with truth, and I learned that truth for anyone is a very complicated thing. Truth has consequences; it forced me to face my fears. Reality also forced me sometimes to attempt avoidance of the unsavory. I will be first to admit that denial and avoidance have sometimes caused me to omit what may be considered significant events, situations, and times from this narrative. What I omitted says as much as those things I included. But then, what lies beyond the margin of any text?

I am an accomplished amateur photographer, and I know the photographer frames the shot as writers frame their world. I doubt that close friends and relatives will object to what I have written (or for that matter, failed to cover). However, some might. Nevertheless, it seems to me that what I have left out was the story's silent twin, and I know that some things are better left unsaid. There are so many things that I have not stated because they are simply too painful...they would generate unnecessary embarrassment.

This trip down memory lane has brought me face-to-face with some bedeviling concepts, such as distinguishing between right and wrong, and good and evil. My spiritual life and work experiences have indelibly stamped on my consciousness that doing the "right thing" isn't always "good," and can often have negative consequences. Moreover, I have pondered how different the country would be if my family had been in the majority group? Would we have placed commerce before humanity? Would we have been fair and honest? Would we have voluntarily shared governance, or would we need to amend the constitution to grant God-given rights to folks who looked different from us? Obviously, we will never know. Yet, because of my station in life, and my life and work experiences, I know what is commensurate with the reality of being a racial minority in America. The early years after the Civil War beginning in 1865, extending to 2020, is the period in which I trace six generations…only 155 years, but I know that good or bad is the derivate result of doing rightly or wrongly. Good or bad results can happen according to prevailing circumstances. The difference is in one's approach, and the result flows accordingly. Good versus evil was the lens through which I saw how my family struggled to be recognized as humans from the end of the Civil War and extending to this day. I hope that the things I have said will soothe the pure truth seekers, or appease them in some way. Stories are compensatory. Studying 155 years of my family's time in America leads me to unapologetically affirm that the world is unfair, unjust, unknowable, and out of control. When writing my memoirs, I attempted to tell my story, and in that process, I attempted to exercise restraint, knowing that I have left a gap, an opening… My draft of the post-Civil War generations of my family is a continuing edit - a current version, but never the final one. For more years that I care to recall, the story of my family occupies my mind during the early morning hours preceding dawn, and at times, I imagine that the silences will be heard by someone else, and the story can continue and thereby be better contextualized. As I write, I offer the silence as much as the written story. Words are the part of silence that can be spoken. The unspoken reflect many resolved issues that I now know may never be resolved while I live on this earth.

Chapter I

MY GENESIS LIES IN THE GORE OF GOREE ISLAND

The gospel writer Luke tells the story of a sermon preached by the disciple Paul in the book of Acts (26:18) in which Paul attempts to convince King Agrippa on the need to "open our eyes, so that we may turn from darkness to light." The book of Kings (2nd Kings 6:17) tells of Elisha's prayer to "open our eyes that we may see." A more contemporary lyric about opening our eyes came from Leon Lumpkins, who prayed that our Maker would "grant us loving peace and let all descension cease." Lumpkins lyrics were popularized in the ballad "Open Our Eyes" as performed by *Earth, Wind, and Fire*, one of the most innovative and successful performing bands in my lifetime. The scriptures and the EWF sound in my head accompanied me during many of my professional travels over more than two decades, when I visited more than a dozen countries on the continent of Africa. However, it was the gore of Goree island on the west coast of Africa that began my transformation from looking to seeing with regard to matters related to my ancestry. Reflecting on decades of questions about my ancestry, I entered the cockpit of my time machine and ascended to thirty-five thousand feet, where seeing soon became a vision, and from that vision, discernment. Of course, it was not the epiphany of the moment so much as it was a lifetime of memory that came together that morning in West Africa.

The sun shone brightly on that warm, cloudless morning in Dakar, Senegal. Humidity was moderate in mid-June, 2005. The temperature was in the upper 70s. My CIMPAD traveling companions and I began the day by journeying from our hotel to the ferry to take the twenty-five-minute trip from the city of Dakar to Goree Island, one of the African slave posts along the Atlantic Ocean in West Africa. Here we would come to know firsthand the gore of Goree Island.

For a visitor, Goree is a rather pleasant setting. With its colonial houses, trailing bougainvillea, baobab trees, sea breezes, and narrow, shady streets, the island is a favorite day trip both for foreigners and residents of Dakar. Some children swam alongside the ferry. When we approached the docking base, children dove for coins in the harbor as the ferry arrived. There are a couple of museums, including a historical museum in the old fort, which even-handedly represents the African involvement in the slave trade as well as that of Europeans. There's a sheltered beach and not a car. The terracotta slave house, where captives were held pending shipment to the Caribbean and American colonies, has been exquisitely restored, deceptively belying its original purpose, shining despite its past cruelties.

Prior to our arrival in Dakar, we had just completed the 5th International Conference on Public Management, Policy and, Development for CIMPAD and were beginning our post-conference travels to the hinterland to learn more about the country where we had been consulted on a series of developmental issues, which the elected officials and non-governmental organizations had previously identified. Senegal is one of the countries from which my pro-bono consultant group had accepted an invitation to visit and to assist them in governance issues as they dealt with various developmental challenges in their quest for advancing their fledgling democratic governments. Our protocol for accepting an invitation from a host African country required the prospective host to identify the issues where assistance was desired. During these visits, which began before the trip to Senegal, I had also come to know some of the locations along the coast of West Africa that had been major holding pens in the slave trade.

The conference in the early summer of 2005 was the venue where a dialogue among African-American and African professionals in government, academia, and business occurred. The conference had presented cutting-edge research ideas and best practices in good governance, health, and economic development policy and related fields for building healthy societies. For more than two decades, I have been affiliated with the Consortium on International Management, Policy, and Development (CIMPAD). The consortium consists of a group of individuals interested in global African affairs who envision opportunities for assisting the development of democracy on the continent, regional planning, healthcare, delivery systems, and transportation. We focus explicitly on sub-Saharan Africa and devour opportunities to observe and compare urbanism in America with urbanism on the Continent. The CIMPAD mission is to "inspire and promote collaborative working relations toward the advancement of knowledge in public administration, public management, public policy, and leadership development among practitioners and academicians in various African countries and the diaspora." Although our work was pro-bono, I am sure that I gained more than I gave. CIMPAD brought me to see about one-fourth of the countries on the continent before I began travels as a Fulbright fellow to Asia, namely to Thailand, Cambodia, and Indonesia. The visit became a "gift" as it fostered informed reflections on my past life. Because I traveled to Goree Island, I was able to connect that place in West Africa to Eucutta, MS, home of my paternal grandparents, and then to connect that place to a story of the descendants of Abe and Calline Sampson and the trials, tribulations, and triumphs of this American family.

On that June morning, I had come to Dakar with a cheerless, morose mindset based largely on my unsettled response to experiences at the conferences and the conversations I had had with my newly found African professorial colleagues a few days earlier. All my past thoughts about African slavery had conditioned me to believe Goree Island would be a sad place. In the final frame, my visits to the continent caused the sacred canopy of what I thought I knew of the African continent to become incontrovertibly shattered.

A few days earlier, June 1-4, 2005, during our conference, we had had conversations with African professors at Gaston Berger University (GBU), or L'Université Gaston Berger (UGB), who told us that their ancestors had not envisioned the permanency of their collusion with the Europeans. I ignored the smell of distance in their clothing and the sound of strangeness in their accent, but I could not ignore the claim that their ancestors had *not* considered the damage done to my ancestors who were captured and sold. It is generally known that there had been a slave trade within Africa prior to the arrival of Europeans; the massive European demand for slaves and the introduction of firearms radically transformed west and central African society. A growing number of Africans were enslaved for petty debts, minor criminal or religious offenses, or following unprovoked raids on unprotected villages. An increasing number of religious wars broke out with the goal of capturing slaves. European weapons made it easier to capture slaves. Thus, it seemed like forever as I tried to hide my puzzlement and embarrassment as I rescued my jaw from the floor.

The place where these conversations took place, UGB, is located some 12 kilometers (7.5 miles) outside a fishing village named Saint-Louis, located some 40 miles from Dakar. The fishing village provided a close view of hardworking groups attending to the repair of their fishing vessels. The fishing village featured a working-class community while the university featured Senegalese intellects.

UGB was the second university established in Senegal (the first being Cheikh Anta Diop University). Originally the University of Saint-Louis, it was renamed for Gaston Berger, a distinguished French-Senegalese philosopher, on December 4, 1996. GBU welcomed its first class of six hundred students on December 17, 1990. The first rector (president) was Ahmadou Lamine Ndiaye, who held office from January 1990 to November 1999. The university is funded by a grant from the government of Senegal.

The school's primary architectural fixture is the central library's tower, which is visible from the surrounding road. The road stretches to the Mauritanian border. The campus is situated in two towns, Sanar Peulh and Sanar Wolof, which are inhabited respectively by ethnic Fulas and Wolofs. Many refer to the university by the name "Sanar" due to its location. Alumni are sometimes referred to as "Sunusanars."

Our trip to the island was meant to be an opportunity for rest and recuperation: soaking in the lessons learned at the conference, visualizing new areas for future consultation, and enjoying our connection to the motherland. I suppose I eventually came to realize each of these opportunities. The visit to the West African country was another opportunity to visit folks who resembled many of the African-Americans one would see while living in the USA. Experiencing their hospitality was another unexpected bonus.

Sitting in the shade of a West African midday and awaiting a delicious underground barbeque luncheon did not find me transfixed on the luring smell of the smoked carnivore. The items on the agenda included smoked pork ribs, lamb, crocodile, and ostrich meatballs. Despite the taste that lingered in my mind, I was instead preoccupied with the unsettling discussions held a few days earlier.

Arriving in Senegal caused me to compare previous visits (2002, 2003 and 2005) to South Africa, trips that included excursions to Robben Island. Robben Island, now a museum, invoked mental pictures of a somber environment. After apartheid, the museum has been transformed from the Alcatraz-like prison on Robben Island. It housed Nelson Mandela for 27 years before his freedom and ascendancy to the presidency of South Africa. It lies seven miles off Cape Town, in the heart of Table Bay. So, I call it "the Alcatraz" of South Africa. At the height of its function as a prison, some 1,500 long-term prisoners had been incarcerated. Of that total prison population of about 1,500, about 500 had been convicted of crimes such as murder, robbery, rape, assault, fraud, housebreaking, and theft. The remaining 1,000 were political prisoners who, in addition to Mr. Mandela, included Ahmed Kathrada, Walter Sisulu, Govan Mbeki, Andrew Mlangeni, Billy Nair, Elias Motsoaledi, Raymond Mhlaba, and Denis Goldberg, all freedom fighters who had been a thorn in the side of the South African government. It was a bleak place in the 20th century.

Robben Island is a waterless, arid patch of land, surrounded by shark-inhabited water. It had been used by South African Government as a place of exile for defeated African chiefs, as a leper colony, as a defense establishment, and then as a "maximum security" prison for "dangerous criminals."

Robben Island prison yard with toilet entry

The prison was championed by Hendrix Verwoerd, the South African prime minister (1958-1966) who worked to ensure white, and especially Afrikaner, dominance in South Africa, to the exclusion of the country's non-white majority. A trained social scientist, he was the chief social engineer of apartheid and justified apartheid on ethical and philosophical grounds while ordering the detention and imprisonment of tens of thousands of people and the exile of further thousands. He banned the African Nationalist Congress (ANC) and the Pan-African Congress, and it was under him that future president Nelson Mandela was imprisoned for life for "sabotage."

Lepers gravesite near the entry to Robben Island

Riding in my time machine at the height of 25,000 feet allowed me to compare the gloom of Robben Island with the West African country of Senegal and see the stark reality. The Senegalese had transformed Goree island in a fashion that reminded me of some parts of Disneyworld! Young children dove into the water as we left Dakar and swam along with the ferry for the twenty-five-minute ride to Goree Island. I was astonished at the sight of the youngsters that swam because previous television pictures of Tarzan and of Africa and Olympic competition had conditioned me to believe that Africans could not swim. The Senegalese swimmers were the first of a number of epiphanies.

Local Dakar merchants waited for us (the Americans) to disembark and expected us to shop for Senegalese souvenirs. There were always serious shoppers in our group, but once we were settled on shore, our guide gathered us around to provide an orientation to the place where we would spend the better part of a day. He led us to a churchyard where African men, women, and children had been warehoused in preparation for the months-long journey across the Atlantic Ocean.

Standing there and soaking in the reality of centuries-old events and the impact they still had was heart-wrenching. At that moment the summer forest of my mind began to soak into Goree Island and grasp its true significance. Soon, we went inside a church where a service was getting underway. My life long memories of a church and religious service did not meet with my expectations. There were no choirs, no scripture reading, nor a sermon. Instead, the service was not so much a worship experience as it was an introduction to the place itself and its role in the slave traffic along the coast of West Africa. I learned about the importance of cooperation between the church and the slave traffickers.

Connecting the dots

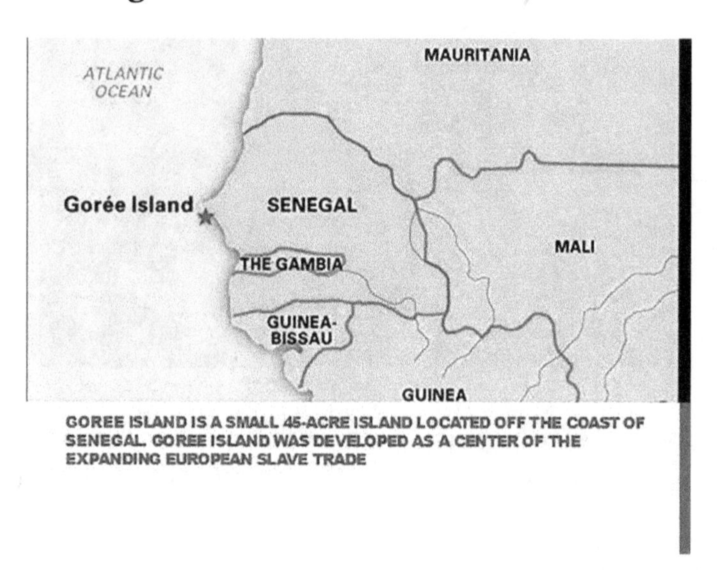

GOREE ISLAND IS A SMALL 45-ACRE ISLAND LOCATED OFF THE COAST OF SENEGAL. GOREE ISLAND WAS DEVELOPED AS A CENTER OF THE EXPANDING EUROPEAN SLAVE TRADE

The history of my family can be traced to that island, first known as Senegambia and now called Goree Island. It is located at the westernmost point in West Africa and had served as a strategic post for the transatlantic slave trade. The island, a short ferry ride away from Dakar, survives through tourism with several museums, including the famous *Maison des Esclaves* (House of Slaves), otherwise known as the Door of No Return. It was there that the lines in the book of Acts and the book of Kings connected to my childhood tapes. It was there that I began to visualize the horror of what that place meant.

During the African slave trade, Goree Island became a slave-holding warehouse that became an important functional center for the trade in African men, women, and children. Millions of West Africans were taken against their will. The main slaving nations were the Western European powers with coasts on the Atlantic Ocean. Africans from many different locations were brought to Goree Island, sold into slavery, and held in the holding warehouse on the island until they were shipped across the Atlantic Ocean. Though accurate totals are unknowable, historians and economists argue that the transatlantic slave trade forcibly displaced 12.5 million between the 17th and 19th centuries; research by historians estimate nearly 11 million survived the infamous Middle Passage across the Atlantic.

Slave ships were draped with the flags of the merchant companies that held monopolies to trade in human capital. The guides told us that it was common for at least thirty slave ships to sit at anchor in the same port of western Africa, awaiting human cargo to be transported from shore and stored in the hull. After several stops along the coast, ships with hulls packed to capacity were ready to set sail across the Atlantic Ocean. The mainline traffickers, being the politically and economically dominant states of Western Europe in the early modern period, also had access to what is now the home of colonies in United States. The colonies had crucial economic interests in the Americas: Spain and Portugal, England and France, the Netherlands and Denmark. In the first couple of centuries, the Iberian nations were the most active, servicing their developing American empires. However, the demand particularly for sugar from the mid-17th century onwards and the rapid colonization of the Caribbean by the northern European powers, led by the British and French, saw the trade dominated by these same nations until the early 19th century. Estimates vary, but all of them place the number of Africans who died while in transit in the millions. My great-grandparents obviously survived.

The point is often made that virtually every African-based port sent a ship into slaving. In England, one can come up with a list including not only the obvious ones like Liverpool, London, and Bristol, but also Plymouth, Exeter, Bridgeport, and locally, Chester and Poulton. The bulk of the activity included ships that sailed Liverpool (5300 voyages), London (3100 voyages) and Bristol (2200 voyages); between them, they accounted for over 90% of the British trade. Clearly, the process of domination seems to have accelerated at the end of the century, with Liverpool not only outstripping its English rivals, but the European competition.

The House of Slaves on Goree Island, Senegal

"The *House of Slaves*" was the moniker assigned to the churchyard in Goree Island where Africans would be sorted, examined for physical fitness, marketed, and shipped by middlemen from mainland West Africa. John Gabriel Stedman studied African slave trade in the 1700s and authored *Narrative of a Five Years' Expedition against the revolted Negroes of Surinam... from the year 1772 to 1777* (London, 1796). In that publication, he noted that in Senegambia, Europeans purchased 6% of all captives in the transatlantic slave trade. Enslaved people came from an immense area of West Africa that stretched from coastal regions drained by the Senegal and Gambia Rivers to the mountainous Futa Toro, Futa Bundu, and Futa Jalon, and farther east to settlements in the Sahel. In Senegambia, as in other regions, the transport of more than 750,000 captives over land and water required an intricate system of auxiliary traders in food and supplies, who kept the slave trade alive along its far-flung routes to the sea.

The traders could rummage and purchase *slaves* before leading them through what is now called the "Door of No Return." Built by the Dutch, the facility is the last slave house still standing in Goree and currently serves as a museum. An estimated 20 million Africans passed through the island between the mid-1500s and the mid-1800s. In a book on the role of history in African ideologies today, Katharina Schramm, called *the Door of No Return* a symbol of "the cultural amnesia and sense of disconnection that slavery and the Middle Passage stand for." The door, she wrote, has become increasingly associated not just with its largely fictional past but with its authentic present as a place of historical "healing and closure," sometimes now described as a "Door of Return" out of slavery's shadow. Historical anthropologist François Richard argues that some people use the history/memory couplet to parse the problem of Goree's House of Slaves (i.e., history concerned with facts and memory with symbolic value and historical gravity, a mode of affective resonance absolutely central to identities in the African diaspora). It's not the most satisfying or cutting way of analyzing the phenomenon, but it has the merit of offering a point of entry. Richards further states that what is important to remember is that while the details about the house may not be entirely exact, they do speak to a deeper historical truth - namely, the experience and infamy of turning humanity into a commodity.

Tourists wait for entry to the House of Slaves

By 2005, I had seen a number of African countries: the city of Addis Ababa, Ethiopia and the hinterlands of Lalibela; the desert in the horn of Africa; fishing bays in St. Louis outside of Dakar; and village life in Gambia. Our CIMPAD travels also took me to the East African countries of Burundi, Kenya, Rwanda, South Sudan, Tanzania, Uganda and Kenya. On separate (non-CIMPAD) trips I traveled to South Africa twice. These experiences allowed me to begin to make informed judgments about comparative quality of life differences between African-Americans and Africans. My travels took me to some of the most beautiful cities in the world, all located on the Continent. I would see evidences of political and social leadership that had never materialized in the USA for African-Americans. Leaders such as Jomo Kenyatta (Kenya), Kwame Nkrumah (Ghana), Julius Nyerere (Tanzania), Patrice Lumumba (Republic of the Congo), and Haile Selassie (Ethiopia) are but a few of the leaders that I could never imagine in America. They all preceded Nelson Mandela's presidency of South Africa.

Our hosts at GBU were also knowledgeable and courteous. Arrayed in their splendid gowns, they took pride in explaining the history of the university and, more importantly, the culture of the Senegalese people.

Historical accounts reveal that the slave trade journey from Senegal across the Atlantic Ocean was about four to six weeks long, depending on ocean turbulence. The human cargo was chained in the hull of the ships during that four-to-six-week time segment. Hearing firsthand from my African brothers, they did not question the fairness of the tribal trade wars in which the loser of an intergroup (tribal) conflict would be sold to the Europeans. The consequences of family separation apparently were never an issue, not then and not now. To this day that revelation caused me great puzzlement. Perhaps it was my brother's latent innocence about the European traders' lack of humanity and the dominance of capitalism and "for profit" motivations which undergirded their interest in slavery. Nevertheless, the tribes that lost a battle in their inter-squad scrimmage became the booty for trade with the Europeans. It never escaped me that the defeated tribes were my ancestors! Upon reflection, I understand that the victors in the tribal wars thought the exchange of humans was temporary and even more did not appreciate the burden of the transatlantic journey and its implication for families and tribes. But even now, that sort of rationalization is difficult to understand. Furthermore, it is ironic that the slavers were largely Christian. I am a Christian, but the nuance of the "rightfulness" of neither American-style slavery nor its Biblical justification ever resonated with my way of seeing justice.

Central Library Tower on the Gaston Berger campus

My American pro-bono consulting group (CIMPAD) was not the only group of visitors to *Maison des Esclaves*; on that June morning, there were visitors from many parts of the world, including those from other African countries. This up-close visit to a place of historical significance proved to be of interest to several folks. To be sure, I was surprised at the level of international interest, but as I compare my other travels on the continent, there were always visitors, especially from European countries. The pleasant sunny day mollified the growing crowd size, and the vendors contained a bit of interesting inventory. Some of the vendors were very aggressive about making a sell. They could not understand "No, thank you" or "I am not interested." In fact, some followed us back to our hotel in Dakar attempting to sell jewelry, postcards, and a host of trinkets. Upon returning to Le Meridian Hotel where we were lodged, we were approached by a group of four female vendors in the lobby. Some of the African-American women in our party were interested in their jewelry and handbags. To be sure, the Senegalese were very well acquainted with capitalism, commerce, and trade. The four Senegalese women were sisters whose age differences (within two years and no twin births) occurred because each sister had a different father. Our party was fascinated by their embrace of polygamy. The Senegalese women stated that they believed a man should have as many wives as he could support.

Our guide was an articulate Senegalese gentleman who explained that Goree Island was a self-sufficient place complete with churches that housed the slaves before they were shipped out. He was careful to relay the stories of past inhumanity; he lifted a rusty cast-iron ball above his head in the courtyard of Senegal's most famous former slave trading house, and in a voice as smooth as riverbed stone, told a story that captured the banal facts behind one of humanity's greatest crimes. "This 17-pound weight used to prevent captives from attempting to flee," he said of the device, which resembled a relic from a medieval dungeon. "For the stubborn, there were neck rings and leg chains that, when attached together, would immobilize several Africans simultaneously. The male captives were usually chained together in pairs, right leg to the next man's left leg, to save space. The chains or hand and leg cuffs were known as 'Bilboes,' which were among the many tools of the slave trade, and which were always in short supply." "The value of a woman was fixed according to the fullness of her breasts. Men were weighed to ensure that they met the minimum requirement of 120 pounds." "After being weighed," he said, "the men were appraised by their age and origin, with certain ethnic groups prized for their hardiness or as supposedly prolific breeders. The Yoruba, for example, were prized as 'stallions.'" He explained that female slaves were segregated from male slaves, and that there was also a compartment for children.

Long before the slaves were boarded and locked in the hull of the ship, white men took sexual liberties with enslaved women and rewarded obedient behavior with favors, while rebellious enslaved people were brutally punished. A strict hierarchy among the enslaved (from privileged house workers and skilled artisans down to lowly field hands) helped keep the slaves divided and less likely to organize against their masters. Even in the 21st century there are remnants of that race-based superior-subordinate relationship. These early behaviors of white supremacy eventually gave rise to slave rebellions such as those led by Gabriel Processor in Richmond, a literate slave blacksmith who planned a large slave rebellion in the Richmond area in the summer of 1800. Information regarding the revolt was leaked prior to its execution, and he and twenty-five followers were taken captive and hanged in punishment. Two years later, Demark Vesey in Charleston devised a scheme to take over Charleston,

South Carolina. Vesey, who had been born in either Africa or the Caribbean in the late 1760s, won a lottery, purchased his freedom, and opened a carpentry shop. Accounts of the reaction said that the local authorities' decision to close the city's independent African church led Vesey to organize his conspiracy. Twenty-eight years later, i.e., 1831, the first successful rebellion was led by Nat Turner in Virginia. In 1831, the "home boys" won, and the grown-ass black maleness in me found a reason to cheer when I read about it. Unfortunately, Turner's "success" in Southampton County, VA was short-lived, and it generated tighter restrictions.

In the midmorning of that mid-June day in 2005, I stood in the portal where slaves had been held until they were loaded on the ships. The reality of where I was standing overwhelmed me. I came face-to-face with the space that opened onto the Atlantic Ocean where ships would begin the month-long trip to destinies in Europe, North America, South America, and the Caribbean.

Me in the portal that my ancestors passed through

As I stood where my ancestors had been shackled, my mind raced to recall the guide's discussion of the conditions my ancestors had experienced. I conjured horrific smells and sounds. For a second time on that day, I was caught in a time warp…I became a time traveler. The experience brought sadness to my soul and tears to my eyes. I did not attempt to hide my tears. In fact, my eyes were not the only ones that expressed sadness and simultaneously, ironic exhilaration. I was not alone in my feelings of contempt. Several of my CIMPAD colleagues were also first-time visitors to Goree Island, and they too were awed by the experience. We experienced an epiphany unlike any previous experience. It was a simultaneous intuitive grasp of reality, an illuminating discovery, a realization, and a disclosure; it was a discerning insight. Altogether it was a revealing moment that changed us all in some way. For me, it was the prescient discussions with our African professor colleagues held a few days earlier. Our discussion about what our African brothers and sisters thought about the resulting slavery of a segment of their kin again became the center of my thoughts. It was/is common knowledge that there had been a slave trade within Africa prior to the arrival of Europeans. Moreover, the massive European demand for slaves and the introduction of firearms radically transformed West and Central African society. A growing number of Africans were enslaved for petty debts or minor criminal or religious offenses or following unprovoked raids on unprotected villages. An increasing number of religious wars broke out with the goal of capturing slaves. European weapons made it easier to capture slaves. How could my African colleagues not envision the outcome of the lengthy journey across the Atlantic Ocean? I was transfixed in a state of near shock for longer than I would have expected. I came to ponder more deeply the impact of time and chance on all of our existence.

The Atlantic Ocean at the Door of No Return

Beyond the portal where slaves were placed on the ships, the Atlantic Ocean lay on the adjacent side of the Door of No Return. Its peaceful appearance momentarily hid the reality of its history. Many of the slaves did not survive the difficult month-long journey from western Africa to the southeastern coast of the US. Many of the slaves did not know their shipmates since they had come from different tribes and various locations on the Continent. They did not have a common language. The ship transportation has been referred to as the "Middle Passage." Historians refer to the "Middle Passage" as a time of in-betweenness for those being traded from Africa to America. The close quarters on the ship and intentional division of pre-established African communities by the ship crew motivated captive Africans to forge bonds of kinship, which then created forced transatlantic communities. The duration of the transatlantic voyage varied widely from one to six months, depending on weather conditions. The journey became more efficient over the centuries; while an average transatlantic journey of the early 16th century lasted several months, by the 19th century, the crossing often required fewer than six weeks.

Typical slave ships contained several hundred slaves about 30 crew members.

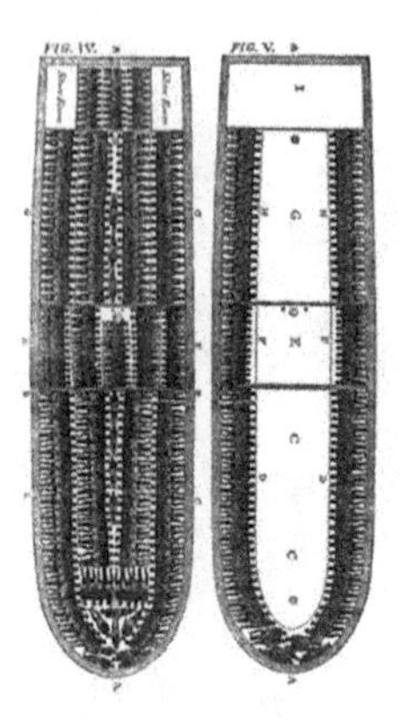

Diagram of a slave ship from the Atlantic slave trade (From an Abstract of Evidence delivered before a select committee of the House of Commons in 1790 and 1791).

At best, captives were fed beans, corn, yams, rice, and palm oil. Slaves were fed one meal a day with water, if at all. When food was scarce, slaveholders would get priority over the slaves (See http://www.pbs.org/wgbh/aia/part1/1p277.html). Sometimes, captives could move around during the day, but many ships kept the shackles on throughout the arduous journey. Aboard certain French ships, slaves were brought on deck to periodically receive fresh air. While female slaves were typically permitted to be on deck more frequently, male slaves would be watched closely to prevent revolt when above deck.

Slaves below the decks lived for months in conditions of squalor and indescribable horror. Disease spread, and ill health was one of the biggest killers. Mortality rates were high, and death made these conditions below the decks even worse. Even though the corpses were thrown overboard, many crew members avoided going to the hole. The slaves who had already been ill-ridden were not always found immediately. Many of the living slaves could have been shackled to someone that was dead for hours or, sometimes, days. Mortality resulted from amoebic dysentery, scurvy, smallpox, syphilis, and measles. The rate of death increased with the length of the voyage, since the incidences of dysentery and scurvy increased with longer stints at sea as the quality and amount of food and water diminished. In addition to physical sickness, many slaves became too depressed to eat or function efficiently due to loss of freedom, family, security, and their own humanity.

The places that gave birth to my family history and the shaping of that history were influenced by a culture antagonistic to our humanity; it revealed to me a new understanding about what I had denied myself while in undergraduate and graduate study. I felt impoverished by my lack of knowledge of the things that mattered to my existence as an African. I told myself I should have taken a richer set of black history courses in undergraduate school. So, with my new sense of hunger and thirst, I set about reading the history books that I had neglected or had not been brought to my attention. In my search for reasons, I discovered the Colonial Williamsburg Foundation (www.slaveryandembrance.org). The foundation details a rich history of dozens of local and regional slave trades in Europe, Africa, and the Americas and their interactions that combined to create the transatlantic slave trade. The collective leaders and facilitators developed an ever-evolving system of people, ships, and goods that deported at least 12.5 million Africans toward destinations in Europe and the Americas over a period of 366 years.

The forced migration of African captives relied upon three complex, intertwined systems that married the interests of European and American investors, traders, and planters with those of African merchants and leaders. Investors in such port cities as Bristol, Nantes, and Salvador da Bahia established Atlantic circuits along which their vessels could obtain captive non-voluntary workers to supply commercial plantations, mines, or factories in the Americas. A second and equally complex system created by African traders and leaders moved captives from nearly all regions of the African interior to coastal markets, where the two systems tragically merged and gave life to one another. A third system joined the others in the Americas, as merchants purchased newly arrived Africans in New World ports and carried them to secondary markets in overland or intercolonial maritime trades that extended the horrific journeys of captives for weeks, months, or even years.

Nearly one third of all slave voyages were outfitted in Liverpool, London, Bristol, and other ports in Britain. French vessels from such ports as La Rochelle, Le Havre, Bordeaux, and Nantes made up another 13%. In the Americas, hundreds of slave ships were sent from the British Caribbean and Rhode Island in North America, and in the 19th century, especially, from the Brazilian port cities of Recife, Salvador da Bahia, and Rio de Janeiro. All told, 90% of captives deported in the transatlantic slave trade were carried in ships from Brazil, Britain, France, Portugal, and the Netherlands.

Just as the circulation of European and American slave ships shifted according to supplies, prices, and political alliances, the movement of captives toward African coastal markets varied in scale and direction from place to place and over time. In nearly all instances, however, the sale of enslaved people to European traders was the result of a long and arduous journey through an extensive network of traders in the African interior.

In Senegambia, European countries purchased 6% of all captives in the transatlantic slave trade; enslaved people came from an immense area of West Africa along the Atlantic

Ocean that stretched from coastal regions drained by the Senegal and Gambia Rivers to the mountainous Futa Toro, Futa Bandu, and Futa Jalon, and farther east to settlements in the Sahel. In Senegambia, the transport of more than 750,000 captives over land and water required an intricate system of auxiliary traders in food and supplies to keep the slave trade alive along its far-flung routes to the sea. In Senegal, there is a monument to the history of enslavement. It is a structure along a main highway in Dakar that features a man waiting for a phone call from those who had left the shores of Senegal. This display suggested to me that the Africans that facilitated the slave trade underestimated the Europeans.

Artistic Figure in Dakar, Senegal

Nevertheless, the Americans who traveled in the group with me were very much appreciative upon learning of the structure and what it meant; our Senegalese brothers and sisters were proud. Shipping ports along the Gold Coast of West Africa supplied 10% of all transatlantic captives, and dozens of European forts and factories tapped into markets of enslaved people who found themselves at the coast only after being sold and transported by any number of middlemen beginning as far north as the Sahel region (today's Burkina Faso). For these people, their transatlantic journey would be yet another passage to endure since their initial enslavement which began weeks, months, or even years earlier.

Likewise, in Central Africa, where nearly half of all transatlantic captives originated, those forced upon ships in Luanda or along the Congo River came from increasingly distant parts of the interior of the continent. Discovering this information, I was able to rationalize my DNA tests which revealed my origins from disparate geographical regions on the Continent. People had been sold from the Atlantic ports of Cabinda and Loango and forced to travel great distances. The "cargo" moved from the interior while connected to local auxiliary trades in ivory or salt, to a greater degree. The people and earthly goods produced by the motherland began a link in the chain of packaging of goods exchanged at the coast and transported east. In this way, the movement of people toward the Central African coast mirrored a reciprocal trade in European goods in the opposite direction.

African captives who survived the Middle Passage were scattered across ports throughout the Americas. Scholars have identified 179 such ports where more than 11 million Africans were transported by European slavers. But, twenty of those ports received more than 8 million Africans. In Brazil, 1,839,000 landed in Rio de Janeiro, and a further 1,550,000 in Salvador da Bahia; Kingston, Jamaica received 886,000 Africans, and 493,000 landed at Bridgetown Barbados; Cap-Francias in Saint-Domingue (now Haiti) was the disembarkation point for 406,000 Africans, and Charleston, South Carolina (United States) 186,000.

These Atlantic ports were the points where enslaved Africans entered the third massive system that shaped the transatlantic slave trade. African arrivals were often quickly sold to planters or speculators on their way toward their final work place. American colonists in frontier settlements of the Caribbean islands, the backcountry of the Carolinas in North America, and the vast Brazilian interior demanded agricultural, domestic, and skilled laborers for their economic prosperity. If the Middle Passage served as the transatlantic slave trade's central artery, the elaborate networks of roads, paths, and waterways in the Americas that transported enslaved people from ports to plantations, mines, and cities were the capillaries - much like the slave routes on the African continent that had ensnared the captives in the first place.

Slave traders forced newly arrived Africans in Buenos Aires, Argentina to trek across the continent to what became Bolivia, Ecuador, and Chile - more than 6400 miles. Traders transported enslaved people from island to island within the Caribbean, then from one location to another on the larger islands in Jamaica, Cuba, and Saint-Domingue as new settlements and crops opened interior locations. What this meant was that colonial slave traders developed complex internal slave trading systems throughout the Americas. Some of them were longer and more protracted than the perilous Atlantic Ocean crossing.

Thus, the forced migrations of Africans and their descendants neither began nor ended with the Middle Passage (though more than 1.5 million Africans died during the Atlantic crossing). Millions of enslaved people were shifted against their will, without their loved ones or visible reminders of home - first in Africa, then across the Atlantic, and in final passages throughout the Americas. I could not separate my views from my Christian belief. So, I began to reconsider high school and college history of Africans and how knowledge of history challenges simple views about man's inhumanity to fellow humans and how such treatment failed to square with Christ's teachings. Knowledge learned from high school and undergraduate teachings, Sunday school lessons, sermons, and the behavior of situations I had witnessed caused me to dig deeper and sharpen my focus. I wanted to do more than just look…I wanted to see.

From these vicarious experiences, I better appreciated the urgency of the lyrics embodied in James Weldon Johnson's "*Lift Every Voice and Sing*" (1899), often referred to as the "Black National Anthem." In it, there is acknowledgement of law-based cultural inhumanity. It is more than ironic that the South African national anthem, "*Nkosi Sikele iAfrika,*" also a bellicose arrangement that rages apartheid in a melodious harmony written by Enoch Sontonga (1897). Both anthems praise tragedy and conflict in a joyful noise. My childhood tapes recalled the Oak Park High School chorus as it belted out the memory of the Johnson lines:

> "Stony the road we trod, bitter the chastening rod,
> Felt in the day that hope unborn had died;],
> Yet with a steady beat, have not our weary feet,
> Come to the Place on which our fathers sighed?
> We have come over a way that with tears has been watered,
> We have come, treading our path through the blood of the slaughtered,
> Out from the gloomy past, 'til now we stand at last
> Where the white gleam of our star is cast.
>
> God of our weary years, God of our silent tears,
> Thou who has brought us thus far on the way,
> Thou who has by thy might, led us into the light,
> Keep us forever in the path, we pray
> Lest our feet stray from the places, our God, where we met thee,

Lest our hearts, drunk with the wine of the world, we forget thee,
Shadowed beneath the hand, may we forever stand,
True to our God, true to our native land."

Two interpretations have emanated from Johnson's classic: For black conservatives, it reminisced that, somehow, black folk's struggle had immersed us in a sort of black honor. On the other hand, for black nationalists, it was reminiscent of a golden age of black Africa where we were kings and queens. It seems to me that neither of these visions are without justifiable criticism. The commonality in these visions is the sense of what Ta-Nehisi Coates refers to as a "pathological bastardization" of black culture. We are not descendants of kings and queens so much as we are the progeny of slaves.

Nearly a decade would pass between my trip to Ethiopia in 2000 before I traveled to Kampala, Uganda. Upon arriving in Uganda at Entebbe International airport, I witnessed the most gorgeous sunrise. I looked forward to the landing since we had been in the air for the better part of 12 hours. My focus on the beautiful sunrise was interrupted as the soft landing gave view to a rusting wrecked aircraft on the adjacent runway. The site of a wrecked plane on the landing strip caused me to move through the summer forest of my mind while our plane landed. As the wheels of that big jet touched the tarmac at Entebbe, I entered the cockpit of my time machine and ascended to 35,000 feet, and I remembered other landings at Dakar, Addis-Ababa, Cape Town, Pretoria, and Johannesburg. After deboarding the jumbo jet, we began the usual routine of international travel, i.e., collecting baggage and clearing through customs.

Sunrise over Entebbe, Uganda

Then, we proceeded via bus and an hour-long, thirty-mile drive into Kampala. Later, while my tapes connected me to my time machine during that drive, I descended to 5,000 feet as I again viewed the carnage on the airstrip at Entebbe in Uganda. My mind raced to news stories I had read and heard about more than 30 years ago. In 1976, an Air France airplane carrying 250 passengers to Paris from Tel Aviv was hijacked by terrorists. The Israeli mission to rescue them, known as Operation Entebbe, was broadcast over wires and carried to the world. A week earlier, on 27 June, a French Airbus jetliner with 248 passengers had been hijacked by two members of the Popular Front for the Liberation of Palestine. The hijackers' objective was to free 40 Palestinian and affiliated militants imprisoned in Israel and 13 prisoners in four other countries in exchange for the hostages. Their plans came to naught. The flight, which had originated in Tel Aviv, was diverted after a stopover in Athens Greece and flown to Entebbe, the main airport of Uganda. Israel's government, led by Prime Minister Yitzhak Rabin, launched a secret mission to rescue the hostages without engaging in negotiation. The rescue mission was pulled off successfully by the Israeli government with all but four of the passengers surviving. In 2007 I could not understand why the debris was still there. For whom was that a trophy? In a way the carnage on the landing strip reflected the ideological differences that characterize world affairs. I, then and now, want to better understand the state of our existence. I pose a question to myself and ask: "Is this really how life should be for an earth-based human? Are all subordinates forever doomed to a squalid place in society?" In reality, the voice of "should have been'" has no vote. "Should" is a verb used to indicate obligation, duty, or correctness, typically when criticizing someone's action. My travels to the continent have brought me face-to-face with many "should have been" situations that would have served as negotiation points between interested parties if I ruled the world. However, meaningful obligations exist within some sort of covenant, i.e., a dyad where quid pro quo is the order of the day. It implies some sort of mutual regard for one another. From the onset of European interest in Africa, it was hardly because of a pact between equally interested parties. The colonizers sought the raw materials that could be used to fuel enterprises in Europe. Among the then reigning tribe leaders on the Continent, material gain from the trade of conquered warring tribes was their focus. Human regard for the Africans was hardly a central consideration for the European colonizers or the African tribe elders. In order to get an above the ground view, I move through the summer forest of my mind and enter the cockpit of my time machine. As I slowly increase my airborne height in my time machine, I ponder these circumstances, and my vision focuses on the children having recess on the playgrounds of the impoverished schools of Kampala on that summer day in 2007. The youngsters were plentiful, and there was evidence that they had neither computers nor books. I saw no opportunity for them to learn critical thinking, though doubtlessly, such a commodity was influenced by my premature creations, based on prejudices I learned in America. Their teachers did not share any negative notions of their students learning skills.

Ugandan School children outside Kampala

In Senegal, I see fishers repairing their boats in the St. Louis fishing village, near Dakar. The placid lake transferred my senses to more pleasant scenes of what could be. Yet, the reality of that circumstance was that St, Louis, Senegal fishing village posed an impossible quandary: stick to Senegalese waters and risk coming back empty-handed, or steal a few miles over the border into neighboring Mauritania and risk getting shot.

I then fly across the Atlantic to a time in the MS past. Scanning the skies, I spot Mt. Zion United Methodist Church located off Highway 16 East on County Road 747, near Money, MS. On June 15, 1964, a routine meeting of church officers was held. As the officers were leaving the church, Klansmen met them outside and ordered them out of their vehicle, where they assaulted J.R. (Bud Cole), Georgia Rush and her son, John Thomas. The church was burned later that evening, leaving only the 40-year-old bell that used to announce the beginning services. Five days later, police officials killed three civil rights workers, James Chaney, Andrew Goodman, and Michael Schwerner. This trio of northerners was offensive to the culture in MS because the trio consisted of a black and two whites. The event became a watershed event that lay down the gauntlet against those who would dare oppose states' rights and the Southern way of life. Local and state officials knew the value of optics. The optic in this instance was the signal that MS was not ready for integration or "outside agitators" who would attempt to change the culture of a segregated South. This set of events, i.e., killing the outside agitators, planted a flag for the Southern way of life. The national Republican party took note and many of those Republicans who sought the Presidency would adopt a Southern strategy in which they supported states' rights while campaigning in the South, which loudly implied that local blacks who opted to upgrade their second-class citizenship through voting and getting a seat at the table where policies were made would be ignored. It was the same nuance that the Southern Confederate Army adopted as they rebelled against the USA during the Civil War, the same nuance that began to bud at the 1948 Democratic Convention where Harry S Truman set forth a civil rights agenda which, in turn, resulted in most white Southerners beginning to change their political indentation from the Democrats to the Republicans. Subsequently in 1980, nearly two decades after the slayings of the civil rights activist, Ronald Reagan disregarded that history and announced his candidacy for president of the US The stench of the thought caused me to return to Africa. However, the scenes of Africa and Mississippi converged, thereby creating yet another stench in my nostrils as I landed my time machine at a fishing village in Senegal. As my mind returned to the village of St. Louis, I saw a group of fishermen whose livelihood depended on harvesting a good haul of fish.

Senegalese Fishers in the village called St. Louis

Although Senegal has areas that bear semblance to Western countries, there is abundant evidence of fishing villages (St. Louis above) and other venues of work that do not have the marks of modern-day industrialization. As the street life that is depicted below shows, traffic flows are not managed, and clean streets are nowhere to be found. On this day, I felt a sense of guilt because I perceived that there was so little I could contribute to a better life (Although "better" unavoidably meant more American-like). When I became a man, I put away childish notions, although I acknowledge that my views are the product of a lifetime of living in America; I had flashbacks to my childhood tapes of the television series *Ramar of the Jungle* as I toured counties in West Africa, including Senegal. My feelings were always mixed: who is to blame for conditions which show severe underdevelopment, and "Is there not something the residents could do to uplift themselves?" I had an insufficient appreciation for cultures different from that which is found in North America.

Prior to arriving on the Continent, I was unknowingly, but significantly influenced by watching 1950s television shows such as *Ramar of the Jungle*, in which a white medicine man carried on the work of his missionary father. As the story goes, Ramar, the white medicine man, had felt obligated to travel to the "*jungle,*" as a doctor, where he would heal natives and bring justice to the bad guys. In one of the stories featured in the mid-1950s through the early 1960s, Ramar hears about a rare substance that halts the effects of aging. The only problem is that the product is exclusively located in territory controlled by the White Goddess, where white men were forbidden to enter. Undaunted, Ramar was determined to make contact with her, with the help of the fearful natives. The television series was one of the dozens of "Colonialist Great White Father" stories that glorified European rule on the Continent. Critical thinking and analysis on these issues came later in life for me. Fortunately, I did not become completely brainwashed; watching the show as an adolescent was mere entertainment, but I would be dishonest or naive to say there was zero influence upon my thinking and processing.

The term *"great white father"* was a title used by colonial powers in North America to refer to the US president. The addition of the word "*white*" may have entered *popular* lexicon via western adventure novels. The first Catholic missionaries in what is now called Zambia were of the International Society of the Missionaries of *Africa*, popularly called "The *White Fathers*" because of their *white* dress. They arrived from what is now called Tanzania in 1891 and established the first mission post called Mwambwe Mwela.

As I fly in my time machine, I see the streets of Mauritania, a West African country northeast of Senegal. There are no demarcations along that thoroughfare devoted to keep traffic flowing in either direction. There are no traffic lights. There are no stop signs. There is no network of controlled highway access that facilitates smooth and orderly traffic flow the likes of which we see in the USA. However, West Africa is not the USA, and the culture of Mauritania (arguably) defied the need for traffic engineers.

Amidst the unkempt streets that had not been monitored by traffic engineers, I saw the beauty of their colorful attire. I saw smiles on their faces as I wondered to myself, "why?"

In South Africa, I recognize Khayelitsha (below) and Guguletha, townships near Cape Town; both townships epitomize inequality. There is no infrastructure for electrical utilities; thus, several houses in a community would be connected to a single source of power as indicated in the photo below.

In southern Kenya and northern Tanzania, the cow dung mud huts that serve as housing for the Maasai people come into view. I want a change of view. Again, I ascend to 35,000 feet and travel across the Atlantic Ocean to the United States. Descending to 5,000 feet, I see, in plain view, the inner cities in Detroit and Compton, and Ward 9 in New Orleans. In Philadelphia, MS, we see, again, law enforcers plotting the murders of Cheney, Goodwin, and Schwerner; in Jackson, MS on a Sunday night, Byron De La Beckwith raises his rifle and assassinates Medgar Evers. In Memphis a month before my graduation from college, James Earl Ray raises his rifle and assassinates Martin Luther King; near Hattiesburg, MS, the imperial wizard of the Ku Klux Klan murders Vernon Dahmer in the winter of 1966; a few years earlier, in the fall of 1963, the 16th Street Baptist Church in Birmingham was bombed by the Klan, killing five young worshippers. During the same time period, Mount Zion Methodist Church in Longdale, Mississippi was torched...For too many of us, the world is a four-cornered room in a central city ghetto.

For much of my adult life, I could not fathom how Christian men could be so concerned about money and material things while evidently disregarding the conditions they forced on their fellow humans, pardon my naivety. In any case, my mind is troubled as I deplane. I rationalize that before, during, and after colonization of the African continent, Africans were, then and still now, not considered to human equals to Europeans. Thus, the 1857 decision in which the Court held that the US Constitution was not meant to include American citizenship for black people, regardless of whether they were enslaved or free, concluded that the rights and privileges that the constitution confers upon American citizens could not apply to them. This ruling and its impact are why I have been tempted to question whether God has failed us when we suffer through marginalization and unending attempts to be recognized as real Americans. However, I have lived long enough to know that our Maker has not failed us, all of us, despite the curse of Donald J. Trump as 45th USA president, the modern-day Strom Thurmond - George Wallace - Nebuchadnezzar, and other outward appearances and circumstances that are characterized by painful, stagnant, or simply unglamorous circumstances. My life and work experiences have brought me face-to-face with the reality of my life in a gap, i.e., that space between promise-stimulated expectation and reality. The gap is a vacuum in which most of us live while on this earth. That space is filled with trials, disappointments, and achievements. In the closing chapter of this memoir, I use my gap experiences to contextualize my life experiences on this planet as a citizen of the USA.

Chapter II

LIFE EXPERIENCES, WORK-RELATED TRAVEL, AND MY CHILDHOOD TAPES

During my career, I have had work-related assignments that required travel to most of the continental United States, many countries in Europe and Asia, and more than a dozen countries on the African continent. One such state-side travel assignment placed me in Salt Lake City in the fall of 1990. Before arriving in Salt Lake City, I realized that the Salt Lake City, Utah-based Mormon Church was the depository for US Census records collected by the US Department of Commerce. I anticipated that the census data would be the beginning point for getting at some some nagging questions about my surname's various spellings and why there was so much spelling differences. So, while in Utah on professional business, I took an advantage of a Saturday morning break when I visited the Mormon Tabernacle Church Library. Since I had had a long-time desire to know what the US government had in its records about my family, this visit provided me such an opportunity.

The decennial census records were computerized such that the researcher had to input surnames and dates to locate the files. I was explicitly looking for documents relating to Jim Sampson, my grandfather. I (foolishly) expected my research agenda would quickly add context to some of the conversations around the dinner table at 115 Melon Street in Laurel, my childhood home (and the "studio" for many of the recording sessions for my childhood tapes). Instead, I spent an entire morning (about four hours) inputting "Sampson," "Samson," and even "Simpson"; none of these keywords generated any data in the 1860 data file. After repeated failure, I remembered how my dad, Plummer, would pronounce his name. He would say, in his distinctive Southern accent, to any new acquaintance: "Sansom is my name," and so, I phonetically used "Sansom," and instantaneously, Jim Sansom's name appeared, and I spent the balance of the day researching. I thought this discovery would lead me to the identification of parents who preceded my grandfather, Jim. I then became aware that African births were not recorded in a fashion that would allow for a fruitful search (https/www.ancestry.com). My ancestors were not important enough to be identified by name! Looking became seeing. I had to (yet again) intellectually confront the reality of slavery and its impact on me.

At this juncture, I revisit the vault which holds my childhood tapes and the library of journeys to the days when I had the ability to look, though I could not see. The first days of "looking" began at 115 Melon Street in Laurel, MS. Before my Goree Island visit, I became aware of Eucutta, MS, the settlement in Mississippi where my father had grown up. Thus begins the story of the descendants of Abe and Kelline Sampson and the trials, tribulations, and triumphs of an American family.

Who am I, what accounts for how CLS came to be?

My legal name is Charles Leon Sampson. The name on my birth certificate is Leon Sansom. There is quite a story about the correct spelling of my family surname. We began as "Sanson," the surname of William C. Sanson, who acquired ownership of my great-grandfather Abe around 1850; custom of the time was that the chattel property would assume the surname of the owner. Since then, we have been "Sansom," "Sampson," and even "Samson." Sometime in 1887, the name was declared "Sampson" by offspring of Abe Sanson, who wanted concrete liberation from the slaveholder. There was no "application" or any other government clearance to formally sanction the action. Yet, the variations continued. My family history is intertwined with the legacy of slavery; record-keeping related to how slaves were counted, and the absence of literary skills in the days and years after the end of the Civil War contributed to the current-day challenge of conducting good research. One reason for the spelling differences is a set of adamant individual beliefs that stare in the face of facts. To be sure, we are a proud, competitive group that persisted despite legal and societal hurdles.

My surname was affirmed as "Sampson" subsequent to my request to become a commissioned officer in the USAF. It was in my senior year of undergraduate study that the United States Air Force conducted a background investigation. Documents pertinent to that investigation included my original birth certificate and public records and the history of school information. My mother enrolled me as "Sampson" in the first grade. I never gave attention to my birth certificate until my application for a driver's license just before my 16th birthday; when the license was issued, my surname was the same as listed in my birth certificate, "Sansom."

My interest in ancestry is attributed to my observations of interactions between my father and his siblings, as well as conversations with my immediate family at the breakfast and dinner table. Substantial records, namely the decennial census, have provided the bulk of information on my family. I have been able to trace my family after the census of 1860 (which was the first to enumerate slaves). Beginning at that point in time and moving forward, I have been able to identify six generations on my paternal side. By the spring of 2016, I had record of more than 425 persons and 100 marriages covering a period of 180 years.

In the beginning...

From discussions around the dinner table at 115 Melon street, my undergraduate studies, and a stint in the US Air Force collectively brought into focus the search I wanted that morning at the Mormon Church library in Salt Lake, Utah. At a desk in that library, I began an organized search for my ancestors. "Childhood tapes" from my adolescence, prompted by family discussions at the dinner table, began to resurface in my mind. I had been told stories of my grandparents (all but one, my paternal grandfather, Jim, were deceased before I was born, and when he passed away in 1948, I was too young to remember seeing him).

The visit to the Mormon Church (The Church of Jesus Christ of Latter-day Saints) occurred because I had come to know that the Mormon Church had long had interest and experience in genealogy, the study of one's ancestors or family history which is thought to be is one of the most popular hobbies in the world. People of all faiths and nationalities enjoy discovering where they come from. For members of Mormon Church, however, learning about one's family history is more than just a casual endeavor. Latter-day Saints believe families can be together after this life.

Thus, they believe it is essential to strengthen relationships with all family members, both those who are alive and those who have died. Latter-day Saints believe that the eternal joining of families is possible through sacred sealing ceremonies that take place in temples. These temple rites may also be performed by proxy for those who have died. Consequently, for Mormons, genealogical research or family history is the essential forerunner for temple work for the dead. In Latter-day Saint belief, the dead have the choice to accept or reject the services performed for them. Since 1894, The Church of Jesus Christ of Latter-day Saints has dedicated time and resources to collecting and sharing records of genealogical importance. Due to cooperation from government archives, churches, and libraries, the Church has created the largest collection of family records in the world, with information on more than 3 billion deceased people. This effort was originally facilitated through the Genealogical Society of Utah and is now facilitated through Family Search, a nonprofit organization sponsored by the Church.

Library holding U. S. Census data

Discussion around the table at 115 Melon taught me that my father's father, Jim, was the son of Abe, and Abe married Calline (Caroline? pronounced "Kell-line"). The history of the Abe and Caroline Sansom family has many twists and turns. It begins on an island first known as Senegambia and now called Goree Island, located at the westernmost point in West Africa. Goree Island used to serve as a strategic trading post for the transatlantic slave trade - African men, women, and children were held and traded on the island before being loaded onto ships to the Americas. The visit to Salt Lake City brought me face-to-face with birth records of Jim Sampson.

Tracing the ancestry of my forefathers requires continuous digging into census files, reading the works of historians, and comparing 21st century culture with that of the 19th and 20th centuries. Compounding this challenge is the fact that records on slaves are limited. While many of my European colleagues can trace their beginnings to the Mayflower and the Continental Congress, the fact of marginalized status of my African ancestors formed an undeciphered wall. The huge gaps in official records did not quell my search for my ancestry. Getting beyond that wall is through the route of deoxyribonucleic acid (DNA), a long molecule that contains our unique genetic code. DNA fingerprinting was invented in 1984 by Professor Jeffrey after he realized one could detect variations in human DNA in the form of mini-satellites. Mini-satellites are short sequences of repetitive DNA that show greater variation from one person to the next. Armed with a kit, a Father's Day gift from my daughter, I followed the instructions on it and sent the specimens off for analysis. I realize that the procedure is not an ancestry test, but it utilizes existing databases that represent the modern world population.

My test results reveal origins in five areas: The dominant region is sub-Saharan Africa, including the countries of Tanzania,

Mozambique, and South Africa, all in the southern part of the continent, and all of which I have visited. There is also evidence of ancestral connection in South America; region two includes Central/South America and Guyana; region three includes the Middle East and North Africa, including Morocco; region four is in Asia, including East Timor; the final region, five, is Europe, including Cyprus. My work as a professor has led me to several countries on the African continent, including trips to some of the ports where slaves were placed on the ships to begin the passage over the Atlantic Ocean, and ultimately, to the USA.

Recalling my travels to the Continent and how they impacted my beliefs

June 3, 2001, is a day I will remember for the rest of my life. That was the day I first arrived on the Continent. Traveling to Addis Ababa, Ethiopia was the first of my journeys to more than a dozen African countries. It began with a 2-hour flight from St. Louis to Newark. At Newark, we boarded a Boeing 767 Ethiopian Airlines carrier. I immediately took notice of the fact that the entire crew, pilots and all, were not American, but Ethiopian. After we had boarded, the Capitan spoke, first in Amharic, then French, and finally, in English. The hosts were polished and behaved in courteous, professional fashion. After a physically exhausting passage over the Atlantic Ocean, the aircraft was refueled in Rome; a new crew, still all Ethiopian, took over. The sleek Boeing 767 aircraft landed on the runway as I awakened in Addis Ababa, Ethiopia. As I gained control of my faculties, I felt a thrilling blessing like nothing I had ever experienced. Ever since undergraduate school, I had longed to travel to the motherland. Ethiopia, upon first glance, was not aesthetically appealing. It is situated in in a high-altitude area with elevations greater than 6000 feet (higher than the city of Denver, CO). What grabbed me was the similarity of the terrain with that of rural Mississippi. The smell of kerosene was in the air, and young men armed with AK-47's stood atop the airport. The grass bordering the runway was nothing like what I had seen in USA; it was unkempt and scraggly. The terminal lacked the capacity to deplane passengers inside, so we deplaned onto the runway and walked a brief distance to the terminal. Our bags were slowly transferred to the conveyor belt (though not unlike most in the USA). Checking through customs, including currency exchange, was not much of a difficulty. One US dollar was equivalent to 22 Ethiopian birr in 2017, but at the time I was traveling in 2001, the exchange rate was 8.43 birr to one US dollar. The difference caught my attention when I traded 200 dollars for $1,686 birr.

Ground transportation was facilitated by school buses that resembled those in the USA. However, the interior was unkempt and the upholstery tattered. Yet, the people were the epitome of hospitality. I was struck by the attractiveness of the Ethiopians. Their distinct facial features, i.e., their cheekbones and tan complexion, caught my attention.

The Ethiopian people represent a rich cultural mosaic with 80 different languages and dialects and as many cultural variations. To the north and south of the country, three different Semitic languages, namely Tigre, Guraginya, and Tigrinya are spoken. Throughout the heartland, the language is Amharic. Ethiopia's official language derived from the ancient Ge'ez, which in this century, survives in widespread use in church liturgy and literature. To the east and other parts of the south are the Oromos, the Afars, and the Somalis, who are Cushitic-speaking peoples, while the associated Sidama languages are spoken to the southeast. To the west and southwest are the Nilotic peoples, each with their distinctive language and culture. Elsewhere around the country, there are many smaller communities or hinterlands, whose cultures, languages, and traditions are related to Ethiopia's long history and, as with all the peoples of the country, to its religions, be they Orthodox Christian, Muslim, or members of pagan communities.

After our group had boarded the bus, we were driven down Africa Avenue in the city of Addis Ababa. The street was packed with cars much like I had seen in Mexico, the Bahamas, and Puerto Rico. Addis Ababa boasts of wide tree-lined streets, fine architecture, a bustling railway station, great weather, and the incongruous donkey trains. Six lanes of motorized and non-motorized vehicles, containing a mixture of cars, trucks, and buses, along with an assortment of domesticated animals including ox driven carts and camels ambling in one direction was quite an introduction to transportation in Ethiopia. With such congestion, the trip to our lodging was as slow as rush hour traffic on Connecticut Avenue in Washington, DC. The long drive in the unair-conditioned trolley blew away some of the heavy smell of kerosene in the air. Finally, we arrived at our lodging facility, an elegant gated Hilton Resort Hotel, for the four-day stay. Our arrival meant getting some rest after traveling for nearly 24 hours. As I had in other international travel, I experienced jet lag, which is inevitable after crossing so many time zones in a day's trip.

My CIMPAD physician team member told me jet lag is also called desynchronosis. Flight fatigue, he said, is a natural byproduct of air travel across multiple time zones. Beside travel fatigue and insomnia, I have experienced anxiety, constipation, diarrhea, confusion, dehydration and a temporary circadian rhythm disorder, a disruption of the internal circadian clock. So, the fact that we had wonderful quarters in a resort hotel was a welcome reality.

Shortly after arrival, I came face-to-face with Ethiopian folk culture, an essential element of Ethiopia in the 21st century. Artists and craftsmen make their own contributions to the country's cultural and social development. Almost every town has its own cultural troupe made up of singers and dancers, poets and writers, and its own cultural hall in which the troupe recreates the song and dance of a bygone age in its particular area. I photographed a housing site in Bahir Dar as our bus took us away from Addis Ababa to the hinterlands. The trip to Ethiopia was devoted to dealing with governance and sustainable development. The theme of nation building was the centerpiece of the conference. Immediate problems revolved around agriculture, food production, and distribution. Civil service reform, one of my specialties, was aimed at ending corruption and nepotism; gender equality and development including issues of women's health, changing the perceived role of women, and enhancing their participation in public policy development, conflict resolution, general healthcare including AIDS prevention and reduction, and the role of non-governmental organizations in the entire enterprise were the substance of our four-day meeting.

Post-conference travel allowed exploration of other parts of the country. The first place we visited was Bahir Dar. We checked out of the Hilton at 5 AM on Thursday, June 7. We were transported to Bole airport for Ethiopian Airlines flight 128, which departed Addis Ababa at 7 AM and arrived at Bahir Dar at 8 AM. We were then transported to the Tana Hotel, a far cry from the comforts of the Hilton Resort. Midmorning began with a tour of Bahir Dar, north of Addis Ababa.

The excursion to the hinterlands brought us to see the weavers/woodworkers market, and later, we enjoyed a visit to an indigenous Ethiopian village located at the mouth of the Blue Nile River. As our trip got underway, I chose a seat in the front of the vehicle. This I refer to as the "shotgun seat," a placement that allowed me to point my camera and take photographs. On many occasions, I would ask the driver to stop and allow me to take some. I must have known that not every one of my colleagues were as interested in photography as I. Moreover, there was a time schedule, but for me, the opportunity to take a permanent impression was more important.

Most of us Americans were new to travel off the beaten path in Africa, so we eagerly looked forward to each new venue. While in Ethiopia, we traveled to the Nile River. The Nile River rises up out of the eastern Africa region, with sources from the Ethiopian highlands. Its basin covers eleven nations: Sudan, Kenya, Uganda, Democratic Republic of Congo, Rwanda, Tanzania, Burundi, Ethiopia, Eritrea, Egypt and South Sudan.

Nile River in Ethiopia

I expected the Nile River to reflect the blue skies, but its brackish brown color meant that the waters were polluted. The sight of Tisisat Falls in Amhara, Ethiopia reminded me of the importance of an environmental protection agency. The pictures I had carried in my mind prior to actually visiting the falls were of a beautiful blue sky refection. I should have known better, if for no reason, but the fact that our bus had to park about five miles away from the sight and we had to hike the rest of the way. The treacherous climb and navigation challenges allowed us to see villages where people lived. The American in me wanted to see highways and interstate arteries, places to shop and eat en route to the sight, but that was not the case. We had to "rough it," and in so doing, I was reminded of creature comforts in the good ole USA!

On June 8, we checked out of the Tana Hotel and traveled to the airport for our trip to Gondar, the capital city of Ethiopia from 1632 to 1855. Gondar is noted for its medieval castles and churches. This time, we checked into Goha Hotel before beginning our tour of the city. Our tour included the unique compound containing a number of 17th century castles, built by various emperors who ruled Ethiopia during that period.

Ruins in the Ethiopian hinterland

Among the sites were the 18th century palace of the Ras Beit, the ruined palace of Kusquam, the church at Debre Berhan Selassie with its unique murals, and the Palace of Empress Mentiwab. This excursion made clear that this place on the Continent contains a distinctive part of world culture. The delicious cuisine accented my exotic experience.

On Saturday, June 9, we traveled to Lalibela and checked into Roha Hotel. Lalibela, Bahir Dar, and Gondar are places in the hinterlands. Sometimes at these facilities, there would be no running water or hot water. It was not unusual to be having dinner when all the electricity would shut off. We were prepared to bring with us such necessities as toilet paper, soap, and other vitals. This is not to suggest that these were not available, but they provided some "insurance" for some of us "ugly" Americans. The photo below is one I captured of a herdsman.

Sunday, June 10 found us checking out of the Roha Hotel to prepare for our trip to Axum. Axum is Ethiopia's most ancient city and the center of a glorious empire that flourished more than 3000 years ago. A quick flight from Lalibela placed us in Axum by midmorning. There we checked into Yeha Hotel, had lunch, and thereafter, began our tour of Axum. Our tour took us to the magnificent stelae or obelisks, the graves of King Kaleb and King Gabre Meskal, and the Queen of Sheba's castle foundations and legendary bath. Axum is a city in northern Ethiopia. It's known for its tall, carved obelisks, relics of the ancient Kingdom of Aksum. Most are in the Northern Stelae Park, including a huge fallen pillar, now in pieces. Centuries-old St. Mary of Zion is a Christian church and pilgrimage site believed to have housed the Biblical Ark of the Covenant. The neighboring Chapel of the Tablet is said to contain the Ark today.

Our guide relayed to us the legendary account of Empress Mentewab. She was born in the Qwara province west of Lake Tana and was thought to have a Portuguese ancestor. Mentewab rose from these origins to become one of the most powerful women in Ethiopian history.

She became the second wife of emperor Bakaffa in 1722 and, outliving him, was crowned empress and co-ruler with their son Iyasu. From the seat of government in Gondar, Mentewab wielded considerable influence in all corners of the empire. Her power is made clear in the opulent additions to the Royal Enclosure at Gondar built under her direction: her own castle, a lavish banquet hall, and in the mountains outside the city at a site called Qusquam, a church devoted to the memory and significance of the Virgin Mary.

She also happened to build another palace for herself adjoining the church. She outlived Iyasu and moved to maintain her clout in the new court of her grandson Iyoas. However, legend has it that her daughter-in-law, Wubit, having been widowed by Iyasu's death but having her son on the throne, challenged Mentewab, believing that it was her turn to be empress.

The conflict escalated, and both women called upon relatives and courtiers for support. Mentewab summoned Mikael Sehul to sway the dispute in her favor, but the move backfired and Sehul seized power for himself, murdering the young boy emperor Iyoas and marrying the youngster's aunt to consolidate power.

In anguish and grief at the death of her grandson by her own undoing, Empress Mentewab fled Gondar and vowed never to return. She lived out the rest of her days in seclusion at her estate and church at Qusquam. From this brief lesson on history and culture of Ethiopia, we came to have an even deeper appreciation for African women in world history. Extending to present time, I muse that the story is evidence of challenges that all women have faced throughout eternity. Unfortunately, the glare of white privilege blinded many before truth could surface.

Church of St. Mary of Zion

We ended our tour with a visit to the 16th century Cathedral of St. Mary of Zion, which is said to hold the original Ark of the Covenant, and is thus the holiest church in Ethiopia. The Church of St. Mary of Zion, with treasures containing the Ark of the Covenant, is the oldest Christian church on the African continent. First built in the 4th century AD in Aksum, Ethiopia, it also bears the distinction of being the most important church in Ethiopia. In the 4th century AD, the Axumite prince Ezana, the first Christian ruler of the Kingdom of Axum (in present-day Eritrea and Ethiopia), was instructed in Christianity by two Syrian monks. The church is believed to have been built in the reign of Ezana and has been rebuilt several times since then, including during the reign of Fasilides in the 17th century. St. Mary of Zion is the place where Ethiopian emperors came to be crowned.

There are numerous relics and evidences of a civilization that occupied the near northern lands of Africa. One of the most prominent of those relics is the Obelisk of Axum. The Obelisk of Axum is a 4th-century AD, 24-meter-tall, 160-ton granite stele/obelisk found in the city of Axum in Ethiopia.

It is ornamented with two false doors at the base and features decorations resembling windows on all sides.

The obelisk of Axum

In ancient times, the name Ethiopia was primarily used to refer to the modern-day nation of Sudan, based in the upper Nile valley south of Egypt, also called Kush, and then secondarily in reference to sub-Saharan Africa in general.

Before our trip, to the Continent, we were under the impression that Ethiopian cultural practices, which had previously barred women from entry to certain places such as the inner sanctum of the churches, etc., would be set aside. That was not the case. When our tour guide brought us to the temple, we were instructed to remove our shoes, and that our female Americans were not welcomed in the holiest of holy places. Perhaps the most startling experience is that after our negotiations failed to allow female entry, we sat on the steps of the temple in an open grassy area, and suddenly, there appeared several men clothed in cultural garb and armed with what appeared to be automatic weapons.

We froze from fright. Then, our guide (also Ethiopian) interacted with the young men, and their communication put us at ease. But this was not the only occasion when my fears of the unknown continent caused anxiety. One such occasion was on Monday, June 11, 2003; as we were preparing to return to Addis Ababa, we came upon army tanks that appeared to have been destroyed in some sort of conflict. Simultaneously we heard the drone of helicopters flying above. It turns out that the helicopters were dispatched by the United Nations. The sounds of upheaval were remnants of the Ethiopian-Eritrean war, an interstate conflict between nations in the Horn of Africa. We learned from locals that there was a long standing "mutual" enmity and suspicion in relations between the people of Tigray proper and Eritrean Tigre people. The root of conflict between Ethiopia and Eritrea was a dispute over border lines. It seemed that the focal point of the conflict was the fact that Eritrea is geographically situated adjacent to the Red Sea and the Gulf of Aden, and Ethiopia is landlocked. Both the Sudan and Djibouti are adjacent to Eritrea. After World War II, Eritrea was annexed to Ethiopia. In 1991, the Eritrean People's Liberation Front defeated the Ethiopian government. Eritrea proclaimed its independence on May 24, 1991. In the days that we had traveled to Bahir Dar and Gondor, we were in the area where the war had been fought. The Eritrean-Ethiopian War took place from May 1998 to June 2000, but remnants of the aftermath of the war remained in 2003 when we visited, the conflict becoming one of the most visible in the Horn of Africa. When we began our departure from Ethiopia, our caravan of buses were stopped by armed soldiers as we attempted to reach the airport to leave for the USA. The soldiers demanded to see our identification; our Ethiopian guides explained to the soldiers that we were indeed USA citizens and that we were not a part of the contending factions. When we were released, we traveled to the outskirts of Addis Ababa. We only stopped when we felt safe and gathered in a circle, where we prayed for safety as we returned. Thankfully, we were able to safely return to our homes in America.

The travel to Ethiopia was the beginning of my excursions on the Continent. Traveling to and through the cities and villages reminded me of assigned readings on urban and regional planning. During my doctoral study, I was introduced to this area of study, a kind of academic program that is closely tethered to both political science and economics. I remembered that upon entering Graduate School of Public and International Affairs at Pitt, I was being prepared for a career in international service. In fact, I was very interested in working with the World Bank, but instead, I accepted an appointment for university teaching and research, and remained there for 38 years. Near the end of my career in the academy, in 2012, I was awarded a Fulbright to teach and research in Thailand.

With the initial introduction to the continent, I would become aware firsthand of the life of my African brothers and sisters. After Ethiopia came visits to more than a dozen countries, all of which provided epiphanies of their own nature, culture, and experiences.

Travels to the southern part of the continent: Mozambique

In the 2000s, the CIMPAD travels had become a staple in my life. In the winter preceding the spring of 2003, our group received an invitation from officials in Mozambique. Mozambique, which was colonized by the Portuguese, was the last African country to gain its independence. It is a Southern African nation whose long Indian Ocean coastline is dotted with popular beaches, such as

Tofo, and includes other offshore marine parks. In the Quirimbas Archipelago, a 250-kilometer stretch of coral islands, mangrove-covered Ibo Island has colonial-era ruins surviving from a period of Portuguese rule. The Bazaruto Archipelago farther south has reefs which protect rare marine life, including dugongs. Our guide explained that on weekends, the air would be filled with the smell of barbeque and other foods that used on weekends for festivals.

The country has a strategic location along the eastern coast of Southern Africa and is gateway to six hinterland countries. I would later learn that Mozambique is one of the African countries where I have ancestral connection. It has abundant natural resources: hydroelectricity, energy, coal, minerals, and timber; additionally, it exports prawns, cotton, cashew nuts, sugar, tea, and copra, as well. The currency exchange was 15,000 meticales for 1 US dollar. So, in this beautiful place, I was walking around as a rich guest in those days in mid-July. However, the carvings, trinkets, and other art pieces barely made a dent in what I purchased, largely because I was not prepared to ship the art pieces back to the USA, and partly because I did not have full confidence in the system of commerce.

Although Mozambican independence was won in 1975, a 20-year civil war ensued, and that meant that the frameworks necessary for government building were delayed. Trusting the system for commerce, I was able to take photographs that keep the memories fresh.

The travel to Maputo, Mozambique included a delay en route, a three day stop in Johannesburg, South Africa. The airport stop took me to South Africa for the first time. It was the last leg of the trip which also had had a refueling and crew change stopover in Dakar, Senegal after beginning in Washington, DC Each leg of the trip ranged from six to eight hours. Refueling was completed to ensure enough fuel to continuously fly 8 more hours before landing in Johannesburg, South Africa. This trip, more than any other, impressed me of the difference between the landmass in the USA versus the African landmass. If it were possible to transport the CONUS to the continent of Africa, the entire landmass of United States would not cover the expanse of the land between Senegal on the Atlantic Ocean and the African countries in northeastern Africa that border the Indian Ocean. After we landed in Johannesburg, we collected our bags and cleared customs. The seventeen-hour journey from the USA left me tired and longing for a bed. The air time between Dakar and Johannesburg was eight hours! Now that we were on the ground, I smelled burning rubber; that did not bother me nearly as much as the unexpected lengthy travel to our hotel and a bed. What would have taken up to thirty minutes in the USA took nearly ninety minutes. I took to heart that one could place the entire continental USA on the northern portion of the African continent and two thirds of the Continent would not be covered! The time difference of seven hours meant that my body did not comprehend that our hosts were ready to entertain us immediately. We were told that our accommodations were not ready, so we traveled to a restaurant. There we met mayors from places in Southern Africa. They were a most impressive and hospitable group: from Angola, Namibia, South Africa and Swaziland; however, none of them spoke the same language. The reception was warm and inviting even though my body was crying for rest. The group of mayors were excited to greet us. Libations and food were plentiful, and soon, they had formed a line dance to the sounds of Wilson Pickett, James Brown, and other American soul music artists. As I first observed the line dance and then became a participant, I was astonished how rhythmically similar were our responses and moves to the music! We were treated to a magnificent barbeque, accompanied by compelling and enlightening conversation, and then transported to our hotel. Finally, a bed and the promise of rest became real.

As I lay in my bed that night, I thought about the challenges of the promise of democracy among so many people that were new to or unfamiliar with the reality of non-colonial self-rule. Formulating rules and procedures for government, advising elected officials, and having an expectation that citizen participation mattered raised my personal appreciation for democracy in America, even with all its flaws. I came to reason that various cultures are variously receptive to democracy. It is important to consider that there are 54 countries that make up the continent of Africa. Most of these are nations of diverse cultures, origins, and languages. Moreover, based on my observations from traveling to many of the countries, there is no ethos that drives individuals to form political unions, despite notions to the contrary. It appears to me that informal social contracts facilitate communication between tribes, and leadership is not universally bound by term limits. European nations carved up the continent to garner natural resources. The Europeans colonized (almost) the entire continent. Each visit to the continent caused me to wonder why and how the African people acquiesced to economic enslavement.

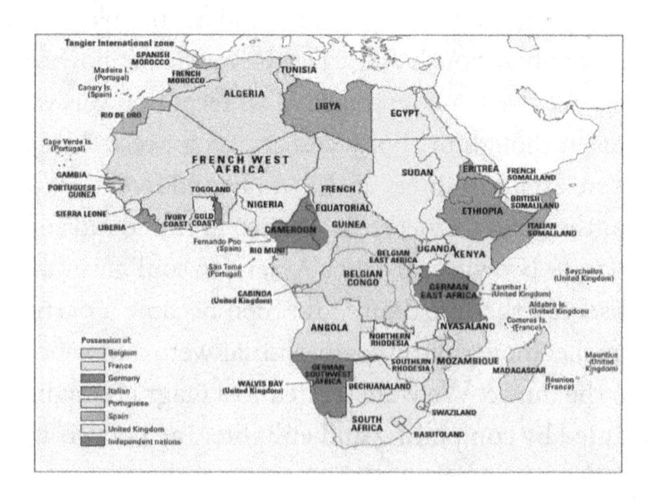

Mozambique is a lovely country with hospitable hosts. The Mozambican ambiance tested my prior beliefs about the country's history. For a long time, I was amazed about how peaceful a group could be amidst such impoverished conditions. Mozambique was special to me because my DNA tests revealed that some of my parentage was connected to this place.

Mozambican men artisans

Lying beside the Indian Ocean, Mozambique is home to artisans of extraordinary talent. Pottery was especially appealing. We came upon a group of gentleman potters, who had completed the pieces displayed in the photo. Even those in our group that were not eager to shop on the Continent, could not resist the beauty of their work. It is clear that there is an export market for their work. I purchased many of the pieces of art that now adorn my study. One of the undeniable aspects of my observation of Southern Africa and Mozambique, in particular, was the apparent inner-spirit of the native Africans. Looking through my American lens, I saw as a deprived people with limited industrialization. I overlooked the ingenuity of the human spirit and the ability to make a way when everything seemed overwhelming. I came to know that the Mozambicans had little idea of resources they would have in a Western type (USA) atmosphere. The native instinct of the African was that if they could not find a means, they would create a means to succeed. I recognize that this is the same spirit that kept many historically black universities afloat with limited resources.

Mozambican women artisans

Archives and oral traditions hold little information about rural African women's history in most African countries. Traveling through Mozambique, we saw beautiful cloth artifacts produced by rural women in Mozambique. Women's contributions to Mozambican culture and history reside in places long invisible to scholars, but in plain view in everyday life. Through their performance of tasks culturally defined as women's work, rural women and girls carve out feminine social spaces where they create historical records with female actions at center stage. Using skills honed over centuries of specialized labor - as mothers, farmers, healers, artisans - they memorialize experiences that archives and formal oral traditions disregard.

The more visible artisans along the commercial paths featured male artisans, as shown in the photo above. To be sure, their work was remarkable, but unfortunately, there is no viable marketing measure that would promote all artisans. In southern Mozambique, men in Magude have been migrating to South Africa in search of mine work since the late 1800s. Known in precolonial times for its agricultural prosperity, droves of cattle, and bustling trade, Magude became, in the 20th century, an increasingly impoverished labor reserve whose patrilineal kinship and marriage rules pressured women to remain on the land and sustain communities in men's absence. The limited archival evidence on these women falls into one of two categories: it either depicts them as powerless, dutiful appendages of their husbands and male kin, or it vilifies the minority of women who "abandoned" their marital homes and fled the countryside to live in town. Free from the "misery" and (according to European commentators) moral constraints of rural life, so-called "town women" earned money on the margins of the colonial economy, making their way as market traders, food vendors, prostitutes, or - for the fortunate few - low-paid factory labor. In the records of the colonial state, as in scholarship relying on archives alone, rural women are the faceless, unchanging background to these events, toiling on in worsening poverty and helpless to improve their lot.

In the early 1900s, women such as Cufassane Munisse walked for days at a stretch to exchange her pottery for baskets of grain (or vice versa), visiting female kin and friends spread throughout southern Mozambique and in neighboring South Africa. In the course of this regional trade, potters also spread new vessel styles and decorating techniques, defying European stereotypes of rural women's passivity, home-boundness, and resistance to technological change. The vessel styles evident in the male potters' work makes its own claim to uniqueness, especially to visiting groups such as CIMPAD. Fairly or not, we did not factor into our buying decisions the rightfulness of whether female members were equally treated. The artisans' work was formed by hand from earth and water and finished in the heat of fire fed by air. Such creations are built without the use of a wheel, instead using a hand-coiling technique. Once ready for firing, the pots are carefully piled up in a shallow fire pit on the ground, then covered over with dry grasses and leaves. The vegetation is set alight, and the pots are fired in a controlled fire naturally ventilated by the air.

As the relief map on the adjoining page shows, before 1800, Africa was controlled by numerous outside countries. However, by 1914, the year of the onset of WWI, all of Africa, with the exception of Ethiopia and Liberia, was under the control of European countries. Ethiopia had up-and-down relations with Italy that could easily cause Ethiopia to be a possession of Italy. Liberia was the country co-founded by the United States. Working in tandem with the American Colonization Society (ACS) in 1817, there emerged a plan to send free African-Americans to Africa as an alternative to emancipation in the United States. In 1820, the first erstwhile US slaves arrived at the British colony of Sierra Leone from the United States, and in 1821, the ACS founded the colony of Liberia south of Sierra Leone as a homeland for former slaves outside British jurisdiction. In 1822, the society established on the west coast of Africa a colony that, in 1847, became the independent nation of Liberia. In 2018, there are some rich countries on the continent, but the bulk of the countries, while politically independent from the Europeans, are still dependent to various extents on commercial and economic ties to Europe. Colleagues who traveled via CIMPAD remarked over dinner that various colonizers provided various levels of human treatment to their subjects.

Our CIMPAD party flew from Johannesburg to Maputo, Mozambique in June 2003. Maputo, the lush capital of

Mozambique, sits on the shore of the Indian Ocean. It was founded as a port town by the Portuguese. The influences of travelers and traders from Africa, Asia, and Europe have made the city a diverse and lively metropolis. The area is famous for its prawns in peri-peri sauce, a spicy concoction made from an especially hot African chili pepper.

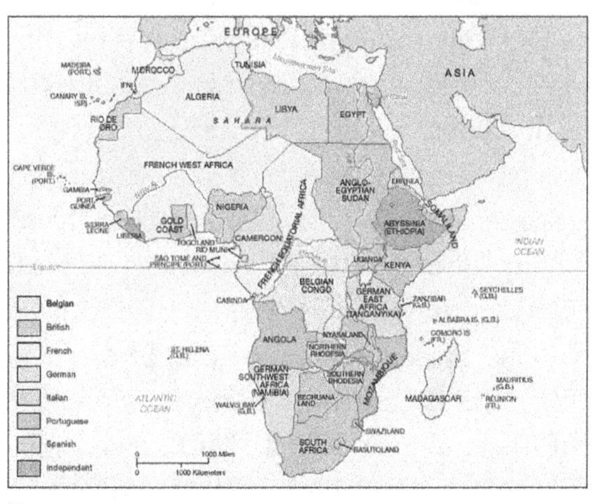

Africa, 1914. Before 1800, Africa was controlled by numerous African states. By 1914, all of Africa, with the exceptions of Ethiopia and Liberia, was under the control or oversight of European powers.

Like many of the other countries we visited, Mozambique displayed the vast differences between the "haves" and the "have-nots." While there were no visibly gated housing developments, it was obvious that wealth disparity was clearly present. Lined up along the streets of central Maputo, Mozambique's capital, are expensive European-style bars and restaurants with sophisticated names like Cafe Continental, Nautilus, 1908 and Mundos. The residential houses and flats in the capital of this southern African nation are a flabbergasting and bewildering array of 1960s modernist and art deco icons, mixed with new-money skyscrapers. Further away in the new, Chinese-built airport in Maputo, which was completed in February, aftershave lotions sell for $230 and bottles of Dom Pérignon cost $320. That is three months' salary for the average worker, who lives on 3,000 meticales ($100) a month.

No figures exist on the wealth disparity here. Mozambique is a jumble of statistical contradictions. It has one of the highest real GDP growth rates in the world, at 7.5%. Yet it ranks 185th out of 187 countries on the 2013 UN Human Development Index by the UN Development Program. It is one of the poorest countries in the world, with more than 55% of its 23.9 million people officially living below the poverty line.

In central Maputo the latest Toyota Pradas, Hiluxes, and Land Rovers drive down avenues named Julius Nyerere, Ho Chi Minh, and Kim Il Sung. These former socialist leaders might be turning in their graves at the wealth disparities to be found here. But who are these new super-rich? They are government ministers; they are friends and relatives of the Front for the Liberation of Mozambique (FRELIMO), the ruling party; they are people working with and for the UN; and a handful are oil and gas investors and associated traders. The international hotels in Maputo are booked to 95% capacity during the week with businesspeople converging here from across the globe: Australia, the US, United Arab Emirates, Norway, Brazil, and China. The majority are here for the country's oil and natural gas - in 2011, Mozambique discovered offshore gas fields.

On our last day in Mozambique, we revisited the beach located on the Indian Ocean. Palm trees swayed in the mild temperatures. In the distance, we could sailors and fishers basking in the sunshine. The world was theirs, and they were oblivious to those who gawked in wonder of the peaceful paradise.

Along the ocean in Mozambique

In 1975, Mozambique had become one of the last African countries to gain its independence from its European colonizer, in this instance, Portugal. Two years later, the Mozambican Civil War began in 1977. The conflict resembled the neighboring Angolan Civil War in that both were proxy wars of the Cold War that started soon after the countries gained independence from Portugal. The ruling party, the Front for the Liberation of Mozambique (FRELIMO), and the national armed forces, according to an account in a 1988 report in *Jump up* entitled "Armed Forces of Mozambique," were the apparent principals in the conflict. FRELIMO was strongly opposed in 1977 by the Mozambique Resistance Movement (RENAMO), which received funding from white-ruled Rhodesia and (later) apartheid South Africa. It is estimated that about a million people died in fighting and from starvation; 5 million civilians were displaced, according to additional reports in *Jump up*; and many were made amputees by landmines, a legacy from the war that plagued Mozambique for more than two decades afterward.

Fighting ended in 1992, and the country's first multi-party elections were held in 1994.

The conditions for our consultant group, CIMPAD, to accept the invitation were to develop via a forum, a research dialogue, and related activities that would facilitate connecting institutional linkages. In the end, our conference aimed at strengthening and promoting sector involvement in the sustainable development of communities. It is still too early to give us a grade, but based on my more recent observations, there has been some progress. I still recall the opening event of our conference. We were greeted by Graca Machel, widow of Samora Moisés Machel, the Mozambican military commander, politician, revolutionary, and first president of Mozambique. Machel died in office in 1986 when his presidential aircraft crashed near the Mozambique-South African border. It was commonly accepted that the South African government was a participant in his death. Mrs. Machel later became the wife of Nelson Mandela in 1998, when Nelson was 80 years of age. After Samora Moises Machel was killed in 1986, Mr. Mandela was still in prison on Robben Island. He later began correspondence with her. She was 27 years younger than him. Perhaps most noteworthy, she is one of the few women to be first lady for two different countries.

Mozambique continues to this date to be an infant democracy. Governmental frameworks, e.g., institutional arrangements for healthcare, public safety, and disaster/emergency management; trade, finance, and development; and natural resources, food security, etc., are in various stages of development. Moreover, there were no political and administrative processes for governance and conflict resolution. My western upbringing told me the needs of the country were dire.

After the conference, we flew to Cape Town, South Africa. Part of me felt guilt; in some weird sense, the travel to

Mozambique was like going to Disney World. My empathy was insufficient for us to make a serious impact on conditions that are indelibly pressed in my memory. In fact, one of the "attractions" of witnessing life on the mother continent ends, and I was able to reflect and fly away. What lay in front of me was a great history lesson, the likes of which I did not receive in all my 24 years of formal education. My travels exposed me to a glimpse of the impact of colonization on a group of African nations.

The history of external colonization of Africa can be divided into two stages: Classical antiquity and European colonialism. In popular parlance, discussions of colonialism in Africa usually focus on the European conquests that resulted in the Scramble for Africa after the Berlin Conference in the 19th century. Between the 1870s and 1900, Africa faced European imperialist aggression, diplomatic pressures, military invasions, and eventual conquest and colonization. At the same time, African societies put up various forms of resistance against the attempt to colonize their countries and impose foreign domination. From the 15th century onwards, most of the countries in Africa came to be colonized by the European world powers, Great Britain, France, Portugal, Germany, Spain, Italy, and Belgium. South Africa was officially colonized in 1652. The more prominent European countries, Britain, Portugal, and France, had already claimed for themselves vast areas of Africa and Asia, and emerging powers like Italy and Germany had done so on a smaller scale. With the dismissal of the aging Chancellor Bismarck by Kaiser Wilhelm II, the relatively low-key colonization became what historians call the Scramble for Africa. The 1885 Berlin Conference, initiated by Bismarck to establish international guidelines for the acquisition of African territory, formalized this "New Imperialism." Between the Franco-Prussian War and the World War I, Europe added almost 9 million square miles - one-fifth of the land area of the globe - to its overseas colonial possessions. A "telling" observation is the fact that Germany, which had at one time various colonies, would later make exchanges with France, Britain, and Portugal. There was plenty of buying and trading among the Europeans. There were six principal colonies of German Africa, along with native kingdoms and polities; they were the legal precedents for the modern states of Burundi, Cameroon, Namibia, Rwanda, Tanzania, and Togo. Parts of contemporary Chad, Gabon, Ghana, Kenya, Mozambique, Nigeria, the Central African Republic, and the Republic of the Congo were also under the control of German Africa at various points during its existence.

Before colonization, Africa was characterized by widespread flexibility in terms of movement, governance, and daily lifestyles. The continent consisted not of closed reproducing entities, equipped with unique unchanging cultures, but of more fluid units that would readily incorporate outsiders into the community with the condition that they accepted its customs, and where the sense of obligation and solidarity went beyond that of the nuclear family. Precolonial societies were highly varied, where they were either stateless, run by the state, or run by kingdoms. The notion of communalism was accepted and practiced widely; land was held commonly and could not be bought or sold, although other things, such as cattle, were owned individually. In those societies that were not stateless, the chiefs ran the daily affairs of the tribe together with one or more councils. The colonization of Africa by Europe brought about many forms of government that are still visible today. Before colonization, however, there were many forms of government in Africa, ranging from powerful empires to decentralized groups of pastoralists and hunters.

The nuance of colonization

Settlements established by Europeans openly characterized the "abjection" of natives (the term abjection literally means "the state of being cast off"). The Europeans created new living arrangements that brought with it governing and academic institutions, as well as agricultural and technological innovations that partially generated the extractive institutions commonly attributed to colonialism by Western powers. In nearly all African countries today, the language used in government and media is a relic inherited from one of these waves of colonization. In the next pages, I introduce data I translated from the World Bank that tell the story of how each European colonizer treated their African subjects.

Observing my research tables below, one can see that the Continent overall is not competitive in the worldwide scheme vis-a-vis adult literacy rates, gross domestic product, and world ranking. These data became building blocks for my determination of the differences that each European colonizer had had on its "subjects". Overall, on the continent, liberation or independence began in the late 1950s, continuing through the late 1980s. What this implies is that British imprint on education, thought, culture, and health would last for years beyond the so-called liberation dates. The adult literacy rates, GDP, and world rankings were extracted from 2010 data as captured by World Bank.

World Development Indicators include data spanning up to 56 years - from 1960 to 2016. *World view* frames global trends with indicators on population, population density, urbanization, Gross National Income (GNI), and Gross Domestic Product (GDP). The purpose of collecting the data is to present indicators measuring the world's economy and progress toward improving lives, achieving sustainable development, providing support for vulnerable populations, and reducing gender disparities.

Between the 1870s and 1900, Africa faced European imperialist aggression, diplomatic pressures, military invasions, and eventual conquest and colonization. By the early 20th century, however, much of Africa, except Ethiopia and Liberia, had been colonized by European powers.

Britain gained control of southern and northeastern Africa from Berlin. From 1880 to 1900, Britain gained control over or occupied what are now known as Egypt, Sudan, Kenya, Uganda, South Africa, Gambia, Sierra Leone, northwestern Somalia, Zimbabwe, Zambia, Botswana, Nigeria, Ghana, and Malawi.

The table below displays the World Bank data relative to liberation dates, adult literacy rates, gross domestic product, and world ranking for the fifteen British colonized territories. The statistic that captures my interest is the adult literacy rate. In the USA, the literacy rate is 99%. The global literacy rate for all people aged 15 and above is 86.3%. The global literacy rate for all males is 90.0% and the rate for all females is 82.7**%**. The world data indicate the average for the African countries that were once colonized by the British was 72.4%; the range was a low of 35% in Sierra Leone to a high of 90.7% in Zimbabwe. Considering that the British-colonized group had better scores across the board cast a disenchanted nuance over the other nations on the continent.

British-colonized African Countries: Liberation Dates, Adult Literacy Rates, Gross Domestic Product and World Ranking

African Country	Liberation Date	Adult Literacy Rate	Gross Domestic Product	World Ranking
Botswana	1966	81.2	14.9 B	109
Gambia	1957	40.1	1.05 B	178
Ghana	1957	74.8	32.2 B	86
Kenya	1963	85.1	40 B	85
Lesotho	1966	84.8	2.39 B	161
Malawi	1960	62.7	7 B	147
Namibia	1990	85	12.2 M	116
Nigeria	1960	68	369.1 B	45
Sierra Leone	1961	35.1	2.58 B	164
South Africa	1910	86.4	3.75 B	28
Sudan	1956	61	67 B	65
Swaziland	1968	83.1	4.40 B	153
Uganda	1962	66.8	20.2 B	104
Zambia	1964	80.6	20 B	106
Zimbabwe	1980	90.7	10 B	135

In 1830, France established its first African conquest after seizing Algiers, followed by several other conquests in Southeast Asia. Other African countries colonized by France include Senegal, Chad, Mali, Gabon, Tunisia, Niger, the Republic of Congo, Cameroon, and several others. The French colonized countries appear below. The French Colonial Empire constituted the overseas colonies, protectorates, and League of Nations mandate territories that came under French rule from the 16th century onward. Competing with Spain, Portugal, the Dutch United Provinces, and England, France began to establish colonies in North America, the Caribbean, and India in the 17th century. A series of wars with Britain and others resulted in France losing nearly all of its conquests by 1814.

French-colonized African Countries: Liberation Dates, Adult Literacy, Gross Domestic Product, and World Ranking

African Country	Liberation Date	Adult Literacy Rate	Gross Domestic Product	World Ranking
Algeria	1962	70	159.4 M	49
Benin	1960	34.7	6.6 M	137
Burkina Faso	1960	21.8	8.8 M	29
Cameroon	1960	67.9	22.4 M	95
Central African Republic	1960	51	2.01 M	163
Chad	1960	25.7	22.8 M	94
Comoros	1975	56.5	562 M	185
Djibouti	1977	67.9	1.04 M	172
Gabon	1960	63.2	13.1 M	112
Morocco	1956	51.7	91.2 M	59
Madagascar	1960	68.9	8.7 M	130
Mali	1964	46.4	9.2 M	127
Mauritania	1960	51.2	3.6 M	154
Niger	1960	28.7	5.5 M	146
Rwanda	1962	70.4	5.6 M	144
Senegal	1960	39.3	12.9 M	114
Togo	1960	60.9	3.2 M	157
Tunisia	1956	74.2	-	-

Windshield observations and a review of related literature reveal that African countries colonized by the French are less well-off than any of the other colonized countries. Having travel experiences in Mauritania, Senegal, and Central African Republic, I could make windshield comparisons with South Africa, Uganda, and Kenya, all colonized by the British, and the differences are noticeable. Of course, South Africa and Kenya are comparatively more "westernized" than most African countries. My reflection does not mean I think the West to be superior. Each place in the globe has its own unique beauty.

These data I collected assisted my assessment of the differences each European colonizer had on its "subjects". Liberation or independence began in the late 1950s, continuing through the 1980s. What this implies is that British imprint on education, thought, culture, and health would last for years beyond the so-called liberation dates. The adult literacy rates, GDP, and world rankings were extracted from 2010 data as captured by World Bank. The French-colonized countries appear below. Data on adult literacy rates were not available to the World Bank for the French-colonized countries.

African countries colonized by the French are less well-off in terms of governing their own wealth and fostering higher standards of living when compared to any of the other colonized countries. As I noted earlier, they can be seen as some of the least "westernized" areas. My reflection does not necessarily mean I think the West to be superior, but when viewed through the lens of the World Bank that measures adult literacy rates, gross domestic product, etc., one can see the impact of colonization on these countries. Those countries colonized by the Portuguese were materially better off than the French but both trailed the British. I have travel experiences in Mozambique and Tanzania (Zanzibar was once controlled by Portugal), both Portuguese-colonized, and we can continue to see differences that could be associated with the individual European colonizer.

Portuguese-colonized Countries: Liberation Date, Adult Literacy Rate, World Ranking 2010

African Country	Liberation Date	Average Adult Literacy Rate **	Gross Domestic Product ***	World Ranking
Angola	1975	67.4	84.4M	61
Cape Verde	1975	76.6	1.6M	166
Guinea-Bissau	1973	42.4	879K	177
Mozambique	1975	47.8	9.5M	124
Sao Tome and Principe	1975	54.9	197M	197
Tanzania	1961	69.4	23B	93

*** USD

It is noteworthy that those countries colonized by the Portuguese were among the last countries to take their liberation; all had late, i.e., post-1970, liberation dates. In fact, five of the last eight countries on the continent to gain their liberation from European control were the Portuguese-controlled ones, while Egyptian liberation had occurred more than 50 years earlier. The time lag or variation in liberation dates can be associated with the colonizing European country itself. While colonization could hardly be characterized as humanistic, historical records distinguish those colonizers that fostered educational opportunity versus those that used the colonies exclusively as free labor. The colonizers had sought domination for economic, not humanitarian reasons. Given that reality, it would be a bit difficult to expect humanitarian support of their workforce. The British found time to provide some education and training, but focused on tribal differences and thereby fueled animosity among their workers. Perhaps the best example is the bloody conflict between the Hutu and the Tutsi in Rwanda in 1994. United Nations data estimate the slaughter of 80,000 to 200,000 Hutus by the Tutsi army in Rwanda and Burundi between 1972 and 1994. In just 100 days, during which Hutu militias targeted Tutsis, between 800,000 and 1 million people were killed.

Belgium-colonized African Countries: Liberation Date, Adult Literacy Rate, GDP, and World Ranking

African Country	Liberation Date	Adult Literacy Rate	Gross Domestic Product	World Ranking
Belgium Congo/Central African Republic	1960	83.8	3.7 M	163

History records that Belgium had, at one time, up to three African countries. The Belgian Colonial Empire consisted of colonies possessed by Belgium between 1901 and 1962. This empire was unlike those of the major European imperial powers, since 98% of it was just one colony (about 76 times larger than Belgium) - the Belgian Congo - and that had originated as the private property of the country's king, King Leopold II, rather than being gained through the political action of the Belgian state. It was, however, the third largest colonial territory in Africa; in contrast, the possessions of Belgium's more powerful neighbor, Germany, came sixth in size.

Belgium itself had only been independent since 1830; prior to that, it was part of the Netherlands (and had a role in that country's colonies) or of France, or was governed by Spain or Austria. By the time independent Belgium might have been in a position to consider an overseas empire, major imperial powers such as the United Kingdom and France already had the most economically promising territories for colonization within their spheres of influence. Leopold II tried to interest his government in establishing colonies, but it lacked the resources to develop the candidate territories and turned down his plans. As early as 1860, he was urging his state to imitate its neighbors in acquiring overseas territory: "Extend beyond the sea whenever an opportunity is offered," he said, "you will find precious outlets for your products, food for your commerce… and a still better position in the great European family" Emerson, (1979). In 1876, he told delegates at an international conference on geography which he sponsored in Brussels that "to open to civilization the only part of our globe which it has not yet penetrated, to pierce the darkness which hangs over entire peoples, is, I dare say, a crusade worthy of this century of progress."

On October 19, 1914, near the Belgian city of Ypres, Allied and German forces began the first of what would be three battles to control the city and its advantageous positions on the northern coast of Belgium during the First World War. As I studied this history, I wondered what the Africans were doing.

Italian-colonized African countries: Liberation Dates, Adult Literacy, GDP, and World Ranking

African Country	Liberation Date	Adult Literacy Rate	Gross Domestic Product	World Ranking
Eritrea	1994	58.6	2.1M	162
Libya	1951	82.6	62.4M	64
Somalia*	1960	37.8		
Ethiopia**	1974	42.7	29.7M	87

*Somalia was partly ruled by Britain

**Ethiopia denies colonization

The Italian Empire comprised the colonies, protectorates, concessions, dependencies, and trust territories of the Kingdom of Italy and, after 1946, the Italian Republic. The genesis of the Italian Colonial Empire was the 1869 purchase, by a commercial company, of the coastal town of Assab on the Red Sea. This was taken over by the Italian government in 1882, becoming modern Italy‘s first overseas territory.

Over the next two decades, the pace of European acquisitions in Africa increased, causing the so-called "Scramble for Africa". At the onset of WWI in 1914, Italy had acquired in Africa a colony on the Red Sea coast (Eritrea), a large protectorate in Somalia, and authority in formerly Ottoman Libya (gained after the Italo-Turkish War). Italy‘s expansion inland from the Red Sea coast brought her into conflict with the Ethiopian Empire, which defeated her first at the battle of Dogali (1887) and again during first Italian invasion of Ethiopia in 1895-96. To be sure Europe was not the only colonizer.

The USA colonized one African country, Liberia, and the table below reveals its liberation date, adult literacy, gross domestic product and world ranking. These facts are not meant to heap praise on the USA. The cause of US colonization would be troubling if I had not known about the race question in America. Africa's first republic, Liberia, was founded in 1822 as a result of the efforts of the American Colonization Society to settle freed American slaves in West Africa. The society contended that the emigration of blacks to Africa was an answer to the problem of slavery and the "incompatibility of the races."

Marcus Garvey, a Jamaican-born black nationalist and leader of the Pan-Africanism movement, had sought to unify and connect people of African descent worldwide. Garvey was born in 1887 in St. Ann's Bay, Jamaica. His father was a stonemason and his mother a household servant. Of the 11 children born to the couple, only Marcus and one sibling survived into adulthood. Garvey attended school in Jamaica until he was 14, when he left St. Ann's Bay for Kingston, the island nation's capital, where he worked as an apprentice in a print shop. He later said he first experienced racism in grade school in Jamaica, primarily from white teachers. In the United States, he was a noted civil rights activist who founded the *Negro World* newspaper, a shipping company called Black Star Line, and the Universal Negro Improvement Association, a fraternal organization of black nationalists. As a group, they advocated for "separate but equal" status for persons of African ancestry, and as such, they sought to establish independent black states around the world, notably in Liberia on the west coast of Africa.

African Country	Liberation Date	Adult Literacy Rate	Gross Domestic Product	World Ranking
Liberia	1847	47.65	986K	174

The USA-colonized African country ranks 174 of 195 countries in the world. Clearly this paltry standing is far below most of the other African countries. One hundred seventy years after Liberia gained its "liberation," the percentage of residents 15 years or older constitutes less than half of the population that can read and write. It is difficult not to lay the blame for this condition at the doorstep of the USA, but it would be equally ignorant to believe that the forces of the Western world had no hand in the state of affairs in Liberia. As I reflect on Garvey's experiences, I can't help but think of the American fighters in my day, e.g., Rap Brown and Stokely Carmichael, who fought for self-sufficiency for black folks.

During each trip to the African continent, I would think of conversations at the table of 115 Melon Street and compare them with my latest experiences. These observations and musings enhanced my childhood tapes. I had never envisioned what I was seeing in those cities, townships, and places in the hinterland. The unseen experiences in the motherland enhanced my childhood tapes. I had never envisioned the beauty of South Africa as it lay astride the Atlantic Ocean on its west coast. Nor had I envisioned the calm of Ngorongoro Crater as I sat upon the ridge between Kenya and Tanzania. My arrival there at the crater occurred after an all-day drive from Nairobi over the worst roads I had ever experienced. The driving distance between Nairobi and the crater is more than 400 miles. It was not a "lovely, scenic drive." We traveled for ten hours in a bus which did not appear to have shock absorbers.

Houses showing lush life in Cape Town

The opulent view of houses along the Atlantic Ocean contrasted sharply with non-European life in the townships where poverty reigned. Khayelitsha, one of the most populous black townships, had no running water in the houses. There is electricity, but it is not unusual to see external electrical cords stretching from house to house. Many citizens of Khayelitsha are not aware of the right to running water. Despite the success of the African National Congress (ANC), which grew into power during the imprisonment of Nelson Mandela, among the rank and file, there is much to be desired in terms of citizens' rights and the delivery of services that are crucial for life as a human being.

Khayelitsha residents preparing meals

Khayelitsha residents were warm and inviting. My host offered to give me a tour of local life in the township. Our first designation was taken to a *shebeen*, an establishment originally understood to be an illicit bar or club where excisable alcoholic beverages were sold without a license. The term has spread far from its origins in Ireland, to Scotland, Canada, the United States, England, Zimbabwe, the English-speaking Caribbean, Namibia, Malawi, and South Africa. During midday, the bar was filled with young men. I was astonished when it became obvious that most of the women had day jobs, but not the men.

While the number of people living the five biggest slums in the world amounts to 5.7 million, this is only just a drop in the ocean. Today, by the most conservative estimates, about 900 million people live in slums. But most experts agree that including different types of informal settlements, the number goes up to 1.6 billion - representing 1/4 of the world's urban population. By 2030, it's estimated that 1 in 4 people on the planet will live in a slum or other informal settlement. The top two of the five largest slums are on the African continent:

- Khayelitsha in Cape Town (South Africa): 400,000
- Kibera in Nairobi (Kenya): 700,000
- Dharavi in Mumbai (India): 1,000,000
- Neza (Mexico): 1,200,000
- Orangi Town in Karachi (Pakistan): 2,400,000

Due to population growth and the migration trend from rural areas to cities, these slums are likely here to stay. In the Khayelitsha, located in Cape Town, South Africa, one toilet is shared by five families on average. Most people use open fields or bushes to do their business, which contributes to the spread of diseases like cholera within communities. It is estimated that the majority of people living in informal settlements worldwide do not have security of tenure or land rights. It's also the best place for criminals to attack. Yet, in my judgment, Cape Town, South Africa is truly one of the most beautiful places on the face of the earth.

Before traveling to South Africa, I had never seen such a natural mountain as Table Mountain. As the adjoining photo details, the top of the mountain is virtually flat. It serves as a tourist attraction for people across the world. As we went on safari, we came into contact with travelers from Sweden, Denmark, Australia, Germany, etc. Based on their vehicles they traveled in, it was easy to assume that they had access to material wealth. All of the obviously well-off and those in my party that felt blessed to be here were in awe of the sights we were observing.

Nor had I ever envisioned the calm of Ngorongoro Crater as I sat upon the ridge between Kenya and Tanzania. Arrival there in 2007 occurred after an all-day drive from Nairobi over the worst terrain I have ever experienced.

Travel between Kenya and Tanzania also acquainted me with the Maasai people. The trip from Nairobi was one of the most uncomfortable, 7-hour trips I have ever encountered. Nairobi was a beautiful city that I would love to revisit. The bus on which we traveled bounced on the rocky roads and only our rest stops provided any relief. Our guides had packed food, and only my hunger caused me to ingest the tasteless morsels of substance. There were no interstate roads as in the USA. I now understood why some of the group chose to shop in Nairobi. After all, my stay in Nairobi was at the Sarova Stanley Hotel, which was located on a street where other American-looking shopping places stood out in the non-daylight hours.

After the day long journey, we found lodging at a hunting reserve where the smell of barbeque was alluring as the door to the loading facility was opened. Our spacious lodgings made the uproarious travel a forgotten memory.

The CIMPAD scout team had worked out a visit to the Maasai tribe. When we arrived, we were unmistakably in the hinterlands I had read about in graduate school. The Maasai people welcomed us, their American brethren, to their home. Maasai are a Nilotic ethnic group inhabiting central and southern Kenya and northern Tanzania. They are among the best-known local populations due to their residence near the many game parks of the African Great Lakes region, as well as their distinctive customs and dress. The Maasai speak the Maa language, a member of the Nilo-Saharan family that is related to the Dinka and Nuer languages. Some have become educated in the official languages of Kenya and Tanzania, Swahili and English. The Maasai population has been reported as numbering 841,622 in Kenya in the 2009 census, compared to 377,089 in the 1989 census. Many of them spoke fluent English.

One of my Kenyan students at University of Missouri, upon learning of my travel to his home, told me of his distress with both the Tanzanian and Kenyan governments, since they have instituted programs to encourage the Maasai to abandon their traditional semi-nomadic lifestyle, but the people have continued their age-old customs. One study has suggested that the Maasai could pass on traditional survival skills such as the ability to produce food in deserts and scrublands, which could help populations adapt to climate change. Many Maasai tribes throughout Tanzania and Kenya welcome visitors to their villages to experience their culture, traditions, and lifestyle, in return for a fee. The Maasai are considered one of the tallest people groups in the world, with an average height of 6 feet 3 inches, according to some reports.

Traditional Maasai lifestyle is centered around their cattle, which constitute their primary source of food. The measure of a man's wealth is in terms of cattle and children. A herd of 50 cattle is respectable, and the more children, the better. A man who has plenty of one but not the other is considered to be poor. A Maasai religious belief relays that God gave them all the cattle on earth, leading to the belief that rustling cattle from other tribes is a matter of taking back what is rightfully theirs, a practice that has become much less common nowadays.

All of the Maasai's needs for food are met by their cattle. It is not uncommon for travel to be halted on a major road while a herd of cattle crosses the road. They eat the meat, drink the milk daily, and drink the blood on occasion. Bulls, oxen, and lambs are slaughtered for meat on special occasions and for ceremonies. Though the Maasai's entire way of life has historically depended on their cattle, more recently, with their cattle dwindling, the Maasai have grown dependent on food such as sorghum, rice, potatoes, and cabbage (known to the Maasai as goat leaves).

The Maasai in Kenya and Tanzania, Xhosa and Sotho in South Africa, Wolof and Fula in Senegal, and Bag and Banyankore in Uganda are among the few tribes I have come across in my travels to the Continent. I have come to believe that tribalism has prevented the development of an African community despite the efforts of such organizations as Organization for African Unity (OAU). Moreover, colonialism exacerbated the distance between countries. I believe that if there had been a United States of Africa, world history would have been significantly different.

Among the countries where my eyes have beheld the beauty of the great continent, none has been more memorable than Cape Town, South Africa. On three separate occasions, I have been able to travel to South Africa. It was this place that captured my fancy, for it so much reminded me of a combination of Toronto and San Francisco. Moreover, the currency exchange meant that one US dollar was equivalent to 10 rand, and there were so many things to buy. The choices in South Africa are far more extensive than any other on the Continent. However, South Africa was the home of apartheid, Nelson Mandela, and Robben Island, the African version of Alcatraz. Robben Island, that desolate outcropping five miles offshore, is a testament to courage and fortitude in the face of brutality, a must-see for any visitor to South Africa. Tours leave Cape Town four times a day, and the trip includes a bus tour of the island and a visit to the prison. Most inmates, including Nelson Mandela, were black men incarcerated for political offenses. The last of these prisoners were released in 1991. The island continued to serve as a medium-security prison for criminal offenders until 1996. In 1997, it was turned into a museum and declared a national monument, and in 1999, it received designation as a World Heritage Site. On each of my travels, I have taken the 45-minute ferry from Cape Town to what is now that museum. On each occasion after arriving at Robben Island, we boarded a tour bus to gain access. The guide would gesture to a bleak limestone quarry on the side of the road. It was here, he said, that Nelson Mandela toiled virtually every day for 13 years, digging up rock, some of which paved the road we were driving on. The sun was so relentless and the quarry so bright and dusty that Mandela was stricken with "snow blindness" that damaged his eyes.

Nevertheless, Mandela and other heroes of South Africa's anti-apartheid movement, such as Govan Mbeki and Walter Sisulu, used their time in this quarry to teach each other literature, philosophy, and political theory, among other things. "This campus may not look like the fancy university campuses you have in America," Tulani said, "but this limestone quarry was one of the great universities of the world." It was a place that served as a toilet and the one place where the prisoners were out of the sight of the guards. Mandela was released after 27 years in prison for fighting for his rights as a human being. Mandela had been in hiding until the CIA tipped off the South African officials about where he was hiding.

The most powerful part of the tour is a visit to Mandela's cell, a 7-by-9-foot room where a bulb burned day and night over his head for the 18 years he was jailed here, beginning in 1964. As Mandela recalled in *Long Walk to Freedom*, he "could walk the length of my cell in three paces. When I lay down, I could feel the wall with my feet, and my head grazed the concrete at the other side."

Many guides at Robben Island are themselves former prisoners, and they speak openly about their lives inside one of the world's most notorious gulags. On my first visit, our prison guide identified himself as a terrorist and reported that he was jailed for burning down a building; "there were no fatalities," said Tulani Mbosa, who stated that he had undergone severe beatings, hunger, and solitary confinement before he was released in 1982. As Tulani stood in the room he once shared with other inmates, he recalled a vital lesson: "Our leader, Nelson Mandela, taught us not to take revenge on our enemies. And because of this, today, we are free, free, free."

In 1985, there was a hue and cry for divestment of American dollars in South Africa since those dollars supported apartheid. Columbia University decided in 1978 to sell investments in companies "which show indifference... to the prevailing repressive racial policies in South Africa," and yet it had nearly $33 million worth of stock in 26 companies doing business there. The protest was not confined to New York. At the University of Missouri and many, many similar institutions and concerns, students raised their voices. At the Missouri University System office, the curators and system president decided to withdraw its holdings from all other concerns except in the University of the Western Cape, an institution of higher learning for coloreds. That was a significant gesture since the investment in businesses in South Africa had strongly supported the retirement program at the university. It is not clear whether the decision was intended to place the American investment in a black university. South

Africa was one of the most segregated places in the world. Each ethnic designation was segregated. Coloreds and blacks were "neighbors." Each non-white community was housed separately in townships. Gugu Lata and Khayelitsha were townships where blacks lived. Khayelitsha is located on the Cape Flats in the City of Cape Town. The name is Xhosa for *Our New Home* and is reputed to be the largest and fastest growing township in South Africa. Adjacent to Khayelitsha is Mitchell, which is a township for coloreds.

In 2005, I was a visiting professor at the University of Western Cape (UWC), and it was this experience that allowed me to compare my experiences with segregation in USA with segregated life in South Africa. The USA was not as distinct in their separation practices as South Africa was. South Africa had a category for each ethnic group; conversely, in the USA, it was largely white and non-whites, with blacks constituting the majority of the non-whites. I took into account the fact that in 1948, the USA began a trek toward desegregation with President Truman's initiative to integrate the Armed Forces. Whereas in South Africa, the government had increased intensity of punishing black South Africans. Between 1948 and the next two decades in America, there was an undeniable shift in government policy toward better treatment of blacks in the USA. The history and origin of the University of Western Cape provided a good example of the difference between USA and South Africa segregation practices. The university was established in 1960 by the South African government as a university for "colored" people only. Other universities near Cape Town are the University of Cape Town (UCT, originally for English speaking whites) and the Stellenbosch University (originally for Afrikaans speaking whites). UCT is *South Africa's* oldest *university,* and it started admitting its first *black* students in 1920. The establishment of UCT was a direct effect of the Extension of University of Education Act of 1959. This law accomplished the segregation of higher education in South Africa. Colored students were only allowed at a few non-white universities. In this period, other "ethnical" universities, such as the University of Zululand and the University of the North, were founded as well. Since well before the end of apartheid in South Africa in 1994, it has laid claim to being an integrated and multiracial institution. When I arrived, there were a number of colored and white professors and administrators, but few blacks. In fact, my friend, Professor John Williams, who was the product of one white parent and one African parent, became the first appointment of a black faculty. John had an extraordinary story. During the uprising, he had to stow away and subsequently leave the country for fear that he would become a fatality. He came to America, where he earned a PhD from the University of Illinois. He is a prolific scholar who was the product of a white parent and an African parent. By the late 2000s, Western Cape extended offers to African doctorates.

How my travels to the Continent shaped my views about slavery

The result of my travels to Senegal, Gambia, Ethiopia, Eritrea, South Sudan, Uganda, Rwanda, Tanzania, Mauritania, Mauritius, Kenya, Mozambique, and South Africa served to defy many of my preconceived beliefs about African life, how slavery evolved, and the intent and impact of the *participating and facilitating* African tribal leaders. I was also intrigued by the vast array of natural materials, oil, gas, tourism, etc., that were under control of Europeans, China, and USA. This experience brought me to know that there were significant tribal and cultural differences on the continent. Not only that, the European colonizers demonstrated cold callous capitalistic behavior as they took advantage of the unsuspecting Africans.

Beyond that, I was interested in what current efforts were being constructed to affirm the viability of the continent. I have often thought if there had been a United States of Arica, the dependence on outsiders would not have developed, at least, as it exists today. When I was a department chair at TSU in 1977, a group of four gentlemen visited to discuss a means of working together with a historically black college or university (HBCU) to begin a student exchange program. Three of the men were African, and one of them was a European who was there to interpret, since each of the men were from different tribes and were not fluent in each other's languages.

Decades later, in 2001, NEPAD evolved as a merger of two plans for the economic regeneration of Africa: The Millennium Partnership for the African Recovery Program (MAP), led by Former President Thabo Mbeki of South Africa in conjunction with Former President Olusegun Obasanjo of Nigeria and President Abdelaziz Bouteflika of Algeria, and the OMEGA Plan for Africa developed by President Abdoulaye Wade of Senegal which was conceived as an apparatus to remove non-African control over the continent. At a summit in Sirte, Libya in March 2001, the Organization of African Unity (OAU) agreed that the MAP and OMEGA plans should be merged.

The UN Economic Commission for Africa (UNECA) developed a "Compact for Africa's Recovery" based on both these plans and on resolutions on Africa adopted by the United Nations Millennium Summit in September 2000; they submitted a merged document to the Conference of African Ministers of Finance and Ministers of Development and Planning in Algiers in May 2001.

NEPAD is now a program of the African Union (AU), which replaced the OAU in 2002, though it has its own secretariat based in South Africa to coordinate and implement its programs. The program advertises four primary objectives: to eradicate poverty, promote sustainable growth and development, integrate Africa in the world economy, and accelerate the empowerment of women. It is based on underlying principles of a commitment to good governance, democracy, human rights, and conflict resolution, and the recognition that maintenance of these standards is fundamental to the creation of an environment conducive to investment and long-term economic growth. NEPAD seeks to attract increased investment, capital flows, and funding, providing an African-owned framework for development as the foundation for partnership at regional and international levels.

Ever since it was set up, there has been some tension over the place of NEPAD within the AU programs, given its origins outside the framework of the AU and the continuing dominant role of South Africa - symbolized by the location of the secretariat in South Africa.

Architects of NEPAD recognize that there have been attempts in the past to set out continent-wide development programs. For a variety of reasons, both internal and external, including questionable leadership and ownership by Africans themselves, these have been less than successful. Today, a new set of circumstances lend themselves to integrated practical implementation.

NEPAD is centered on African ownership and management. African leaders have set an agenda for the renewal of the continent. The agenda is based on national and regional priorities and development plans that must be prepared through participatory processes involving the people. To achieve these objectives, African leaders have vowed to take joint responsibility for strengthening mechanisms for conflict prevention, managing these mechanisms at the sub-regional and continental levels, and ensuring that these mechanisms are used to restore and maintain peace.

Efforts are also underway which are devoted to revitalizing and extending the provision of education, technical training, and health services, with high priority given to addressing the problem of HIV/AIDS, malaria, and other communicable diseases, as well as building the capacity of the states in Africa to set and enforce the legal framework and to maintain law and order. Significantly, the numbers of democratically-elected leaders are on the increase. Through their actions, they have declared that the hopes of Africa's peoples for a better life can no longer rest on the magnanimity of others. For the betterment of the world, NEPAD needs to be successful, but eons of memory do not spark overwhelming expectations for success.

Views about Slavery as influenced by the Bible

The continent's future is obviously better than its past. Yet, there are remnants of the past that must not be eliminated from the rear-view mirror. The center of that statement is the role of slavery in the history of the continent. Past European leaders misapplied lessons from the Bible in order to give a kind of approval to African slavery. Henry G. Brinton, a pastor at Fairfax Presbyterian Church in Virginia and contributor to the Washington Post and USA Today, writes that "the Bible was used a weapon by both the North and the South before and during the Civil War." Brinton says some contemporary Americans are making the same mistake their Civil War ancestors did by twisting the Bible to support their own battle cries.

Brinton, author of "*Balancing Acts: Obligation, Liberation, and Contemporary Christian Conflicts*," says both the Union and the Confederacy invoked the Bible to justify their positions on slavery. Slaveholders justified the practice by citing the Bible. They asked who could question the Word of God when it said,

> "slaves, obey your earthly masters with fear and trembling" (Ephesians 6:5), or "tell slaves to be submissive to their masters and to give satisfaction in every respect" (Titus 2:9).

Brinton further argues that Christian opponents of slavery elevated Biblical principles of justice and equality above individual passages that approved exclusion. What many proponents of slavery fail to take into consideration is that slavery in the Biblical world was complex and very different from the slavery practiced in the 18th-to-19th-century Western world.

Christian views on slavery are varied both regionally and historically. Slavery in various forms has been a part of the social environment for much of Christianity's history, spanning well over eighteen centuries. In the early years of Christianity, slavery was a normal feature of the economy and society in the Roman Empire, and this persisted in different forms and with regional differences well into the Middle Ages. The Bible uses the Hebrew term *eved* and Greek *doulos* to refer to slaves. *Eved* has a much wider meaning than the English term *slave*, and in many circumstances, it is more accurately translated into English as *servant* or *hired worker. Doulos* is more specific but is also used in more general senses as well: of the Hebrew prophets (Revelations 10:7), of the attitude of Christian leaders toward those they lead (Matthew 20:27), of Christians towards God (1 Peter 2:16), and of Jesus himself (Philippians 2:7).

Historically, slavery was not just an Old Testament phenomenon. Slavery was practiced in every ancient Middle

Eastern society: Egyptian, Babylonian, Greek, Roman, and Israelite. Slavery was an integral part of commerce, taxation, and temple religion.

In the book of Genesis, Noah condemns Canaan (Son of Ham) to perpetual servitude: "Cursed be Canaan! The lowest of slaves will he be to his brothers" (Genesis 9:25). T. David Curp notes that this episode has been used to justify racialized slavery, since "Christians and even some Muslims eventually identified Ham's descendants as black Africans." Anthony Pagden argued that "this reading of the Book of Genesis merged easily into a medieval iconographic tradition in which devils were always depicted as black." Later pseudo-scientific theories were built around African skull shapes, dental structure, and body postures, all to find an unassailable argument - rooted in whatever the most persuasive contemporary idiom happened to be: law, theology, genealogy, or natural science - why one part of humanity should live in perpetual indebtedness to another. As I process this enigma, I don't believe that the evils of slavery were central in my African brothers' thoughts when they worked with the Europeans to establish the western slave trade. My discussions with my Senegalese brothers in 2005 led me to believe their forefathers had not fathomed the permanency of family disruption that would occur when the captured brethren would be stored in the hull of a ship en route to the far west via the Atlantic voyage. I acknowledge that my thoughts could be based on my naivete and my never-ending search for humanity.

Other lessons from the Old Testament on slavery

From passages in the Old Testament, we learn that the Canaanites settled in Canaan, rather than Africa, where Ham's other sons, Cush and Put, most likely settled. Noah's curse only applied to Canaan, and according to Biblical commentator Gleason L. Archer, this curse was fulfilled when Joshua conquered Canaan in 1400 BC (see *Encyclopedia of Bible Difficulties*, Zondervan Publishing Co., 1982). Although there is considerable doubt about the nature and extent of the conquest described in the early chapters of the book of Joshua, the post-Flood story did supply a rationale for the subjugation of the Canaanites. It is possible that the naming of 'Canaan' in the post-Flood story is itself a reflection of the situation of warfare between peoples in the time when the written form of the story took shape.

Some forms of servitude, customary in ancient times, were condoned by the Torah. Hebrew legislation maintained kinship rights (Exodus 21:3-9 and Leviticus 25:41, 47-49, and 54, providing for Hebrew indentured servants), marriage rights (Exodus 21:4 and 10-11, providing for a Hebrew daughter contracted into a marriage), personal legal rights relating to physical protection and protection from breach of conduct (Exodus 21:8, providing for a Hebrew daughter contracted into a marriage; Exodus 21:20-21 and 26-27, providing for Hebrew or foreign servants of any kind; and Leviticus 25:39-41, providing for Hebrew indentured servants), freedom of movement, and access to liberty.

Hebrews would be punished if they beat a slave causing death within a day or two and would have to let a slave go free if they destroyed a slave's eye or tooth, force a slave to work on the Sabbath, return an escaped slave of another people who had taken refuge among the Israelites, or slander a slave. It was common for a person to voluntarily sell oneself into slavery for a fixed period, either to pay off debts or to get food and shelter. It was legitimate to enslave captives obtained through warfare, but not through kidnapping for enslaving them. This part of Biblical guidance was obviously not observed by the western slave traders. Children could also be sold into debt bondage, which was sometimes ordered by a court of law.

The Bible does set minimum rules for the conditions under which slaves were to be kept. Slaves were to be treated as part of an extended family; they could celebrate religious festivals such as Sukkot and Shabbat, Israelite slaves could not to be compelled to work under inhuman conditions, and debtors who sold themselves as slaves to their creditors had to be treated the same as a hired servant. If a master harmed a slave in one of the ways covered by the guidelines for treating slaves, i.e., lex talionis, the slave was to be compensated by working off their indebtedness; if the slave died within 24 to 48 hours, it was to be *avenged* (whether this refers to the death penalty or not is uncertain).

Israelite slaves were automatically granted freedom after six years of work, and/or at the next Jubilee (occurring either every 49 or every 50 years, depending on interpretation), although the latter would not apply if the slave was owned by an Israelite and wasn‘t in debt bondage. Slaves were released automatically in their 7th year of service. This provision did not include females sold into concubinage by impoverished parents; instead, their rights over/against another wife were protected. In other texts, male and female slaves are both to be released after the 6th year of service. Liberated slaves were to be given livestock, grain, and wine as a parting gift. This 7th year manumission could be voluntarily renounced. If a male slave had been given another slave in marriage, and they had a family, the wife and children remained the property of the master. However, if the slave was happy with his master, and wished to stay with a wife that his owner gave to him, he could renounce manumission, an act which would be signified, as in other ancient Near Eastern nations, by the slave gaining a ritual ear piercing. After such renunciation, the individual became his master‘s slave forever (and was therefore not released at the Jubilee). It is important to note that these are provisions for slavery/service among Israelites. Non-Israelite slaves could be enslaved indefinitely and were to be treated as inheritable property. Whether these kinds of statements represent an active encouragement of enforced slavery upon foreign nations or simply recognition of a fact is difficult at this distance to know with certainty.

New Testament

Early Christians reputedly regarded slaves who converted to Christianity as spiritually free men, brothers in Christ, receiving the same portion of Christ's kingdom inheritance. However, this regard apparently had no legal power. These slaves were also told to obey their masters "with fear and trembling, in sincerity of heart, as to Christ." (Ephesians 6:5 KJV). This verse was used by defenders of slavery prior to the American Civil War. Slaves may have been encouraged by Paul the Apostle in the first Corinthian Epistle to seek or purchase their freedom whenever possible (1st Corinthians 7:21 KJV). However, as Christians held no formal power before the 4th century, this recognition probably had no more significance other than as a network to assist escaped slaves.

Chapter III

THE US CENSUS, A PATH TO CONNECT MY EARTHLY ORIGINS

Beginning in 1860, some seventy years after the initial United States census had been authorized in 1790, slaves were counted individually. Slaves were included by gender and estimated age on slave schedules, listed by the name of the owner. Most of these reports do not provide names; individuals were simply numbered and could be distinguished by age, sex, complexion, and perceived ability to work in the house or in the field. Individual recognition on par with white male citizens was nonexistent. Slaves were parts of a production group… a chattel property. The Federal Constitution stipulated that a slave counted as three-fifths of a person for purposes of taxation and apportionment of the House of Representatives. Only the heads of free households appear in these records. All others, including slaves, are noted statistically under the head of household or reported owner.

The 1790 authorizing legislation required the name of the head of the family and the number of persons in each household of the following descriptions: free white males of 16 years and upward (to assess the country's industrial and military potential) and free white females, all other free persons, and slaves. Under the general direction of Thomas Jefferson, the Secretary of State, US marshals took the census in the original 13 States, plus the districts of Kentucky, Maine, and Vermont, and the Southwest Territory (Tennessee). Both George Washington and Thomas Jefferson expressed skepticism over the final count, expecting a number that exceeded the 3.9 million inhabitants counted in the census.

Sometimes, the listings for large slave holdings appear to take the form of family groupings, but in most cases, slaves are listed from eldest to youngest with no apparent effort to portray family structure. The census counts almost never provide conclusive evidence for the presence of a specific slave in the household or plantation of a particular slaveholder. A reflection on this state of affairs makes me proud of our family's survival, but it also troubles me that in a nation that professed to be Christian, tolerance for such marginalization was the order of the day.

My American beginnings can be traced to the slave quarters in Richmond, VA. This assertion derives from interpretation of historical documents; thus, I can't lay claim to being absolutely certain. However, based on what I have been able to gather, Abe Sanson's father was born amid inhuman living conditions in what is now the state of Virginia, according to the US Census for 1860. My characterization of the Virginia colony as "inhuman," as it relates to the treatment of Africans, is manifested by the history which states that Virginia and Maryland were among the first colonies that saw the connection between forced labor and profits. In 1669, nearly two centuries before my great-grandfather was born, Virginia became the first colony to declare that it was *not* a crime to kill a slave while the slave was being punished. These practices were the fruit of legalized marginalization, and centuries later can be connected to lynching black folks.

Africans first appeared in Virginia in 1619, when 19 black slaves were sold to the colonists at Jamestown in 1619. A Dutch vessel had captured them from a Spanish ship and decided to get rid of their "cargo" by selling them to the English. These Africans were not actually treated as "chattel slaves." Rather, they joined the indentured servants of Virginia (by that time almost 1000 people). They later earned their freedom, owned land, and unfortunately, some even owned a slave themselves.

The transition to a formal institution of "chattel slavery," in which blacks were formally and legally condemned to generational slavery, happened gradually. In 1656, there was an interesting trial in Virginia. Elizabeth Key, a slave of mixed race, gained her freedom. It was reported that she said she was held in slavery illegally, so she hired a lawyer and took her case to court. She proved that her father was a free, English subject (Thomas Key). English law did not bind the children of English subjects to slavery, so she was declared a free subject. After that, however, Virginia began to institutionalize slavery based on race (mostly against black Africans, but also against North American Indians). In 1662, the laws of Virginia stated that all descendants of a slave mother would be born into slavery. The Virginia Slave Codes of 1705 defined slaves as those taken from non-Christian nations, as well as anyone taken from the Indians.

Cultural and religious transformation began as the Africans were baptized and embraced Christianity; initially, they were treated as indentured servants, a status that placed a sunset on servitude. The first laws regarding slavery of Africans were passed in the 17th century and codified into Virginia's first slave code in 1705. Among laws affecting slaves was one enacted in 1662, which said that children born in the colony would take the social status of their mothers, regardless of who their fathers were. This practice contrasted with English common law of the time and resulted in numerous generations of enslaved mixed-race children and adults, some of whom were majority white. Among the most notable were Sally Hemmings and her siblings, fathered by planter John Wayles, and her four surviving children by Thomas Jefferson. Thus, slavery in Virginia was simultaneous with the first appearance of the Africans in 1619, soon after the founding of Virginia as an English colony by the London Virginia Company. The company established a headright system to encourage colonists to transport the time-based indentured servants to the colony for labor; they received a certain amount of land for people whose passage they paid to Virginia. The headright practice was created in 1618 in Jamestown, Virginia. The practice complemented the emergence of tobacco farming since a large supply of workers would be needed. Headright settlers who paid their way to Virginia received 50 acres of land.

Some historians believe that some of the first blacks who arrived in Virginia were already slaves, while others say they were taken into the colony as indentured servants. Historians generally believe slavery did not begin as an institution until the 1660s. Given the history of Africans in America, it is difficult to believe that a substantial proportion of them were free. The Emmanuel case shows the differences in treatment between Negro and European indentured servants. In 1640, the General Virginia Court decided the Emmanuel case. Emmanuel was a Negro indentured servant who participated in a plot to escape along with six white servants. Together, they stole corn, powder, and shotguns but were caught before making their escape. The members of the group were each convicted; they were sentenced to a variety of punishments. Christopher Miller, the leader of the group, was sentenced to wear shackles for one year. White servant John Williams was sentenced to serve the colony for an extra seven years. Peter Willcocke was branded and whipped, and was required to serve the colony for an additional seven years. Richard Cookson was required to serve for two additional years. Emmanuel, the Negro, was whipped and branded with an "R" on his cheek. All the white servants had their terms of servitude increased by some extent, but the court did not extend Emmanuel's time of service. Many historians speculate Emmanuel was already a servant for life. While Emmanuel's status is not defined in the records, his being branded shows a difference in how white servants and black servants were treated. Though this case suggests that slavery existed, the distinction of lifetime servitude or slavery associated with Africans or people of African descent was not widespread until later.

From 1776 to 1789, the Revolutionary War and the adoption of the constitution brought national independence and established the basic political framework within which the nation would be governed ever after. From 1861 to 1877, the Civil War and Reconstruction affirmed the integrity of the Union, ended slavery, and generated three constitutional amendments that, at last, laid the foundation for honoring the Declaration's promise that "all men are created equal." Between 1929 and 1945, the Great Depression and World War II utterly redefined the role of government in American society and catapulted the United States from being an isolated, peripheral state into the world's hegemonic superpower. Between 1957 and 1965, there was established a bureaucracy for implementing and monitoring civil rights legislation, and a decade later, the Voting Rights Act, i.e., Public Law 89-110, approved by the US Congress in 1965. To understand the logic and the consequences of those four grand transitions is to understand much about the essence and the trajectory of the totality of American history. I will discuss these four phases in history as I continue my discussion of how each impacted my family's situation. Because these transformative acts occur chronologically, I will discuss each in the time context consistent with events in my family history.

To place these events in perspective, I again summoned the summer forest of my mind and became a time traveler. I become a pilot on that aircraft and again climbed to 35,000 feet. This time, I seek to get a view of American history to better determine how certain events have influenced my family. Because I have been trained as a social and political policy analyst, I look through the lens of policy formulation and subsequent impact. Thus, I see four policy actions, i.e., public laws that influenced the shape of the long arc of American history, that have significantly impacted the course of USA development, and subsequently affected the experiences of my family. Such policy actions mounted by the national government are scattered through the centuries that cover my family. These policies can be said to coexist with events that could be called "social movements,"; however, social scientists have defined a *social movement* as a sustained, organized collective effort that focuses on some aspect of *social change*. Sociologists argue that social movements exemplify actions that promote racial justice, defend the rights of diverse groups, attack the government, or advocate particular beliefs. The events I focus on were not intended to advocate for the uprising of the underclass. My understanding of social science and history causes me to consider that these policies respectively distilled the experience and defined the historical legacy of a century. Each embraced a pair of episodes with lastingly transformative impacts. I define transformative acts to be public policies, i.e., those acts that a government proposes or opposes, and in doing so, improves a condition for the betterment of the populace or makes difficulty for another segment of the population.

Transformative Act I: From the Constitution to the Revolutionary War

When I closely study and consider the state of racial inequality extant in the United States, I find a set of circumstances which foreshadowed legalized inequality among whites and non-whites. These circumstances are closely aligned with the structure of the American political system. They were imbedded within the culture and include the rules under which it operates and the interests it represented. To begin an explanation of my view, I believe that classism existed before racism in America, largely because the only persons who "counted" were Europeans. Consider Adam Smith's views on the importance of government. He argued that the importance of government was shared by "men of substance" in the late 18th century. During the period between the Revolution and the Constitution, the rich and the well-born set the dominant political tone in the USA. Smith (1776) noted in *Wealth of Nations*:

Their power was born of place, position, and finance. They were located at or near the seats of government, and they were in direct contact with legislatures and government officers. They influenced and often dominated the local newspapers which voiced the ideas and interests of commerce and identified them with the good of the whole people, the state, and the nation. The published writings of the leaders of the period are almost without exception those of merchants, of their lawyers, or of politicians sympathetic with them.

In my high school and undergraduate studies, I was taught that the United States of 1787 was an "egalitarian" society, free from the extremes of want and wealth which characterized the European world. If I am unkind in my subsequent analysis, I say this nuance represents a fractured fairy tale. If I am kind, I say the nuance was an aspirational or normative attempt of a definition. History does not state that the opulent and corrupt kings and bishops were found in North America, but there were landed estates and colonial mansions which bespoke a munificence of their own. Although land was abundant when compared with Europe, there was no equal opportunity in acquiring it. From the earliest English settlements, men of influence had received vast land grants from the Crown. And through their control of the provincial governments, they had gained possession of the western parts of their states. By 1700, three-fourths of the acreage in New York belonged to less than a dozen people. In the interior of Virginia, seven persons acquired a total of 1,732,000 acres. By 1760, fewer than 500 merchants in five colonial cities controlled most of the trade on the eastern seaboard and themselves owned most of the land (Aronson, *Status and Kinship in the Higher Civil Service*, 1964).

Here and there were "middle-class" farmers, tavern keepers, distillers, and shop owners who, by the standards of the day, might be described as "comfortable." However, the great bulk of the small yeomen, composing of nearly 85% of the white population, were poor freeholders, tenants, squatters, indentured servants, or hired hands. The cities had their share of their poor and their poorhouses, along with their cobblers, weavers, bakers, blacksmiths, peddlers, laborers, clerks, and domestics who worked long hours for little money. As of 1787, property qualifications left more than a third of the white male population disfranchised. Property qualifications were so steep for holding office that most voters were prevented from qualifying as candidates (see Michael Parenti, *Democracy for the Few*, 2010).

Creating the US Constitution

The American Constitution was framed by financially successful planters, merchants, lawyers, bankers, and creditors. These white men resisted the practice of primogeniture, the culture and social order that placed the bulk of inheritance in the hands of first-born sons. These non-first-born sons desired and created a new order. It was based on a new type of patriarchy. Race was not a factor since most of the subjects were white men. Through the years on the new land that was to become the United States, they developed ties that were linked by kinship and marriage, and by years of service in the Congress, the military, or diplomacy. They met in Philadelphia in 1787 for the recognized purpose of revising the Articles of Confederation and strengthening the central government. There was a powerful desire to build a nation, and by their explicit intent on doing something about the increasingly insurgent spirit coming from their experiences in Europe. Blacks, per se, were not in the calculus.

Although the framers facilitated the creation of the American Constitution long before the Civil War, the nuance of position with the social order, i.e., social class, did not evidence themselves more clearly than the onset and aftermath of the Civil War. The distinction between the haves and have-nots did not achieve full moon status until that time. To be sure, the Constitution was framed by financially successful planters, merchants, lawyers, bankers, and creditors, many of them linked by kinship and marriage, and by years of service in the Congress, the military, or diplomacy.

Challenge and significance of the political context

To further understand the inhumanity experienced by the former slaves, we must delve deeper into the history, culture, and politics in the country that existed between the 1776 and the Revolutionary War that extended into the next century. During that time, there was an environment in which little thought had been given to the possibility of non-Europeans as meaningful participants in social and political life. After the Civil War, which ended in 1865, and the subsequent issue of what to do with the former slaves, white Southerners resented being ruled by Union military governors and Freedmen's Bureau officials. They sought to restore white patriarchal self-rule. Their fight against the Union was so fervent that strains of that resistance can be felt centuries later as manifested by establishing the Confederate flag and Confederate holidays, as well as constructing statues that honor Confederate figures, such as Robert E. Lee, P.G.T. Beauregard, and Jefferson Davis, in cities where slavery as an institution brought economic value to those areas. Consider that in June 2015, Dylan Roof, a self-declared white supremacist, entered the Emanuel African Methodist Episcopal Church in Charleston, South Carolina and proceeded to kill nine black people who were engaged in Bible study. Before he opened fire, Roof had posted photos of himself online waving the Stars and Bars and spitting on the American flag. The images made a direct link between racial hatred and Confederate symbolism.

In the aftermath of the Civil War, much of the Confederacy railed against policies that sought to "even the playing field," such as implementing teaching of important life skills to former slaves. Perhaps the most vigorous acknowledgement of my claim is the push for "states' rights" in the years immediately after the Civil War and continuing to the 21st century, when black churches were victims of massacres, burnings, and bombings. During the summer and fall of 1865, most of the old Confederate states held constitutional conventions. President Andrew Johnson's reconstruction plan permitted only white men to vote for convention delegates or participate in the framing of the new state governments. Not surprisingly, none of the state conventions considered extending the right to vote to the new freedmen. South Carolina's provisional governor declared at their state constitutional convention that "this is a white man's government."

By the end of 1865, most of the South began to conduct state elections under the new state constitutions that reflected supremacy of the national government. The center of the new movement toward legalized egalitarianism was the Nineteenth Amendment, which granted voting rights to women. The *Nineteenth Amendment was* originally introduced in Congress in 1878 by Senator Aaron A. Sargent. Forty-one *years* later, in 1919, Congress submitted it to the states for ratification. It *was* ratified by three-fourths of the states a *year* later, with *Tennessee*'s ratification being the last needed to add the amendment to the Constitution. During the interim, ex-Confederate leaders stood for and won elections for state government offices and the US Congress. Political power held in their hands meant hostility toward the first generation, and a slowing down of the pace towards equality.

Transformative Act II: From the 1840s (pre-Civil War developments) to 1877 (the Civil War and Reconstruction)

The end of the Civil War marked the end of slavery for 4 million black Southerners. However, the war also left my ancestors landless and with little money to support themselves.

Former slaves had no memories of being independent and being able to go and come without permission. In short, they were not acclimated to freedom; they had no experiences to draw upon that would be the beginning of skill development for citizenship in a capitalist society. A further complicating fact was that white Southerners were slow to accept the ex-slaves as competitors for earning a living in their America. In their bid to maintain control over the free former slaves, white Southerners devised special state law codes. Many Northerners saw these codes as blatant attempts to restore slavery. Thus, the culture was strengthened by the reality of law, i.e., the Black Codes of 1865-66 which became the enabling legislation for Jim Crow laws.

There was no robust governmental action, i.e., public policy, that was devoted to ending slavery or to recognizing the plight of the workers who had toiled for them for the entirety of their lives. There was not even a modest public policy aimed at providing assistance to the new group of citizens. Little thought had been given to the needs of the newly emancipated slaves. This was in part because neither Southern nor Northern legislators were committed to the notion of transforming the skills of the slaves to benefit themselves and the economy of the country. I must recognize that shortly before the end of the war, Congress created the Freedmen's Bureau. That agency of the federal government furnished food and medical aid to the former slaves. It also established schools for the freedmen. By 1870, a quarter million black children and adults had attended more than 4,000 of these schools in the South.

The Freedmen's Bureau also helped the former slaves in the workplace. It tried to make sure that the former slaves received fair wages and got to freely choose their employers. The bureau created special courts to settle disputes between black workers and their white employers. It could also intervene in other cases that threatened the rights of freedmen. Perhaps most significant was the fact that the bureau opened the way for teaching the former slave to read.

The newly formed state legislatures quickly authorized many needed public projects and the taxes to pay for them. Among these projects was the creation, for the first time in the South, of free public education. However, the public schools excluded black children. Thus, the first traceable generation in my family that extends from 1847 through the end of the 19th century lived in a hostile environment. As I carefully absorb these data, my childhood tapes direct me to the lyrics in James Weldon Johnson's *Lift Every Voice and Sing*, also referred to as the Black National Anthem: "stony road enduring the chastening rod, felt in the days when hope unborn had died."

Transformative Acts III and IV occurred much later and will be discussed as I develop the chronology where those policies impacted my family's development.

Chapter IV

THE FIRST GENERATION

I have only been able to document my family from the years immediately following the Civil war. My research on the first generation includes the period beginning in 1847 and continuing to around 1882. It is clearly evident that my grandparents had lived prior to the end of the Civil War, but up to that point in time, they were victimized by not having a seat at the bargaining table. The white population, both Northerners and Southerners, still held questions about our humanity in the mid-to-late 1800s. Ironically, Abraham Lincoln's presidency of 1860 left much to be accomplished vis-a-vis the pathway for my ancestors' quest for citizenship. It is true that Mr. Lincoln led a movement for freeing the slaves, but because slavery was crucial to the economic well-being of the United States, many historians fail to take into consideration the impact of Lincoln's home environment and personal attitude and how those factors may have influenced him as he attempted get a buy-in from so many Americans on the need to change the paradigm. Consider that the "Great Emancipator" believed that American democracy meant equal rights and equality of opportunity, but he drew a line between basic natural rights, such as freedom from slavery, and political and civil rights, like voting. He sounded the clarion call of 21st century states righters when he expressed his belief that it was up to the states to make such a decision. In fact, Lincoln may have also been known as the "Great Colonizer." He supported a proposal to move Africans to Liberia. Arguably, he was influenced by his wife Mary, whose father was a slave owner in Kentucky; such collateral influence stripped him of vibrant passion about black folks. I focus on the leader of the country, but he had the responsibility to listen to all the people on the subject of slave versus freedom, and all these matters add up to the reason I have difficulty researching my ancestry.

My main research tool on my ancestry is the Decennial Census. The first US census was conducted in 1790, a year after the inauguration of President Washington and shortly before the second session of the First Congress ended. Congress assigned responsibility for the 1790 census to the marshals of the US judicial districts under an act which, with minor modifications and extensions, governed census taking through 1840. The law required that every household be visited, that completed census schedules be posted in "two of the most public places within [each jurisdiction], there to remain for the inspection of all concerned," and that "the aggregate amount of each description of persons" for every district be transmitted to the president. However, there were many limitations of the methodology: recorded information was not always fully accurate or complete, information was recorded orally, unfamiliar accents and pronunciations caused misspellings, people did not always cooperate, residents were not always at home (traveling, moving, working) and might not be counted, and neighbors sometimes gave erroneous information to census enumerators.

There were at least two limitations specific to African-Americans during the period 1790-1860:

1. Some aspects of African-Americans in the census differ from that of other groups (particularly before 1870). This is due to the enslaved status of most of the black population and the legal marginalization of those who were free prior to the 1870 census. Even after 1870, the census often undercounted the black population.
2. During slavery, the Federal Census did not list the names of slaves (although there were rare instances where a first name is provided by the owner). Since most blacks were enslaved in the decades prior to 1870, the names of the majority of African-Americans were not recorded in the census before that year. Free African-Americans were documented.

Sometimes, the listings for large slave holdings appear to take the form of family groupings, but in most cases, slaves are listed from eldest to youngest with no apparent effort to portray family structure. The census counts almost never provided conclusive evidence for the presence of a specific slave in the household or plantation of a slaveholder. The generations I have identified began in the years immediately following the end of the Civil War. My data comes from the census records of those days. My paternal great-grandfather, Abe Sanson, is the patriarch of the first generation. He was born on a plantation in Mississippi. His father, whose name is not recorded in census documents, was born on a slave plantation in Virginia, where his life was an uphill climb to the bottom.

The cold reality of learning that there were no records of my family until the federal government allowed the counting of slaves revealed to me that my family was not recognized as being worthy of a census count. That epiphany brought to mind the existence of a "stone wall," which meant that researching the records was possible but hardly probable; that I could not advance my search with confidence for the parents of Abe. What I have is oral history and scattered records. Based on traditions passed down verbally, I learned that Abe had four siblings who grew up on MS plantation(s): Solomon (Sol), Dave, Oliver (Ol), and a sister whose name remains elusive, although some family records contain the moniker "Sis." Exhaustive searches have failed to produce names of his parents. That search is yet underway. To be sure, "family" was not a distinction granted to slaves. Abe was chattel property. The institution of the slave trade was clearly racist, but it was also sexist. Females were producers of the babies that became investments for the slave owners. Thus, tracking the maternal side of the family was fraught with great challenge.

My paternal great-grandmother, Calline, wife of Abe, was born around 1851. She achieved young adulthood about the time when slavery was legally ended. She, like most of the former slaves and similarly situated black folk, had been denied a formal education because there was no compulsory school attendance law for these former slaves; in fact, it was illegal for slaves to be educated. They were literally the outcasts of Jasper County, MS: a forlorn and forgotten race of people. The government had little interest in developing an accurate census of non-whites. This absence of record-keeping serves as a roadblock to learning about Abe Sanson's parents. The first federal census of slaves dates to 1860, the Eighth Census of the US government; there was not as much care for acknowledging the importance of family lineage.

Slaves were enumerated separately during the 1860 census, though most schedules do not provide personal names. In most cases, individuals were not named, but were simply numbered and can be distinguished only by age, sex, and complexion; the names of owners are recorded. The fact of public disinterest in accounting for slaves in such a manner is understandable… the dominant culture and the resulting laws considered slaves as property. Even when the constitution was being constructed, former slaves were counted as three-fifths of a white man. The Three-Fifths Compromise was a formal agreement reached between delegates from southern states and those from northern states during the 1787 United States Constitutional Convention. The debate was over whether, and if so, how, slaves would be counted when determining a state's total population for legislative representation and taxing purposes. The issue was important, as this population number would then be used to determine the number of seats that the state would have in the United States House of Representatives for the next ten years.

According to research published by Kenneth N. Addison in 2009, and replicated by political scientists for decades, the effect was to give the southern states one third more seats in Congress and one third more electoral votes than if slaves had been ignored, but fewer than if slaves and free persons had been counted equally, allowing the slaveholder interests to largely dominate the government of the United States until 1861. The compromise was proposed by delegates James Wilson and Roger Sherman.

The convention had unanimously accepted the principle that representation in the House of Representatives would be in proportion to the relative state populations. However, since slaves could not vote, white leaders in slave states would thus have the benefit of increased representation in the House and the Electoral College. Delegates opposed to slavery proposed that only free inhabitants of each state be counted for apportionment purposes, while delegates supportive of slavery, on the other hand, opposed the proposal, wanting slaves to count in their actual numbers. The compromise that was finally agreed upon - of counting "*all other persons*" as only three-fifths of their actual numbers - reduced the representation of the slave states relative to the original proposals but improved it over the Northern position, according to Paul Finkelman writing in the *Rutgers Law Journal* in 2013. An inducement for slave states to accept the compromise was its connection to taxation in the same ratio so that the burden of taxation on the slave states was also reduced. It is also worth considering that the failure of the framers to recognize the humanity of the slaves accounts for the futile search for parents who were born before 1860. Moreover, the three-fifths decision by the framers is an irony of bondage; slaves were valued only to the extent that they furthered the monetary or political advantage of their owners.

My interpretation of the census data and my experience researching slave history allows me to extrapolate that Abe descended from parents who were born on a plantation in Virginia. The US Census for 1900 shows that his father and his mother were birthed in Virginia. Slaves were property and were not counted as humans, nor was there formal governmental accounting of their lives as humans. As a lad, he was sold to William C. Sanson around 1850. So, the first 15 years of his life were as a slave on plantations in MS. What is not clear is whether the transaction to William C. Sanson included his entire family or whether they were individually parceled out. Most slave owners had limited regard for "family" among their chattel property. The 1860 US Census lists William C. Sanson as owner of about 14 slaves in Jasper County, MS. Sanson, a farmer, was born in 1829 in Alabama. He was 18 years older than my great-grandfather, Abe Sanson. Sanson, the owner of the chattel property that was the first traceable generation of my family, had personal and real estate holdings estimated to be about $25K in 1860. Inflation calculations put that amount to be about $600K in today's dollars. Census records that account his holdings appear below. William

C. Sanson was not among the wealthier plantation owners. The task of tracking the number and grade of slaves was a management technique that began when the census of slaves first began.

The matter of wealth among slave owners is significant since the wealthier slave owner had comparatively greater resources than the less well-off slaveholder. Caitlin C. Rosenthal writes in her book *From Slavery to Scientific Management: Capitalism and Control in America* (Harvard University Press, 2018) about the evolution of modern management techniques and practices usually associated with good old-fashioned intelligence and ingenuity - "a glorious parade of inventions that goes from textile looms to the computer" – that were built on the backs of slaves. According to Rosenthal, the history of detailed record-keeping on plantations goes back to at least the 1750s in Jamaica and Barbados and facilitates a history of capitalism. It was characterized by the behavior of wealthy slave owners in the West Indies and required productivity reports from their overseers by requiring regular reports about how their businesses were faring. This subtle change marked the beginning of an early instance of separation of ownership and management.

Table 1. Top Twenty-five slave owners in 1860 US Census		
Owner	**Location**	**Total number of slaves**
Col. Joshua John Ward	Georgetown, SC	1130
John Burneside	Ascension, LA	940
Dr. Stephen Duncan	Issaquenna, MS	858
Meredith Calhoun	Rapides, LA	709
William Aiken	Colleton, SC	700
Gov. John L. Manning	Ascension, LA	670
Col. Joseph A.S. Acklen	West Feliciana, LA	665
Gov. Robert F. Withers	Georgetown, SC	631
Joseph Blake	Beaufort, SC	575
John Robinson	Madison, MS	550
Jerrett Brown	Sumter, AL	540
Arthur Blake	Charleston, SC	538
John J. Middleton	Beaufort, SC	530
Elisha Worthington	Chicot, AR	529
Daniel Blake	Colleton, SC	527
J.C. Jenkins	Wilkinson, MS	523
J. Harleston Read	Georgetown, SC	511
John Butler	McIntosh, GA	505
Alfred V. Davis	Concordia, LA	500
O.J. Morgan	Carroll, LA	500
Charles Heyward	Colleton, SC	491
Levin R. Marshall	Concordia, LA	484
D. F. Kenner	Ascension, LA	473
Mrs. Mary Sterling	Pointe Coupe, LA	465
R. R. Barrow	Lafourche, LA	399
Average Number of Slaves		575

With the average number of slaves being 575 among the top twenty-five, Sanson's 14 paled in comparison. What this implies is that my slave ancestors had been the property of less well-off masters that could not or would not provide creature comforts ranging from comparatively better lodging and food to access to leisure.

Slave owners were able to collect data on their workforce in ways that other business owners could not because they had complete control over their workers. They did not have to worry about turnover or recruiting new workers, and they could experiment with different tactics such as moving workers around and demanding higher levels of output, even monitoring what they ate and how long new mothers breastfed their babies. The slaves had no recourse. When this kind of tracking technique was tried on Northern laborers, they'd just quit, says Rosenthal.

The widespread adoption of these accounting techniques is partly due to a Mississippi planter and accountant named Thomas Affleck, who developed account books for plantation owners that allowed them to make sophisticated calculations and measure productivity in a standardized way.

Tracking this information allowed planters to determine how far they could push their workers to get the most profit. Using those account books, slave owners could see how many pounds of cotton each slave picked and compare it to their output from previous years, and then create minimum picking requirements based on these calculations. The table on the previous page shows the twenty-five largest slave owners as reported in the 1860 US Slave Census Schedule.

Wilma King, a distinguished professor of history, colleague, and personal friend, authored *Stolen Childhood (Indiana University Press, 1997)*, a book that focused on enslaved children in a fashion that allows an understanding of their lives and their development as a unique group apart from their enslaved parents and the society in which their masters lived. Her book helped me to envision my grandparents when they lived as enslaved children.

The role of slaves in the US gave new life to capitalism. In such an economic system, the government plays a secondary role. Slave owners made the decisions and owned the land and other property. Moreover, in a capitalistic society, the means of production are largely or entirely privately operated for profit. Slaves' lives formed an identifiable progression of stages controlled and influenced by slave owners. They worked in all kinds of weather. It was never too hot nor too cold, it could never rain, blow hail, or snow to make it too hard to work. Norman R. Yetman (1970), stated that "work can rightly be called the thief who stole the childhood of young bondservants." Enslaved children accomplished many jobs that any adult could complete, even if it took two or more children. Slave children were more valuable than their parents. Consider the Virginia planter's 1849 property inventory that included 70-year-old Daniel, who was escribed as an "old and crippled half-hand," and a partially blind 50-year-old slave was described in the inventory with the designation as a quarter-hand. In that same inventory, Little Bob and Julius, 12-year-old boys, were valued at $800 each. Although I am not an historian, nor an economist, I believe slaves' work is best examined through the lens of labor since slave labor was the overarching reason for slavery.

An overseer expressed the opinion that chores made children "acquire habits of perseverance and industry." Furthermore, the overseer expressed the additional belief that chores or work "kept them from mischief." Enslaved youngsters differed in that their parents, who did not benefit directly from their efforts, made few, if any decisions about their own work and that of their offspring. Slave owners, who benefited from their toil, often preferred young slaves in order to indefinitely reap the rewards of work. The US

Congress passed the Fair Labor Standards Act in 1938 regulating the employment of those under 16 or 18 years of age, and the Supreme Court upheld the law after a challenge was placed in the courts. It is ironic that while the 1938 labor law placed limits on many forms of child labor, agricultural labor was excluded.

Entry into the work place entitled youngsters to additional food commensurate with extra responsibilities. One planter specified that "full allowances" should go to "small children that work in the field," while children that did not work in the field received a "half allowance." Terry Leak, a Mississippi plantation owner authorized "store orders" based upon age and work. Enslaved children who were not working received a fifty-cent allowance while children under the age of ten years received an allowance of one dollar. Some slave owners provided a rooster and several hens for slave couples. When their children were "large enough to go to the field," the overseer was directed to increase their "stock" by one hen. Once children reached the age of fifteen, they could have their own stock, if the owner vouched for their worthiness. This treatment became the fertilizer or catalyst for conflict among the enslaved children and their parents.

I recall listening to my father describe his memories of his grandparent discussing slave life. "Us chillen start to work soon's us could toddle. First us gather firewood. Iffen it's freezing or hot, us have to go to toughen us up. When we's gits bigger, we had to tend de cattle and feed hosses and hogs. By the time us good sprouts, us picking cotton and pulling corn." My dad would mimic the voice sounds of his father as he remembered them, and that was fascinating to me.

Revisiting the Transformative Acts as they impacted my family history

Earlier in this narrative, I introduced what I consider the four greatest transformative acts that impacted my family's quality of living, both as slaves and freemen. The first generation of my family evolved during the second great transformative act, i.e., the Reconstruction, which saw closure around 1877. My family experiences personify George Eliot's *Silas Marner* (1861) character who described a group of destitute people, as "remnants of a disinherited race." Marriage, education, and earning a living was new for the freed people. In 2006, Darlene Goring authored an article entitled "The history of slave marriage in the US," where she opined that the American paradigm of legally permissible marital relationships was shaped by the African-American slave experience. Colonial and antebellum legislation and jurisprudence prohibited marriages between bonded slaves. It was the end of the Civil War, and the passage of the Thirteenth Amendment that brought postbellum recognition of marriages between emancipated African slaves. Legally, black families did not exist in the eyes of the law until the late 1860s.

Slaves were chattel; they were considered items of private property with little to distinguish them from horses, cows, or farm equipment. During the antebellum period, each slave-holding state of the Union regulated the condition and legal status of slaves through slave codes. These codes governed every facet of slave life. Slaves could not own, rent, or transfer real property, own individual property, make or enter into any civil contracts, or be a party to a suit, except indirectly when a free person represented him in a suit for freedom. In court, he or she was not considered a "competent witness," except in a case involving another slave. They had no civil rights, no political rights, no claim to their time, and no freedom of movement. Life, liberty, and the pursuit of happiness simply did not seem consistent with the practice of chattel slavery. It is ironic that a group of people felt so passionate about these inalienable rights, yet maintained the brutal practice of human bondage.

In 1827, George M. Stroud stated, "the cardinal principle of slavery is that the slave is not to be ranked among sentient beings, but among things - an article of property - a chattel personal." Nor could the former slaves be lawfully taught to read or write or exert dominion over their physical body or surroundings. Moreover, they could not receive real or private property either by inheritance or testimony. The slave's lack of capacity was affirmed by the Supreme Court in *Hall v. United States (1871)*, wherein the Court refused to enforce a claim made by a former slave against the estate of his master. The Court agreed that a slave was not entitled to political or civil rights while subject to the condition of servitude. The slave's acquisitions belonged to his master; he had no ability to contract or be contracted with and could therefore make no binding contract with his master. Before Lincoln's signing of the Emancipation Proclamation and congressional passage of the Thirteenth Amendment, slaves were human anomalies. This attitude and nuance lasted beyond the days of slavery and extended during the Reconstruction period. Further, the residue of that sentiment can be found in many corners of US society in the 21st century.

The right to marry that African-Americans enjoyed in the postbellum is best understood within a cultural context in which marriage and the family were institutions employed by the larger culture to promote certain social and economic values (See https://academic.udayton.edu/race/04needs/family03.htm). Reform of the law of marriage during this period played a key role in advancing these agendas. African-Americans were granted the right to marry at precisely the moment when that right was being radically transformed in such a way that the public interest in marriage took priority over private interests in the creation of autonomous intimate partnerships (See William Wells Brown, 1814-1884 for broader narrative.).

The nuance among 19th-century white policymakers extolled the virtues of slavery as a tool to uplift the characters of Africans in America: "[Slavery in America] has been the lever by which 5 million human beings have been elevated from the degraded and benighted condition of savage life... to a knowledge of their responsibilities to God and their relations to society," stated a Kentucky congressman in 1860. These sentiments were echoed by abolitionist Northern officers not three years later when the institution of marriage was lauded for its civilizing effect on the newly freed men and women: "[Marriage] is the great lever by which [the freed men and women] are to be lifted up and prepared for a state of civilization."

Ironically, the institution of marriage among the former slaves was the forerunner of prosecution and incarceration of African-Americans - more often men than women - for violating laws regulating matrimonial morality. The aggressiveness with which African-American men were prosecuted for matrimonial deviance can be seen as an epiphenomenon of changes in white masculinity and agency that were taking place in postbellum industrializing America more generally. If the integrity of white male agency could no longer be anchored as the antinomy of Black chattel slavery since all men were now, at least in theory, free market actors, then white masculinity required new ground against which it would be set off. This task was complicated by the fact that wage laborers in the Gilded Age were in a famously weak position to negotiate with industrialists over wages and working conditions. Thus, as Nancy Cott and Amy Dru Stanley have argued, white men needed to construct a new domain other than slavery against which to contrast masculine agency. Marriage and the domestic sphere of the feminine became that fiction. It would have been calamitous for African-American men to be able to opt out of this important regulatory regime. Thus, African-Americans entered the domain of marriage just as its institutional boundaries became heavily freighted in "innovative ways."

The institution of marriage was not the only area where African-Americans experienced a hostile government and society. In 1822, the state of Mississippi invoked penalties of a year in prison for teaching the former slaves the ability to read and write. In Alabama, the penalty for attempting to teach any free colored person or slave to spell, read, or write was a fine of not less than two hundred and fifty dollars nor more than five hundred dollars. Other states, e.g., Virginia, mandated that "any slave or free colored person found at any school for teaching, reading, or writing, by day or night, may be whipped, at the discretion of a justice, not exceeding twenty lashes." As I examined the census documents, I observed that one of the questions was whether the person could read or write. There were few instances in the 1860 census that elicited an affirmative response; as time moved forward into the 20th century, most of the family members were literate. In sum, the dominant theme that characterizes the first generation evolves from slavery to apprenticeship, sharecropping, and second-class citizenship. These practices epitomized the dominant culture, and the subsequent behaviors lasted from the end of the Civil War until adoption and passage of Public Law 89-110, the Voting Rights Act of 1965, nearly 100 years.

What's more, the institutions of government, including the courts, were not inclined to be advocates for advancing opportunities for citizenship readiness for the former slaves. Court litigation could have been tools or means of assisting the transition from slavery to citizenship. During the course of the Reconstruction, both the US Supreme Court and the lower level federal courts faced the task of interpreting Reconstruction legislation, including the Thirteenth, Fourteenth, and Fifteenth Amendments, and the Enforcement Acts. The *Thirteenth Amendment to the United States Constitution* officially abolished and continues to prohibit slavery to this day. The *Fourteenth Amendment* declared that all persons born or naturalized in the *United States* are *American* citizens including African-Americans. *The Fifteenth Amendment* prohibited governments from denying US citizens the right to vote based on race, color, or past servitude. By the end of Reconstruction, the Supreme Court had defined these groundbreaking pieces of legislation in a conservative manner that negatively impacted the former slaves. Clauson (2015) researched the Court's handling of the Thirteenth, Fourteenth, and Fifteenth Amendments and argued that while Federal District Courts had moved to broaden the nationalistic meaning of these Amendments, the US Supreme Court was antithetical to such a direction. Things came to a "head" when *United States v. Hall* (1871) was heard by the USSC. There had been Ku Klux Klan violence in Green County, AL, and prosecutors sought to bring to justice the rioters under the enforcement acts of 1870. Federal prosecutors challenged the judges to make a broad, nationalistic interpretation, which would have enabled the federal government to protect the rights of the former slaves for the long haul. The issue at hand was, what were the privileges and immunities of national citizenship? Did the Fourteenth Amendment apply the Bill of Rights to the states? Were these rights protected against the state governments? However, constitutional protections still met the force of a national culture that refused to acknowledge their rights as citizens. Culture trumped law. Ultimately, the government failed to secure a conviction of the white rioters, and justice was denied yet again.

Amidst these impediments, the union of Abe and Calline evolved as a family of twelve children; the offspring included daughters Mandie, Annie, Laura, and Liza and sons Jim (my grandfather), Jake, Matthew, Will, and Albert, as well as three other children that were fathered by the white plantation owner. Two of the latter were twins, Ed and Ellis. Abe and Calline's union and subsequent parenthood came to maturity at the onset of the 1880s. Abe had no means of reacting to the fact of the role of the plantation owner in the production of the children in the family. Moreover, there were no courts that would take seriously any such plaintiff.

Given the disregard of the sanctity of marriage among African-Americans, it is ironic that they were members of the first traceable generation who could have been the first "beneficiaries" of the Thirteenth, Fourteenth, and Fifteenth Amendments to the Constitution. The amendments were important in implementing the Reconstruction of the American South after the war. Culture, then and now, is stronger than law. It was the national culture and the electoral college that "approved" the presidential election of 1876, in which the popular vote was won by Samuel Tilden against Rutherford B. Hayes (although the decision by the electoral college was and is constitutional; it reflects the framers' distrust of democracy). However, Tilden did not win the electoral college. History calls it the "Hayes-Tilden compromise" in which Hayes agreed to overturn government policies that were designed to assist the transformation of the former male slaves to freedmen. The "compromise' was the prerequisite or condition for Hayes' elevation to the presidency. My history lessons teach that from 1861 to 1877, the Civil War and Reconstruction affirmed the integrity of the Union, ended slavery, and generated three constitutional amendments that at least laid the foundation for honoring the Declaration's promise that "all men are created equal." But, what is written and what is taught barely acknowledge the nuance of that period.

In addition to legislative acts that diminished and marginalized the newly freed men, women, and children of color, there were also court deliberations, which had a nefarious impact on my family. When I remember my American history, there was a perilous time during the years leading up to the Civil War which was manifested in the litigation being considered by the US Supreme Court. Perhaps the most important litigation was the Court's ruling in the Dred Scott case (*Scott v. Sanford*). Dred was a slave who escaped to a "free state" (Missouri) and then sued for his freedom. The year was 1857. Abe Sanson was 10 years old when the courts ruled that "Negroes" had no rights that white men were obliged to recognize.

Here is the background: In 1846 (the year before my grandfather Abe was born), an erstwhile former slave named Dred Scott and his wife Harriet sued for their freedom in a St. Louis city court. The odds were in their favor. They had lived with their owner, an army surgeon, at Fort Snelling, then in the free Territory of Wisconsin. The Scotts' freedom could be established on the grounds that they had been held in bondage for extended periods in a free territory and were then returned to a slave state. Courts had ruled this way in the past. However, what appeared to be a straightforward lawsuit between two private parties became an 11-year legal struggle that culminated in one of the most notorious decisions ever issued by the United States Supreme Court.

On its way to the Supreme Court, the Dred Scott case grew in scope and significance as slavery became the single most explosive issue in American politics. By the time the case reached the high court, it had come to have enormous political implications for the entire nation.

On March 6, 1857, Chief Justice Roger B. Taney read the majority opinion of the Court, which stated that slaves were not citizens of the United States and therefore could not expect any protection from the federal government or the courts. The opinion also stated that Congress had no authority to ban slavery from a federal territory. This decision moved the nation a step closer to Civil War, and in 1861, the Civil War began and continued through to 1865.

The decision of *Scott v. Sanford*, considered by progressive legal scholars to be the worst ever rendered by the Supreme Court, was overturned by the Thirteenth and Fourteenth Amendments to the Constitution, which abolished slavery and declared all persons born in the United States to be citizens therein. The challenge was to have all members of American society accept the nuance of the law and see the good in it for everyone. In order for that new language to have meaning, it would require a supportive culture. More than 150 years after the Constitution was amended, I am sad to opine that the American culture does not vigorously (or for that matter tacitly) embrace what equality under the law means. The truth of the matter is that we live in a plutocracy where the dollar bill reigns supreme. Even when the more progressive policy supporters make a move to protect workers' pensions and provide health insurance for all citizens regardless of their station in life, the cries of "Socialism" curtail movement in that direction.

Chapter V

TRACING THE HISTORY OF THE SECOND SAMPSON GENERATION

The beginnings of my second paternal generation overlap the final decades of the 19th century and extend through the middle of the 20th century. This second generation of Sampsons came to maturity as the 1800s ended. The family unit evolved into a household headed by Jim and Corine Lindsey Sanson; Jim, who was fondly called "Grandpa Jimmy," was born in 1880; Corine Lindsey, who was born in 1884, would eventually give birth to 10 children. In the early years of their marriage, the family lived in the town of Eucutta, MS in Jasper County, nearly ten miles northeast from Sandersville in neighboring Jones County. Jim and Corine's journey blazed the trail as their generation was the first to come into existence as free people. As did many women who gave birth to children in the late 1800s, births were not likely to occur in hospital settings. Thus, Corine served as a midwife for all the Sampsons as they spread across the Southeast. She was serving in that role months after the birth of her last daughter,

Annie Laura, and according to her daughter Iola, passed away after contracting an illness in the mid-1930s.

Jim Sampson (*né* Sanson) was known for his craftmanship and ability to earn a living with his hands. He made railroad ties, fences, wagon wheels, caskets, and chairs, as well as maintaining a farm and raising livestock. When harvest and slaughter time came, he shared the fruits of his labor with all in the community who were in need. Jim and Corine's offspring are listed below.

Wiley, the firstborn (died from a rabid dog bite at nine years)
Plummer (1904-1995) my father, married Lurline Gavin in 1927. They had one daughter and seven sons.
Lurelia (1908-1997) married Nathan Arrington, and they had two sons and three daughters.
Milton (1909-1990) married Alice Nixon, and they had four sons.
Lucius (1911-2006) married Ella Mae Morgan (1916-1965), and they had three sons and three daughters.
Iola (1914-2000) married Walter Martin.
Abraham (1919-2005) married Lula Bunch, and they had three sons and three daughters.
Annie Laura (1923-1997) married Hubert Marsh, and they had three sons and two daughters.
Nettie Mae (birth date unknown)
Sylvester (died in infancy)

The second Sampson generation without a doubt was chronologically positioned to "enjoy" the "benefits" of the Thirteenth, Fourteenth, and Fifteenth Amendments to the Constitution more so than their parents. Even so, those constitutional protections still met the force of a national culture that refused to acknowledge them as people, not to speak of their rights as citizens. It was the national culture that "approved" the presidential election of 1876 in which the popular vote, but not the electoral vote, was won by Samuel Tilden against Rutherford B. Hayes. History calls it the "Hayes-Tilden compromise," in which Hayes agreed to halt government policy that supported the needs of the former slaves as they worked to become productive citizens. In exchange for Hayes' elevation to the presidency, he agreed to put a stop to government policy that would advance the condition of the former slaves. The second generation could have joined with James Weldon Johnson when he penned the phrase "sing a song full of the faith that the dark past has taught us," but they chose to "sing a song full of the hope that the present has brought..." They married, raised families, and earned a living by the sweat of their brow. They withstood the "Black Codes," Ku Klux Klan, Jim Crow, and unequal access to educational opportunity. There was a reliance on God, spirituality, religion, and their wit, sweat, and muscle. A story has been widely retold about their reliance on God's faithfulness: during a tornado that tore through Eucutta, the wooden framed structure where Sampson resided was lifted off its blocks, and all inside were in danger of being seriously injured or killed. Corine prayed for mercy, and legacy has it that the house was placed directly back on its foundation. The heroic actions of my grandmother doubtlessly became one of the planks in the infrastructure for interrelationships among my dad and his siblings. Overcoming odds became a hallmark for the group. Overcoming adversity results in character building. It shapes us into who we are and who we will become. It creates the confidence to overcome and the learning mechanisms to deal with the things that don't go our way. Further, it creates resilience, i.e., learning to deal with and address adversity. There were few traditional tools in my grandparents' kit to ward off adversity; particularly in short supply was walking around money, e.g., means to develop opportunities for leisure time.

From the end of slavery and continuing five generations later, the greater portion of my family were members of the working class engaged in wage or salaried labor, especially manual labor. As with all members of working-class families, members rely on their income exclusively to feed and maintain families. Discretionary spending for leisure lagged behind spending for subsistence, e.g., food, shelter, and clothing. The period from 1894 to 1915 was one in which white working-class workers in the United States began to have more leisure time than their predecessors. When I consider the time period beginning in 1894 regarding discretionary spending, I note that there were few occasions revealed in oral history about the family member "who made it," yet there were accounts of overcoming disadvantage. My mind was filled with "why", so I consulted studies conducted that attempted to explain the state of Black America in the 1890s. My inquisitiveness led me to the work of Carter G. Woodson and Lorenzo Greene, whose 1930 studies generated the publication *African-American Wages by Occupation*. From their work I learned that wages were scant in all the wage categories, e.g., blacksmiths in 1890 earned 27 cents an hour, carpenters 32 cents, machinists 24 cents, and day laborers 15 cents. These were the averages for whites. It does not take much imagination to discern that blacks in these positions did not earn the same as their white counterparts. Thus, I conclude that black working-class families did not join the expanded membership of the working class that had the good fortune of leisure time. Fast forward to my childhood days, my childhood tapes contained memories of few social occasions where the family gathered to celebrate one another. Moreover, there were no photographs of daily life for the past generations. Thus, I conclude that expanded membership of the working class with leisure time came as a result of the ability to engage discretionary spending. There were funds for staging family picnics, and attending *a* variety of entertainment activities such as state fairs, revival services, and motion pictures. Such was not the case for my 1890 ancestors. Access to leisure and photography did not trickle down to black working folks in the same proportion as it did to white working-class families. Thus, the nature of family influence in black working-class members is a function of their social class and access to more income. The family is the strongest influence on leisure and relationships among family members.

When asked about most important leisure, individuals, regardless of age or culture, typically indicate that time spent or activities pursued with family are most valued. It is within families that individuals learn leisure skills, interests, attitudes, and behaviors, and research has indicated continuity of recreation and leisure interests learned in childhood and adolescence across the life course. In addition, family and family members are common or frequent leisure companions throughout the life cycle. Families also construct time and opportunities for leisure, as well as constraints. However, the family‘s influence on leisure is often distinguished by gender, social class, age, race/ethnicity, and culture. Families shape leisure meanings and participation across the course of life and time in a myriad of ways. Family is both a source of leisure opportunity and constraint, reflecting the tension between individual wants/self-determination and societal norms/expectations of others. These are all factors that subsequently influence intergroup relations. I conclude these factors predict how my future ancestors interacted with one another. My childhood tapes do not contain memories of family gatherings, except at funerals. In a subsequent chapter, I discuss my first family vacation, which happened to be a first for my parents as well.

Tracing my maternal lineage

The maternal side of the second generation consisted of the unit in which Calvin Gavin was the bread winner. The Gavins were distinctly different from the Sampsons. My mother loved to read; she planted dreams in her children's heads. Conversely, my father seemed to accept the reality of his station in life. He was not bitter or resentful, and he certainly was not afraid of physical labor. He epitomized the phrase of working "from sunup 'til sundown." He felt it was his natural obligation to provide for his wife and children. My parents' different visions of their place in the gap characterize the varied gifts I gained from each of them. To be sure, there is a sharp contrast that distinguishes the history of my mother's family background from that of my father. A hyperbole is to suggest that my dad was from Mars and my mother from Venus. Despite such differences, they complemented each other in a way that benefited my siblings and me.

My mother's lineage, the Gavin family, can be traced to South Carolina before the Civil War. Sharon Morgan (2016), a genealogical researcher and Gavin descendant, traced the Gavin lineage from Ross Cromarty, Scotland to Virginia around 1695. Morgan's work reveals that the white Gavins are inseparable from the black Gavins, and that many of the white Gavin men fathered children with black women who worked as slaves.

More than two centuries would pass before my mother, Lurline Gavin, was born. She was an attractive, witty lady with a keen sense of humor. She read and recited poetry. My older siblings also remember her sense of humor. She had "good" hair and a brown complexion. From the time that my mother was twenty-three years old to two decades later, she gave birth to one daughter and eight sons, all but one surviving into adulthood.

She was a great homemaker and a wonderful cook who could do wonders with blackberries and fried chicken.

Lurline was a descendant of slaves. Records indicate ownership of slaves who were great-grandparents to her father, and my grandfather, Calvin Gavin. A book authored by David Gavin, entitled *David Gavin Diary, 1855–1874*, details the European part of my maternal family history. David Gavin was born in 1811, the son of John and Ann Gavin. He had three brothers: Charles (b. 1815), who lived in Florida; John (circa 1819-1858); and William (1829-1861). Gavin lived in the Colleton District of South Carolina, in the area between what is now St. George (called George's Station in the diary) in Dorchester County and Canaday's Crossroads in Colleton County. He was a planter and a lawyer who made frequent trips to the court in Waterboro. Gavin's legal work, his work as an appraiser of slaves in estates, his work as a surveyor, life on his plantation, and other matters were recorded in his diary. From his writings, we learn that the white Gavin men fathered many children with their female slaves. The collection is one volume, consisting of Gavin's diary, 1855-1871; personal accounts, 1856-1874; and about 150 brief entries giving vital dates and other information about family members, friends, and acquaintances. Diary entries discuss family members and neighbors, Gavin's political views (he apparently was a member of the American Party), election results for Colleton District, S.C., etc. Included are notations on the daily tasks of slaves, their illnesses, and the remedies used to treat them, and Gavin's problems with a runaway slave. Social and legal experiences of women are also occasionally noted.

The *David Gavin Diary* has two references to Chloe, a mulatto (a derisive term applied to offspring of mixed parentage, i.e., white and black) girl left to Bathiah Byrd Gavin in her father's will. Chloe became Bathiah's cook, moved with her from South

Carolina to Mississippi, and died there (in Perry County) in 1843 or 1844. David Gavin described Chloe as a yellow woman. While in South Carolina, Chloe had a child, Landy, whose father was a Frenchman named Dentinac. Landy´s complexion was said to be light, and his hair was described as black and curly, not kinky. At some point, Landy paid Hesakiah Byrd $900 for his freedom and went to Indiana. Richard Lackey speculated that Landy, once in Indiana, "passed for a white man" (Byrd genealogy article from David Schankin, 2014).

Chole gave birth to Friday Gavin, my great-great-great-grandfather. Friday is the father of all black Gavins in MS. In 1843, Friday (1770-1856) became the property of Bathia Byrd Gavin. Friday died on September 13, 1856 from dropsy in the chest (an old term for the swelling of soft tissues due to the accumulation of excess water). In years gone by, a person might have been said to have dropsy, which is now recognized as edema due to congestive heart failure. David Gavin's entry in the diary read:

13 Sep 1856 - "My old man Friday died this morning, before day, of dropsy in the chest… I have had him in my possession since February 1843; he carried my keys and attended to feeding the horses and attending to my cattle, hogs, and stock general as long as he was able, and a great manager of hogs he was, and could remember more about the stock than I could… He served my grandfather and grandmother Gavin, my father not having come into possession of him because he died in 1838 before his mother died in 1842. His (Friday's) mother was my grandmother Gavin's cook, and died in Perry County, MS, 1843 or 4. He seemed like a connecting link between me and grandfather and grandmother Gavin, for he could talk to and tell me of the acting and doing of them and others of the olden time, about the connections of the family, their names, and where they lived and moved to or

from. He says he was large enough to open the gate for people in the Revolutionary War and was at the defeat of Gen. Sumpter (at Fishing creek) during the revolution, and that his master had to run, and his mother Chloe got an old woman to claim herself and children to keep the Tories and British from taking them...." (Source: David Gavin Diary, p. 44)

Friday cohabitated with Peg Inabnet-Gavin during the period of 1798 while living in South Carolina, and then while in Mississippi before 1880. During slavery, slaves were not allowed to be married. Peg was transported to MS with all but one of her children (Mary Elizabeth stayed behind). She cohabitated with Charles Gavin (1785, SC) after migration to MS. Peg and Charles did not have any children together.

One of David Gavin's diary entries describes an incident with Peg, who served as his cook. The entry is indicative of the culture and mores regarding slaves who dared to seek their freedom during those years:

> 18 Feb 1857 - "Yesterday we were hunting my and Mr. Rumph's Team, but did not start them; we caught H. Inabnet's Peg and chased Jonas. Peg was so scarred with the whip, and wishing to catch our own Negroes that we left her and hunted for our own, but did not find them." (Source David Gavin, p. 54)

Friday and Peg had nine children, many of whom established families in MS.

William 1811 - married Nicy and then Susan; no children found

Chloe1819 - married Peter and had nine children

Joseph 1822 - married Ann and had ten children; then married Elsie Brewer

Nathan 1824 - married Frances and had one child

Abby 1825 - served as cook for John Edward Gavin; no children found
Mary Elizabeth 1825- remained in SC; inherited land from David Gavin (was he her father?)
Moses 1828 - unknown spouse + one child (my great-great-grandfather)
America 1830 - married Jacob, then Sandy Gavin (1833) and had three children
Harry ???? - probably died as a child of catarrhal fever, a respiratory condition
Morgan (2016) claims that the entire group of black Gavins were offspring of Friday and Peg. So, my maternal lineage is as follows:

Friday was the father of Moses (1828);
Moses was the father of Wash (1845);
Wash was the father of Calvin (1875), who was my mother's father and my maternal grandfather.

It is noteworthy that I can trace my mother's family for more than six generations and that the ability to do so was due to the records of the white Gavins.

My mother's personal family history was not delightful. Discussions at the dining room table and front porch discussions when cousin Ernest Newell would visit are recorded in my childhood tapes. Replaying them in my middle school years, I recalled Langston Hughes poem "Mother to Son." This poignant contribution to American literature resonates with the stories of the household of Calvin Gavin, my maternal grandfather.

"Well, son, I'll tell you:
Life for me ain't been no crystal stair.

It's had tacks in it,
And splinters,
And boards torn up,
And places with no carpet on the floor__
Bare.
But all the time
I'se been a-climbin' on,
And reached landin's,
And turnin' corners,
And sometimes goin' in the dark
Where there ain't been no light.
So, boy, don't you turn back.
Don't you set down on the steps
"Cause you finds it kinder hard.
Don't you fall now_ _
For I'se still goin' honey,
I'se still climbin',
And life for me ain't been no crystal stair."

My mother and her sister, my Aunt Corrine (my absolute favorite aunt), would often tell me of the difficulties they encountered as children. Most poignant was the fact of losing their mother in 1914, who at the time was 33 years old. She had given birth to eight children, seven of whom were alive at that juncture. My mother was 7 years old when her mother passed. Searching the 1910 Decennial Census, I learned that Ella Gavin had married my grandfather when she was about 14 years old. Her oldest was her son Edward, who was 20 at the time of her death; second son Herbert was 19; first daughter Mamie was 15; Corrine, the second sister, was 11; son Herman 9; daughter Geneva 6; and the youngest was Chalmers Jeffry, who was 4 years old. Chalmers was a twin brother to Charlie Jasper, who was deceased at birth.

Thus, in 1914, Calvin Gavin was a 38-year-old widower with seven children: three young children, three adolescents, and one young adult. Attempting to control the pain of mourning, Calvin moved his family to Mobile, AL, close to his sister to get some help maintaining his household. In the meantime, Corrine, the second daughter, aged 11 years, assumed much of the care for her younger siblings. But Calvin's mourning was not over; six years after losing his wife Ella, his oldest daughter Mamie succumbed at the age of 20 years. Eventually, he returned to the Jones County, MS (Sandersville/Errata) area where he married Lucinda Jones, who was twelve years his junior.

Calvin and Lucinda had a combined seven children in their care, two of hers and five of his. Listening to my mother and Aunt Corrine, I learned that Calvin Gavin's children did not always feel sufficiently nurtured by their stepmother.

The 1930 Decennial Census reveals that Calvin and Lucinda had an "empty nest" when the census taker visited them; they lived as husband and wife until Calvin's death in 1939 at the age of 64. Lucinda would live until her 99th birthday in 1985. I remember her from our visits to her in Sandersville in the early 1960s. My mother called her "Miss Lucinda." There was little evidence of a close maternal relationship between her and my mother even though Lucinda had been her stepmother from early adolescence until adulthood in 1928 when Lurline and Plummer married. Lucinda did speak fondly of my grandfather Calvin, her late husband.

I heard many stories about my grandfather Calvin; he was unique in the Errata community largely because he could read. He was described as smart, opinionated, and critical of many of those who lived around him. The census reports that he was always employed and had completed high school at a time when few African-Americans had the opportunity, considering that the Freedmen's Bureau was created in 1865 during the Lincoln administration by an act of Congress called the Freedman's Bureau Bill. It was passed on March 3, 1865 to aid former slaves through food and housing, oversight, education, healthcare, and employment contracts with private landowners. President Andrew Johnson, who succeeded President Lincoln, vetoed a stronger version of the freedman's legislation on February 19, 1866, and Congress failed to override that veto on the following day. In July 1868, Congress voted to again extend the Freedmen's Bureau but, a couple of weeks later, decided to limit its functions to processing claims and supporting education. Four years later, in June 1872, Congress voted to completely shut down the Freedmen's Bureau by the end of that month. These events tell the story of impudent public policies that could have meant massive boosts to public education for the former slaves. My grandfather was born the year after the demise of the Freedman's Bureau. Nevertheless, he learned to read, and he qualified for appointment as postmaster, but the offer came during the days after he lost his wife. His daughters Corrine and Lurline were proud of his legacy. One of their stories recalled the time when a neighbor received a telegram but could not read it, so he, like many others in the community, came to Calvin Gavin to interpret for him. My grandfather was in the middle of his evening meal. The neighbor is said to have stated, "Mr. Gavin, dey brought dis to me and dey say it is important. Would you be kind enough to tell me what it says?" Without looking at the visitor, Calvin demonstrated his annoyance at his neighbor's request. "Can't you see I am eating? Sit down and wait until I am finished." Minutes later, Calvin turned to the neighbor and snarled, "let me see what you got here." After reading the telegram, he turned to his neighbor and stated in a nonchalant voice, "your brother in Chicago died."

Grandpa Calvin was a religious man. After the family moved to Laurel, he began to worship at St. Paul Methodist Church. Later, he would serve as Sunday school superintendent. St. Paul was then and is now a respected place of worship that was founded to serve black Methodists in Laurel. St. Paul served as the worship place for most of the black teachers, physicians, and business owners in Laurel. Perhaps the most notable was the family of Leontyne Price, the opera diva who was born in Laurel. Over the years, when significant public figures, such as Dr. Martin Luther King, Jr., would visit Laurel (1964), one of the venues would be St. Paul. Thus, my grandfather's legacy was affirmed by my mother and her sister.

I only took mandatory psychology courses in undergraduate school, none in graduate study, and thus, I have more anecdotal evidence about healthy psychological life than has been generated by research or deep study. Yet, it is safe to believe that having a parent die at a young age, as was the case with my mother at the age of five years, is a life-altering experience that can make children feel different from their peers. Feeling socially isolated can negatively impact a child's self-esteem, which can put them at risk for anxiety, depression, and substance abuse. I never saw any evidence of anxiety, depression, or substance abuse in my mother's life.

As children grow and mature into healthy adults, a crucial part of their development is learning to form intimate relationships. The roots of a child's ability to form interpersonal relationships often depend on the quality of the relationships that children have with their parents. Attachment theory teaches that young children need to form a strong attachment to at least one primary caregiver who can provide unconditional love and support that allows them to form and develop relationship skills as they grow older. Whether or not children develop later problems often depends on the surviving parent and how well they can help their children overcome grief and learn to move on with their lives. It appears that my mother and her sisters had a very close bond with their father despite a not-so-close bond with their stepmother who came into their lives within three years of losing their mother.

Transformative Act III 1929-1945: The Great Depression and the onset of World War II

A substantial portion of my childhood tapes capture dinner table discussions of my parent's memories about the Great Depression and subsequent failed government policies that had been legislated to counter the financial challenge of those days. Between 1929 and 1945, the Great Depression and World War II utterly redefined the role of government in American society and catapulted the United States from being an isolated, peripheral state into the world's hegemonic superpower. The rise of the United States did not mean that all citizens equally enjoyed the benefits of the burgeoning new power. Among the white population, the masses therein did not enjoy the meteoric rise, and certainly the African-American population as a whole experienced deferment of dreams of economic and political self-sufficiency.

American prosperity in the 1920s was real, but it was not nearly as pervasive as legend has portrayed. The millions of European immigrants who had swarmed into the nation's teeming industrial cities in the preceding decades remained culturally parochial and economically precarious in gritty ethnic ghettoes. Most black Americans, including my grandparents, still dwelled in the eleven states of the old Confederacy, the poorest and most disadvantaged people in America's poorest and most backward region. And well before the Great Depression, almost as soon as the Great War concluded in 1918, a severe economic crisis had beset the farm belt. It did not entirely lift until the next world war, more than twenty years later. The long-suffering countryside was home to nearly half of all Americans in the 1920s; one out of every five workers toiled on the nation's fields and farms. Virtually none enjoyed such common urban amenities as electricity and indoor plumbing. In fact, it was the mid-to-late 1950s when my house first had an indoor toilet, bathroom, and black and white television.

At the same time, other foreboding signs began to appear, faintly at first, but with mounting urgency as the depression began to unfold. A ramshackle, woefully underregulated private banking system, a legacy of Andrew Jackson's war on central banking, had managed to wobble its dysfunctional way into the modern era. Some twenty-five thousand banks, most of them highly fragile "unitary" institutions with tiny service areas, little to no diversification of clients or assets, and microscopic capitalization, constituted the astonishingly vulnerable foundation of the national credit. As for government, public spending at all levels, including towns, cities, counties, states, and the federal government itself, amounted only to about 15% of the gross domestic product in the 1920s, one-fifth of which was federal expenditures. Ideology aside, its very size made the federal government in the 1920s somewhat like a ninety-pound weakling in the fight against the looming depression.

Yet, for most of the 1920s, the mood of much of the country, impervious to news of accumulating international dangers and buoyed by wildly ascending stock prices, as well as the congenital optimism long claimed as every American's birthright, remained remarkably upbeat. Then, in the autumn of 1929, the bubble burst. That was two years after my father and mother were married. The Great Crash in October sent stock prices plummeting and all but froze the international flow of credit. Banks failed by the thousands. Businesses collapsed by the tens of thousands. Millions - nobody knew at first how many, so primitive were the government's fact-finding organs - went unemployed. Herbert Hoover, elected just months earlier amid lavish testimonials to his peerless competence, saw his presidency shattered and his reputation forever shredded because of his inability to tame the depression monster.

By 1932, some 13 million Americans, one out of every four able and willing workers in the country, were out of work. My parents had been married four years and were parents to Mazie, Plummer, Jr., and James Calvin (Jim), who was born in mid-November as the year came to an end. Even those horrendous numbers could not begin to take the full measure of the human misery that unemployment entailed. Given the demography of the labor force and prevailing cultural norms that kept most women - and virtually all married women - out of the wage-paying economy, a 25% unemployment rate meant that, for all practical purposes, every fourth household in America had no breadwinner. Many Americans came to believe that they were witnessing not just another downswing of the business cycle, but the collapse of a historic economic, political, and social order, perhaps even the end of the American way of life. Yet curiously, as many observers noted, most Americans remained inexplicably docile, even passive, in the face of this unprecedented calamity. The Great Depression spurred the rise of African-American political activism and the Civil Rights Movement in the 1950s and 1960s. The popularity of President Franklin D. Roosevelt and his New Deal Program was instrumental in convincing African-Americans to switch their GOP political allegiances to become a core part of the Democratic Party's voting bloc.

Chapter VI

THE THIRD GENERATION

The Great Depression, World War II, and the Cold War hovered over the third generation of the modern-day Sampsons, and the aftermath of those challenging times lingered until that generation grew into adulthood. It was the early 1900s when the offspring of Jim and Corine began growing into adulthood, and by 1950, all of their grandchildren had been born. As I reflect on the times and the people who preceded me, I have come to the belief that the third generation epitomized the Horatio Alger myth, the "classic" American success story and character arc, the trajectory from "rags to riches." It comes from the novels of Horatio Alger, Jr., which were widely popular after the Civil War in the United States. Lest I be remiss in my reporting, my family never transcended from rags to riches, they made do with rags and rode out the financial storm.

As the Cold War unfolded in the decade and a half after World War II, the United States experienced phenomenal economic growth. The war brought the return of prosperity, and in the post-war period, the United States consolidated its position as the world's richest country. Gross national product, a measure of all goods and services produced in the United States, jumped from about $200 billion in 1940 to $300 billion in 1950, and to more than $500 billion in 1960. The GNP/GDP figure in 2010 was $15 trillion dollars! More and more Americans now considered, themselves, part of the middle class.

The growth resulted from many sources. The automobile industry was partially responsible, as the number of automobiles produced annually quadrupled between 1946 and 1955. A housing boom stimulated in part by easily affordable mortgages for returning servicemen fueled the expansion. The rise in defense spending as the Cold War escalated also played a part.

After 1945, the major corporations in America grew even larger. There had been earlier waves of mergers in the 1890s and the 1920s; in the 1950s, another wave occurred. New conglomerates - firms with holdings in a variety of industries - led the way. International Telephone and Telegraph, for example, bought Sheraton Hotels, Continental Baking, Hartford Fire Insurance, and Avis Rent-a-Car, among other companies. Smaller franchise operations like McDonald's fast food restaurants provided yet another pattern. Large corporations also developed holdings overseas, where labor costs were often lower.

Workers found their own lives changing as industrial America changed. Fewer workers produced goods; more provided services. By 1956, a majority held white-collar jobs, working as corporate managers, teachers, salespersons, and office employees. Some firms granted a guaranteed annual wage, long-term employment contracts, and other benefits. With such changes, labor militancy was undermined, and some class distinctions began to fade.

Farmers, on the other hand, faced tough times. Gains in productivity led to agricultural consolidation, as farming became a big business. Family farms, in turn, found it difficult to compete, and more and more farmers left the land.

As I learned of the challenges the third generation faced, I was simultaneously angered and awed. Rarely have so many done so much with so few resources. Their belief in God was the hallmark of their being. Deacons and preachers could be counted among them. They were adolescents during WWI, witnessed Herbert Hoover's Great Depression in the 1930s, joined the Armed Forces in support of WWII in the 1940s, and afterward initiated the migration from the cotton fields of Mississippi to the industrial Midwest. They inherited the consequences of economic inequality, i.e., the disparity of wealth or income between distinct groups within a society. Porter (2014) states that economic inequality is characterized by the aphorism "the rich get richer while the poor get poorer"; however, the phrase refers more specifically to the gap on income or asset between the poorest and the richest. Their "inheritance" of economic inequality tempered their dreams and ambitions, and ironically grounded them in such a fashion that they were able to "eke out a living" and rise above the circumstances of inequality. Nevertheless, in my estimation, there are several disadvantages associated with economic inequality. First, where there is economic inequality, there are decreases in educational attainment. Most of the third generation did not graduate high school; nations with a high degree of economic equality and a relatively small low-income population tend to have a substantially higher level of education (Thorbeck and Charumilind, 2002). Second, economic inequality increases political inequality when wealth distribution becomes concentrated in a small number of hands as political power tends to become skewed in favor of that small wealthy group. High-income groups are able and incentivized to manipulate government in their favor through both legal processes and corrupt practices. Impoverished or working-class groups are simultaneously less able to become educated or participate in the political process as economic means become increasingly depleted. Third, inequality decreases the chances for viability in health: impoverished members of society are subject to disproportionate occurrence rates of certain kinds of illnesses, while access to quality healthcare and healthy food is sometimes limited or unavailable for poor individuals.

The result of a substantially poor population, a defining feature of economic inequality, is a less effective lower-income workforce, higher disease and mortality rates, higher healthcare costs, and progressively deepening poverty for afflicted groups. Fifth, inequality_increases crime. Studies establish a positive relationship between income inequality and crime. According to a survey of research conducted between 1968 and 2000, most researchers point to evidence showing that economically unequal societies have higher crime rates *(Denning, 2011).* That survey concludes that inequality is "the single factor most closely and consistently related to crime." Sixth, inequality stifles growth. An elevated level of economic inequality means a higher level of poverty. Poverty is associated with increased crime and poor public health, which burdens the economy. In the face of increasing food prices and lower incomes, support for pro-growth government policies declines *(International Institute for Labor Studies, 2008).* Moreover, wealthy citizens maintain disproportionate political power compared to poorer citizens, which encourages the development of inefficient tax structures skewed in favor of the wealthy while unequal income distribution increases political instability, which threatens property rights, increases the risk of state repudiated contracts, and discourages capital accumulation *(Thorbecke and Charumilind, Economic Inequality and Its Socioeconomic Impact, 30 World Development 1477, 1484, April 22, 2002).*

Finally, a widening rich-poor gap tends to increase the rate of rent-seeking and predatory market behaviors that hinder economic growth, i.e., the use of the resources of a company, an organization, or an individual to obtain economic gain from others without reciprocating any benefits to society through wealth creation, such as when a company lobbies the government for loan subsidies, grants, or tariff protection.

Despite the reality of these foreboding lessons from basic economics, or perhaps because of their existence, there were decisions to marry and raise families. There was also time for building community and rising from the canvas as they battled social and political forces that, on their face, outmanned them. Jim and Corine saw adulthood come to Plummer, Lurelia, Milton, Lucius, and Iola. Abraham was a lad when their father passed away, and Annie Laura was a toddler.

From these offspring came entrepreneurs, farmers, laborers, all endowed with a strong work ethic. The older brothers, i.e., Plummer, Milton, and Lucius, found employment at Masonite Corporation beginning in the 1940s. Lurelia, the first-born sister, also elected to marry and reside in Laurel. The last three, i.e., Iola, Abraham, and Annie Laura, made a life for themselves in Dayton.

Left to Right Annie Laura, Plummer, Lurline seated, Abraham, Lucius and Iola

This group of the third generation shown in this photo were well into their senior years in 1995. Annie Laurie, the youngest in the family; along with my dada, Plummer, Sr.; Abraham, the youngest son; Lucius; and Iola gathered at Deeds Carillion Park in Dayton, along with my mother (seated), and were all present at a family gathering that occurred on my birthday. More than three dozen Chicago relatives chattered a bus and traveled to Dayton that weekend. I cherish that occasion because it was the first time that my extended family sang happy birthday to me on my birthday.

Several of the third generation were trailblazers; perhaps the most outstanding enterprise was the religious ministry. Because of the strong Christian beliefs among Black Southerners, it followed that preaching was idealized. A family legend goes back to the second generation and includes the story of Rev. Charlie "Sin-Killing" Lindsey. Reverend was a sibling of my grandmother Corine Lindsey. Conversations around the dinner table at 115 Melon about Uncle Charlie focused on the fierceness of his message and his ability to reach the unsaved, thus the moniker "Sin-Killing." He blazed the trail for the ministers in the subsequent generations of my family. Those in the fourth generation that accepted their calling to the religious ministry included my brother Therman and my cousin ML.

As an institution, the black Church evolved from the clutches of slavery, as had all other institution and agencies in USA. Those who led society were slow to embrace equality between Africans and Europeans. Thus, as time and inevitability brought about a society of emancipated black folk, there was also a need for a theology that would address the needs of this new group of non-European Americans. Such a theology was long in the making as honest men and women grappled with the "Negro problem." In about 1845, the decade leading up to the Civil War, southern slaveholders and slavery sympathizers established the Southern Baptist Church. Black members accounted for about 100,000 of the 350,000 Southern Baptist church members, according to Baptist historian William Whitsitt's estimate published in the 1895 SBC Annual. The estimate was based on Whitsett's extrapolation backward from 1852 statistics compiled by Baptist statistician J.L. Burrows.

Mostly former slaves, those black Southern Baptists were often allowed to vote on matters of church discipline and admission of new members to their churches, according to Southern Baptist Theological Seminary historian Greg Wills in his 1997 book, *Democratic Religion*. They also served on church committees and were recognized as messengers by some Baptist associations.

Despite signs of incremental acceptance of Africans as human beings, slavery in the 19th century was the most critical moral issue dividing Baptists in the United States. Struggling to gain a foothold in the South after the American Revolution, a generation of white Southern Baptist preachers accommodated themselves to the leadership of southern society. Rather than challenging the gentry on slavery and urging freedom of the slaves (as did the Quakers and Methodists), they began to interpret the Bible as supporting the practice of slavery and encouraged good paternalistic practices by slaveholders. They preached to slaves to accept their places and obey their masters. Before the Nat Turner Rebellion, white Baptists had welcomed slaves and free blacks as members. After the Rebellion, whites worked to exert more control over black congregations, and state legislatures passed laws that required that black congregations be overseen by white ministers. There was clearly no separation of state from the church when it came to slave management policy. In the decades before the Civil War, there were arguments and policies among church leaders that resulted in a compromise of sorts: there was a policy of neutrality concerning slavery. Yet there were strong contrary arguments advanced by many white Baptist preachers in the South who argued in favor of preserving the right of ministers to be slaveholders. Such policy stances were completely contrary to a Black theology for that latest group of Americans. The up-and-down, push/pull policy debates would continue in some form or another for decades to come.

When it came to membership growth in the Southern Baptist churches, black membership dwarfed that of whites, according to Baylor University historians Thomas Kidd and Barry Hankins in *Baptists in America*. Still, churches expressed their belief in the "social inferiority of African-Americans" by making them sit in the worst seats during worship and treating them "like children," wrote Wills (1997). Some historians argue that many of those slave church members likely were forced "to be a part of the church" and received incomplete Biblical teaching, with sermons and Bible lessons aimed at maintaining subservience on the plantation. Consequently, when slaves gained their freedom at the end of the Civil War, black Southern Baptists "looked for a comparable emancipation in their church life," according to LeRoy Gainey, pastor and educator. Much of African-Americans' spiritual growth, Gainey said, occurred in "hush harbors," secret churches in the woods that taught the whole counsel of God.

The churches in Beavers Meadow (Jasper County, MS) and adjoining Shady Grove (Jones County, MS), where my parents and their parents belonged, are among the "hush harbors" to which Gainey refers. In the decades leading up to the Great Depression, these churches provided opportunities for black ministers to develop, and they also made for opportunities for other young men and women to "court." Worship or going to church was more than getting saved, it was also a time to find a marriage mate. The wood frame churches were, in addition to places of worship, community centers for nearby residents. Horses and buggies were the modern means of transportation. During the summer months in Jasper and Jones Counties, there would be summer revival, a week-long event beginning on Sunday when families and young ladies would bring dinner in baskets to be served in the afternoon, following Sunday morning worship. I loved hearing my dad talk about how he would ride his horse to church. He spoke proudly of his beautiful horse, which was a statement of his eligibility as a bachelor seeking a mate. He would later tell me that he and my mother met during a worship meeting. The churches were small, accommodating less than a hundred folks. Thus, sometimes, the sanctuary was standing-room only, therefore, many young men would stand outside and look into the ongoing service from the windows.

My parents, Plummer and Lurline: first members of the third generation

My father, Plummer, was a dark-complexioned, lean muscular man who thrived on hard, physically demanding work. He was the oldest of seven siblings that grew into adulthood. When he was born on August 15, 1904, Theodore Roosevelt was president, the average annual income was $1056, a new car cost $800, a new house $3395, a loaf of bread was 0.03 cents, the Dow Jones Average was 79, and life expectancy was 47 years. His father, Jim Sanson (my grandfather), was 21 years old when he and Corine were joined in holy matrimony. From the union of Jim Sanson and Corine Lindsey came eleven children, including three that were fathered by the white plantation owner. My dad and his siblings Lurelia, Milton, Lucius, Iola, Marie, Abraham, and Annie Laura grew into adulthood and formed the backbone of the third generation. After first-generation Grandmother

Caroline passed away in the latter years of the 1920s, Grandpa Jimmy sold his 120 acres to Masonite Corporation in the mid-to-late 1930s. Although unlettered, Jim acquired considerable material possessions. When Jim was in his late forties, he owned a large acreage in northern Jones County, near Eucutta. After Grandpa Jimmy sold his acreage, he moved to the outskirts of Laurel, and the migration from Eucutta and Sandersville began in earnest. Grandmother Corine enjoyed much social capital in her community. She was a midwife, a practice that placed her at the birth of many in her community.

My parents were first of the third-generation members to marry on March 3, 1927. When my mother passed away in 1992, she and my dad had been married 65 years, and she had parented nine children. Their union and the unions of dad's and mother's siblings modeled a type of perseverance which was important to the production of my generation, the fourth. Their "fertile" ground flourished amidst the turbulence of the "roaring twenties," a decade when American economic growth, technological change, and the loosening of social codes encouraged a lively and uninhibited youth culture centered around the automobile, jazz music, and bootleg liquor. As I recall family discussions, I am convinced that the uninhibited youth culture and bootleg liquor description that historians use was remote from the experiences of my dad and his new bride. Of course, the end of the 1920s was the time the stock market crashed, and the Great Depression persisted the entirety of the next decade. When the market crashed, they had been married less than two years. For each of these new families, it was a challenge to rise above the strains of social and political inequality as manifested in the circumstances of the Depression and Jim Crow.

Lynching, the practice of murder by extrajudicial action, was the practice of law designed to keep black folks in order.

Lynchings in the United States began after the American Civil War in the late 1800s, following the emancipation of slaves; they declined after 1930 but were recorded into the 1960s. Lynchings most frequently targeted African-American men and women in the South. They were most frequent from the 1890 to the 1920s. In the state of Mississippi and Jones County, perhaps the most poignant was the case of Willie McGee. Although there were no night riders that burst into McGee's residence and hung him, there was little chance of getting a fair trial when the accused was black, and the alleged victim was white. McGee was an African-American grocery delivery driver who was electrocuted for the rape of a white woman. Alex Heard, a native of Jackson, MS, wrote *The Eyes of Willie McGee: A Tragedy of Race, Sex, and Secrets in the Jim Crow South* (HarperCollins, 2010).

Alex Heard's research led him to multiple resources of information, among them the Mississippi Department of Archives and History and the archives of the communist Civil Rights Congress in Washington, DC (The CRC paid for McGee's defense, and former Congresswoman Bella Abzug was his lead attorney, adding interesting historical twists to the case.). There, he discovered trial transcripts, FBI documents, and archived newspapers. There were many questions that were never resolved although there were three trials before the execution: 1) Did grocery delivery driver Willie McGee crawl through a window, wake mother of three Willette Hawkins from her sleep as she held her infant daughter, and rape her? 2) Or did Hawkins wake up after a nightmare and believe it actually happened? 3) Did she make it up? The majority of Laurel's African-Americans believe McGee was innocent while the majority of whites believe he was guilty.

Decades later, the story remains a sore subject in Laurel. In interviews, Alex Heard reports: "'Willie McGee was a man who liked women and they liked him,' Cleavan Jordan, an acquaintance of McGee stated, 'along in there after the war, he got messed up with a white woman and her husband found out. So, she called rape on Willie to save her own neck.'"

Heard gives examples of how the corrupt justice system of the time favored whites, as in the case of Laverne Yarbrough. "At around 6 PM on December 6, 1946, a 24-year-old white male named Laverne Yarbrough showed up at a small grocery store in the Queensburg section of town. The store's owner, F.A. Hendry, didn't know Yarbrough, but he noticed that he had a bottle of whiskey in his pocket," Heard writes. Hendry closed the store for the night. Moments later, two African-American boys witnessed Yarbrough walking past them holding a little black girl by the hand. He proceeded to pick her up and take her into the woods, where he raped her.

Prosecutors sought the death penalty for Yarbrough, but an all-white jury sentenced him to life. The end of the story is that a white man rapes a helpless child, and his life is spared, yet a black man questionably charged with raping a white woman is executed. This state of affairs in 1940s and 1950s MS affirmed the decision of my uncles and several others to leave Mississippi for a more desirous alternative.

The 1940s Migration to the North and Midwest

Uncle Hubert and Uncle Abraham initiated the migration from the fields of Mississippi to the industrial Midwest (Dayton, OH and Chicago, IL). Other cousins whose parents were siblings of Grandpa Jimmy also began to leave Mississippi in the 1940s, heading to the West Coast. Both the westbound and northbound migrators had to cross their Red Sea. The Red Sea metaphor was an actual place in Biblical times, and both in Biblical times and in the 1940s, the Red Sea was a turning point in the history of God's relationship with his people. The Israelites claimed salvation as they passed through the parted waters of the Red Sea. For my uncles, the Mason-Dixon Line was their Red Sea. What is more, life was not a crystal stair. Those family members who remained in the South, including my father Plummer, his brothers Milton and Lucius, and his sister Lurelia, continued in farming, but the gradual transition brought on by the Industrial Revolution would eventually transition employment to non-farm jobs. Both the migration ventures and those siblings that remained in Mississippi were impacted by the Industrial Revolution.

What were some of the watershed events in the development of the third generation? Without a doubt, the most consequential were the migrations to the Midwest and the West Coast after the end of WWII. My uncles were veterans of the war and had been stationed at bases in northern Kentucky. These gentlemen were yet in their twenties as they sought alternatives to the fields of Mississippi. For them, basic lessons in economics were overshadowed by the harshness of second-class citizenship in Mississippi. The alternative was the industrial city of the Midwest, Dayton, OH.

After cessation of hostilities associated with WWII, Dayton's growth expanded to encompass a logistical center for manufacturers, suppliers, and shippers. Wright-Patterson Air Force Base (WPAFB) would become a host for significant research and development in fields such as industrial, aeronautical, and astronautical engineering that led to many technological innovations. There was an abundance of defense concerns and plants; Dayton was a center for the auto sector and was economically diversified and friendly to unionization, a set of conditions that spawned a respectable number of jobs which paid more than my family members would make as small-scale farmers in Mississippi. Dayton also had foundries, electrical equipment makers, and machine builders.

Between the 1940s and the 1970s, the city saw significant growth in suburban areas from population migration. Advancements in architecture also contributed to the suburban boom. New modernized shopping centers and the Interstate Highway System allowed workers to commute greater distances and families to live further from the downtown area. More than 127,000 homes were built in Dayton and Montgomery County during the 1950s. For my uncles Abraham and Hubert, it was the land of milk and honey. Abraham (1919-2005) had resided with his parents Jim and Corine in Jasper County, MS before enlisting in the army and reporting to Camp Shelby near Hattiesburg in 1942. After his discharge, he married Lula Teressa Bunch (1922-2002), also of the Jasper County area, and they made their home in Dayton. They had six children together.

Hubert C. Marsh (1923-2019) married Grandpa Jimmy's youngest daughter Annie Laura (1924-1997), who was my father's youngest sister. Hubert, son of John and Lottie Marsh, enlisted in the US Army in 1944 and served at Fort Benjamin Harrison in Indiana. Hubert and Annie Laura also had six children. Both Abraham and Hubert brought with them the strong work ethic they learned from their respective parents, as well as a strong motivation to escape the living conditions in MS. The decision and vision of Uncle Hubert and Uncle Abraham spawned hundreds of family members who would be born in, and work in, reside in, and contribute to the quality of life in Dayton.

Skills that Hubert Marsh and Abraham Sampson brought with them to Ohio

Both Abraham and Hubert were tall handsome black men who took pride in their appearance. In their young adult years, they had become accustomed to an entrepreneurial spirit. In retrospect, the aftermath of the Great Depression and its barrenness facilitated a connection between starvation and the necessity of bringing to market the skills that would put food on their tables. In Plato's Republic, we read that "a need or problem encourages creative efforts to meet the need or solve the problem." They learned the skill of barbering while serving in the military. Being able-bodied, they were laborers and unafraid of physical working conditions. During the time they were struggling to make a life for themselves in the brave new world, the US government was putting in place the Marshall Plan, a program by which the United States gave large amounts of economic aid to European countries to help them rebuild after the devastation of WWII. It is more than ironic that Abraham and Hubert joined the Armed Forces and were among many of the black soldiers that contributed to the successful conclusion of WWII, but there was no Marshall Plan for them. There have been varying levels of support for governmental policy necessary to maintain white supremacy in the face of black claims to equal treatment. For example, general citizen support for white supremacy was demonstrably less prevalent after World War II than after World War I. After World War I, black soldiers returned to a country where lynching was common, where the KKK could muster thousands of members in white robes to march down Pennsylvania Avenue in Washington, DC, and where this same organization could elect and control the government of a Midwestern state (Indiana). Violence was a preferred measure for maintaining white hegemony in the South. After World

War II, racial supremacy that required extreme violence for its support had been brought into question by Hitler's death camps, and the absolute right of whites to rule over blacks because of supposed competency differences had been undermined by the experience of Southern white soldiers returning from the Korean War's integrated military experience. Yet, there was an undeniable bent toward either ignorance of white supremacy or tacit acknowledgement of its reality. There wasn't a policy nuance that supported equality among the races after WWII. It was that context that faced my uncles, Abraham and Hubert, as they were honorably separated from the Armed Forces. Thus, the conditions of second-class citizenship persisted and became important connecting pieces that put in place ripe conditions for them to migrate from MS to OH. In the mid-1940s they achieved young adulthood, and they, like my father, their older brother, had no formal education beyond middle and high school; there were no social programs that took into account how the masses of blacks would elevate themselves to become productive taxpaying citizens. However, as the job market in Dayton was flourishing in the aftermath of WWII, both men found employment with the Veterans Administration. Iola Sampson Martin, their middle sister, was also a self-starter and an entrepreneur who worked as an elevator operator at Ohio Bell before going on to successfully develop her own businesses.

Transformative Act IV 1945-1965: Administrative Infrastructure (Bureaucracy) for the Civil Rights Movement and PL 89-110, Voting Rights Act of 1965

In previous chapters, I identified what I argue were the most transformative acts, i.e., public policies that have impacted

African-Americans. The first was the Constitution and the period continuing through the Revolutionary War. This was a period of class dominance in the USA; I asserted that classism was in force in the American culture before racism and that its forces were evident. During the time when the idea and framework of American democracy surfaced, European men were the undisputed captains of the time. White men who were not the first-born in their families, and thus not the direct inheritors of family wealth, rebelled and sought their fortunes in a new land. They were not infatuated with King George and the structure of society that did not favor them. Women and racial minorities were not significant factors in the main calculus.

The second transformative act was the chronological period focusing on those events leading up to the Civil War and the days of Reconstruction. It was during this time that the muscle of the African slaves were key factors in the economic well-being of American society. Some argue that the Civil War was not generated by slavery but by resistance of those who were opposed to a strong central government and instead favored states' rights and the Southern way of life. The main ingredient in each of these nuances is the presence of free labor provided by slave law. Consider that, after the Civil War, there was strong resistance of the South to any legislation that would assist the former slaves in their quest for citizenship. The reconstruction period was short lived, and its demise came before a policy and cultural course correction could form institutions that would lead to better education; in fact, for a long time in many states, there were laws against educating black Americans. After the Civil War, there arose the Black Codes which affirmed second-class citizenship and racial segregation. These movements were the soil for the Jim Crow laws.

The third transformative act occurred during the onset of the Great Depression and WWII. In the latter years of the 1920s, the American economy failed. Nearly every citizen felt the pangs of loss. FDR replaced Herbert Hoover, and "alphabet legislation" came into being. Nearly three dozen agencies were authorized to enact the New Deal legislation in 1933. CCC, WPA, NIRA, TVA, DRS, FERA, and FSA were a few of the agencies. They were the embodiment of an American welfare state. Blacks entered into the new political order as part of a class coalition rather than as an exploited racial group. The founders of the legislation failed to recognize that those who dwelt in the basement of American society were domiciled there because they were black; their condition was the fruit of Jim Crow and Black Codes. Thus, while some in society began to find rungs on the ladder that removed them from the direst straits of poverty, blacks as a group did not similarly benefit from the legislation.

The fourth transformative act is the modern Civil Rights Movement as it was strengthened by a federal bureaucracy (a second chance for modern reconstruction) and, most importantly, Public Law 89-110, the Voting Rights Act of 1965. Agency and institutional muscle were put in place to ensure that access to housing, work, and a voice in public affairs (through voting and public office). Each of the foregone periods constitute the social DNA that affected my family as Americans.

Focus on the "main ingredient": Transformative Act IV

The US government and the thrust of its social and political public policies always impacted the quality of life for Africans, and my family was no exception. It was during the period after WWII that the government turned attention away from the promises of the Fifteenth Amendment (which were forgotten or disregarded shortly after first passed). The decades between the Great Depression and WWII had to be characterized by the time of unmitigated Jim Crow laws and second-class citizenship.

For the working-class African-Americans, jobs took precedence over public accommodations, open housing, and school integration. For most of them, the franchise (the vote) was a luxury... the stuff of dreams. For the people who lived on Melon Street when I was a child (and for those generations before), the guidance of Maslow's hierarchy of needs accurately described the situation/condition that most of us Melon Street residents felt. During my undergraduate study of psychology and social science, I learned that the Maslow research (1943) theorized that there is a ladder of needs each human has. The needs range from basic to self-fulfillment. In my study of psychology in my early college years, I came to understand that *physiological needs* were the basics/ bedrock of human existence; thus, breathing, water, food, sleep, clothing, shelter, and sex were of primary importance. Then came *safety needs*, e.g., personal security, emotional security, financial security, and health. The third rung on Maslow's ladder was *social belonging*, i.e., membership in a family or a community, were all more important than pursuit of first-class citizenship which would entitle them to a voice in social and political governance. For a people who had not been allowed access to education, voice and voting were not what they first sought. For most of them, there was no connection between self-fulfillment and citizenship. The top of the pyramid was a pipe dream; it was the stuff of "self-fulfillment," a condition characterized by fully mature beings that had acquired all the in-between needs and were en route to achieving all that a person can be, i.e., creating and contributing to the well-being of society.

A full century stood between the end of the Civil War (1865) and passage of voting rights for citizens of color, i.e., Public Law 89-110, the Voting Rights Act of 1965. It is more than ironic that the only group of individuals that did not have to have legislated access to the vote were white men. Such a state of affairs cannot help but foster a condition of privilege. The residue from that era waters the soil which produces vegetables of disregard for non-whites, as well as for women, in our society. The century-long pathway to voting rights for people of color contains three distinct threads:

Fragmented laws from irresponsible Congresses: Arguments posed by forces that were strongly opposed to voting for any group other than white men were always successful at whittling down language that would otherwise grant full citizenship to non-white males.

Presidential campaigns and transitions were characterized by simplistic and irreconcilable proposals. The dominant culture did not favor equality for non-whites, which subsequently generated narrow visions in successful presidential campaigns.

3) Excessive preoccupation with short-term issues that carried no long-term advances for the former slaves.

After the end of the Civil War and the public laws that repealed the Reconstruction, there were "hits and misses" devoted to voting access for the former slaves. In 1919, during the 66th Congress, the amendment to grant suffrage to women passed, though not before it failed in vigorous efforts to have that law apply to white women only. The Tennessee General Assembly voted to approve the Nineteenth Amendment on August 18, 1920. Nevertheless, for black women, suffrage was not affirmed at the federal and state level until 1965 when the Voting Rights Act (Public Law 89-110) passed the US Congress.

Between 1947 and 1965, efforts began in earnest to establish a federal bureaucracy to oversee administration of civil rights that would facilitate legal access to the polls for descendants of the slaves. This "movement" became the precursor to the 1965 Voting Rights Act. The path toward full-fledged citizenship for non-whites moved very slowly. Progress toward this goal dispassionately incremented, reflecting the lack of political empathy for black Americans. After World War II, President Truman had ordered integration of the US Armed Forces, and segregation as public policy was coming under attack. African-Americans had served honorably in World War II and returned to the USA country as civilians with expectations of overcoming Jim Crowism. At the same time, some municipalities had begun to elect black mayors. The 1940s saw the election of black mayors in a few nearly all-black towns: Easton, Texas; Grambling, Louisiana; and Mound Bayou, Mississippi. The period of time that occurred immediately following World War II was not a time of silence with regard to civil rights in general or right to vote, in particular. In public forums, media, and church meetings, competing groups were visibly concerned about civil rights and voting, yet the dominant interests, e.g., White Citizen Council(s), the Ku Klux Klan, and leadership of the Federal Bureau of Investigation, were politically active enough to maintain the equilibrium of stability over equality.

Post-WWII legislating would eventually see Southern lawmakers co-opted, and they subsequently set aside their antagonism toward the overall advancement of blacks in public accommodations, open housing, and school integration in favor of the single act of voting. The Omnibus Act required the antagonists to choose options, and otherwise determine which of the fronts would command their attention, since their entire way of life was on the legislative and policy agenda. They contented themselves with having "confined the federal activities to the field of voting and kept the withering hand of the federal government out of the schools and social order," or so it was reported in congressional record (1957). Strom Thurmond, then the Democratic (now Republican) Senator from North Carolina, filibustered for 24 hours against the legislation. When the issue was finally voted on, it passed by a margin of 52 to 38.

Congressional passage of the 1957 Voting Rights law proved that law alone would not miraculously enfranchise blacks. This act sought to protect black voting by allowing blacks to engage litigation to request injunctions when there was evidence their rights had been violated. It also empowered the US Attorney General to seek court injunctions against practices that deprived blacks of the right to vote. Symbolically, the legislation demonstrated that the federal government was willing to help blacks secure the right to vote and protect them in their efforts to do so, as reported by Lawson. However, the substantial change did not occur immediately, in part because of anemic presidential leadership during the Eisenhower Administration. Laws were passed in increments. Three years after the 1957 initiative, a civil rights bill was passed which extended federal authority to promote voter registration by permitting federal judges or special referees to register qualified blacks that had not been enrolled by local officials. Another three years later, the 1960 Civil Rights Act also allowed access to local voting records by federal officials in the event of prosecution of local officials based on discriminatory practices. These measures would form the framework for the 1965 Voting Rights Act. Between 1965 and 1985, the number of black elected officials grew after each election. Support from moderate Republicans and Democrats enabled a fostering of support for policies that resulted in a "second Reconstruction." However, as has been the case with every piece of legislation that fostered equality for African-Americans, all good things have to come to an end. It has been the sunset provision in the law that requires periodic review by the Congress that has facilitated the surgical removal of the muscle that supported voices and representation in lawmaking bodies. There is an apparent belief among conservative Republicans that too much has been done for the sons and daughters of the former slaves. This belief is now held by many conservative Republicans that favor black and minority voter suppression and dilution.

Chapter VII

FAMILY ETHOS AND CORE VALUES

My father and mother were God-fearing, honest working-class people who always wanted the best for their children. They were married January 27, 1927, in Jasper County, MS. After a courtship, which my dad took pride in telling me about repeatedly while I lived at 115 Melon, he would recall his request for my mother's hand in marriage. He stated to his prospective father-in-law, "Mr. Gavin, me and Lurline have made out to get married, and we want your blessing," to which my grandfather replied: "Well, I can't say I am surprised, and I do believe you come from a good family. Who is going to perform the marriage ceremony?" My childhood tapes of my father's version recall that he told his prospective father-in-law of their choice for a minister, and my mother's father replied, "I wouldn't let that man marry a dog of mine! I will ask Reverend Fox to perform the ceremony." Calvin Gavin, according to both my parents, was a strong willed, opinionated man.

We lived in a typical patriarchal setting in which my father farmed and worked in a factory. My mother never held a job outside the home. Unlike many households in the black community, my mother never took in washing and ironing for white families who lived on the other side of the railroad tracks, nor did she work as a day maid in those houses.

My older brothers told me that after my birth, my dad became a devoutly religious Christian. I recall conversations with Ezell in particular about dad's chuch attendance. I don't know if his conversion was due to the scare of my birth or having an ephinany and realizing how far he had traveled since the Great Depression to the blessing of raising a household in spite of a harsh culture and limited political capital. Whatever was the case, he had little tolerance for laziness. He was a serious-minded man who distinguished right from wrong; the absence of a formal education coupled with an ethos that sought family as the most desirable manly attribute colored his views about social issues and politics.

We were indoctrinated into the ethos of believing we could do whatever we prepared ourselves to be: to never hate the oppressor and to work hard. My mother, who lost her mother when she was 5 years old, always wanted her children to achieve, to make something of ourselves. Her endearing expression was, "if you cannot be the 'bell cow,' you should gallop in the ring." Another expression I heard was, "I will be glad when every tub can sit on its own bottom." I always thought this expression of hers that she learned from her father was his exasperation that reflected the burden of care for his children as a widower. Both expressions were manifestations of a desire for individualism, self-sufficiency, and pride, part and parcel of the larger American ethos.

Our central family place was the dining room table. Before each meal, my dad would offer thanks for our meal, and each person seated at the table would repeat a Bible verse. Some traditions hold that grace and thanksgiving impart a blessing which sanctifies the meal. In English, reciting such a prayer is sometimes referred to as "saying grace." The term comes from the Ecclesiastical Latin phrase *gratiarum actio*, "act of thanks."

In Christian theology, the act of saying grace is derived from the Bible, in which Jesus and Saint Paul pray before meals. The practice reflects the belief that humans should thank God, who is the origin of everything. I was a mature adolescent before I would find out that the practice of stating a Bible verse, while a staple at 115 Melon, was not universal even in households that professed to be saved and claimed to also be Christians. The practice of memorizing a Bible verse as a part of our grace protocol was said to complement our knowledge of the Bible and would keep us close to our Lord and Savior.

A typical Sunday meal would consist of several courses, e.g., macaroni and cheese, fried chicken, green vegetables such as turnips or collards, cornbread, squash (in summer), and blackberry cobbler, banana pudding, or coconut cake. One other practice that I grew up with during meal time was placing one's food on the plate one dish at a time. When I traveled as a young man to other venues which featured a meal, the plate would contain all the items at one time.

Conversation would cover such topics as how we were fairing in our educational pursuits, the pastor's Sunday sermon, challenges to my dad earning more so that he could better support his family, civil rights, and public accommodations (lunch counters at all eating facilities in downtown Laurel such as Woolworth and all other restaurants were segregated, and particular effort was meant to observe segregation forever). In the early 1960s, there were the days of the freedom fighters from the north who came to registration for voting by black folks, but there was much effort on the part of white officials to prevent Negroes from the franchise. We never talked about women's issues; during the 1950s, there was not much acknowledgment or awareness of the role women played in society. Women were expected to stay home, raise the children, cook, and "keep house." The lyrics to the song *Family Reunion* popularized by the O'Jays captured the nuance:

> "You know the family is the solution to the world's problems today
> Now let's take a look at the family
> In the family the father is like the head, the leader, the director
> Not domineering, but showing love, guidance
> For everyone else in the family
> Now if we could get all the fathers of the world
> To stand up and be fathers
> That would be great
> Then we have mothers
> Who are the right arm of the father
> They're supposed to-to-to do the cooking
> Raise the children, do the sewing
> And help the father to guide and direct
> Then there's the son
> The son, most sons are like imitators of their father
> So we're back again to the father
> And he is guiding in the right way
> The son is definitely gonna be alright
> Then we have the daughter
> Watching her mother
> Be-because sooner or later she's gonna be a mother
> And she'll have her own sons and daughters..."

The O'Jays' *Family Reunion* was recorded decades after my experiences at 115 Melon, but the song ignored the nearly universal inequality in mother and father roles. Decades would pass before there was an embrace in black families that elevated the role of women to the same level as men.

At 115 Melon, we were middle-class oriented, and we never thought ourselves as second-class citizens. We aspired to be tantamount to the white families as depicted in *Leave it to Beaver* and *Ozzie and Harriet* television shows. Within the recesses of our consciousness, there must have been acknowledgement of the gap between what we valued (racial equality) and the reality of culture and public policy. We were oblivious to inequalities including social discrimination and isolation, and unequal access to healthcare, employment, and housing, and thus experience negative mental and physical health outcomes due to these experiences. We faced obstacles to being first-class citizens; the residue of common Jim Crow laws included literary tests, poll taxes, and the grandfather clause, which were all restrictions on voting meant to keep black men from casting a ballot. Access to first-class citizenship is/was the right to vote, a right not fully exercised until the Voting Rights Act of 1965 which was eviscerated by the USSC in 2013 (*Shelby v. Holder*). Growing up in MS, we were the embodiment of William Earnest Henley's poem, Invictus: "In the fell clutch of circumstance, we did not wince nor cried aloud. Under the bludgeoning of chance, our heads were bloody, but unbowed. Beyond the place of wrath and tears, looms the horror of the shade, and yet the menace of the years found and shall continually find us unafraid." In fact, it mattered not how narrow, tight, or difficult the path to citizenship, nor the dishonest reasons for the inditement. We instinctively knew we were the masters of our fate, and the captains of our souls. In our prayers, we thanked God for our unconquerable souls.

In March 1977, my parents celebrated 50 years of marriage. The photo above captures parents and offspring: from bottom left and moving up and across, my sister Mazie, Plummer, Jr., James Calvin (Jim), Therman (who officiated the ceremony), Ezell, Clarence, myself, and Wylie. The photo below shows some of the attendees of the 50th anniversary we held for our parents in March 1977 at Friendship Baptist Church in Laurel.

It is fair to say that the Plummer Sampson, Sr. household was a group of black conservatives; as I reflect on what we experienced as a people and as a family, conservatism, per se, would hardly be justified in my view. Contemporary black conservatism in the United States is a political and social movement rooted in the African-American community, and the ethos aligns largely with the American conservative movement. Since the African-American Civil Rights Movement (1954-1968), the black community has generally fallen to the left of the right-wing conservative movement and has predominantly favored itself on the side of liberalism and civil rights. Black conservatism emphasizes traditionalism, patriotism, capitalism, free markets, and strong social conservation.

One of the main characteristics of black conservatism is its emphasis on personal choice and responsibilities above socioeconomic status and institutional racism. Such line of thought or philosophy identifies with the Booker T. Washington (1856-1915) school of thought. Washington, who was based at Tuskegee Institute in Alabama, is historically famous for his 1895 Atlanta Compromise speech in which he urged "Negroes" to "drop down their buckets where they were," arguing that

African-Americans would be strategically advantaged to learn practical skills, particularly trades and agriculture skills, rather than university education and voting rights. He believed that this approach would be favorable to whites, who would in turn be more amenable to working with colored citizens in their efforts at advancement. Contrary to this school of thought was that advanced by W.E.B. DuBois (1868-1963), a founder of the NAACP and a critic of Washington. DuBois focused his efforts on the "talented tenth," the 10% of African-Americans who could most likely benefit from a formal education. The rest were, unfortunately, beyond his purview. Washington's strategy was frankly more pragmatic for the majority of African-Americans as it included the 90% that was beyond the DuBois purview, but it did so while offering little to advance the status of the black man in the quest for full citizenship. Thus, in the tradition of African-American politics and intellectual life, black conservatives tend to side with Booker T. Washington as contrasted with W. E. B. DuBois. For most black conservatives, the key mission is to bring repair and success to the black community by applying the following fundamental principles:

The pursuit of educational and professional excellence as a means of advancement within the society,

Policies that promote safety and security in the community beyond the typical casting of a criminal as a "victim" of societal racism,

Local economic development through free enterprise rather than looking to the federal government for assistance, and

Empowerment of the individual via self-improvement (virtue), conscience, and supernatural grace.

At our dinner table, the Booker T. Washington ethos had a small edge over W.E.B. DuBois' more progressive nuance. Interestingly enough, black conservatives may find common ground with black nationalists through their common belief in black empowerment and the theory that black people have been duped by the welfare state.

On the other hand, some of the policies advocated by black conservatives conflict with some of the key points in the common social, economic, and political positions that a high percentage of African-Americans favor. For example, black conservatives typically oppose affirmative action, which is supported by most of the African-American communities. They tend to argue that efforts to obtain reparations for slavery are either misguided or counterproductive. Moreover, black conservatives - especially black Republicans - are often accused of being Uncle Toms. *Ebony* in their May 2001 "100+ Most Influential Black Americans" issue, did not include several influential African-Americans such as Thomas Sowell, Shelby Steele, Armstrong Williams, Walter Williams, and Supreme Court Justice Clarence Thomas. Black conservatives favor integration of African-Americans into mainstream America and, consequently, disagree with black nationalism and separatism. Black conservatives are more inclined to support economic policies promoting globalization, free trade, and tax cuts.

According to a 2004 study, 13.7% of blacks identified as "Conservative" or "Extremely Conservative" (see *Brian Greenberg, Linda S. Watts, Richard A. Greenwald, Gordon Reavley, Alice L. George, Scott Beekman, Cecelia Bucki, Mark Ciabattari, John C. Stoner, Troy D. Paino, Laurie Mercier, Andrew Hunt, Peter C. Holloran, Nancy Cohen. (23 October 2008). Social History of the United States [10 volumes]. ABC-CLIO. p. 360. ISBN 978-1-59884-128-2)*, with another 14.4% identifying as slightly conservative. However, the same study indicated less than 10% identified as Republican or Republican-leaning in any fashion. Another study (Pew Research Center) survey showed that 19% of blacks identify with the religious right. In 2004, the Pew Research Center indicated only 7% of blacks identify as Republican.

As I view the differing ethos, I recognize the angry portion of my mind in which antagonism dominates; I see whites having power over blacks regardless of whether the Washington or DuBois precept prevails. Arguably, the European culture controls everything we believe, whether it is education, news, media, entertainment, and most important, the image of our selves. Such a paradigm allows whites to inundate blacks with disinformation designed to instill the myth of white superiority coupled with black self-hatred. Fortunately, such a paradigm or frame of mind does not stand the test of critical thinking, but there are remnants of this nuance today in the 21st century.

From Reconstruction (1865) up until the New Deal (1932), the black population tended to vote predominantly Republican, particularly in the South. Until 1948 and the coming of Harry S. Truman on the national scene, the Republican party was more racially liberal than the Democratic Party, primarily because of the role of the southern wing of the Democratic Party as the party of racial segregation and the Republican Party's roots in the abolitionist movement. Blacks started to shift in significant numbers to the Democrats with the election of Franklin D. Roosevelt. He was the major architect of the New Deal, legislation that could have benefited economically disadvantaged minority communities. FDR's leadership helped forge the New Deal Coalition which dominated American politics for the next 30 years and continued with the elections of John F. Kennedy and, subsequently, Lyndon B. Johnson. This shift was also influenced by Herbert Hoover's practice of firing loyal African-Americans from positions within the Republican Party to increase his appeal to racist Southern white voters. The pendulum appears to be swinging in the direction of appeasing a portion of the white population at the expense of African-Americans and other minorities as Donald Trump promises to make America "great again."

The African-American church has traditionally been an essential element of social and political movements in the black community. These generally have been identified with persons of the left or liberals, like Adam Clayton Powell and Jesse Jackson, but this has not always been the case. On issues concerning homosexuality, black Protestants are more socially conservative than other groups, except white Evangelicals (see *"American President: Franklin Delano Roosevelt: The American Franchise". Millercenter.org.*). Their view on the issue of homosexual teachers changed less than any other segment based on religion or race.

My siblings and I grew up in Friendship Missionary Baptist Church. My father was a deacon, and his name is placed upon the cornerstone of that church in Laurel, MS. I was baptized at Friendship Baptist Church as a lad of 11 or 12 years old. We always attended church. If the doors were open, we were there. My mother taught Sunday school classes at Friendship Baptist Church and sang in the senior choir, while the deacon board and church business meetings would rarely find my father absent.

Membership and attendance at FBC were my introduction to the Baptist tradition. The church was founded in 1915 under the leadership of founding pastor, Rev. Robert Hunter Reid. He was assisted by his wife, Mrs. J.H. Reid, and Mrs. Larcenia Reed, and deacons John Washington, John Barlow, along with Rev. Jessie Lee. Hunter Nobles, A.J. Hightower, and L.C. Lee served as trustees. Brother Jessie Lee was Sunday school superintendent. In the formative period, worship services were conducted under an arbor brush on a plot of land on Jefferson Street. As the months passed, membership continued to increase. In May 1916, a new building was erected at 154 Jefferson Street. That facility served as the church building until 1956.

My mother, along with Sunday school teachers at FBC, molded my journey to Christianity. In addition to my mother, others who nurtured me were Mrs. Gertrude Clark, Sunday school teacher and future superintendent who saw something in me; Melvin McCoy, my Sunday school teacher during junior high school days who impressed me by the way he prepared and delivered his classes; my neighbor, Columbus Nicholson, who was kind and demonstrated what I would later come to know as the Christian walk; and Gus Deloach, Sunday school superintendent during my high school years. From all these individuals, I learned precepts and behaviors that have guided me all the subsequent years of my life. They were more influential than the ministers.

During my K-12 days, FBC had "preaching" Sundays on the second and fourth Sundays. We had a circuit rider clergy. In the earliest years of the United States, preachers were assigned to travel around specific geographic territories to minister to settlers and organize congregations. Although we were Baptists, the circuit rider clergy was modeled from the practices in the Methodist Church. The preacher thus did not live in our community. The preacher would be hired by the deacons in the Baptist Church. Once a pastor was employed, it was his responsibility to conduct worship and visit members of each church in his care on a regular basis, in addition to possibly establishing new churches. The routine of second and fourth Sundays morning preaching and evening worship services was what we had at FBC. On the other hand, Sunday school was conducted every Sunday. Rev. I. C. Allen was pastor during my final years in high school. He and the previous preachers were consistent in teaching the necessity of repentance, baptism, and the golden rule. The combined effect of this experience led me to believe in forgiveness and grace. To be sure, as I grew older and "wiser," I strayed from their teachings, especially when I went off to college. But by then, the seed had been planted. My life was conformed to the description in Paul's letter to Timothy (2nd Timothy 1:5) in which he recognized the influence of family teaching. Being Baptist meant worship services on the second and fourth Sundays that lasted for three hours. Worship services in African-American churches have historically represented a cultural institution through which African-Americans have been able to express themselves freely and without constraint (Mays and Nicholson 1933; Lincoln and Mamiya 1990; Frazier 1964; Lincoln 1974). There is a great deal of evidence that the church is the most conservative institution in the African-American community; thus, it is logical to assume that ritual services, including the mode of worship and style/ function of music, would be most likely to be preserved in their least changed form. Many cultural ties of the African ancestral lineage have been maintained within the enclave of the African-American folk church. Pearl Williams-Jones characterizes the folk church as:

. . . a mystical, invisible body of believers unified by a common Christian theology as well as a visible body and community of black people unified by common cultural ties. We may consider the black folk church as being an institution controlled by blacks which exists principally within the black community and which reflects its attitudes, values, and lifestyle. It is a church of everyday people and one of any denomination (1977: 21).

Many of the ritual practices that we commonly associate with the African-American folk church - such as freely structured services, dance, improvisational music, the emotional and musical style of delivery of some preachers' sermons and prayers, and spontaneous verbal and non-verbal responses by preachers and congregations - have clearly emerged from African values and aesthetics.

For most African-American preachers, church-pastor-ship was their first significant public exposure. Joyce Marie Jackson, a folklorist/ethnomusicologist professor who teaches in the Department of Geography and Anthropology at Louisiana State University, published an article in 2016 that captured the description and essence on black preaching as a powerful instrument for accelerating the pace of slave conversions as well as providing a certain degree of freedom for those charismatic enslaved men who could preach. The evangelical cast of this religious form stressed the conversion experience rather than the process of religious instruction, which made Christianity more accessible to illiterate enslaved people and (often barely literate) slaveholders alike. In this form of Christianity, a converted heart and a gifted tongue were more important than the amount of theological training received. The black Church was and still is the "cultural womb of the black community."

From this culture and experience emerged a preaching style that was lengthy and included colorful narrative prayers developed earlier during the institution of slavery. The chanted sermon style - once held to be altogether European in origin - actually has historic precedent in several groups in West, Central, East, and Southern Africa. Because many African cultures emphasize oral traditions, the artful manipulations of "the word" - from the precolonial epics of the West African griot to contemporary playing the dozens or rapping in the streets - is a highly prized skill among people of African descent. Although both African-Americans and Anglo-Americans perform the folk chanted sermon - and may go beyond chanting to actually singing - the tradition has been most fully developed in the African-American community.

My observation of preaching and pastors that appear in my childhood tapes attest to the tenacity of certain traditional belief structures, among them the continuing importance of "the call," the concept that one has been "chosen" by God as His intermediary or messenger. The nature of the call manifests itself in a mysterious way through a "sign," through healing powers, through conversion, or just by hearing the "voice of God." From these evolved a preaching style that became the signature of that preacher. The sermon was usually a Biblical experience. The oratory tradition of African-Americans has its roots in the black preaching experience. The church and faith were incontrovertibly the centerpiece for the black community. Like many pastors, my first experience with public oration was in the black Church, e.g., Easter speeches, choir solos, and dramatic presentations, as well as youth participation in worship services.

It was not unusual in many black Baptist churches that the preacher had a musical gift, which complemented his delivery of a sermon. The sermon would be the focal point of worship in the black Church, and all other aspects of worship are subsidiary. Singing, however, is second only to preaching as the magnet of attraction and the primary vehicle of spiritual transport for the worshippers. In the more traditional folk church, even the sermon or parts of the sermon will be sung or chanted in a ritualistic cadence where, on occasion, the organist joins in to accompany the minister's sermon, especially towards the climatic end. Rhythm and timing were among the most significant aspects of the preacher's musical art. Timing was a vital factor in the building of the entire sermon, which began in prose and moved into metrical verse. To be effective, the rhythm of the lines had to be maintained and properly paced throughout the sermon.

Worship service would begin after Sunday school, with devotion led by the deacons. Deacon Andrew "Coon" Williams would begin with a call-and-response hymn. In his deep baritone voice, he would begin, "come and go to dat lan," and the congregation would then join in with the call-and-response mode. They would all stand at the end of the litany, and my dad would read the scripture, which always seemed to be John 1: 1-5. My mother taught my dad to read after they were married, and by the time I became of age, my father had adopted Joshua 24:15, "as for me and my house, we will serve the Lord." Deacons James Dace, Alfonzo Nichols, or Fred Collins could always be counted on to give stirring prayers. Sometimes, I would be puzzled at the hymns (beginning and concluding) because the lyrics were foreboding, even scary, for an adolescent, e.g., "dat awful day will shurly (surely) come," which would signal the end of the devotional service and the chorus of the congregation would join in. After the concluding hymn that completed the devotion, the choir would process, followed by the preacher, to their respective places. Two or three songs by the choir and the reading of announcements and welcoming visitors by the church clerk, Sis Minnie M. Jones, would easily consume 30 minutes, or at least seemed so, although I never used a stopwatch to verify the amount of time. Following the announcements, either Ida Mae Davis (Laurel's Aretha Franklin) or Walterine Cobb (Laurel's Patti Labelle) would belt out soulful spirituals such as "Peace Be Still" or "I Stood on the Banks of Jordan." With Mildred Thigpen and, later, Willie Maurice Bender on keyboards, the congregation would begin to feel the spirit, and they would be ready to praise the Lord. A successful sermon always contains interaction between the preacher and the congregation, often in the form of call-and-response patterns. The structure of the preacher's chant depends upon the message, the length of the performance, and the degree of congregational participation.

The prelude to the beginning of the pastor's sermon was "Amazing Grace" sung in modified largo. The congregation would stand as the song was concluded. These preliminaries would be followed by a spirit-filled sermon, usually more than thirty minutes. The congregation's response plays a key role in the structure of the preacher's rhythmic delivery.

Many worshippers would "get happy" and shout, exclaiming gratitude at how they had been saved and blessed. Shouting usually involved the same worshippers; most prominent in my memory is Sister Alberta Clay, a senior member known for her size. The shouting many times became a distraction. Restoring a semblance of order would require the muscle Brother John Boyd, a strong male usher of some considerable girth, to finally calm down Mrs. Clay. Along with intense fanning by some of the female ushers, the worship service gradually calmed down. The once unrestrained emotions would subside, and the pastor would "open the doors of the church" to the "lost" among the worshippers. I don't think the intent of the pastors message was to instill fear in the hearts of the worshippers, but expressions such as "brother, you are going to die with your shoes on," or that sinners would be "thrown into the blazing furnace" (Matthew 13:50), or as cited in 2nd Thessalonians 1:9, urging the parishioners that salvation was the only antidote against "punishment with everlasting destruction," and other characteristic exhortations caused personal anxiety, and I suspect that I was not alone. Yet, my anxiety was lessened as I came to understand that each of us must pray and seek God and repent of our sins until we know for ourselves that God has forgiven and saved us. Most important for me and my spiritual development (which continues to this day) is that man does not convict man and cannot tell them when God forgives and saves them. From the pulpit and dinner table discussions, we were taught that men (and women) must work out their own soul salvation. My anxiety dissipated when the closing of the sermon invoked the message that when God saves the individual, the individual knows without anyone telling them, whether the preacher, loved ones, or any friend.

The seating pattern in the church sanctuary was indicative of practices from a century earlier. Men would be seated on the left side of the pulpit while women would be seated across on the right side. The mother of the church was a senior member, and she would be dressed in white for most of the services. The front bench was usually empty; it was designated the "mourners' bench," a place where sinners who were repenting and anticipating church membership would sit. The highly spirited sermons were intended to communicate how to obtain true salvation; they emphasized a sense of trouble, conviction, and condemnation set up by God in the heart of the unsaved person.

I was among the last cohort of members to be baptized at the 154 Jefferson Street location. Later on, i.e., during the mid-to-late 1950s, the federal-funded highway construction project empowered the city to claim eminent domain and take the church property for building the corridor for the Laurel portion of US Interstate highway 59.

Relocating the Jefferson Street church site to 115 Custom Avenue

President Dwight D. Eisenhower signed the Federal-Aid Highway Act of 1956, popularly known as the National *Interstate* and Defense Highways Act. The Interstate System would eventually become part of American culture as construction projects expanded transportation arteries. The Eisenhower initiative put in motion the United States government's efforts to construct a national network of highways, which began on an *ad hoc* basis with the passage of the Federal Aid Road Act of 1919 that provided $75 million over a 5-year period for matching funds to the states for the construction and improvement of highways. The nation's revenue needs associated with World War I prevented any significant implementation of this policy, which expired in 1921.

In December 1918, E.J. Mehren, a civil engineer and the editor of Engineering News-Record, presented his "A Suggested National Highway Policy and Plan." In the plan, Mehren proposed a 50,000-mile system, consisting of five east-west routes and ten north-south routes. The system would include 2% of all roads and would pass through every state at a cost of $25,000 per mile, providing commercial, as well as military, transport benefits.

The automobile culture was the center of the developing economy; however, construction of the Interstate Highway System was a thinly disguised public works program designed to prevent a severe post-war recession or, worse, the return of economic depression that characterized the pre-war decade. Core to the road-building philosophy was the belief that a prosperous society must be a mobile society and that the construction of roads, specifically interstate highways, could be a means to remove urban decay and promote prosperity.

Eisenhower's initiative was lobbied for heavily by a coalition of vehicle, oil, tire, cement, steel, and union interests. With the transportation arteries, it was expected that the suburbs would increase in number and offer new opportunities to the American people. There was a downside to the planner's ideas, though; there were people who couldn't move to the suburbs. To further complicate the challenge for African-American residents, there was the routine denial of home loans by the federal government in certain areas. A practice called redlining and the enforcement of restrictive covenants prevented homeowners from selling to certain types of people, often including African-Americans. Moreover, they were also denied jobs and other opportunities that would have allowed them to afford to buy a home in the first place. In the first 20 years of the federal interstate system alone, highway construction displaced 475,000 families and over a million Americans. Most of them were low-income people of color in urban cores. When it came to places such as Laurel, these restrictions left African-Americans crowded into small all-black neighborhoods. They essentially weren't allowed to move anywhere else.

The I-59 corridor was designed to run through communities where the black and poor whites resided in the city limits of Laurel. It is a north-south route that spans 445.23 miles from a junction with I-10 and I-12 at Slidell, Louisiana to a junction with I-24 near Wildwood, Georgia. It connects the metropolitan areas of New Orleans, Louisiana and Chattanooga, Tennessee, running closely parallel to the older US Route 11 corridor for the entire distance. Approximately one third of the route, spanning 153 miles from Meridian to Birmingham, overlaps that of the east-west I-20.

South Laurel, where elementary schools, middle schools, and high schools for blacks were located, was also home for many working-class, professional, and blue-collar individuals. It was the home for upwardly achievement-oriented blacks including teachers and physicians who lived in Laurel and were displaced by the development of the Interstate Highway System (even though our elected leaders and those who operate the bureaucracy have been reluctant to reckon that highway projects played a key role in ripping apart underprivileged communities around the country). The long-time structure that housed Friendship Baptist Church (154 Jefferson Street) was taken by eminent domain so as to make room for the interstate highway, I-59. Subsequently, the congregation began having Sunday morning services in the auditorium of Sandy Gavin School. Land for relocating the church to Custom Avenue was purchased. An architect was selected, and the deacons and trustees of FBC were on their way to constructing the Custom Avenue facility which is the current location of Friendship. I remember the dedication services that were held in May 1957; my father was a deacon, and his name is listed on the church cornerstone. He was very proud of his involvement in finding a place for relocating the church.

My mother had grown up in the Methodist church where her father was superintendent of the Sunday school. St. Paul Methodist has a long and proud history. Many of the upwardly mobile Negro residents claimed membership at St. Paul. On the other hand, my dad was a functional illiterate; my mother was the "reader" in the house. She taught my father to read. They both valued education. They viewed Mississippi as the land of opportunity, i.e., the first opportunity for their children to leave Laurel should be exercised. At the time I became a thinking, observing individual, my parents had been a unit for more than nineteen years. They had become jaded given their experiences with second-class citizenship. During discussions at the dinner table at 115 Melon Street, we were taught that the way out of second-class citizenship in Jim Crow Mississippi began with getting a good education. In early 1950s when I began elementary school, I was not as jaded as my parents; after all, my life and work experiences had been quite brief! I was enthusiastic about life and about going to school. Perhaps the influence of worship at Friendship Baptist Church, particularly with the influence of my Sunday school teachers, was a factor in my spiritual and mental health development. I don't believe any of these influential spiritual mentors had thought about how both religion and spirituality could have a positive impact on mental health. In my graduate course on research methods, I learned that there are four ways of knowing anything: Sense/Perception, Language, Emotion/Intuition and Logic/Reason. The philosopher Charles Peirce framed the basic ways of knowing as: 1) the method of tenacity, 2) the method of authority, 3) the method of intuition, and 4) the method of science (Buchler, 1955). Whether it was tenacity or reason, intuition or emotion, sense or perception, or logic or reason, I was continuously evolving, from first grade to the present, and have come to know that both religion and spirituality have helped me tolerate stress by generating peace, purpose, and forgiveness.

Chapter VIII

GROWING UP IN THE "FREE STATE OF JONES":

Laurel and its history and culture

Laurel is the county seat of Jones County, Mississippi. As of the 2010 decennial census, the city had a total population of 18,548. It is located northeast of Ellisville, the first county seat and current location of the county courthouse.

The population trends reveal the growth of 89% between 1900 (3,193) and 1960 (27,889). Since 1960, the population has decreased by about one third. It is the principal city of a Micropolitan Statistical Area. Its major employers include Howard Industries, Sanderson Farms, Masonite, Family Health Center, House Implement, Thermo-Kool, and South Central Regional Medical Center. Laurel is home to the Lauren Rogers Museum of Art, Mississippi's oldest art museum, which was established by a family that made its wealth in timber. It is the headquarters of the Jones County Sheriff's Department, which administers tax collection and a variety of public services for residents of the county.

Laurel began as one of the nameless mill towns along the railway to New Orleans. It was founded in 1882 as a lumber town, as the industry harvested yellow pine forests in the region (Payne, 1990). The city was named for laurel thickets near the original town site (Gannett, 1905). By the turn of the century, the city had become a site of cotton mills that processed and manufactured textiles from the state's commodity crop of cotton. The city population grew markedly during the early 20th century, as rural people were attracted to manufacturing jobs. Mechanization of agriculture reduced the number of farming jobs. The city reached its peak of population in 1960 and has declined by about one third since then.

Unlike many of the other Southern "cut-out-and-get-out" lumber operations, Laurel endured and eventually prospered. Northern industrialists not only moved their business dealings south to Mississippi, but also permanently relocated their families to the region. This complete relocation convinced the new arrivals to invest heavily in Laurel's infrastructure. Whether self-serving or not, the capital investment provided by the new Northern arrivals eventually benefited the community as a whole. This community investment explains how unlike many of the South's other timber communities, Laurel avoided many of the pitfalls of poor community morale and substandard labor conditions. Biracial investment and philanthropy displayed by the city's benefactors stood in stark contrast to the views of most white Mississippians. The benefactors' progressive outlook transcended traditional racial divisions and helped create a town of the "New South" in the heart of the Piney Woods. Like all Southern cities, strict racial separation kept the citizens of Laurel apart. The Northern-born members of the community adhered to the "separate-but-equal" policies, but they also implemented programs and institutions that would help foster Laurel's African-American community.

Laurel historian Cleveland Payne, who wrote the book *Laurel: A History of the Black Community: 1882-1962* (Laurel: privately printed, 1990), argued that although Laurel's black residents still lived under a system of regional and national injustice, Laurel provided them with opportunities unavailable to blacks in many other parts of the "Old South."

The city, like the rest of the state, embraced racial segregation. Housing, public education, public accommodation, and voting policy specified racially-divided facilities, and that edict was culturally, politically, and socially accepted. For me, this meant that I did not experience a white student or teacher until the onset of my undergraduate education. I was born decades after passage of the New Deal and came to know only when I was in college that my family was poor. As an undergraduate, I qualified for support under the policies of the Great Society. What this meant was that my family was accustomed to living on the lower rungs of the political, economic, and social ladder. While we believed that education was central to any hope for advancement, we were literally oblivious to the disadvantage of not having access to first-class educational facilities, lunch counters, and housing.

My childhood residence

I was born at 115 Melon Street, Laurel, Jones County, MS and resided there until I graduated high school and subsequently began my undergraduate degree. The town of Laurel served as the home of my parents, Plummer and Lurline Sampson, from the early 1940s until their passing in 1992 (Lurline) and 1995 (Plummer). The legal description of 115 Melon, the homestead of Plummer and Lurline Sampson, is described as:

Lot 10 of Block A of the Debardeleven and Rhodes Subdivision, as per plat thereof now on file in the office of the Chancery Clerk of the Second Judicial District of Jones County, Laurel, Mississippi.

Public Records index it as:

Lot 10, Block A of the Debardeleven and Rhodes Subdivision, Second District of Jones County, Mississippi also known as 115 Melon Street, Laurel, MS 39440

The early years: life in the "Free State of Jones"

There were always chores to be done at 115. Although my family lived in an urban area, our lifestyle was more rural. In our backyard during the late 1940s were two mules, Mack and Blue. My dad used them to cultivate and plant crops in the adjoining rural community called Mt. Olive. As time went on, my older siblings were achieving young adulthood, and they were enrolling in college and joining the Armed Service. With the growing "shortage of labor," my dad sold the mules. Cows and goats replaced them as occupants of our small cramped backyard. It was a daily responsibility to milk the cows and put them out to pasture in a grassy area alongside the railroad tracks at the end of our street. The cows provided fresh milk and butter. A laying-hen, whose sole purpose was to provide, did so, and her chicks also were consumed by my family. Also, alongside the railroad tracks were hog pens. My family, as did many others in the community, fed their livestock on the land that was owned by the railroad company. Most of the people who lived on Melon and adjoining streets in the Debardeleven and Rhodes Subdivision had hogs and other livestock. The hogs provided protein. They were fed by collecting food waste from neighbors (a.k.a. picking up slop) because there was no waste management system in the community. The late fall of each year was hog-killing time. The slaughtered carcass brought about an abundant supply of meat for the family. Before refrigeration became commonplace, smokehouses and curing barns were used to store the meat. The slaughter allowed harvesting every imaginable portion of the pig, from chitlins to pork chops and ham.

There were about 20 families living on Melon Street. All of the houses contained men and their wives and offspring. These men found work at the mill and wood-processing factories. My dad, just as Mr. LeRoy McCann, Mr. Mose McCormick, and Mr. Dan Thigpen, worked at Masonite. I never knew where Mr. John Adams worked. Our culture was to call all adult men "mister" and all adult women as either "miss" or "Mrs." Only Mr. Columbus Nicholson, a widower, did not have a spouse. On Melon Street, few of the women worked outside the house. They were full-time mothers and caregivers.

Across the street from our house were the Itsons. Mr. Lonnie was the bread winner at the house across the street, and Mrs. D was the matriarch of the house (I never knew what the "D" stood for). The Itson household contained eight children. Just as many other neighbors did, the children, upon reaching their late teen and young adult years, found jobs cleaning houses; the better jobs were plucking chickens at the local poultry. Mr. Lonnie drove a truck for the Rural Electric Association (REA); in the 1930s and 1940s, few farms were connected to the electricity grid. During the New Deal era, a system of electric cooperatives was established, and the offshoot of REA was jobs of many kinds. It was thought then that for a black man to drive a truck for REA was a high accomplishment. Through the sharing of resources, the nation's rural communities were electrified. When Mr. Lonnie would drive home for lunch, the children would race to sit in the truck and play. Next door to us were the Denham family, Mr. Jace and Mrs. Lucy. Unlike most of the households, the Denham house had only one daughter, Miss Willie Mae. Miss Willie Mae was an attractive woman, and many male taxicab drivers attempted to get her attention.

Around 1959, my parents vacationed in Dayton, where they posed for a photo with some of their grandchildren. The photo captures the offspring of Plummer, Jr. (Michael and Michelle); Jim (Gregory, Tyree and Tyrone); and Clarence's firstborn (Jerry). The first time my family had the funds to take a family vacation was 1959. The vacation was a trip to Dayton to visit relatives.

In 1984, my siblings and I encouraged our parents to relocate to Dayton, OH due to health challenges of our father. Although it was clear that there was a need for step up vigilance related to my dad's healthcare, most evident was the fact that my mother would not be able to individually provide that vigilance, particularly given the fact that Dayton, OH is a full day's drive (15 hours) from Laurel. My parents resided at 241 Shoop, in Dayton, one of the residences of my brother Ezell.

From about 1966 until 1984, Plummer and Lurline were not required to pay property taxes because of the Mississippi Homestead Exemption Act, which excused real property tax liability for individuals who were at least 65 years of age and who occupied the property. After their relocation to Ohio, there was no payment of property tax, and subsequently, the property was placed on sale for delinquent taxes in 1991. I learned from my high school classmate Carolyn Moody, an official in the Jones County Tax Office, that the county was about to to sell the property at its routine tax auction. I then informed my siblings, and we interceded by paying the delinquent taxes and thereby retaining the homestead. After paying the delinquent tax, Plummer, James, Therman, Ezell, Clarence, and Charles made tax payments each year from 1992 until Plummer's passing in 2012. After that, the other five continued payments until Therman's passing 2014. From January 2015 until August 2015, James, Ezell, Clarence, and Charles continue to meet all fiscal responsibility for taxes, insurance, maintenance, and upkeep.

My siblings, first-born Mazie

From 1928 to 1948, my mother gave birth to one daughter and seven sons. For fifty-two years, I enjoyed the comfort and support of our parents. My sister Mazie, the first-born child of Plummer and Lurline and first grandchild of Jim and Corine Sanson, signaled the beginning of the fourth generation of my paternal family. She was the only daughter among eight children. I am told that my sister Mazie was the "apple" of my paternal grandparents' eyes.

Being the first grandchild of Jim and Coreen, she was the recipient of the adulation of the Sampson grandparents and the Gavin grandfather. As I reflect on my family, I am quick to remember that the marriage and childbearing began when the country was facing the worst economic time in the previous century and the decades that followed. These "externalities" did not factor into whatever equation my parents were following. Beginning with Mazie, there was twenty-one years of childbearing, most of which occurred during the Great Depression. The last three of us (Clarence, Wylie, and me) were the ones born after the Great Depression and experienced its aftereffects. The depression ingrained in us the desire to "live above" our circumstances, and that ethic would serve us well as we experienced financial, political, and race-based challenges. WWII was over when my 17-year-old sister and her husband began their family. When I was born, my sister Mazie had moved from the house as she had begun her marriage and family with Peter Thomas. In the next nineteen years, she gave birth to eight children: five sons and three daughters. Mazie's birthing pattern was very much akin to what our parents had modeled. Unlike our mother, who never worked outside the home, Mazie was gainfully employed in the poultry industry while she raised her children. Her first son was the beginning of the fifth generation, a cohort of 34 grandchildren that would call Plummer and Lurline, granddad and grandmother. All her children would graduate high school in Laurel and become gainfully employed contributors to the Dayton economy.

Being the only daughter meant that she could "boss" her brothers around, largely by constant reminders of "I am your only sister!" So, we all catered to her wishes and commands. She has a fiercely independent character that propelled her to arduous work and devotion to her role as a mother.

Unlike her brothers who opted to leave Laurel at the earliest opportunity, Mazie elected to remain in Laurel. She did so until her children, all of whom who subsequently migrated to Dayton at first opportunity, left the Magnolia state. In Mazie's latter years, she acquiesced to the years of relatives campaigning and joined them upon her retirement. The decision was in no small part attributable to her medical needs that were becoming more evident, a situation that was compounded because none of her offspring could easily assist at a distance. She did move to Dayton after the death of her husband, Amos Jones, but her move to Dayton occurred after she had built a strong relationship in the community of Vossburg. Mr. Amos' passing was a real blow to Mazie. After their marriage in 1968, he became the father figure for her three youngest children. Moreover, Amos and Mazie complemented each other very well. He liked the open space of rural MS and the opportunities for hunting, fishing, etc., that were not readily available in the urban North. Thus, his death meant a change in Mazie's way of life. Our parents' migration to Dayton in 1984 left her as the only family (other than me) who did not reside in the city which is famous for America's pioneering airplane development.

The relocation to Dayton meant she was surrounded by all her offspring and their families, 21 grandchildren, her brothers, and her aunts and uncles. Among the uncles and aunts were my father's younger siblings who knew her and loved her from the time she became the first grandchild. She lost her firstborn, James Russel Thomas, unexpectedly in 1995, a loss that was grievous and would endure years before there was "acceptance" of his untimely passing. At that juncture (1995), her daughters and sons rallied around her, and we were all tasked with the challenge of living beyond our circumstance.

Plummer Sampson, Jr. (1931- 2012) was the first son, born March 15, 1931 in Sandersville, Mississippi. He passed away on the last Saturday of December 2012. Plummer was a role model for his younger brothers. When he graduated Oak Park High School in 1949, he headed to the University of Dayton to begin his undergraduate study. The fact of moving from Laurel, a rural Southern town where second-class citizenship for blacks was the accepted norm, to Midwestern Dayton meant that he was faced with the task of blazing a trail for his siblings. The entirety of his education had occurred in a system that was not adequately funded so as to deliver a competitive education. OPHS was a segregated high school; in fact, everything about Laurel was segregated. The University of Dayton (UD) was greater than 98% white in the fall of 1949, so he had to learn a new culture and new traditions that are rarely thought of as challenges until one must confront them. The 1949 edition of Laurel was characterized by Jim Crow laws, second-class citizenship, and the absence of public accommodations for non-whites. This set of circumstances was intractably placed in his mind, but he was determined to rise beyond his circumstances. He departed Laurel with the burden of expectations on his shoulders. Around the dinner table at 115 Melon, my mother encouraged his dream of becoming a physician, while others thought he should become mayor of Dayton. Little did we know the nature of investments necessary for a medical education, nor did we take into consideration the challenge of electoral success for those seeking public office, particularly for blacks during the 1950s. Thus, there were few black role models for him to emulate. Time passed through nearly six decades (until June 2005) before Laurel would seat Melvin Mack as its first black mayor.

Becoming a physician, on the other hand, was not quite as daunting; there were two Negro doctors in Laurel during the late 1940s through the late 1950s, Dr. Barnes and Dr. Nave. During the Jim Crow era of legalized segregation (1887-1964), black physicians in the former Confederate states, like their black patients, experienced a violent form of racial discrimination. According to a study conducted by Bond (2018), such invidious discrimination was enforced not only by state and local governments, law enforcement, and hate groups, but also by white colleagues and professional organizations, including the American Medical Association (AMA). The role of black physicians in the American Civil Rights Movement has yet to be fully appreciated. Moreover, their ability to practice during this period was determined by the effectiveness of their strategies to remain in the favor of local white physicians and to avoid appearing too successful or pretentious to the greater white community. For instance, in 1918, after 18 years of practice in Vicksburg, Mississippi, Dr. J.A. Miller, a black graduate of Williams College and the University of Michigan School of Medicine, lost favor.

A group of "leading citizens" tarred, feathered, and paraded him through town, put him in jail, and then banished him from the city under threat of death. White mobs also drove black physicians out of Indianola in 1903, Laurel around 1925, and Meridian in 1925. Moreover, access to medical care for blacks was further compromised when the number of "black medical schools" in the United States decreased from 10 to 2 after the Flexner Report of 1910, and the number of black physicians in Mississippi decreased proportionately. The first black person native to Laurel to be awarded the MD was Deborah Hyde, who graduated OPHS in 1966. She became a neurosurgeon in 1977. Nevertheless, around the dinner table at 115 Melon, we believed that "a man's reach should exceed his grasp."

The inability to meet rising tuition costs at UD forced Plummer to volunteer for the US Armed Forces at the end of his sophomore year. The Mississippi lad spent four years as an enlisted member and returned to UD to complete his BS and MBA degrees. He also earned the PhD in Allied Health and Clinical Pathology from the Union Graduate School in Cincinnati, Ohio.

When Plummer left home to go to undergraduate study at the University of Dayton, I was a toddler, but I came to love and admire him as I followed his achievements. Remarks about him from my parents around the dinner table were always warm and loving. When he would return to 115 Melon, he always brought me gifts. I was always struck at his "proper talk," i.e., correct usage of the English language. We all thought the slow Southern drawl that dominated the discourse in Laurel did not sound like a person who was really educated. Expressions such as, "oh, for crying out loud" instead of "good gracious," or "ooo wee" were hard to overlook. Being educated by teachers in Laurel that had a vision for us to be successful in life complemented the influence of his

"Northern talk." His gifts to me as a lad were the beginning of his lifelong generosity toward me. His contributions went beyond material things (I recall having an accident while driving his car miles away in Alabama when I was out of college, and what was most remarkable was his forgiving nature). Both Plummer and my late brother Therman gave me aspirational dreams as I began my undergraduate study. It was the two of them that planted the notion that turned out to be my undergraduate major.

After returning from his initial tour of duty in the air force, he married Marjorie Heywood of Gurley, Alabama. Marge birthed a son and two daughters, and they were married for more than fifty years when Plummer expired on the last Saturday in December in 2012 at the age of 81. Plummer's funeral occurred in early January 2013. His wife and children facilitated his homegoing that would suit any dignitary. Plummer retired as Chief of Program Control at Wright Patterson Air Force Base (WPAFB). He defended the country during the conflict popularly known as *Desert Storm*. He had been an adjunct faculty member at Sinclair Community College for several years. Dr. Sampson's community involvement also included administrative roles at First Dayton Little League, where he was instrumental in the acquisition of a new baseball park. He served on the City of Dayton Priority Board for many years. My brother, though having grown up in Baptist tradition, became a Catholic and was a faithful member of St. Benedict the Moor Catholic Church. He was a lifetime member of the Theta Lambda Chapter of Alpha Phi Alpha. His fraternal membership introduced the idea of fraternity to me, and I subsequently pledged Alpha Phi Alpha as well.

James Calvin Sampson, (1932-2021) who was named for both his grandfathers (Jim Sampson and Calvin Gavin), is the second brother. I admire all my brothers, but none more than

Jim. The "hand" that was dealt to him was unlike any of his siblings. When he was 17, he left OPHS, with the "blessing" of our dad, and traveled to Dayton in 1950. He was the only one of his siblings that did not graduate high school at OPHS; he competed his HS diploma at Roosevelt High School in Dayton. Jim and Plummer lodged with Aunt Iola Sampson-Martin, my dad's sister who had migrated to Dayton shortly after Uncles Abraham and Hubert. Iola owned a house where she rented out rooms. Jim and Plummer partially defrayed their room and board by performing chores around the house. Less than two years would pass before Jim enlisted in the US Army. He was honorably discharged and returned to Dayton, gaining employment at Ohio Bell as a janitor. His work ethic was remarkable, and his superiors became aware of that quality; he subsequently worked himself from being one of the first black lineman for Ohio Bell and then a telephone installer and repairman to being plant manager before his retirement.

He married Helen Smith, who had migrated with her parents from Georgia as a child; they provided a home for six offspring that grew into adulthood. As their children developed from toddlers to teenagers, Jim and Helen left the Baptist Church and became members of the Church of Christ, where Jim rose to the stature of elder. After forty-six years of marriage Helen succumbed in 1998. Unfortunately, Jim would bury a second wife, Iva, in 2015 after seventeen years of marriage.

All our family members had been members of the National Baptist Convention, a movement that came to recognition in the days of segregation. Jim, because of his membership in the Plummer and Lurline household, was also a National Baptist. Jim's decision to affiliate with the Church of Christ as a young adult would ultimately give rise to lively conversations with those whose loyalties lay with the National Baptist Convention and the theological difference between the two church organizations. National Baptist Church history traces back to Saturday, November 22, 1880, when 151 persons from 11 states met in Montgomery, Alabama and organized the Baptist Foreign Mission Convention. A strong motivation was the desire to foster preaching the Gospel of Jesus Christ on the mother soil of Africa.

On the other hand, Churches of Christ, founded in Independence, Missouri in 1864, are autonomous Christian congregations associated with one another through distinct beliefs and practices. Represented chiefly in the United States, they were associated with the American Restoration Movement. They claim Biblical precedent for their doctrine and practice and trace their heritage back to the early Christian church as described in the New Testament.

Prior to the US Religious Census of 1906, all congregations associated with the Restoration Movement had been reported together by the Census Bureau. But as the movement developed, tensions grew between those who emphasized unity and those who emphasized restoration, resulting in a division between those who used musical instruments in worship (known as the Christian Church) and those who believed a cappella singing to be proper (Churches of Christ). While this was the most visible distinction between the two groups, there was also disagreement over the appropriateness of organizational structures above the congregational level, such as those of missionary societies and funding orphanages.

Crawford (2013) argues that slavery was not viewed as immoral among the founders of the 19th-century Restoration Movement, also known as the Stone-Campbell Movement, the religious awakening that birthed Churches of Christ. He shares the following comment written by Alexander Campbell in 1845:

"There is not one verse in the Bible inhibiting it, but many regulating it. It is not, then, we conclude, immoral."

Crawford goes on to reveal how Southern slaveholders were encouraged to evangelize the enslaved as a means for creating a more compliant slave. He argues that this sentiment transcends the institution of slavery and is alive throughout the history of Churches of Christ, even now. I believe there is a residue of that nuance in the 21st century.

Both the Church of Christ and the National Baptist Convention were distinctly different from James H. Cone's *Black Theology* (1969) and its relevance to civil rights. Black theology embraced the reality of black people on the earth and their suffering and humiliation. Even though the Church of Christ had at times claimed virtual immunity from the pressures of its social and historical context, the ever-present and powerful confrontation between white and black greatly affected the formation of Churches of Christ identity. One could argue that there were slight degrees of difference between the Church of Christ and the National Baptist Convention in comparison to the Cone paradigm. Despite the differences in theological paradigms, Jim embraces his Baptist, Catholic, and Methodist siblings.

Therman C. Sampson, (1935-2014) was born in Sandersville, MS as the 4th child of eight. He was an energetic, loquacious lad whom my father would to refer as "the radio." Therman was born when the Great Depression was in its midst. Farm wages estimated by the statistical abstract show that the weighted average salary was $23.45 per month, but the seasonal nature of farming meant that the annual salary was less than $2,000 annually. The family of six was fed by the sweat and muscle of my dad sharecropping as they lived in rural Jones County. As the turn of the decade occurred, the family opted to move to Laurel for an employment opportunity at Masonite Corporation as a laborer. Therman was educated at the public schools in Laurel, earning his high school diploma in 1953. In the fall of that year, he enrolled at Alcorn State University in Lorman, MS. As Plummer had experienced before him, the dollars for tuition, room, board, and books could not be sustained despite part-time jobs held by him and my dad. Thus, Therman interrupted his undergraduate studies to volunteer for the US Army. Two years later, he was honorably discharged and returned to Dayton, where he enrolled to study electrical engineering. It was there that he met Ethel Martin, a Georgia native whose dad resided in Dayton. They were married in 1959 and were a devoted couple for 55 years when he passed away in 2014. Sadly, Ethel passed away in 2019. Therman and Ethel's offspring became the first to be "orphans." To their fold came three daughters, a son, and eleven grandchildren. He was funeralized on what would have been his 80th birthday.

Therman's siblings and friends recall his sense of humor and fashionable dress. He emulated our dad, and for a brief time following the passing of mother, he, Ethel, and children welcomed dad to live with them so that my dad's stark loneliness could be muted. Therman was an adolescent in the mid-1950s when the use of slangs reflected the changes in time. Phrases such as "agitate the gravel," reflecting the male penchant for fast cars; "back seat bingo," meaning necking in a car; and "beatnik," which characterized the beat culture, were popular. As a teen, he was influenced by James Dean, the actor and cultural icon who drew attention to teenage disillusionment and social estrangement, as expressed in the title of his most celebrated film, *Rebel Without a Cause*. In the early *1950s, James Dean* was heralded as the new heartthrob of women. Almost overnight, the *effects* of Dean's movies sent shock waves through the country; suddenly, *teenagers* underwent transformations of mind-blowing proportions. During the *1950s*, jeans evolved into a symbol of *youth* rebellion. It was fashionable for teenaged boys to wear their jeans low around the waist (though not as low as the "saggers" of the 21st century that expose their buttocks) and their shirt collars turned up. As his younger brother, I watched his every move, and his teen years were very impressive. However, this was a fad that passed quickly as he moved into adulthood.

He was awarded the Bachelor of Science degree in elementary education from Central State University in June 1969. A two-track employment thereafter began. He began his teaching career at Jefferson Elementary and soon after was appointed mathematics supervisor for the Federal Emergency Aid Act (ESAA) Title V and VI Program. This experience advanced him to supervisor of the computer laboratory at Miami Chapel and, subsequently, assistant principal, and then principal in the Dayton public school arena.

Despite Therman's success as an educational administrator, his life as an educator took second place to his calling in his religious ministry. As a lad, he (like all his siblings) was influenced by worship and Sunday school at Friendship Baptist Church in Laurel, where as a youngster, he was influenced by the late Reverend I.C. Peay, a dynamic and gifted young man. Decades would pass before he acknowledged his call to preach the gospel. Under the guidance of a new mentor or father in the ministry, Rev. Reed Hagan, he began the trail from assistant pastor to senior pastor at New Zion Missionary Baptist Church, where he served for 41 years. He eulogized our mother in 1992 and our father in 1995. Over the years, he earned graduate degrees from University of Cincinnati and Union Graduate School; he completed his Master of Divinity degree at Payne and the Doctorate of Divinity from Faith Baptist College in Anderson, SC.

When he passed away, and plans for his final service were being considered, his children and their mother asked me to speak as a brother. I noted that he was born on the first Monday in 1935 and passed away on the last day in 2014. The total number of days between the first Monday in 1935 and the last day of 2014 is 29,213 days or 79 years, 11 months, and 24 days. That equals to 20,867 weekdays and 8,346 weekend days, or 4,173 weeks and 2 days. There was joy inside my pain on the day we laid his body to rest on what would have been his 80th birthday. He loved New Zion Baptist Church and devoted forty years to its development. His was a shoulder on which I could bring my woes; at all times, he was faithful to the creed of brotherhood. Tired moments found his humor a delightful treat; at all times, he was a shrine of understanding.

When I was a lad, we talked about life, the hereafter, education, health, and relations with all humankind. During those conversations which lasted over the years of my youth, he and my late brother Plummer created dreams about what I should study in college and were not shy about offering me their idea about marriage for me.

January 7, 2015 was one of the coldest days I have ever experienced. It was an overcast day with blowing winds that reduced the temperature to the 10s. Parishioners at New Zion Baptist Church, representatives of the Ohio Association of Elementary Principals, Dayton Ministerial Alliance, and Theta Lambda chapter, Alpha Phi Alpha Fraternity, Inc., made for standing-room only final services.

As I traveled through the summer forest of my mind that day, I saw Therman's soul on the final day of 2014 as it slipped the surly bonds of earth and danced the skies on laughter-silvered wings. Sunward his soul climbed and joined the tumbling mirth of sun-split clouds. His soul hovered there and chased the shouting wind.

Up the long delirious skies he topped; the wind swept heights with easy grace where neither lark nor eagle flew. After 42,066,720 minutes of life on earth, with swift silent lifting, he traveled beyond the sanctity of space and saw the face of God.

Ezell Sampson (1937-2018) is the fifth child. Talk of his intelligence was often a topic at the dinner table at 115 Melon. As the story goes, when Therman, who was two years Ezell's senior, was enrolled in first grade, he would promptly return home and teach to Ezell what he had learned. Thus, when Ezell enrolled in first grade, he had read the lessons in the book. His teacher became aware of his ability to read and spell and promoted him to the second grade. The result of the early promotion placed Ezell as the youngest in all his classes through to graduation from Oak Park in 1954. Despite his reputation for being smart, he was never arrogant about his blessing. He was a favorite among his peers, as is observed when he visits Laurel during the occasion of the Oak Park School reunion, held during the first of July biennially. He was called "Groundhog" by his classmates, and that moniker sticks to the present day. Groundhogs are also known as woodchucks and are akin to the squirrel family. In some parts of the country, they are called whistle pigs. Their eyes, ears, and nose are located at the top of their heads for safely peering out of dens to spot danger. But it was not the squirrel characteristics that gave rise to the nickname; instead, the brown winter coat he wore reminded them of a groundhog.

Based on discussions at the 115 Melon Street dinner table, the 1930s in the Plummer Sampson, Sr. household was a time when the pangs of the Great Depression were felt by everyone in the family. The family subsisted on my dad's ability to grow vegetables and keep a cow and hogs. In 1937, unemployment continued to drop to 14.3%, dropping some 6.7% from the previous year. The average wage per year was $1780.00, gasoline was 10 cents a gallon, a loaf of bread was 9 cents, and the average price for a new car was $760.00. These were some of the externalities that, in the final analysis, never deprived the household of hope and a desire to rise above present-day circumstances. For Ezell, it was a time of continuing his high school education, participating in the OPHS football team, where he earned a place on the team as a quarterback. Then, he became "Hog, QB number 40." He was not the first in the family to have an interest in football, though; Plummer, Jr. also played football at OPHS. In the fall of 1954, he enrolled at Alcorn College, as had Therman before him. And as Therman and Plummer, Jr. before him, tuition was too much for the household to support. Thus, after his sophomore year, he, like his brothers before him, joined the US Armed Services.

The US Army facilitated an opportunity for international traveling. He traveled to Germany. While there, he went to the World Fair in 1957. At the age of 22, he was honorably discharged from the Armed Forces. He then considered the completion of his undergraduate degree, but life got in the way; he married and had a daughter and a son, and the degree pursuit was again put on hold. In fact, it was more than 50 years later when he earned his baccalaureate degree from Antioch College. This was all after he had begun work as a letter carrier for the US Post Office, and he, like Jim, rose through the ranks of his organization and became postmaster in Xenia, OH. He was also active in the masonry where he achieved 33rd degree and worshipful master acclimation. It is ironic that Ezell passed away on December 31, 2018, close to the same hour on the date on which, four years earlier, Therman had passed away (on December 31, 2014).

Ezell's daughter Sharon asked me to reminisce at the homegoing. My heart was broken, but I certainly would not say no to Sharon. As I traveled through the summer forest of my mind, I recall Abraham Lincoln's Gettysburg address and paraphrased

"The world will little note, nor long remember what we say here, but we can never forget the contributions of my brother Ezell to the quality of life among all whom he touched. It is for us the living, rather, to be dedicated here to the unfinished work which Ezell, who fought here, nobly advanced. It is rather for us to be here, dedicated to the great task remaining before us - that from this honored brother, husband, father, and cousin, we take increased devotion to that cause for which he gave the last full measure of devotion." His weary wanderings are over. He has reached his promised rest. No more moving tents, fiery serpents, or howling wilderness. He has arrived in the land that flows with milk and honey and has eaten the produce of the land.

To be with Christ and rest while waiting for the people of God is a joyful hope indeed, and to expect this glory to come soon, a double joy... Unbelief shudders at the Jordans we all must cross, but rest assured as Ezell would tell us: he experienced more ills than death at its worst can cause us. So, let us banish every fearful thought, and rejoice with exceeding gladness that we too can look forward to that time when we will be with the Lord forever.

"Homegoing Service," Homegoing Celebration, or Homegoing Ceremony is a Christian funeral or memorial in which friends and family celebrate the deceased "going home" to heaven or glory, to be with the Lord. This term is frequently used by the African-American religious and church community. "Homegoing" - the title is taken from an old African-American belief that death allowed an enslaved person's spirit to travel back to Africa - is rooted, like the Bible, in original sin. Homegoing services/funerals are not events that we look forward to, yet these events demonstrate to a large extent that the deceased was regarded by family and friends. Following the funeral service, there is an occasion for a repast, a meal. The repast for Ezell demonstrated how beloved he was to family and friends alike.

Most of his nephews, nieces, and cousins (many who lived in places other than Dayton) gathered in the Fellowship Hall of New Zion Baptist Church to rekindle relationships and mourn while celebrating. Offspring from each of his siblings were on hand to demonstrate their fondness for Uncle Ezell. I know why he was thought of as a cherished uncle, cousin, or brother; his generosity knew no end. As I participated, it occurred to me that funerals or homegoing services in our family meant a reunion. I just wish we could find the energy to congregate when there is no one being eulogized!

Ezell was a great comfort to his family; every one of us was a valued companion. This was never more evident than in the year 2000 when our baby brother, Wiley, passed away. During his last days, Wiley asked Ezell to be with him, and Ezell was present in April 2000, as he transitioned.

Clarence J. Sampson is the sixth child; born exactly one year after Hitler's Nazi attacked Poland and after the "end" of the Great Depression. When he was 15 months old, the USA entered the war on December 7, 1941 after the Japanese attacked Pearl Harbor. Thus, it is fair to state that world events influenced his early childhood and the Sampson household. My dad was thirty-six years of age when his sixth child was born; thus, he was too old for the draft, and his child-rearing responsibilities would have negated any military service. Shortly after Clarence's birth, my dad was hired as a laborer at Masonite Corporation. Working at Masonite meant solid wages for the first time in thirteen years of marriage. It also meant moving to Laurel and purchasing a home.

Clarence was intended to be the last of the children. As Clarence grew up, the local economy was improving; being the youngest in the house meant he was nurtured by his siblings. As a young lad and as a teenager, there evidenced his interest in entrepreneurship, financial independence, and civil rights. He was called "ba bro" (Baby Brother), and the moniker continued until I was born five years later. I recall overhearing a conversation between my parents in 1949. Dad was observing my mother and was concerned about what obviously appeared, to him, to be a possible new pregnancy. In a way in which only Plummer Sampson, Sr. could, he asked, "dat ain't anutter one is it?" My mother softly assured him she was not pregnant.

The early to mid-1940s was a period of transition in the country and the Sampson household. The move to 115 Melon meant a larger space within the city limits. It also meant electric lights, which meant that the kerosene lamps could be retired. Eventually, there was running water in the house, but there was no indoor toilet. Although the availability of electricity in Mississippi began in the 1920s, at that time, 35% of American households had electricity; by 1935, less than 1% of Mississippi households had electric power. The federal government took the lead in electrification during President Roosevelt's first term in 1933. Although the idea of providing federal assistance to accomplish rural electrification gained ground rapidly, it would be more than a decade before my family was able to wire the house for electricity. Getting electricity soon meant getting a radio, while winter heating came via a wood fire in a potbelly stove. As I reflect through the lens of my seventy-plus years of travel, education, and experience, I see this phase as our family's initiation to the finer physical things in life. This new exposure really meant that we could work harder and more efficiently. There were no weekend trips to the Gulf Coast barely 100 miles away, nope. There were no vacations. We were able to go to the Jones County Fair in the fall when there was scheduled a day for Negro or Colored entry.

"I - D - E - A! I - D - E - A!" was Clarence's melodious jingo; characteristic of a teen with an active imagination, he fantasized about two-way wristwatch radios and vision-enhanced telephone calls long before they became staple in America life. He made slingshots, pipette shooters, and many gadgets. As a boy scout, he earned many merit badges and advanced to Eagle Scout rank, the highest achievement in that organization. What I remember vividly was his insistence in becoming active in the Civil Rights Movement. My parents did not encourage his interest (lynchings were prevalent in MS, and Emmet Till, who was in Clarence's age range, had been killed by white terrorists in Money, MS in 1955). The fact is that my parents were afraid for Clarence's safety, yet they allowed him to join the NAACP youth choir. Many black parents resisted their children's participation in civil rights. Many feared their offspring would become the next Emmitt Till. Emmitt Louis Till was a 14-year-old African-American who was lynched in Mississippi in 1955 after being accused of offending a white woman in her family's grocery store. It was no secret that the choir did more than perform for entertainment; they assisted voter rights projects and recruited participants for sit-in demonstrations.

After graduating OPHS, he married his high school sweetheart and fathered his firstborn. In late fall of 1959, he migrated to Dayton and became a police cadet. He became a Dayton police officer and retired after more than twenty-five years of service.

Wylie R. Sampson (1948-2000) was the eighth child. He was the real *baby brother*, the only one born in a hospital, and the first of his siblings to pass on. He was born in the year in which the State of Israel came into existence, Mahatma Gandhi of India was assassinated, and the Berlin Blockade was instituted by Russia. Additionally, Harry Truman was elected president and racial segregation in the US military ended.

Wylie's birth occurred after twenty-one years of marriage. The Great Depression and FDR's New Deal had come and gone;

World War II was over. The average income had increased from $2400.00 in 1927 (the year of parents' marriage) to $2936.00 in 1948, an increase of nearly 18%. Consumer Price Index (CPI) data provided by the Bureau of Labor Statistics of the United States government shows how the cost of products has changed over time and includes everything from a gallon of gas to milk, bread, etc. Reviewing these data reveals that when my parents were first married, if they enjoyed the average annual income, they would have had $1200.00 each. By 1948, the average annual income was about $3000.00; thus, the household of 10 would have had about $300.00 each. We were income-poor, and had been since the family unit had begun; nevertheless, Wylie (and all of us) were rich in nurturance and desire to live above our financial, social, and political reality. Being the baby of the family meant he was the recipient of heightened adoration from his parents and siblings.

Dad's employment at Masonite Corporation, coupled with his farming, meant we had a level of comfort not before realized in our household. We had electricity and running water including indoor toilet facilities when Wylie was ready to enroll in elementary school (1954). We also had an automobile, a 1947 Buick Roadmaster, and a black and white television set in our living room. In our backyard was a milk cow (Butsy), a couple of goats, and a full henhouse.

After Clarence graduated from OPHS, Wylie and I were the only ones at home. We lived at a time when dad was earning more than a teacher in the public schools. Dad bought Buicks every three years or so: 1949 Buick, 1952 Buick, and 1956 Buick. We had a color television and indoor plumbing facilities. Despite our newfound fortune, we still had a cow and chickens in our backyard. I shall never forget the Easter Sunday incident when only Wylie and I were living at home.

It was customary on Easter Sunday to have a play commemorating Christ's triumph over the cross. However, in the weeks leading up to the date for the program, I had found a way to avoid participation in the program, as just about every child that attended Friendship Baptist Church would like to have done, but Wylie could not "worm" a way out and had to get to church with my parents that morning. Thus, I was alone with the responsibility to get the cow to grazing pastures that were located along the railroad track near our house. The normally cooperative cow that had allowed one of us to milk her daily was, on that Easter Sunday, in estrus. I was in for a most eventual morning. When I opened the gate to put feed in her trough, she leaped out and ran across town. I chased after her, but she was too fast for me. Near noon, I finally found her in a white neighborhood. I was able to put a chain on her halter, and I had the embarrassing task of bringing her back to our house. That trip took me past the houses of several of my OPHS classmates. Upon their seeing me, I was greeted with uproarious laughter. It seemed that my parents were the last family on Melon Street to have livestock in our backyard, and therefore, the tasks of milking, feeding the pigs, and staking out the cows to graze in the grasses that lay at the end of the street, all before getting dressed and walking the three-mile trek to OPHS. These duties commanded our attention at our house until I was a freshman in high school. My Easter experience was hilariously funny to my classmates and neighbors. The worst of the "shame" was having to walk down the street where a group of OPHS band majorettes had gathered at the McCormick house, and they saw a side of me that I dreaded… walking down the street with a cow in tow. It was nearly noon before life returned to normal. Worst of all, I had to tell my parents what had happened. Wylie's guffaw seemed to last forever. My parents were sorry that I had that incident, and that was probably the saving grace for that day. It was the last year that we had livestock in the backyard. The following year, we built a brick home on Melon Street among shotgun houses.

Perhaps more than any of his siblings, Wylie would question authority. Authority in our household was my parents, particularly my dad. Wylie and I were assigned farm duties, e.g., harvesting hay to help with the cost of back-to-school expenses, planting sweet potatoes, harvesting watermelons, making syrup from the cane patch, etc., Afterward, my dad would take us downtown (Laurel) to purchase supplies for the upcoming fall term. On one occasion when Wylie and I were shopping for clothing and miscellaneous school supplies, Wylie resisted my father's insistence upon the style of shoes or particular clothing items. The "confrontation" occurred in a downtown store. My dad won the stand-off, but I was surprised at dad's willingness to compromise. Another instance of his defiant spirit was demonstrated after graduating OPHS in the spring of 1966. Like Therman and Ezell before him, Wylie expressed an interest in enrolling at Alcorn State University in Lorman. Dad drove him to the campus that fall and placed tuition, room, and board dollars in his hand. Sometime between dad's drive back to Laurel and the first week of class, Wylie decided not to enroll and opted instead to migrate to Dayton.

He moved in with Clarence, and that transition put in process the trek to the Dayton Police Academy. En route to police officer status, he began his family when his two daughters were born. He served in the Dayton Police Department from 1968 to 1982, when he went to Jefferson Township as chief of police. He served as chief for three years before transferring to Cleveland, where he served as chief of the Cleveland Developmental Center. After that, he taught at the Ohio Peace Officers Training Academy in London, OH, specializing in criminal investigations and cultural diversity from 1988 until 1993. From 1993, he served as Yellow Springs, OH police chief; he also taught at Sinclair Community College and rejoined the Trotwood department as administrative captain for special projects. In September 1996, Wylie was hired as captain of the Trotwood Police Department. Before his arrival, there was some resentment brewing in the ranks because an "outsider" was being hired as a captain and, in the process, took away a promotion possibility within the Trotwood Police department. He was eulogized by his colleagues who reminisced about his commanding presence and dapper look, coupled with his resounding bass voice. His eulogizers told those gathered at his homegoing that "it took Wylie only about a week to win over even the most avid of complainers. Before long, it became common knowledge that Captain Sampson could be counted on to champion any worthwhile cause." The eulogizer concluded that he could not find a single word to describe Plummer and Lurline's youngest son, but it was appropriate to include "proud, brave, deep, and more than anything else, compassionate." Like his siblings and parents, he was thrifty and embraced principled work. When he was a cadet in training for the Dayton Police Force, he learned that advanced (pirated) copies of the promotion test were available. Wylie wanted to earn his appointment without getting any assistance, especially if it came from what he determined to be a dishonest source. He did so, but I think that he lost some friends within the force when he acted so courageously. He enjoyed the opportunity to visit the White House at the invitation of President Bill Clinton to participate in a conference on hate crimes. He lost his battle to cancer in April 2000, leaving two daughters and his wife to cherish his memory.

Growing up in Laurel, my family did not have the leisure to have much "life after work." The leisure time we had as children was to go to a movie and sit in the balcony at the Strand Theater.

It did not occur to us that balcony seating reflected our standing in society. My siblings and I considered it a treat and a rest from chores. Summer holidays would most likely give us time to go to the "show," as we referred to those occasions. The Strand Movie Theater located in downtown Laurel was a major part of social life in our town.

The left door on the photo above was our entry point to buy a ticket and walk up the stairs to the balcony.

Public education in Laurel

I am indebted to the dedication of the K-12 teachers that were keenly aware of differences between the white and colored educational experiences. What they lacked in financial resources was nearly matched by their devotion to their role as teachers. At every grade, I experienced teachers that encouraged us, fostered upward middle-class values, and used their meager salaries to supplement our education. My teachers were my surrogate parents.

When I was growing up in Laurel, there were four public schools for "colored" citizens: 1) Sandy Gavin Elementary, which was named for my mother's uncle; 2) Southside Elementary; 3) Nora Davis Elementary and Middle School, which housed grades 1-6 for those residing in the Kingston neighborhood and became the sole location for sixth-grade colored students after a fire destroyed Southside; and 4) Oak Park High School, which facilitated the educational experience for grades 7-12.

The issue of financial resources may best be understood by taking a ride in my time machine and soaring to 35,000 feet. We then focus on the time period as the 19th century ended, the period between 1882 and 1899. At that point in time, the population of Laurel grew rapidly, and in 1899, Laurel's first public school was built. It began operating as an attendance center for whites. The following year there was a "Negro Education" provision adopted that would provide a public facility for blacks in the city. The first facility was a rental of space in "Odd Fellows Hall," which was black-owned. It soon came to be called "Laurel Colored Schools," marking the beginning of the black and white educational system in Laurel. This was the beginning of the separate and unequal educational system blacks inherited. Inequality of resources were not only seen in buildings, books, and laboratory equipment passed down to our schools after they had been first used by the white students in the Laurel public school system.

Elementary School Days

My first school was Sandy Gavin Elementary. Sandy Gavin School was built in 1907, and it housed grades one through five for the Negro citizens who lived in the city limits. My family is connected to the man for whom the school is named, Sandy Gavin. My grandfather, Calvin (1873-1941), and Sandy were first cousins once removed. Their common ancestors are Friday (1770-1856) and Peg Gavin. Friday was the father of Moses (1828), who was the father of Wash (1845), who was the father of Calvin Gavin (1873-1939), as I previously discussed.

Sandy Gavin was revered in the city of Laurel due in no small part to his leadership in the field of education. As a lad, I heard my mother and Aunt Corrine, her sister, speak of Sandy Gavin and the connection between Sandy and Calvin, their father and my grandfather. These sisters were proud of their ancestry and the Gavin contribution to the elevation of the community in Laurel.

In September 1929, a newspaper story in the *Laurel Morning Call* focused on Superintendent of the Laurel Public Schools R.H. Watkins, who spoke to a "gathering of nearly one thousand whites and darkies" that had gathered at Sandy Gavin School on the occasion of Sandy Gavin's funeral. According to the newspaper, other dignitaries included L. J. Rowen, president of Alcorn College for Negroes, and colored physician Ben Leonard. Other "Negroes made short talks," according to the newspaper story published September 18, 1929.

Sandy Gavin was a man among men. He was a dignified functionary when there was little dignity associated with being "colored." From the pulpits, I observed on more than one occasion, the expression that a married colored man was little more than a "big boy around the house." Certainly, the tenor of the stories carried in the newspapers about people of color reflected the low regard for African-Americans during that time. My maternal ancestor, Sandy Gavin, was not among the most marginalized in Laurel. In his limited way, he opened the doors for a wide swarth of colored inhabitants of Laurel and Jones County.

Chapter IX

THE FOURTH GENERATION: MY CHILDHOOD AND MY SIBLINGS

A viable partnership for the Church in 1950s Laurel was with public educational institutions. These organizations shaped the lives of the black community in Laurel. My first teacher was Mrs. Idella B. Washington, who was also principal of Sandy Gavin Elementary School. The class was designated as the primer; it partially covered kindergarten and first grade. Many of my classmates that were born after WWII or did not attend a kindergarten were assigned to the primer.

A school day for preschoolers was either from 8 AM to noon, or noon to 3 PM. For first graders and above, the hours were 8 AM – 3 PM.

SCHOOL DAYS 1951-52

I was enrolled there until completion of the fifth grade. During that phase of my formal education, I learned to read. I also liked going to school. There, I met classmates from the south side of Laurel, some of whom remain my friends today.

The school day began when the bell would ring, and we were required to form a line, cease talking or playing, and quietly march into the building. No talking was allowed once we were in our lines. If there was inattention to the task of marching into the building or unhallowed talking, the enforcer of the edict was Mrs. Pigee. She was a stern disciplinarian who brandished a strap to enforce her role as a learning figure. I was never a target of her "enforcement" for whispering or otherwise failing to pay attention to the lesson at hand. Upon assembling into our assigned seats, we would have devotion consisting of a song and a prayer. During this time, I became aware of classmates who had good singing voices. At recess each day, the class could go outside; the playground was separated based on gender. As it turned out, my first-grade teacher was Mrs. Maudie Mae Pigee-Jones.

The first grade consisted of morning and afternoon sessions. Reading, learning cursive writing, and spelling were part of the curriculum. The time seemed to fly by at Sandy Gavin. I completed the first grade and was promoted to second grade. The second-grade class teacher was Mrs. Mabel O. Lott. She was much kinder than Mrs. Pigee. Students requiring disciplining would be referred to the principal's office. In each of the grades, decorum and civic responsibility were parts of the curricula. The practice of devotion meant either we were affirmed by the importance of the Christian religion, or there were a few who were not impressed enough to turn the lives over to Christ. When I was promoted to the third grade, a neighbor, Mrs. Idella Hodge was my teacher. She was a good friend to our family and grandmother to one of my first friends, and for many years, she helped my father prepare his income tax filing. She was a teacher that cared about her charges' minds and souls. She also possessed a leather strap, but I do not remember her using it. Once the students knew about behavior enforcement practices, just the knowledge of the teacher's strap was enough to maintain law and order.

Completing the third grade meant enrolling in Sandy Gavin Annex, which was annexed to Sandy Gavin. When I was a second grader, Southside Elementary burned and had to be replaced. Southside had housed grades four and five. Now, grades four and five were in a new building, andboth the old Sandy Gavin and Sandy Gavin Annex were brick facilities. Sandy Gavin Annex also had a cafeteria, and this meant instead of going home for lunch, I could buy a meal for 25 cents each day.

Nora Davis middle school

Nora Davis Elementary School was established in 1948. It is in the north of Laurel and was authorized to provide education for black citizens residing in the Kingston neighborhood encompassing grades one through six. It served as the sixth-grade center for all Laurel residents. These arrangements produced a transportation challenge to residents that lived in southern Laurel.

Reported in the 1951-52 book *American School and University* is a chapter called "America's Outstanding School Buildings (built since 1945)." In that chapter was a series of school photos and a longer listing of "best" schools in each state. Southern education administrators attempted to "equalize" the schools for black and white students to preserve segregation. During the late 1940s and extending through the next decade, this span of time included, preceded a period of school building that's very important in Mississippi's history. This school construction was intended to pre-empt the outcome of public school desegregation battles that were solved by the ruling in *Brown v. Board of Education*. The 14-room facility was constructed at a cost of $135,000.00, according to news stories in the Jackson (MS) Clarion Ledger in 1949. The building contained an auditorium with a 600-seating capacity along with a cafeteria and "adequate offices" for the teaching staff.

In September 1949, Ms. Nora Davis, a respected educator who had taught in the Laurel public schools for 40 years, was honored by naming her principal of the school that was to bear her name. The Jackson Clarion Ledger carried a prominent story on page 3 of the June 3, 1949 edition. "Topflight" news writers from Jackson, Memphis, and New Orleans were invited to attend the June 5 dedication. The program included R.H. Watkins, former superintendent of the Laurel school system; D.U. Maddox, president of the Laurel school board; and L.T. Ellis, superintendent of the Oak Park "Negro" high school in Laurel. Maddox paid tribute to Ms. Davis during the dedication. Ms. Davis was born in 1884 and expired in 1952. She, like Sandy Gavin before her, was highly regarded within the community. Her body was buried in a cemetery that bears her name.

My attendance at the school began in the end of the 1950s. Transportation to and from the Nora Davis middle school campus was a particular challenge; there was no public conveyance for black students. My family resided on the south side in a neighborhood called the "Neck," a distance of about four miles from Nora Davis. The black students who resided in Queensberg and other South Laurel communities either walked or had parental carpools as the basic travel modes. Beginning that fall, I began to walk to Nora Davis every school day. That would last until January, when my Christmas gift was a bicycle, and that became my mode of travel from January to May of my sixth-grade year, 1958-59.

On to high school

Oak Park High School (OPHS) was the center of social and educational development for me from 1959 to 1964. It had been founded in 1882 when John Kamper, a wealthy contractor, built a mill to provide timber to complete the Northern and New Orleans Railroad. The workforce for the construction was predominantly black. In 1891, the Eastman-Gardiner Company of Clinton, Iowa, purchased the Kamper Mill Properties. The enterprise consisted of baron brothers, George and Silas Gardiner, and brother-in-law Lauren C. Eastman. In 1893, another brother-in-law named Wallace joined the company. After the "critical period" had passed in 1896, the company seemed to have had a favorable future. In 1897, Rogers started a weekly newspaper called *The Laurel Chronicle. The Laurel Chronicle* that carried a column entitled "Progressive Colored Citizens"; this made it the first white-owned newspaper in the state of Mississippi to highlight the contributions of black citizens in a positive way. The column encouraged blacks to come to the city of Laurel to work in the timber and railroad industries. It continued through the 1960s. A "prominent" member of the colored community, Mrs. Hattie V.J. McInnis, served as the editor of the section that was labeled "Negro News of Interest."

The population of Laurel grew rapidly, and in 1899, Laurel's first public school was built. It began operating as an attendance center for whites. The following year, the "Negro Education" provisions were completed by renting the "Odd Fellows Hall," which was black-owned. It soon came to be called "Laurel Colored Schools," marking the beginning of the black and white educational system in Laurel. Laurel's population increased from 3,198 to 13,027 inhabitants - mostly in the black communities. In 1900, the "colored school" had 43 students instructed by one teacher/principal. In 1920, the school consisted of 100 students taught by 18 teachers and supervised by two principals covering grades 1-8. It soon became clear that more buildings were needed to keep up with the increasing enrollment of black students.

By the 1920s, Laurel had become the "#1 industrial town in the state of Mississippi" and was later called the "yellow pine" capital of the world. Between 1920 and 1925, Laurel's population grew 32%, and the school-aged population grew 27%. Laurel approached the 19,000-resident mark. Plans to solve overcrowding problems resulted in the St. Elmo Church Library Project, completed in 1922 as Southside School. A second plan resulted in the building of the Southside School #2. This institution became the Sandy Gavin School and began operating in 1925, and it has continued to the 21st century. Sandy Gavin was the principal at Sandy Gavin School. His mother, America, born in 1830, was sister of Moses Gavin, born in 1828. Moses was my maternal great-grandfather, father of my grandfather, Calvin Gavin. Moses and America were two of nine children born to Friday and Peg Gavin. As the nation was enjoying the "roaring twenties" with booming development, so was Laurel. The St. Elmo Church Library Project was a contributor to education for "coloreds," and its completion solved a smaller problem, but the black community was still in need of a high school. By 1925, there was ongoing confusion between the whites and a then well-defined black middle class. The interaction between the two, although there was disagreement, was characterized as always respectful by Laurel historian Cleveland Payne, who authored *the Oak Park story 1928-1970, a cultural history*. The two groups agreed first on the establishment of the Queensburg Academy for Colored Students. Queensburg was built in 1925 and later became Oak Park Vocational High school. The Oak Park Vocational High School, under the supervision and jurisdiction of the Laurel City school system, opened in September 1928. Oak Park consisted of 325 students and 10 teachers. A board of trustees controlled the grounds on which the school was built. Funds were put aside for the school's support system. J. E. Johnson became principal and was later assisted by J. H. Mosley (*Oak Park Story* 7-13).

What a difference time and chance make! Compared to our predecessors, those of us who became the fourth generation were born with "silver spoon(s) in our mouths." Civil rights once again gained prominence on the national legislative agenda. Open housing laws, public accommodations, LBJ's Great Society, the War on Poverty, and the transition from being "colored" or Negro to black. Public Law 89-110, the Voting Rights Act of 1965, paved the way for the election of mayors, council persons, and members of state legislatures, US Congress, US Senate, and even the presidency of the US. Entire households could boast of college-educated offspring. Those who chose not to go the college route found rewarding lives. Jobs became positions and appointments. Middle-class life was enjoyed by most, though not all. There was a reliance on family values and educational attainment, both of which were complemented by active involvement in church matters.

My first family vacation

The summer of 1958 was the first time I traveled away from the state of Mississippi. I was, at that time, coming upon my eleventh year. My mother took me and Wylie on a train trip to Cincinnati, Ohio. The trip became a watershed event in my development. It was the first time in my life that non-Mississippi public accommodations allowed us to use a restroom facility without being subject to arrest. The twelve-hour trip culminated at the Cincinnati Union Terminal, which was a significant development in the history of Cincinnati rail transportation. Cincinnati historians argue that the terminal was one of the last great train stations built in the country. Union Terminal has had a long and storied history, from welcoming soldiers' home from WWII to several other noteworthy occasions. Wylie and I could only stare up and admire the largest half-dome in the Western Hemisphere. We were met at the terminal by Plummer, Jr. and Jim, who drove us to Dayton some 50 miles away. The week-long stay introduced us to the Northern lifestyle and all the related amenities such as wide paved streets, sidewalks, and neighborhood swimming pools. We saw how my dads' siblings lived... two-story houses, large neighborhoods, public parks with swimming pools, beautiful well-kept-lawns, and fewer reminders of Southern Jim Crow and second-class citizenship. This new exposure meant there was a yearning for a vacation/family reunion the very next year. As a child, I recall that here was little time for celebrating or vacationing, yet we had much to thankful for.

I researched vacations in general and vacation choices to provide a contextual understanding of vacation frequencies and types experienced by other American families. I read a number of scholarly papers written by social science (largely sociology) researchers. I found that social science literature has acknowledged racial differences in leisure preferences and vacation experiences for decades. Moreover, as is the case with many other facets of life in America, the role of race is pivotal to understanding the connection of leisure and vacation differences among American citizens. One social science author, Lee (1972), found that some leisure activities and settings could be distinguished or explained as naturally black or white. Additionally, Schuman and Hatchett (1974) showed that African-Americans participated in different leisure activities, even in integrated neighborhoods. In a widely cited study, Washburne (1978) found that African-Americans were significantly less likely to spend vacations in less developed, more natural outdoor recreation areas such as camping out in nature, at a regional or national park, such as Yellowstone or the Colorado Rockies, etc. A 1989 study by West showed that African-Americans were more likely to use city parks but not regional parks or national parks as venues for leisure and vacationing. Interracial relations factors also explain leisure and vacation choices and the subsequent underrepresentation by minorities in regional parks" (p. 11). From a similar viewpoint, Philipp (1995) found that the appeal of many leisure activities to African-Americans and the comfort felt while doing these activities, might be lessened by feelings of discrimination which were associated with the activities. In fact, much of the discussion in the literature over this extended period has focused on explaining racial differences in leisure behavior using either "marginality" (e.g., income, social class, access) or "ethnicity" (e.g., subcultural values, language, traditions) theories. All the foregone are important to understanding why African-Americans did not "go on vacation" in the same proportion as white families. Unsurprisingly, this body of literature ignores the role of perceptions and emotions of African-Americans in different leisure activities and locations. Many of the sociological studies avoid discussion of the interactive effects of prejudice and discrimination in shaping African-American leisure behavior despite the historical significance of racial discrimination in the United States over the last several hundred years. West (1989) refers to this situation as the "cognitive tyranny of the dominant paradigms in leisure research on minorities" and states that the separation of the races in "choices" related to leisure places is due in part to the dominance of the subcultural paradigm, a stark fact that is overlooked in much of the sociological literature. In addition, "a consistent body of evidence in support of either marginality or ethnicity has not emerged" over several decades. I conclude that a different conceptual approach is needed to move the literature beyond the present theoretical boundaries of marginality and ethnicity to provide a more complete understanding of African-American leisure behavior and, more specifically, why race matters. Such a conceptual framework would acknowledge the power of racial discrimination in the formation of African-American attitudes and behavior, and then address African-American perceptions of racial acceptance and discrimination which may be associated with leisure activities and locations. Most tangibly, the role of money also connects with leisure and vacation choices. In short, most of the black people I knew did not have a supply of disposal dollars to invest in travel, leisure, or vacations.

Nevertheless, planning for and anticipating the 1959 trip generated a wealth of enthusiasm. Dad was earning more money from his job at Masonite Corporation than at any time before, and with only Wylie and I living at home, there were fewer claims on his dollars. The combination of increased monetary resources, five offspring and grandchildren living in Dayton, and his younger siblings Iola, Abraham, and Annie Laura with big houses and good jobs made for an insatiable appetite for a road trip the following year. So, in midsummer, 1959, we piled into our 1956 Buick Roadmaster and began the 15-hour trip on Highway 11 to Dayton. The trip was significant for several reasons. This would be the first family reunion in my memory, although the term "reunion" was never mentioned as I check my childhood tapes. However, Uncle Lucius and Uncle Milton also motored to Dayton during that same week. I never knew the extent to which it had been planned. All the siblings were there except for Aunt Lurelia. One of her sons, Jimmy Earl, came with us to assist with the drive. My mother packed a heavy lunch bag of fried chicken, potato salad, coconut cake, and other goodies. I was unaware of the impact of Jim Crow laws that would prevent us from using rest facilities and restaurants along the way while we were south of the Mason-Dixon Line. Not until we were inside the state of Ohio were there public facilities for all races. Thus, when we traveled through Mississippi, Alabama, Tennessee, and Kentucky we would avail ourselves along some wooded area during the dark. Nearly ten years would pass before we could use facilities while traveling between the South and the North.

We had several first cousins who had grown up in Dayton: Jerry, Geraldine, Barbara, and Larry, offspring of Uncle Abraham and Aunt Lula T.; and Helen, Darlene, Hubert, Jr., Raymond, and Anthony, offspring of Uncle Hubert Marsh and Aunt Annie Laura. Jerry, LeRoy, Helen, and I were the "same year's children," as my mother would say. Those were magical days when my two male cousins and I could explore manhood and physical development during our early teen years. Of my brothers, Plummer, Jr. and Jim were married and had their own families; Therman was just married to Ethel Martin, a Georgia student who had enrolled at University of Dayton; Ezell was not yet married; and Clarence was in transition. My sister, Mazie, was mothering her children in Mississippi; thus, they were not part of the gathering. In late August, when LeRoy and I returned to Laurel, we longed for more Northern exposure, but we were destined to complete our education in Laurel.

Oak Park High, home of the Dragons

At the onset of my seventh-grade school year in the fall of 1959, I enrolled at Oak Park. At that juncture, L.T. Ellis was principal. My study at Oak Park was one of the most impactful experiences in my life. Going to school at OPHS meant having to walk about three miles from 115 Melon. OPHS was the only public school that "colored folks" could lawfully attend. In northern Laurel, where the Kingston community was located, and in "Cross-the KC," Dunnigan's Bottom, South Side, Queensburg, and the Debardeleven district where I lived, there was a sizable number of students that walked daily to OPHS. Public officials were preoccupied with maintaining segregation; J. P. Coleman was governor. Although the *Brown v. Board of Education* had been decided by the Supreme Court, making integrated education the law of the land in 1954 during Governor Coleman's administration, the legislature, in response to concern about school integration, passed a resolution of interposition which authorized the state to prohibit the implementation of the *Brown* decision in Mississippi. The legislature also created the State Sovereignty Commission to carry out the intent of that resolution and to promote states' rights. He was successful in maintaining racial segregation during his four years in office.

There was no rabid interest in the business of policy-making; after all, segregation was what we had experienced since birth. Thus, we were inured to the way of life in 1950s Mississippi. Fortunately, we had dedicated instructors who themselves did not approve of Jim Crow laws and second-class citizenship.

All our teachers, i.e., civics, social studies, life sciences, mathematics, etc., made us aware of what was going on in the outside world; the NAACP Youth Council worked to increase awareness about civil rights, but the revolution was years away. Most of us desired to get an education and either go to college or find a "good" job. Several activities took our eyes of the prize, including sports, e.g., football, and the desire to become recording artists. Another distraction was daytime radio from WNOE New Orleans. Among other sounds, they piped in Bill Doggett, the organ impresario, with his hit "Honky Tonk"; in addition, the station would broadcast Little Richard singing "Good Golly Miss Molly," the Chantels singing "Maybe," and Little Willie John's "Talk to Me." During the nighttime, WLAC from Nashville could be picked up on the radio. Each of these AM radio stations was external to Laurel; the point is that local radio stations such as WMAL did not broadcast Rhythm and Blues (R&B), or what had been called "race music." My first year at OPHS was 7th grade. That experience began in Second Baptist Church, a prominent church in the black community. The facility was located across the street from what had been the OPHS campus. Since the summer after my sixth grade, OPHS was destroyed by fire. Two years would pass before the new facility was completed.

Traveling through the summer forests in my mind in my time machine, I recall my eighth-grade experiences at OPHS, which seemed to be dominated by civic studies with Ms. May Frances Spencer, who arranged debates on social issues as part of her teaching style. They were always spirited and substantive. The junior high civics molded my focus of civil rights and public policy. I grew up in a conservative house, but my introduction to civics education introduced me to progressive and liberal activity. We had not been exposed to the importance of civil rights, voting, and citizen participation in government

The ninth-grade experience was distinct for two reasons: 1) my dad taught me drive a car, and 2) I became a student under the guidance of Malcolm Black, the band director who graduated from Jackson State. Under him, I learned to play the alto saxophone. Gaining fluency in a musical instrument opened the door to many opportunities, but learning to drive was the beginning of life as an adult. Driving a car, as conjured in my 15-year-old testosterone infused mind, meant that my manhood was being shaped. I fantasized that the ability to drive a car was a signal of my movement forward in life. Obviously, it is a means of transportation, but more than that, it was a signal of independence. My dad knew about my exuberance to drive, and he would allow me to drive on rural roads outside the city of Laurel. This I did when we would travel to the farm plot of land where he cultivated "truck crops" in the community of Mt. Olive. The dirt roads and their curvature through heavily-wooded areas where there was never any ongoing traffic was ideal for my training to drive. I would drive inside the city limits when my dad would go to meetings at the church during the week. I would be the only adolescent at business meetings, but the experience was worth it since it afforded driving on paved roads where there was ongoing traffic. Dad was a patient and thorough teacher. At the dinner table, he would debrief mother and Wylie on how I had done. Once, while driving home from Mt. Olive, I drove the car into a parked truck. The truck was parked on the side of the road and was not encroaching the path for traffic. To this day, I cannot understand how I managed to crash into that parked vehicle! Fortunately, there was no damage to either vehicle, but the incident brought my driving lessons to a halt for a while. Soon, I regained dad's confidence, and he agreed that I could go to the examining station at the highway patrol office to take the test for a license. Now, that meant that I could ask dad for the car to independently transport me to events of interest. On rare occasions, he would accede.

As I now see it, my parents had a binary child-rearing style. When the first group of my siblings was born, my parents relied on what they had experienced with their parents. That meant "tough love." Using Maslow's hierarchy of needs model, we notice that the most basic were of needs were physiological, e.g., food, water, warmth, and rest. As I understand the environment in which they grew up, these needs, along with safety and security, were their focus. Moreover, their marriage came while the Great Depression was in full swing. This circumstance coupled with the burden of second-class citizenship and Jim Crow laws meant that their parenting style was shaped by the influence of those times and considerations. My mother gave birth to children over a span of twenty years. The final three of us were born when financial times began to get better. My parents began to focus on psychological needs of their offspring, e.g., belongingness in the community and self-esteem. More than with the first set of children, the second set was influenced by the activities that brought WWII to an end. Things were better for all of us, but for Clarence, Wylie, and me came the "gift" of motherly concern in a fashion that was more difficult with the first edition. I jokingly state that my parents conducted research and development of proper rearing styles and embraced a more liberating set of guidlines for those who brought up the rear. Thus (mainly through the influence of my mother), self-actualizing and achieving were more important, thus my claim that my parents had a binary rearing model. My enrollment at OPHS manifested the impact of more liberal parenting, coupled with a group of educators in the lives of the final three children. None of this meant that they were horrible or cruel in their earlier years as parents, though.

Music instruction in my freshman year meant the beginning of Malcolm Black in my life. To this day, he remains one of my favorite teachers. Mr. Black was just out of undergraduate study at Jackson State University. He is a gifted and accomplished arranger and musician who later earned his doctorate from University of Wisconsin. Learning to play saxophone was my entry to the OPHS marching and concert band. Participation in the marching band meant I was committed to attending Friday night football games since the band provided half-time shows at home and, sometimes, on the road. That "commitment" was a new one for those of us who had resided at 115 Melon. Some of my older brothers were talented and developed a longing for playing football for the OPHS Dragons, but they would have a tough time getting permission to go to a football game, and there were plenty of obstacles in getting parental permission to play football. For me, reading and playing music opened a door to a creative side that lay hidden in my consciousness. By my tenth grade, Mr. Black had given me an opportunity to play in a "swing" band/combo on the weekends. All of the other men in the band were older high school teachers, so as I learned improvisation and an understanding of the mechanics of music arranging, I was also getting a view of the world that was invaluable to my future development as an adult. By the end of my sophomore year, I had achieved the "first chair" in the alto saxophone section. I was eager to get solo performances with the concert band, and thus, my knowledge (as little as it was) was impressive enough that Mr. Black arranged for me to receive a band scholarship to attend Jackson State, his alma mater, upon completion of my senior year.

The OPHS band was the first organized team in which I was a member. Being accountable for members of my section fostered an appreciation of the fact that there is no "I" in team. Several of my classmates were also in the OPHS band: Jerry

Donaldson, a talented budding musician who later earned a scholarship to DePauw University, with whom I have remained friends; my cousin LeRoy, who played the single bass drum; and John Moody, who demonstrated snare drum skills that are present in my memory to this day. Each time I hear a marching band at a football game today, I pay attention to the rhythm patterns of their cadence. Otis Windham, who has been my friend since 6th grade, played baritone horn. Jerome Wyatt's trumpet would, in retrospect, point to his leadership in the community. Charles Magee, a truly superior trumpeter, went on to play and record professionally on the east coast.

Malcom Black was not the only teacher who was a blessing for me. In my sophomore year, I was fortunate to be a student in Ms. Bertha Marshall's tenth-grade English literature class. When she was appointed to teach at OPHS, she was a fresh baccalaureate. Interpreting literature and using the written word to stimulate intellectual development broadened my self-worth. Ms. Marshall was also director of the Thespian Society. When she directed her plays, I would be assigned a lead role. The nurturing I continued to get from Mr. Black and Ms. Marshall would not be the end of teachers shaping my contributions to the world in which I live. Mr. Sammy Malone was a former football coach and college athlete who taught algebra and trigonometry. Between class discussions with LeRoy, John, Jerry, and Alfred Williams, as well as other classmates, would often revolve around the underlying life lessons and philosophy Coach Malone would use to explain the logic in trigonometry. When Sammy Malone became our teacher, his rotund figure and graying hair emphasized the wisdom of a man who had seen a lot in life; he was a beloved teacher who saw the good individually in each of us and attempted to uphold the promise our lives demonstrated. Teaching was not confined to the classroom, and it was not limited to the subject matter in his course outline. "A man's grasp should exceed his reach"; this was a favorite expression of his. To the second-string football players in his class that complained about playing time, he would state, "many flowers are born to blush unseen and waste their sweetness on the desert air." My mentor group of Malcolm Black, Bertha Marshall, Mae Frances Spencer, and Sammy Malone would expand to Jeff Rockette, a man who did not teach me in a class but served as advisor to OPHS chapter affiliation to the High School YMCA, better known as Hi-Y.

High School YMCA

The Hi-Y, a well-established YMCA program aimed at school-aged children, had its roots in early YMCA youth programs. The term Hi-Y was first officially used in 1927, but the YMCA had been active with youths since the 1850s. Hi-Y stands for High School YMCA, and it was for boys only. Tri-Hi-Y (the female version) started soon after the Hi-Y program. During my high school junior year, my extra-curricular activities included the Hi-Y. Participation in this group afforded me one of the most significant experiences of my life. That life experience also served to garner memories that would cause me to reflect on them decades later.

At the end of chapter one in this writing, I argued that most of us live in a gap between promise stimulated expectation and on-the-ground reality. The expectation is born of what we have been taught about right and wrong, and good and evil. These subjects were the stuff of discussions around the dinner table, Sunday school lessons, and the Bible and civics courses that began early in life. We had been taught that we had our head in the lion's mouth; that we were human citizens, but our country had not come around to accept that. There was always something missing in the discussions, I thought, when our roles as subjects rather than citizens prevailed.

Living in Laurel, we were literally within an earshot of the hostility aimed at the African-American community in Mississippi and in the nation itself. I muse that many of us in Laurel (definitely not all) personified the saying, "been down so long, the bottom looks like up"; all the while my classmates and I imperviously basked in the warmth of teacher mentorship, there was a fight for our civil rights an hour's drive away. Part of that mentorship came from Mr. Rockette, who urged me to run for Mississippi Hi-Y president; the bid was successful. So, in the early summer of 1963, two events would change my life forever. The Mississippi delegation met in Jackson on June 17 to drive to the national meeting of the Hi-Y at St. Olaf College in Northfield, MN. The watershed event was the assassination of Medgar Wiley Evers, an African-American civil rights activist from Mississippi who worked to overturn segregation at the University of Mississippi and enact social justice and voting rights. In the driveway outside his home in Jackson, Mississippi, Medgar Evers was shot to death by white supremacist Byron De La Beckwith. In 1964, the first trial of chief suspect De La Beckwith ended with a deadlock by an all-white jury, sparking numerous protests. When a second all-white jury also failed to reach a decision, De La Beckwith was set free. Three decades later, the state of Mississippi reopened the case under pressure from civil rights leaders and Evers' family. In February 1994, a racially mixed jury in Jackson found Beckwith guilty of murder. The unrepentant white supremacist, aged 73, was sentenced to life imprisonment.

During World War II, Evers volunteered for the US Army and participated in the Normandy invasion. In 1952, he joined the National Association for the Advancement of Colored

People (NAACP). As a field worker for the NAACP, Evers traveled through his home state, encouraging poor African-Americans to register to vote and recruiting them into the Civil Rights Movement. He was instrumental in getting witnesses and evidence for the Emmitt Till murder case, which brought national attention to the plight of African-Americans in the South. On June 12, 1963, Medgar Evers was killed. Amid this national tragedy, five days after the assassination, the Mississippi delegation convened in Jackson. Evers' assassination was not an isolated event. In retrospect, most of us had been sheltered from the nearby activity in Hinds County; we were comparatively unconnected and uncommitted to the civil rights ferment 80 miles away in Jackson. It was the largest city in Mississippi in 1960, with 250,000 residents, 50,000 of whom were black. Evers, a field secretary for the Jackson chapter of the NAACP, began to build up NAACP youth councils at colleges and high schools in the area since 1961. Since the Congress on Racial Equality (CORE) and the Student Nonviolent Coordinating Committee (SNCC) were in other parts of Mississippi, the NAACP was the only consistent nonviolent group in Jackson. The NAACP presence placed the Civil Rights Movement against the politically and socially powerful white establishment. The white establishment was asked to desegregate all public facilities, public schools, and lunchroom counters, hire blacks on the police force, upgrade the salaries of municipal workers, employ black crossing guards for school zones, and form a biracial committee. This was the "backdrop" that clouded our drive to Northfield, MN five days after the assassination. What I learned was that not all whites were opposed to our liberation, but unfortunately, too many of them were too quiet. Near the end of the week in Northfield, on the campus of St. Olaf College, Dick Cunningham, a newspaper reporter for the *Minneapolis Tribune*, wrote an article for his paper on July 2 entitled "Hi-Y Voluntarily Acts to Integrate." The transcript of that article is listed below.

"The National Hi-Y council Monday passed a motion against racial discrimination following a spontaneous groundswell of excitement over racial questions at the National Hi-Y Congress... meeting at St. Olaf College here.

The council elected Charles Sampson, a Negro from Laurel, MS, as its president.

> The 1,200 members approved the motion overwhelmingly last night and cheered the election of Sampson. The council is the legislative body with one member from each of the 50 states representing 350,000 members aged 15-18, of Hi-Y and Tri-Hi-Y
> (girls) in 11,000 clubs. Only 5% of the clubs are segregated.

The Council passed the resolution with only three dissenting votes after its president George Fletcher, Lubbock, TX, assured a southern member: "This is not forced integration (of the individual clubs) for the very simple reason that that would kill Hi-Y in the United States.

> The resolution calls upon the YMCA's National Committee to
> work with school youth to carefully consider this resolution and develop recommended steps to enable appropriate action to be
> taken by area, state, and local councils, individual clubs, and individual members.

> The resolution was not on the agenda for the annual meeting, which has been held here in connection with the congress, which

meets every three years. The resolution grew spontaneously out of
discussion groups in the congress.

In pre-congress questionnaires, an overwhelming majority of the delegates put racial relations as the topic they most wanted
to discuss during the six-day meeting.
On Sunday, the interest became intense after the Rev. Charles C.
Noble, Dean of the Hendricks Chapel at Syracuse University, spoke
on "the measure of a Man." An informal bull session started Sunday afternoon under the elm trees outside the west door of Boe Memorial Chapel. It ranged from 10 to 150 members, all during the afternoon, with groups drifting off to take up the theme elsewhere on campus.

One group wrote the resolution Sunday night and had it accepted by the council officers yesterday morning. Dr. Noble warned youngsters… to do some spadework with their parents, but "do it gently. Go in the back door." He also told them to (1) take the issue to regional conferences, (2) exchange students in districts where Negroes and whites go to different schools, (3) desegregate their own clubs, (4) correspond with friends from congress to maintain interest, and (5) initiate core "freedom conferences" where such issues can be discussed "openly and fairly."

Other officers elected to leadership in the 1963-64 National Hi-Y in addition to Sampson were Bruce L. Kahl, Sacramento, CA, vice-president; Janet Ellis, Houston, TX, secretary; and Dave Hansleman, Angola, IN, treasurer."

Returning to Laurel, in that hot summer of 1963, I became a near-celebrity. There were several requests to speak at church and other civic gatherings. The *Laurel Leader Call* newspaper carried an article in the "Negro News of Interest" section of its paper which was edited by Hattie V. J. McInnis, a music teacher at OPHS. Publishing the story in the Leader Call affirmed the authenticity of the experience at St. Olaf and Northfield, MN. Despite my experiences, there were challenging days ahead. Public accommodations, voting rights, and integration lay in the future. Jim Crow was on life support, but its venom remained.

My senior year at OPHS

In the fall of 1963, I began my senior year in high school. My "homeroom" teacher was Ms. Essie Mae Harry, also my English instructor. She was a no-nonsense learning facilitator who had a compelling countenance. Ms. Harry spoke with precise diction, and every one of her students respected her. Often, when a passage of literature that contained either simile or metaphors loosely or tightly connected to our life experiences would cause Jerome Wyatt (Tommy Tomorrow) to quip about getting our liberation, Ms. Harry would quickly warn us: "Students, you have your head in the lion's mouth." She was not discouraging our desire for first class citizenship, just pointing out that we should consider the outcomes of our actions and think before we leaped. She was a stickler for prompt and timely attendance; when one of us was late to class, she would, without breaking her lecture delivery rhythm, say upon the errant classmate, "a diller, a dollar, a ten o'clock scholar… Mr. Arrington, you may see me at three" (Marvin Arrington was a star athlete and would often arrive nattily dressed so that he was certain to be the center of attention). Tardiness, however, was rare among our group, 12A. Placement in section A began in 6th grade and had been designated for college-bound students. We had been fed a strong curriculum, and instilled in us were Coach Malone's words: "A man's reach should exceed his grasp"; this further instilled within us that we had the ability to go further.

Mrs. Katherine Showers, who taught civics and history, complemented Ms. Harry and Coach Malone. She was an energetic lecturer who was an accomplished teacher in her own right. In retrospect, I have come to revere my high school instructors as I grew older (and hopefully wiser). Mrs. Showers would many times "teach the test"; when she would say, "you all better stick a pin in this," we came to know some of the items/questions that would appear on a subsequent examination. My teacher's encouragement built self-confidence that served me through undergraduate school.

Completing my senior year, I was occupied with my studies and extra-curricular activities, including Hi-Y and concert and marching band, as well as the Thespian Society. Because of my Hi-Y, there were travels to many locations around the country. Because of these "obligations," I experienced travel on an airplane and to New York City for the first time. The return trip was as memorable as the week when Medgar Evers had been assassinated in June 1963. On September 15, during a plane change in Birmingham, I learned of a bomb blast at the 16th Street Baptist Church in Birmingham, Alabama. The blast had killed four African-American girls during church services. At least 14 others were injured in the explosion. Subsequently, riots broke out, and two African-American boys, Virgil Ware, 13, and Johnny Robinson, 16, were also killed. In all, at least 20 people were injured from the initial bombing and the ensuing riots. Alabama Governor George Wallace dispatched 500 National Guards and 300 state troopers to the city. The next day, they were joined by 500 police officers and 150 sheriffs' deputies. The season of carnage was in full bloom. On September 16, President John F. Kennedy responded by saying: "If these cruel and tragic events can only awaken that city and state - if they can only awaken this entire nation to a realization of the folly of racial injustice and hatred and violence, then it is not too late for all concerned to unite in steps toward peaceful progress before more lives are lost." JFK would himself become the subject of yet another assassination two months later.

On Monday, September 16, 1963, Dr. Martin Luther King, Jr. held a press conference in Birmingham, saying that the US Army "ought to come to Birmingham and take over this city and run it." Justice was in the distant future. In 1965, four suspects were identified: Bobby Frank Cherry, Thomas Blanton, Robert

Chambliss, and Herman Frank Cash, all Ku Klux Klan members. Not surprisingly, witnesses were reluctant to talk, and physical evidence was lacking, so no charges were filed. A decade after (1976), the Alabama attorney general reopened the case and, subsequently, the three former Ku Klux Klan members were convicted of murder for the bombing.

The Evers assassination, the bombing of the Sixteenth Baptist church, and increases in civil rights demonstrations (lunch counters) and the "outside agitators", i.e., busloads of freedom fighters arriving in MS to facilitate voter registration, captured my attention and that of my classmates during my junior and senior years at OPHS. At the same time, our parents and OPHS insulated us from being casualties of the fight for civil rights in Mississippi. When I asked permission from my father to participate in the lunch counter demonstrations, he became livid. It would be years before I understood his fear of me becoming a casualty of the unrest. Soul and R&B recordings kept our eyes off the prize. Stevie Wonder's "Fingertips," Martha Reeves and the Vandellas' "Heat Wave," Garnet Mims and the Enchanters' "Cry Baby," and the Chiffons' "He's So Fine" would be playing on the jukebox at Howards Cafe and at house parties the parents would sponsor.

However, none of the music could draw my attention away from that November, the week before Thanksgiving, when in Dallas, TX, President Kennedy was assassinated. A shroud of sadness covered America. I remember being in a band class when the principal's office intercom announcement interrupted Mr. Black's preparation for a concert band performance. A pall fell over the nation as details of the assassination were made public. The assassination of John F. Kennedy remains one of the few unmistakable signal events from the second half of the 20th century. More moments - some thrilling (the moon landing, the fall of the Berlin Wall), others horrifying (the assassinations of Martin Luther King, Jr. and Robert Kennedy, within two months of each other, and the *Challenger* explosion) - have secured their places in the history books and, even more indelibly, in the memories of those who witnessed them. But, nothing in the latter part of "the American century" defined an era as profoundly as the rifle shots that split the warm Dallas air on November 22, 1963 and the sudden death of the 46-year-old president. I recall some of my teachers openly grieving when the announcement of his death was made. I shall never forget the sound and tempo of the drum cadence the soldiers played as the flag draped casket was drawn down Pennsylvania Avenue.

A few weeks later, the nation would segue into the Christmas holiday season, but the sadness of the loss was unmistakable. The war in Vietnam and my effort to avoid becoming a casualty in conflict impacted a host of decisions as I was leaving OPHS. The Vietnamese conflict had its origins long before I was born and involved every presidential administration from FDR to LBJ, but most US presidents had avoided direct participation in the skirmish. The origins of US participation in the war began in August 1945 after Japan surrendered to the Allies. Ho Chi Minh then began to fight a variety of political factions for control of major enclaves. A few days after the Vietnamese "revolution," nationalist forces entered the north and, as previously planned by the allies, established an administration in the country as far south as the 16th parallel. There were other significant steps following the end of WWII; on September 26, 1945, Office of Strategic Services (OSS) officer Lieutenant Colonel A. Peter Dewey, who was working with the Viet Minh to repatriate Americans, was captured by the Japanese. Col. Dewey was mistaken for a Frenchman, shot, and killed by the Viet Minh. These actions were the forerunner of the Allies versus the Communists.

Fast forward to 1961, when the new administration of President John F. Kennedy remained essentially committed to the bipartisan, anti-communist foreign policies inherited from the administrations of Presidents Truman and Eisenhower. During 1961, his first year in office, Kennedy found himself faced with a three-part crisis: the failure of the Bay of Pigs Invasion in Cuba, the construction of the Berlin Wall by the Soviets, and a negotiated settlement between the pro-Western government of Laos and the Pathet Lao communist movement. Fearing that another failure on the part of the US to stop communist expansion would fatally damage US credibility with its allies, Kennedy decided that Southeast Asia would be the venue for fighting back. Following JFK, LBJ and Nixon would be burdened by the action in Southeast Asia. The 20-year war did not end until 1975. These external events resulted in the deaths of 2 million civilians on both sides and some 1.1 million North Vietnamese and Viet Cong fighters. The US military estimated that between 200,000 and 250,000 South Vietnamese soldiers died in the war. More than 58,000 Americans were killed. That is more than twice the size of my hometown, Laurel.

Although I had always intended to go to undergraduate school, the 1960s events in Southeast Asia spurred and enhanced my ambition to complete a college degree. Too many of my high school classmates and other OPHS graduates lost their lives in the jungles of Southeast Asia. When the US Congress passed the Gulf of Tonkin Resolution by the US Congress in 1964, it authorized LBJ to take any measures he believed were necessary to retaliate and to promote the maintenance of international peace and security in Southeast Asia.

In the meantime, my senior year at OPHS was coming to an end. The spring discussion at 115 Melon dinner table was whether I would accept a scholarship to attend Jackson State or choose some other institution. Mr. Black had recommended me for the scholarship, but many of my classmates, e.g., LeRoy, Alfred Williams, Sam Hudges, Rodney Rockette, John Moody, Anita Burnett, and Jerome Wyatt were interested in Tennessee State University. I was not interested in four years of playing in a college marching band. I was fortunate that my mother was supportive of my wishes; she completed an application for study at Tennessee State for me, and the rest is history.

My activities and responsibilities with the Hi-Y, concert and marching bands, my chores at 115, and my studies kept me busy. In the spring of my senior year, my brother Therman brought home his new bride, Ethel. We were all excited to see him and the pretty young lady that accompanied him. They were driving a new automobile, a Renault Dolphin, and to my delight, they would come to OPHS during class hours. During those times, it was not unusual for visitors to gain entry to the halls while class was in session. Their visit generated a vicarious experience. I imagined that, one day, I would have a beautiful bride to introduce to my friends and family. When my male classmates saw my sister-in-law, the "dog" in them caused howls that only a teenage male would utter.

Later in that spring was the occasion for the senior prom. This was the ultimate social event of the season. It was a celebration and declaration of adulthood. For some, it meant unfettered access to alcohol; over the years there had been automobile accidents that left some crippled for life. The majority of my male classmates were getting measured for formal white jackets while female classmates were planning for that gala dress that would highlight their God-given physicality. The prom was held in the school cafeteria; thus, there was an effort to decorate the room to complement our interpretation of an exotic night in some far-off place. Many of my male classmates would lobby for use of the automobile. I was no different. For weeks in advance of the date, I would find an opportunity to appeal to my dad to use the family car for that night.

My prom date, Nanette Wilson, was my girlfriend since my sophomore year. She celebrated my achievements, loved to talk on the telephone, and was studious, proud, and progressive. Her mother and father, like my mine, were "helicopter parents"; thus, we were chaperoned at every turn. There were few, if any movie dates; we relied on walks to and from school and being able to see each other during school events. During my junior year at OPHS, I had convinced my parents that I could be counted upon to be mindful in being a responsible teenager. My conduct demonstrated while worshipping at FBS must have been a crucial factor in their calculus. Frequently, I was a delegate to church conventions, active in Sunday school, and performing my chores. "Preaching Sundays" were on 2nd and 4th weeks; therefore, on 1st and 3rd Sundays, after attending 5:00-6:30 Baptist Training Union on those weeks, I could go to the Wilson household and "court" Nanette. Marvin and Girtha Wilson lived in the housing projects in Laurel, and their daughter and I would sit on the steps to the living room a few feet away from where Mrs. Wilson sat, out of sight but not out of hearing.

The 10 PM curfew imposed on me as a resident of 115 Melon required me to leave the Wilson household to make the fifteen-minute walk to my house. Thus, like clockwork, my walk home would begin shortly after 9:40 PM. Between my house and Nannette's was Howards Cafe and Taxi Stand, otherwise known as "the block" or "Howards Corner." The cafe sold hamburgers and sodas, and the jukebox would blare the latest R&B hits. On typical summer and fall weekends, boys and men would gather and brag about either their athletic prowess or sexual exploits. Few, if any girls would be among the patrons. Bobby "Blue"

Bland's "Cry, Cry, Cry" or "I Pity The fool," featuring trumpet, saxophone, and blues guitars with boss base sounds, would ring in my head long after I was out of earshot, having walked from Jefferson Street to Masonite Drive and, finally, to Melon Street.

Little did I know that during these weekend "dates," I was investing (building up) social capital with the Wilsons. The extent of my social capital was manifested in the extent to which they trusted me, and that trust was most important on prom night. While I had been able to get permission from my dad to use the family car for the prom, neither my dad nor I were aware that our late-model shiny Buick would encounter an engine shutdown. I was able to drive the car to Nanette's driveway, where it went dead. I was horrified and embarrassed. Mr. Wilson saw me from his bedroom window, and my anguish was undeniable. He came out and said to me, "drive my car." Disaster was averted, but it would be a longer time before my ego could return to its normal state.

A few weeks later was our graduation from OPHS. The week of May 24-28, OPHS conducted its 36th Commencement beginning with the commencement sermon. My class of 82 graduates processed into the auditorium under the sound of the concert band that Sunday morning. We had, as did all previous classes, developed a motto: "Knowledge Comes, but Wisdom Lingers." Reverend Paul Exkano, pastor of East Jerusalem Baptist, spoke to us and extolled the virtues of faith in a hostile world. On Thursday, May 28, we again processed into the OPHS while the concert band played Giacomo Meyerbeer's Coronation March. The regal sound was august and captured the tone of what we thought of ourselves. During such ceremonies, it was also customary for James Weldon Johnson and John Rosamond Johnson's "Lift Every Voice and Sing" to be sung in unison while all stood acknowledging the song, which was written in 1900 and came to be recognized as the Black National Anthem.

To be sure it was a somber occasion as we were prompted by Dr. C. C. Armstrong, an administrator and faculty member at Alcorn College, to understand the gravity of commencing; that completion of high school was the beginning rather than the end.

Most of those in 12A were college bound, with the majority choosing either Jackson State or Alcorn in Mississippi. Our valedictorian, Jerry Donaldson, was the recipient of the prestigious Masonite Scholarship and an additional scholarship to attend DePauw University in Greencastle, IN. In my judgement, it is remarkable that there was only one of us in the class of 1964 to apply for undergraduate study at a predominantly white institution. The rest of us applied to historically black colleges or universities (HBCUs). A sizable number of my classmates in homerooms 12B and 12C chose undergraduate study, and a significant portion elected military service.

Despite the commencement speakers' warning that high school completion should not signal the end, it was the end of childhood and adolescence, as well as the end of my relationship with my girlfriend, Nannette; 1964 was the last year I lived in Laurel. The rest of the summer I spent planning for and daydreaming about undergraduate study in Nashville, TN, a place I had driven through once or twice en route to Dayton, OH.

Leaving Laurel meant my parents had sent out all their children except my baby brother Wylie. They were approaching their sixties, living in a relatively new brick home with central heating and air, and experiencing grandparenthood that included 16 children living in both Laurel and Dayton, OH.

Leaving Laurel also meant I was leaving one style of Deep Southern segregation. From birth until the summer of 1964, I lived and became of age in the black community. There is an irony in the fact that the federal government had legislated public policies aimed at lifting US citizens from segregation and second-class citizenship. Before I was born, FDR's New Deal was intended to assist poor blacks as they strove to survive and feed their families; during my life, the US Supreme Court had even rendered a judgment in the 1954 *Brown v. Board of Education* case which outlawed segregation in education. When my class completed our high school education ten years after the decision, there was no indication from elected officials in Mississippi that they would comply. In fact, segregation of public education facilities in the state continued until 1972. When the class of OPHS graduated in 1964, Paul B. Johnson, Jr. was governor. As did all his predecessors, there was no inclination to provide fair and equal treatment to African-Americans. Johnson had, for a Southerner, a liberal early record. He supported Harry S. Truman for President in 1948 (Truman received just over 10% of the vote in Mississippi) and Adlai Stevenson in 1952. He ran for governor three times, in 1947, 1951, and 1955, but was unsuccessful.

In 1959, Johnson ran for lieutenant governor and won, serving under Governor Ross Barnet, who became a segregationist icon. Johnson played a prominent role in trying to prevent James Meredith from enrolling at Ole Miss in 1962, physically blocking (for the benefit of photographers) the federal marshals who were escorting the African-American veteran. The nature of the leadership of Johnson and his predecessors is, in large part, the explanation for persistent enforcement of Jim Crow laws in Mississippi. After his unsuccessful attempts to gain the state house, he ran for governor again in 1963. He defeated former governor James P. Coleman by tying his opponent to JFK's 1963 civil rights legislation. During the campaign, he asked voters to "stand tall with Paul" against those wanting to change Mississippi's "way of life," in reference to his confrontation with federal marshals at Ole Miss. But a change in culture was in the winds. The *Civil Rights Act of 1964* (Public Law 88-352, 78 Stat. 241) was enacted July 2, *1964*. That landmark *civil rights* and US labor *law* in the United States outlawed discrimination based on race, color, religion, sex, or national origin. The new public accommodations legislation was the reward for the persistence, fortitude, and bravery of the lunch counter and sit-in demonstrators that had paved the way. When the shift began in earnest, I was on my way out of Mississippi for the third time, but this trip was not a summer vacation.

As I was headed out of Laurel, I had many warm memories, and there would be many more to come. When my class of 1964 graduated, there would be only eight other commencements. The 1970 Oak Park High School commencement was the last one. OPHS became a "victim" of the 1954 US Supreme Court *Brown v. Board of Education* decision. The overarching theme in the plaintiff's brief was to overturn the "separate but equal" doctrine that their predecessors had endorsed in the Court's infamous 1896 *Plessy v. Ferguson* decision. The 1954 case was conceived in the 1930s by Charles Hamilton Houston, then Dean of Howard University Law School, who brilliantly executed a series of cases by his star pupil, Thurgood Marshall, over the next two decades. The US Supreme Court's decision in *Brown v. Board of Education* marked a turning point in the history of race relations in the United States. The high court's decision stripped away constitutional sanctions for segregation by race and made equal opportunity for education the law of the land. A great deal of irony accompanies justice. Once, there were African-American principals, teachers, coaches, and band directors employed in the Mississippi public schools, but the desegregation order resulted in black principals, coaches, and directors becoming assistants or getting relieved of their employment. White power, privilege, and colonial legacy, which had never gone out of existence, resurfaced in abundance as a result of the court's order. Its resurgence surprised only the naive. The bottom line is that OPHS became an elementary school, while Laurel High School absorbed that which was left from the decision.

Pursuant to these developments, the National Oak Park High School Alumni Association was formed in 1980. The overriding purpose was to host a schoolwide reunion to attract alumni and their families. A group of dedicated alumni established biennial reunions that coincided with Independence Day. A special initiative was organized to recognize Oak Park graduates that "have brought honor, prestige, and fame to the legacy of Oak Park High School." This initiative gave birth to National Oak Park High School Hall of Fame beginning with the reunion in 1992. The Hall of Fame has fourteen (14) categories: business, community service, civic/social, education, engineering/ technology, government, journalism, law, medicine/health, military, performing arts, religion, and sports.

In 2004, I was selected to become a member of the hall of fame in the area of education. To be sure, I was dumbfounded when the selection committee told me that I had been nominated and unanimously selected. At that point, I joined former teachers, opera diva Leontyne Price, and world-class Olympic member Ralph Boston. When I was inducted in July 2004, there were eight individuals: Dr. Mary L. Balthazar (education), class of 1954; Edward Collier (government), class of 1946; Clinton Collins (government), class of 1946; Dr. Armendia P. Dixon, a former teacher of mine who represented the class of 1956; Dr. Gerald Ellis (education), class of 1954; and Dr. Leander T Ellis, Jr. (medicine), class of 1946. These recipients had far more life and work experience than I. I have before then and since been on the receiving end of accolades, but being selected by my classmates for this honor brings smiles to my face years later.

Chapter X

BECOMING "JOE COLLEGE"

College days swiftly pass, imbued with memories fund, and the recollection slowly fades way (Simpson 1915).

The slang dictionary (1932) states that the phrase "Joe College" described a young man whose "dress and manner betokened the non-academic aspects of college life." I liked the simile as well as the sound of the alliteration of the phrase, but that is not what "Joe College" meant to me. The young men that were my freshman classmates looked forward primarily to the academic aspect of undergraduate study. However, to be sure, the non-academic aspects did have their attraction; such was unavoidable when there were so many pretty girls from all over the country who were our co-eds.

Traveling by Greyhound from Laurel to Nashville

It was early September when my parents drove me to the Greyhound bus terminal to purchase a ticket. The ticket agent, a white woman, stared at me with hatred in her eyes and her voice.

I was startled since I had never seen her prior to that Saturday evening. Her verbal and nonverbal behavior reflected the worst of race relations in Mississippi. I completed the transaction by paying for my ticket, and my parents and I went into the "colored" waiting room. The public accommodations act, Title II of the Civil Rights Act of 1964, designated public accommodations to include a limited number of facilities which are open to the public. Examples include hotels, motels, restaurants, theaters, and all other public accommodations engaged in interstate commerce (including the Laurel Greyhound Bus Terminal), exempting private clubs without defining the term "private." However, that recent law was not recognized in Mississippi.

My "sendoff crowd" was sparse, but in addition to my parents and my brother Wylie was Nanette and one of her sisters. I walked over to their car, where the radio was playing Curtis Mayfield's "Long, Long Winter." The soulful, mournful lyrics, sung the way only Curtis Mayfield and the Impressions could, were poignant and difficult to dismiss.

It‘s gonna be a long, long winter
For me, for me
A long, long winter for me
You see
To my surprise she‘s left me
And from her eyes I could see
That‘d it be a long, long winter, for me

It‘s gonna be cold, cold and dreary
Every day, oh yeah
But somehow, I don‘t feel, she wants it that way
Lord I hope I‘m right
For I can‘t stand these lonely nights
And it‘s a long, long winter for me

Now that she's gone
The nights are not dark at all
And now that's she's gone
The days are not all it seems
My girl is gone from me
And my heart's in misery
And it's a long, long winter for me, oh yeah

My girl is gone from me
And my heart's in misery
And it's a long, long winter for me, ooh ooh
A long, long winter for me, yeah yeah yeah yeah
A long long...

The sound reverberated in my head for the first few hours after our departure, but I was beginning to learn how to compartmentalize, and by the time the bus arrived in Birmingham, I was focusing again on what my freshman year would hold. In the days and weeks leading up to the Saturday evening departure, there had been cautious tales warning us to be careful when we would arrive in Birmingham. The warning was prophetic. Walking to the restroom, a man approached my TSU-bound classmates and me, claiming to be in need of some sort of assistance. He asked us to go outside to his car and said that he would pay us for our assistance. One of us remembered the prior warnings, and we resisted what we later surmised was a planned robbery.

Early on Sunday morning, we arrived at the Greyhound terminal in Nashville and were met by baggage transportation teams that chauffeured us to the campus for the first time. Prior to my arrival, I had been assigned to live in a new dormitory, Watson Hall, room 320. I had not given thought to room assignments requiring three students in a room, but fortunately, I arrived early enough to get the single bed by the door. By midday, my bags had arrived, and I could shower, change clothes, and find the cafeteria. Walking across campus, I came face-to-face with students from around the country. The "brain drain" had not yet materialized, so my freshman co-eds were among the best and brightest black students in the country who could not afford tuition costs at places such as Howard or Morehouse. Likewise, the "muscle drain" had not begun, so HBCUs like TSU attracted talented athletes.

Freshman week meant orientation, standing in long lines, and getting class enrollment cards, but the "eye candy" took away the drudgery of the waits. I had never before seen so many attractive black women in one place. Fortunately, when I graduated fours later, I had married one of those pretty girls. My cousin-brother LeRoy with whom I had begun elementary and graduated high school in Laurel experienced the scenery of the campus. It was during freshman orientation week that he met his future bride, Rebecca Stanley.

Tasting freedom and independence

Being a college man caused me to realize that my 10 PM curfews imposed by my parents, while living in Laurel, no longer existed. There was no one to grant permission where I went or when. The TSU campus always had plenty of local students; one such was Curtis Rutherford. His father was a professor, and Curtis had use of an automobile. Thus, on the second Saturday evening, Curtis gave us a tour of the campus and its surrounding area. The tour included night spots, such as the Wigwam, and other student hangouts that sold beer. While my life in Laurel had introduced me to beer, drinking it was a rarity, one that I never had the occasion to share with my parents. Being 18 years old meant we could buy beer, and buy we did! We drove to some location where we opened the beer and began to consume; before we could swallow, it became apparent that we had been profiled by a pair of local policemen. We learned that possession of an open container of any alcohol in a car was against the local law. The officers lectured us and released us to return to the campus. The experience was sufficient for me to keep my eyes on the prize, an undergraduate degree. In retrospect, we were fortunate; there were so many bright young men whose college life was aborted because of freedom, independence, and alcohol.

Freedom and independence also meant being referred to as "Mister". Professor Juanita Horner was my freshman English instructor, and she addressed her students as Mister or Miss. This was a sure sign that we were thought of as adults. My first week of class also caused me to come to grips with the fact of talented co-eds whose prowess surpassed my experiences at OPHS. LeRoy and I were in awe of college life; he would muse aloud about whether he was "college material" before and after his arrival at TSU. At the end of the first grading period, I had a C+ average. In high school, I never had a grade that was less than B! That end-of-term grade got my attention; this timely epiphany helped me to adjust to the academic side of college life. For the balance of my years as an undergraduate, reality kept coming with challenging academic assignments; however, I found my groove by the end of my freshman year. En route to the completion of the frosh year, we received some troubling news; shortly after returning from our Christmas holiday break, I received a telephone call from Mrs. Della Hodge, who told me of the passing of my Aunt Ella Mae, mother of LeRoy. It was my burden to tell LeRoy this sad news. We immediately boarded the Greyhound bus and left Nashville to return to Laurel. The announcement was a shock for me, and I know that it was a shock for LeRoy. There had been no warning of any illness of Aunt Ella Mae two weeks earlier, during our Christmas holiday visit. We rode through the night on what seemed like the longest journey ever, and fifteen hours later, we were back in Laurel. LeRoy and his father and siblings completed arrangements for a homegoing ceremony. To be sure, most homegoing ceremonies are wrenching, regardless of whether the occasion is a surprise or if it had been anticipated. The loss of a mother is especially painful. The Lucius Sampson family was especially close-knit. Thus, as I would later attend to the passing of my mother, I knew then in 1965 that Ella Mae Morgan's passing would cause pain that time barely heals. LeRoy returned to TSU via Uncle Abraham's new Buick. I returned a day or so earlier. I told Rebecca of the tragedy, and she promised to be mindful of what LeRoy was experiencing. When I lost my mother in 1992, I thought of what LeRoy and all his immediate family had gone through seventeen years earlier. There is no quick cure for grief; my late brother Therman likened grief to a long walk in the woods. The path is uncharted, but there is eventually a learning how to deal with the loss.

Worship services at TSU

Although parental supervision was not there to "police" my behavior, I maintained worship attendance. Professor James Simmons, who taught philosophy, was campus minister. The ecumenical service (like many of my new experiences) was a change from the Baptist worship to which I had been accustomed, yet it was serious and anchoring. During my senior year at TSU, I had come an assistant to the university minister, Dr. Simmons, and he saw "promise" in me, I guess, because I could help him by reading scripture and eventually delivering a sermon he had written. Sunday worship was a delight for me, in part because the services would be filled with pretty girls.

Moving to Dayton after my freshman year

The summer after the first year of undergraduate school was the real beginning of freedom and independence. At the end of my freshman year, I contacted my parents to get their permission to move to Dayton for the summer. There was no resistance; job opportunities in Dayton were far more plentiful than opportunities I would find in Laurel. I boarded a Greyhound bus and traveled to Dayton. The timing of my arrival could not have been more fruitful. On the day of my arrival, I was offered a job at Aunt Iola's laundry. I worked there for a week before my brother Plummer arranged for me to find work at Wright Patterson Air Force Base (WPAFB). Indiana University had been awarded a contract to assist the "man in space program." Research facilities at WPAFB attracted many major universities. There were work opportunities for college students in the laboratory where Plummer worked as chemist. I was one of two undergraduates that collected air samples from sacrificed animals that would be useful in gravity studies crucial to the astronauts as they traveled in space. The job paid $100 dollars per week, more than what my dad earned at Masonite. I was sitting on top of the world!

The move to Dayton became the confluence of several developments in my young life. My brothers were supportive of me in every way possible. I lived with my brother Clarence, Plummer led the effort to get me a research assistant job at WPAFB and transported me to work each day, and I ate meals at Jim's, Therman's, and Ezell's. There was also my uncle Abraham and his family, who opened their home to me. My aunt Iola was good to me, as was my aunt Annie Laura. All wished me well and ensured that I had few, if any, out-of-pocket expenses. The result was that I was able to save funds for my return to my sophomore year. When the time came for me to return to Nashville, my brothers bought clothes for me. This was the situation each summer between each of my undergraduate years.

When time came for my sophomore year, I returned to campus and found that because I had grown up in poverty, I was eligible for participation in the student work-study program. It had never occurred to me that I was disadvantaged while we lived in Mississippi; I knew that my father worked hard and was never fairly remunerated, but I had grown up in a two-parent household (although highly parochial/non-egalitarian) with a supportive set of schools, church, and community. As a point of fact, I had both my parents until I was 45 years old. My mother never worked outside the house, and my father and his brothers were adamant that their wives would not wash clothes for white families, as was the case in many other black households. As I became more aware of the import of the federal government in facilitating opportunities for advancement of underserved populations, coupled with the historical refusal of state governments to adopt some policies that would begin to erase the gap in quality of living, brought to my attention in living technicolor the impact of a culture of national complicity that overlooked second-class citizenship. I knew that the efforts of Dr. Martin Luther King, Jr., the Southern Non-violent Coordinating Council (SNCC), the Congress of Racial Equality (CORE), Stokely Carmichael, Rap Brown, and the Panthers answered the times that were calling for someone to step forward. In my sophomore year, I became more acutely attuned to the fact of a lifetime of marginalizing public policy. I did not feel I was personally entitled, but I began to understand how being one of the last of my siblings put me on a pathway to being the first to be able to graduate OPHS and complete an undergraduate degree in four years, a privilege that was not available to my brothers. I also became more acutely aware of the war in Vietnam and the resistance of many Americans against participating in the war in Vietnam.

The "socio-temporal" context was extremely challenging. On the one hand, LBJ was exhorting the Congress: "Unfortunately, many Americans live on the outskirts of hope, some because of their poverty, some because of their color, and all too many because of both. Our task is to help replace their despair with opportunity." What Congress subsequently passed was the program that afforded me an increased chance for completing my degree; thus, my reliance on my parents for financial support was almost eliminated. With that burden being lifted, I could devote time to "being in college" and taking advantage of opportunities for people of color in the USA. My academic performance was enhanced. I earned recognition on the academic dean's list every term in my sophomore, junior, and senior years. The flip side of the "socio-temporal" conundrum was the ever-increasing war in Vietnam. Nevertheless, at the end of my sophomore year, I returned to my summer job at WPAFB.

My first white mentor

In high school literature, I was assigned the essay "Civilization" by Ralph Waldo Emerson, which argued that a highly organized man, characterized by supreme delicacy of sentiment in practical power, religion, liberty, sense of honor, and taste, avoids conformity and false consistency and follows native instincts and ideas that live beneath the surface. Emerson argued that to accomplish anything of excellence, one must lean on a principle and borrow its omnipotence; thus, "hitch your wagon to a star" and avoid things that have little meaning. Instead, we must discipline ourselves and work rather for those interests which the divinities honor and promote - justice, love, freedom, knowledge, and utility. Most of us are not aware of our innate inclinations. It is at this stage of personal growth, whether it comes at age 20 or age 60, that we learn the value of a mentor. Mentors, through their expertise and enthusiasm for sharing that expertise, invested in what they felt I could become. In my life, I have been blessed to have a number of mentors that have helped me prepare, grow, find, and achieve closure. My mentors have been my parents, my brothers, and other men and women of many hues and ethnicities.

Summer, 1965 was the time I became aware of Dr. Raymond Murray, MD., M.A.C.P, who was principal investigator of a USDOD-funded research program at WPAFB. He was an inspiring and talented physician who graduated from Harvard Medical School in 1948 after serving in the Navy Medical Corps during World War II. A specialist in cardiology, Dr. Murray had worked in private practice in Grand Rapids, Michigan before moving to the Indiana University School of Medicine. There, he rose to become a tenured professor, chair of community health sciences, and director of the Krannert Institute for Cardiology. I met him when he hired me to work in his laboratory at WPAFB in the summer of 1965. He was my first, but not my only, white mentor. He chose to mentor me, being inquisitive of how I was fairing in undergraduate school. He was different from any white male I had encountered. His influence upon me caused me to distinguish between individuals and groups. Near the end of my senior year, he encouraged me to seek entry to graduate or law school. He prepared me for the graduate school interview process and even bought me a suit to wear when the interview was held. Dr. Murray was a gracious and cultured man, a good friend, a valued counselor, and a dedicated mentor. By my senior year, I had an opportunity to be commissioned to be an officer in the USAF; thus, my entry to graduate study was temporarily put aside.

After my graduating from TSU and accepting my commission as an officer in the Air Force, I learned that Dr. Murray passed away. He had contributed funds to establish an endowment which was devoted to further study for minority PhDs and MDs in physical and life sciences. Given Dr. Murray's generosity toward me, I was not surprised that his family would carry on his legacy after his passing.

Social science research uses the term "socio-temporal" to contextualize the importance of time and events in assessing a phenomenon. I use that lens to better understand myself and the events of the day while I was still an undergraduate. It was in the mid-1960s, a time when there was elevated consciousness about being black and within the diaspora in America. The elevation of consciousness preceded (if it was not a precursor to) that time when "colored" and "Negro" were thrown aside for "African-American" and, soon, "black." During that time of social upheaval, we were being proselytized about our blackness (or the absence of the characteristic in our daily lives); it was during that time when black people generally agreed that the white man's greatest power over blacks was that they control everything that blacks believe. Whites, many asserted, controlled our education, news, media, entertainment, and the image of "proper", i.e., what constitutes "acceptable," for black folks. Such a position of real dominance allows whites to inundate blacks with disinformation designed to instill the myth of white supremacy and black self-hatred into our minds. It allows a psychological warfare program that serves to protect white dominance. I took all these into consideration even when I was the recipient of Dr. Murray's benevolence. Because of the way he treated me and all that I had ever been accustomed to, I began in earnest to critically examine my life as a member of the human race that resided in the USA. That critical thinking and processing continues to this day. One of the stronger influences in my critical examination was the book *The Mis-Education of the Negro*, which was originally written as a dissertation by author Carter G. Woodson, who wanted to investigate the efficiency of the education structure for African-Americans. In substance, Carter Woodson produced a definitive and constructive critique of the educational system, with special reference to its blighting effects on Africans that came to USA as slaves, and the term he used, *mis-education*, was the most apt and descriptive word available. Now, however, this concept is loudly articulated by many voices of whites and blacks alike who challenge the system. The thesis of Dr. Woodson's book is that the blacks of his day were being culturally indoctrinated, rather than being educated in American schools. The most imperative and crucial element in Woodson's concept of *mis-education* hinged on the education system's failure to present authentic black (Negro, back then) history in schools and the bitter knowledge that there was a scarcity of literature available for such a purpose. Most history books gave little or no space to black man's presence in America. Some of them contained casual references to blacks, but these generally depicted them in menial, subordinate roles, more or less sub-human. Such books stressed their good fortune at having been exposed, through slavery, to the higher (white man's) civilization. There were derogatory statements included relating to the primitive, heathenish quality of the African background, but nothing denoting skills, abilities, contributions, or potential in the image of the blacks, whether in Africa or America. Woodson considered this state of affairs deplorable, an American tragedy, dooming the Negro to a brainwashed acceptance of the inferior role assigned to him by the dominant race and absorbed by him through his schooling. Moreover, the neglect of African-American history and the distortion of the facts concerning blacks in most history books deprived the black child knowledge of the significance of our race as a heritage, relegating us to nothingness and "nobodyness." This contradiction between the contending forces between the history of my people and my then present-day reality became a conundrum because of the way Ray Murray treated me. Such treatment stared into the reality of all that I had ever been accustomed to. I began in earnest to critically examine my life as a member of the human race who lived in the USA. Woodson did not support the once popular view that in matters of education, "Negroes" were subjected to the will of others on the presumption that such poor people are not large taxpayers and must be content with charitable contributions that uplift them. On the contrary, Woodson argued that the consumer pays the tax, and as such, every individual of the social order should be given unlimited opportunity to make the most of herself. Moreover, that opportunities for black advancement should not be determined by outside forces but should be determined by the makeup of the individual and what his environment requires of him.

As Woodson discusses throughout the book, every ethnic group brought their own strengths and characteristics, which helped the United States propel itself into a superpower. However, African-Americans will never be able to build upon their strengths if they are not made aware of it through education and will always fall behind as they react to conform to the styles of their white counterparts.

Woodson, Malcolm X, and Jamil Abdullah Al-Amin, in each of their own ways, favored truth over a lie, justice over injustice, and righteousness over the reward of evildoers. I came to a point in my development that the Dr. Murrays of the world were crucial to my advancement and for the advancement of many of my friends who were similarly situated. My experience fostered my empirical knowledge that many Americans are fair minded individuals despite a contradictory barrage of evidence.

In the fall of 1966, I returned to Nashville for the start of my junior year. My college job was to serve as a member of the TSU debate society. Participation on the debate team required the development of research skills, rigorous attention to detail, and the readiness to argue either side of a proposition. That experience, as much as any, prepared me for graduate school. As determined by the National Debate Tournament, the 1965-66 debate topic was *"resolved that the federal government should establish a national program of public work for the unemployed."* The challenge of exercise was to be able to convincingly argue either side. I came to appreciate opposing points of view, especially when I brought my prejudices on the front end. The ability to successfully argue either side of an issue required intensive preparation, especially where the competition was keen. Most of our competition came from institutions that had sponsored debate teams many more years than had TSU. Moreover, the competition almost always came from predominantly white universities, a situation that was a source of uneasiness on my team. The members of my TSU team had come from backgrounds with the prevalent notion that "white was *always* right." Thus, we had to overcome ideas that had been crucial to maintaining a mindset of intellectual inferiority. We came face-to-face with the verity of an observation of Dr. John Henrik Clarke (1915-1998), who stated, "to control a people, one must first control what they think about themselves and how they regard history and culture… when your conqueror makes you ashamed of your culture and history, there is no need for prison walls…" Thus, after some early drubbings during our novice rounds of debate, team members James Montgomery, Lewis Myers, Dorothy Williams, and I studied the outcomes of debates against David Lipscomb College, Lambeth College, and East Tennessee State. We strategized based on what we had observed in preparing for case presentation, rebuttal, etc. Successively, we were getting better prepared for our next debate practice sessions and actual contests. We agreed that Professor Troy Jones, our faculty advisor, focused on our diction, but was not as effective at focusing on nuance and other subtle tactics we had experienced. Montgomery, who later became a practicing attorney, was my debate partner. Lewis Meyers also became an accomplished attorney. Montgomery and I went on to defeat Jackson State, Tougaloo, and Yale University. The team won six victories in the Intercollegiate Forensic Association that year. Most important was gaining a sense of self-worth while learning critical thinking skills. All the team completed the undergraduate degree and earned commissions as officers in the USAF, while most us went on to either graduate or law school.

The ignored elephants in 1968

Despite our accomplishments in academic non-curricular outings and in our individual studies, there were two undeniable externalities. One of them had to do with the future of TSU as a historically black university. On May 15, 1968, Rita Sanders Geier became the named plaintiff in a well-publicized lawsuit brought against the University of Tennessee on behalf of "current and future students" of Tennessee State University by her attorney, George Barrett. The case of *Geier v. University of Tennessee* continued for nearly 40 years, and it would ultimately transform public education in Middle Tennessee. The lawsuit represented a seminal event that flew just beneath the radar in the spring of 1968, one month before I graduated TSU. The outcome of this litigation would become the bane of my existence in the decades that lay before me. Geier, then Rita Sanders, had graduated from Fisk University and earned a master's degree in history at the University of Chicago before joining the TSU faculty in the late 1960s. "I had just returned from the University of Chicago, so I was idealistic in my view of what college education should be," she recalls. "Tennessee State was suffering from decades of benign neglect, and it offered a stark, negative, and different picture. The physical plant was terrible, the curriculum stagnant and inadequate to offer a real quality education. The technical programs were either missing or weak." Geier also "discovered" that faculty salaries were significantly lower in comparison to other state-supported institutions of higher learning. "In fact, the whole funding base for the school was less than at the other comparable state universities," she said. "The UT system received the lion's share of state funding, and there was no participation by any black school in that system."

Geier's critique had merit, but it was difficult to absorb the argument that we had somehow been miseducated. However, there were "holes" that needed attending in our curriculum and in the terminal-degree faculty who taught the courses. While I was an undergraduate majoring in political science, my student colleagues and I were taught by several Vanderbilt graduate students and law students since resources were insufficient to hire full-time faculty at TSU. At that point, political science was a unit in the History, Political Science, and Geography Department. During my senior year, fellow students began to ask for a separate department for Political Science, but for many black students at TSU, the effort to bring about a change "got in the way" of their educational goals. Moreover, many black faculty members had acquiesced and become inured; they had mortgages and family responsibilities; they were not energized for facilitating such a change in the social and political order. We had been down so long that the bottom looked like up. To be sure, speaking out about injustice positions one in an onerous position.

The lawsuit featured a "David v. Goliath" contest that challenged the culture of the educational delivery system in Tennessee. The University of Tennessee was the unchallenged flagship institution, and efforts to change that situation would not eventuate until after a social and political tsunami.

The opening argument in the litigation (filed by both black and white plaintiffs) was to enjoin the proposed construction and expansion of the University of Tennessee-Nashville Center. The plaintiffs alleged, *inter alia,* that Tennessee Agricultural and Industrial State University, now Tennessee State University (hereinafter referred to as TSU), was originally established under state statute[2] as a state public higher education institution for the education of blacks, for which the statute was prima facie evidence of racial discrimination, that TSU was being maintained by state officials as a segregated black institution contrary to the Fourteenth Amendment to the Constitution of the United States, that appropriations for TSU were not provided on a basis equal to those of the State's predominantly white institutions, and that the new construction and expansion of the predominantly white University of Tennessee-Nashville Extension Center would serve to perpetuate TSU, also located in Nashville, as a segregated black institution which would ensure the continued existence of a dual system of public higher education in Tennessee. Based on the foregoing reasons, and others, the plaintiffs requested that the state be enjoined from expanding the Nashville Extension Center, from providing unequal educational facilities, and from maintaining racially segregated institutions of higher education in Nashville. The matter remained in the courts for decades. The lawsuit challenged the culture of the educational delivery system in Tennessee. Ironically, TSU, the Goliath figure in the litigation, became the public whipping boy through taunts and letters to the local newspaper decrying the change.

The other elephant was the same that had caused consternation as I was graduating from OPHS in 1964: the war in Vietnam. US involvement resulted in the draft of many high school and college classmates, too many of whom did not survive the war. At the beginning of 1966, the number of US military personnel in South Vietnam totaled 184,314. South Vietnamese military forces totaled 514,000 including the army (ARVN) and the Regional Force and Popular Force (the "Ruff-Puffs") militias. The North Vietnamese Army (PAVN) numbered 400,000, mostly still in North Vietnam; 50,000 North Vietnamese cadre and soldiers infiltrated South Vietnam during 1965. The war was criticized roundly on college campuses; antiwar demonstrators would chant, "hey, hey, LBJ, how many have you killed today?" Walter Cronkite, CBS news anchor, would provide daily casualty reports at 6PM. In 1968, there were 16,592 killed and 87,388 wounded. Cronkite would also read stories of the Ho Chi Minh trail, an elaborate system of mountain and jungle paths and trails used by North Vietnam to infiltrate troops and supplies into South Vietnam, Cambodia, and Laos during the Vietnam War. Many Americans became victims of the trail. All told, there were more than 58,000 American casualties, a number which was two times greater than the population of my hometown. My brothers Plummer and Therman advised me to join the Reserve Officers Training Commission (ROTC) while in undergraduate school to ensure I would not get drafted. I followed their advice; the result was a commission as an officer in the US Air Force and uninterrupted time to complete my undergraduate work. Subsequently, my service obligation did not begin until after my degree had been conferred. In fact, I did not travel to Southeast Asia until I had been awarded a Fulbright to teach a graduate governance course at Khon Kaen University in Thailand in 2012, more than forty years later. During my Fulbright assignment, I traveled to Laos and Cambodia, and during my travels, I observed the groves of thick banana trees and other foliage that hid the North Vietnamese during the war. My 2012 observations triggered my childhood tapes, replaying the decades-old conversations with my brothers, in particular Plummer and Therman, who were also US military veterans, both of whom had their undergraduate work interrupted by a stint in the Armed Forces. Both not only completed their respective undergraduate degrees but also went on to complete graduate work.

My tumultuous and eventful senior year of undergraduate study began in the fall of 1967. In August, we buried my first cousin Jerry, son of Uncle Abraham. Jerry was just 21 years old, and when he succumbed to cancer, our family was distraught. Jerry, LeRoy (son of Lucius), and I were born the same year, and we had become best friends; our comradery reflected the relationship between my father, Uncle Lucius, and Uncle Abraham. Jerry was Abraham's first-born son. His passing was not a surprise, but it was definitely not welcome. So, my early fall pathway in the fall was covered by a cloud of sadness. The routine of class, debating, and participating in the student council, where I chaired the student judicial committee, kept me busy. The anti-war fervor on campus had become so intense that ROTC cadets were advised to change to civilian clothes after the cadet class was completed. Thus, I would run from the field house where the ROTC classes were held to my dormitory, Watson Residence Hall. Our experiences in Nashville were not isolated. There were worldwide protests, beginning early in 1968, characterized by an escalation of social conflicts, these predominantly being popular rebellions against military and bureaucratic elites, who responded with an escalation of political repression. In the USA, these protests marked a turning point for the Civil Rights Movement and produced revolutionary movements like the Black Panther

Party. In reaction to the Tet Offensive, protests also sparked a broad movement in opposition to the Vietnam War all over the United States, and even over in London, Paris, Berlin, and Rome. Mass socialistic movements grew not only in the United States but also in most European countries. On campus, the ROTC building was firebombed, and some students were organizing strikes and shutdowns of administration buildings. The cry that was heard across campus: "On strike, shut it down!"

By the end of the first semester of my senior year, the Christmas holiday provided a reprieve. I traveled to my hometown to share the holiday with my parents. At that time, Wylie was the only one living full-time with my parents. The improved quality of the physical life was unmistakable.

Dad and mother had just built a new house at 115 Melon in my junior year of high school. This time, there were no hogs to feed or cows to milk. I always enjoyed my siblings, especially at Christmas, but this time, I was able to distance myself from the revolution and prepare for my final semester at Tennessee State University. So, in early January, I boarded the Greyhound bus and returned to Nashville.

The Sigma Rho Sigma gathering, meeting Joy and completing my Bachelor of Art (A.B.) degree

Amid the cacophony of my senior year at TSU, I began to seriously consider a life beyond undergraduate school. Professors were constantly finding opportunities and urging that we take advantage of them. It was during this time I found myself at a gathering of the Sigma Rho Sigma Honor Society for the Social Sciences; during that occasion, I met the woman whom I would marry. At least a semester before that fall meeting in 1967, I would see her in a crowd of students as classes were changing. TSU had a bevy of very attractive women, but Joy stood out among them. She was a junior majoring in sociology. Her physical attraction was only part of her countenance; she was an articulate, self-assured, and outstanding intellect. I would soon come to know why I had become transfixed as I would see her walking across campus nattily dressed before we were introduced. The fact of our interest in the social sciences meant that we would have long conversations about the evils of the world and our personal responsibility for making things better. The sound of revolution was in the air in my personal life and in the social fabric of the Western world. There would be protests in France, in which students joined up with wildcat strikes of up to 10 million workers. For a few days, the movement seemed capable of overthrowing the government. In Northern Ireland, Mexico City, and Brazil, there were protests, dictatorships, state repression, and colonization. In the socialist countries, there were also protests against lack of freedom of speech and violation of other civil rights by the Communist bureaucratic and military elites. In Central and Eastern Europe, there were widespread protests that escalated, particularly in the Prague Spring in Czechoslovakia, in Warsaw (Poland), and in Yugoslavia.

As form follows function, the arts and entertainment world began to give expressions that complemented the times. James Radno, Gerome Ragni, and Galt MacDermont produced the Broadway musical "Hair." *Hair* was a product of the hippie counterculture and the sexual revolution of the late 1960s. Several of its songs became anthems of the anti-Vietnam War peace movement. The musical's profanity, its depiction of the use of illegal drugs, its treatment of sexuality, its irreverence for the American flag, and its nude scenes caused much comment and controversy. The musical broke new ground in musical theater by defining the genre of "rock musical," using a racially integrated cast, and inviting the audience onstage for a "Be-In" finale.

Hair tells the story of the "tribe," a group of politically active, long-haired hippies of the Age of Aquarius" living a bohemian life in New York City and fighting against draft into the Vietnam War.

While the mainstream media focused largely on the hippie lifestyle and the new social revolution, simultaneously, there had been building up in the black community the "Black Power Movement." Outer manifestation was the long natural hair worn by both men and women; the "afro" had come of age. Miniskirts, bell-bottom trousers, and platform shoes replaced the more conservative garb on campus. Stokely Carmichael, H. Rap Brown a.k.a. Jamil Abdullah Al-Amin, Huey Newton, Eldredge Cleaver, Bobby Seal, and like-minded "liberators" countered MLK's non-violent approach to freedom. As we began forcibly "taking" our liberation, we encountered inimical forces of racism and hatred. There was a culmination on the night of April 4, 1968 when Dr. Martin Luther King, Jr., was assassinated in Memphis. With this round of events, we got fed up.

Just after 6 PM on April 4, 1968, Dr. King was fatally shot while standing on the balcony outside his second-story room at the Lorraine Motel in Memphis, Tennessee. The civil rights leader was in Memphis to support a sanitation workers' strike and was on his way to dinner when a bullet struck him in the jaw and severed his spinal cord. King was pronounced dead after his arrival at a Memphis hospital. He was 39 years old.

In the months before his assassination, Martin Luther King became increasingly concerned with the problem of economic inequality in America. He organized a poor people's campaign to focus on the issue, including an interracial poor people's march in Washington, and in March 1968, he traveled to Memphis in support of poorly treated African-American sanitation workers. On March 28, a workers' protest march led by King ended in violence and the death of an African-American teenager. King left the city but vowed to return in early April to lead another demonstration.

On April 3, back in Memphis, King gave his last sermon, saying: "We've got some difficult days ahead, but it really doesn't matter with me now because I've been to the mountaintop… And He's allowed me to go up to the mountain. And I've looked over, and I've seen the Promised Land. I may not get there with you. But I want you to know tonight that we, as a people, will get to the promised land."

One day after speaking those words, Dr. King was shot and killed by James Earl Ray. As word of the assassination spread, riots broke out in cities all across the United States, and National Guard troops were deployed in Memphis and Nashville. Within a few hours, our dormitory was surrounded by National Guards who swept every floor; the residents had done no wrong, but the state took precautionary steps. My roommate, James Woodall, was an avid photographer, and while we were obeying the troopers who demanded that we sit on the hallway floor, Woody began his photographing. A trooper saw the flashes of the camera; simultaneously, Woody saw the trooper, took the undeveloped film out, and gave it to me, knowing the law enforcement group would confiscate his camera. NEED PHOTO FROM THAT EVENT

On April 9, King was laid to rest in his hometown of Atlanta, Georgia. Tens of thousands of people lined the streets to pay tribute to King's casket as it passed by in a wooden farm cart drawn by two mules. Once again, a drum major for freedom had been silenced. Two months later, the nation would again lose a freedom fighter. Four days before the TSU commencement, June 5, 1968, Robert F. Kennedy was assassinated in Los Angeles after he had just won a crucial victory in the California Democratic primary. He was gunned down by a 22-year-old Palestinian militant named Sirhan Sirhan. The killer later said he murdered Kennedy because he believed the senator played a key role in oppressing the Palestinian people. Senator Kennedy lay immobile for several agonizing minutes, his blood staining the floor in a horrendous image captured by news photographers and transmitted around the world.

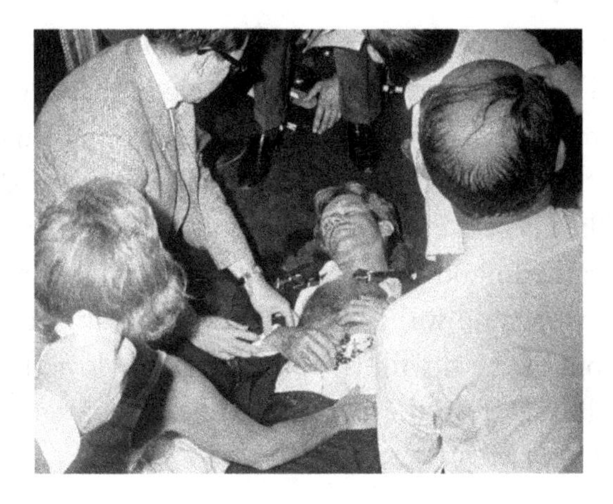

It is an understatement to state that 1968 was a traumatic year. The United States suffered a national nervous breakdown. MLK and RFK were two men committed to change within the system that were killed for their effort. The two killings seemed to make a compelling argument to many that the peaceful path was a dead end and that the resort to violence was now acceptable. Violence had become a toxic and permanent virus infecting American society; something had gone profoundly wrong, and that the road to peaceful change had become blocked by madmen, evildoers, and fanatics. Optimism plummeted.

Such turbulence required a refuge. My refuge was my budding relationship with Joy. During the entire final term at TSU, our primary attention was focused on each other. In the late spring of my senior year, the annual dinner-dance featuring the ROTC meant dressing in formal wear and demonstrating our best behaviors. I was proud to be seen with Joy at that event, and we enjoyed each other's company at other events. We would find places for picnics, watch movies, and go to concerts. Recalling those days brings to memory some of the lyrics of the record "Groovin," as the title tells it all. We were grooving on sunny afternoons, and we really couldn't get away too soon from the classroom and other mundane events then. We couldn't imagine anything that was better; the world was ours whenever we were together. There were always things we could see; we realized that if we kept spending sunny days that way, we would talk and laugh our time away. I felt it coming closer day by day. Soon, life would be endless ecstasy for Joy and me. Those moments in time, we walked hand in hand across campus, dreaming of the time when we would walk right up to the sun. I pledged to pull the moon out of the sky for the promise of her love; I pledged to take the rainbow from the sky, and if one was not good enough, I promised her two.

Fulfillingness' first finale

Soon, it was Sunday, June 9, 1968, commencement day. Plummer and Therman brought their wives to join in the celebration, and of course, I then introduced my girlfriend. The days of being "Joe College" were coming to an end. During commencement, I was commissioned a 2nd lieutenant in the USAF in addition to earning my baccalaureate degree. Four years had come and gone in a flash. A week later, I was on a Greyhound bus en route to Laurel. I was excited that I would be able to visit my parents, particularly since my mother had to have a surgical procedure that prevented her from attending my graduation ceremony. I was attired in Air Force dress blue with my bronze officer bars on my shoulders; the shoes were shined and glossy. I felt a sense of accomplishment upon my return. Four years earlier, I was a high school senior with promise, and now I had a degree, a commission, and a girlfriend. My parents and my brother Wylie were proud. That sentiment would carry me through the summer as I awaited the date of my active duty.

Because of my impending service date, permanent employment was elusive. My summer job at WPAFB in Dr. Murray's laboratory became available, and I was assigned to a facility in Pittsburgh for about a month. Soon, I "discovered" the limitations of public transportation, and I wanted personal transportation. I raised the concern with my father, and he advanced me funds sufficient for a down payment. A few weeks later, I strolled into Jim Reed Chevrolet in Nashville and drove off the lot in a new 1968 Chevy Malibu. This was my first car, and I adored its seafrost-green color with a black roof.

Lieutenant Sampson reporting for duty

My initial active-duty assignment was at Keesler AFB in Biloxi, MS, which is 100 miles from Laurel.

The assignment required eight weeks attendance in preparation for administrative officer training. The curriculum concerned itself with managing an administrative unit within a headquarters section in the US Air Force. I had never managed anyone previously since I was fresh out of college and inexperienced about the ways of life in general. Nevertheless, I did not spend a single weekend at Keesler; on alternative weekends, I would drive home to visit dad and mother and to Nashville to see Joy. The trip from Biloxi to Nashville was lengthy and tiring, but I somehow seemed oblivious to the strain. As the eight-week assignment drew to a close, I was faced with reporting to Nellis AFB in Las Vegas, my permanent duty assignment. During weekends in Nashville and days in Biloxi, I began to visit jewelry stores in search of an engagement ring; I had never asked Joy to marry me, but I believed that since we were in love with each other, she would not disappoint me. Thus, in early October, I made reservations for dinner at the Embers in Printers Alley, a fashionable restaurant in downtown Nashville. It was on this occasion that I proposed amidst a candlelit dinner. I took the box holding the rings, opened them, and asked, "will you marry me?" Joy rapidly said yes, and we placed the engagement ring on her finger. I remembered that when I first met her, I looked for a ring on her left hand, and there was none.

The next months were colored with exhilaration and anxiety. My reporting date to Nellis AFB was fast approaching; I packed all my belongings in the trunk and back seat of my new Malibu and began the two-night three-day drive to the desert. Oklahoma City and Albuquerque were my stops before the arrival in Las Vegas. There was nothing remarkable about OKC, but arriving in Albuquerque after a twelve-hour drive, I came upon the most magnificent sunset. On the third day, I drove upon Hoover Dam, just outside of Henderson, Nevada and the Arizona border. I had never seen such an impressive manmade structure. Hoover Dam was originally known as Boulder Dam between 1933 to 1947; it was officially renamed Hoover Dam by a joint resolution of Congress. It is a concrete arch gravity dam in the Black Canyon of the Colorado River. It was constructed between 1931 and 1936 during the Great Depression and was dedicated on September 30, 1935 by President Franklin D. Roosevelt. Its construction was the result of a massive effort involving thousands of workers, and it cost over one hundred lives. The dam was named after President Herbert Hoover. It impounds Lake Mead, the largest reservoir in the United States by volume (when it is full).

Traffic around the dam was congested (I have driven through the dam several times in the past forty years, and traffic has always been congested). An hour after driving across the dam, I found myself driving on North Main Street in the city of sin. The days of "Joe College" were truly past, and I was on my own. When I checked in the office of my commander, Colonel Arthur Schultz, I saluted and stated, "Lieutenant Sampson, reporting for duty, Sir" (as I had learned the protocol while a cadet in undergraduate school, where I became commissioned on my graduation day, June 9, 1968). Colonel Schultz responded (barked), "you are late, Lieutenant; you were to be here a week ago!" Schultz was a gruff, no-nonsense senior officer. I had misunderstood my orders and taken a delay en route after leaving Keesler Air Force Base. The delay (one week) meant that I reported to duty a week late. I did not know that my new commander had to authorize the request. Thus, my first day got off to a rough start. The encounter with Colonel Schultz became a signal to pay attention to detail in all I read and did. "Joe College" days slipped further into the past. Yet, I learned from Colonel Schultz, and I am delighted to report that he grew to respect and appreciate my work. By 1971, Schultz had retired, but he was asked by the placement office at UNLV to provide a confidential on me. Colonel Schultz provided me a copy of his report for the University of Nevada's evaluation of me. I was frankly astonished. Arthur Schultz's confidential recommendation of September 30, 1971 went:

"Charles Sampson exhibits a normally neat appearance. He has a pleasing personality, reticent upon initial contact. Insofar as my personal knowledge of this young man is concerned, his character is unimpeachable; he is a hardworking and adaptable to most situations. His scholarship is evidenced by the time he has invested in his education, having earned his master's degree during his off-duty hours while under my command. Charles Sampson was assigned as my administrative and executive officer under my direct supervision for a period of two (2) years. His adaptability was demonstrated when as a young, inexperienced officer, he made the transition from a school environment to a large military organization.

Responsibilities were many and demanding, being charged with the responsibility of consolidated administrative section serving a large industrial complex and the supervision of eight (8) secretaries and clerks. Smooth integration and handling of large quantities of correspondence reportsand support documentation, and last but of most vital importance, the raining of subordinates, were handled in a professional matter.

The administrative section for this organization handled an average of 13,000 transactions monthly, and in fact, this organization received recognition after having no discrepancies, which attests to this young man's abilities. Some of his duties include security, which entailed obtaining background and medical clearance on 1,300 assigned personnel, and planning and publishing security measures to respond to thereafter, sabotage, and espionage threats. He is well versed in personnel management procedure and has demonstrated the strength to offer his personnel where needed by his subordinates and to terminate employment when this became necessary.

I would be most pleased to have this man in my employ, should the occasion arise in the future."

Such was Colonel Schutz's appraisal of me and my efforts in the Field Maintenance Squadron at Nellis AFB. It was more gratifying than any of the biannual officer evaluations I received while he was on active duty. Upon Schultz's retirement, Colonel Roy Kephart became my commanding officer. Colonel Kephart was very supportive of my career in the military. Soon, he began to rely on me to write for his written and oral presentations. He would take me with him when he needed to get his flying time done. As I sat in the navigator's seat on the plane, there would only be he and I. He was in command when I was promoted to captain.

My job was to be administrative officer for the 57th Field Maintenance Squadron (57FMS); the squadron's mission was to repair aircraft, and there were 1,100 enlisted men and eight officers assigned to the unit. We were supporting the war in Vietnam by keeping the F-15 jets in a ready state to contribute to the mission some 7,700 miles and 21 hours away.

Bachelor life in Las Vegas

When I arrived in Las Vegas in the fall (October) of 1968, it was the farthest west I had ever traveled from Laurel, MS. I drove for three nights and two days before arriving in Las Vegas. My first stop was Oklahoma City, the second day consisted of another eight-hour effort of driving far more than half the day across Texas before finding lodging in Albuquerque, NM. On the third day, I arrived in Las Vegas, a city that was only 58 years old. The desert metropolis was built on gambling, vice, and other forms of entertainment. When it attained just over a century of existence (it was incorporated in 1911), it had drawn millions of visitors and trillions of dollars in wealth to southern Nevada. In the early 1970s, the weather in Las Vegas would be either a large part of its appeal or the reason for not wanting to live there, depending on the time of the year. The city is located in the desert and in a valley. There was almost no humidity; thus, the dry heat that plagued the city turned out to be much more tolerable than the Southern and Midwest humid conditions I had been accustomed to all my life.

My mission was to successfully complete my active duty commitment, which required dedication and talent. While adjusting to the military routine in Nevada, my mind was still in Nashville. Joy and I would exchange letters several times a week, and we spent a fortune on long-distance telephone calls. The gist of my letters declared that "if I had a dime for every time I dreamed about her, I would be a wealthy man..." I declared that there was a spark of magic in her eyes, that Heaven appeared each time she smiled. "I never thought that fairy tales came true, but they come true when I´m near you. You´re a genie in disguise, full of wonder and surprise. You´re the one that I´ve been waiting for; forever and ever will my love for you keep growing strong. If I could, I´d catch a falling star to shine on you, so I´ll know where you are; order rainbows in your favorite shade to show I love you, thinking of you... Write your name across the sky; anything you ask I´ll try."

The city was founded by ranchers and railroad workers, but it quickly found that its greatest asset was not its springs but its casinos. Las Vegas' embrace of Old West-style freedoms - gambling and prostitution - provided a perfect home for East Coast organized crime. Beginning in the 1940s, money from drugs and racketeering built casinos and was laundered within them. Visitors came to partake in what the casinos offered: low-cost luxury and the thrill of fantasies fulfilled.

From the early 1900s, Nevada was known as a place where unhappy couples could get a relatively quick divorce. Las Vegas embraced the concept of an even quicker marriage, with no blood tests or waiting periods. The Strip's first wedding chapel, the Little Church of the West, opened in 1942.

As the 20th century came to a close, the San Pedro, Los Angeles, and Salt Lake railroads arrived in Las Vegas, connecting the city with the Pacific and the country's main rail networks. Nevada outlawed gambling in 1910, but the practice continued in speakeasies and illicit casinos. By the time gambling was legalized again in 1931, organized crime already had roots in the city.

In 1931, construction began on the massive Boulder Dam (later renamed the Hoover Dam), drawing thousands of workers to a site just east of the city. Casinos and showgirl venues opened up on Fremont Street, the town's sole paved road, to attract the project's workers. When the dam was completed in 1936, cheap hydroelectricity powered the flashing signs of Fremont's "Glitter Gulch."

Shortly after the completion of the Hoover Dam began the development of the famous Strip. In 1941, the El Rancho Vegas resort opened on a section of US-91 just outside the city's jurisdiction. Other hotel-casinos soon followed, and the section of highway became known as "the Strip." Most were built around the regional or Old West themes that were popular on Fremont Street. In 1946, mobster Bugsy Siegal, backed by East Coast Jewish gangster Meyer Lansky's Mexican drug money, opened the Flamingo, a swank resort that took its cues from Hollywood.

Siegel was murdered in 1947, but his vision for Las Vegas lived on: During the 1950s and 1960s, mobsters helped build the Sahara, the Sands, the New Frontier, and the Riviera. Money from organized crime combined with funds from more respectable investors - Wall Street banks, union pension funds, the Mormon Church, and the Princeton University endowment. Tourists flocked to the resorts - 8 million a year by 1954 - drawn by performers such as Frank Sinatra, Dean Martin, and Elvis Presley, and by rows of slot machines and gaming tables.

From the 1940s onward, Las Vegas enjoyed a military boom as World War II bases gave way to the Cold War, the state of political hostility between countries in the then Soviet bloc countries and the US-led Western powers from 1945 to 1990. These cold war hostilities were manifested in the activities surrounding the Nevada Test Site, where over 100 nuclear bombs were detonated above ground between 1951 and 1963. Mushroom clouds were often visible from the hotels on the Strip, and postcards proclaimed Las Vegas the "Up and Atom City." There was little evidence of that past when I arrived in the late-1960s, although there was evidence signifying distrust between the Russia and the United States. My arrival preceded the impact of Howard Hughes, whose fortunes ushered in an era in which mob interests were displaced by corporate conglomerates.

In the late 1960s when I arrived, food and entertainment were inexpensive. There was no state or local income tax; sales tax on grocery was about 3%. The low-cost dining and readily available amusement were the perfect ingredients for a young man from the South. Upon arrival in the city and on the base, I began to understand the lyrics to a song we would hear my senior year at TSU. Tony Clark popularized "The Entertainer," written by Billy Joel. It was the story of an entertainer who had been forced to perform even as he experienced a broken heart. While I was not an entertainer, I related to what I believe was the nuance of the song, being isolated and having no social capital from which to draw sustenance. For me, it was absence of meaningful social capital which would allay my concerns about being isolated and alone. Having been in an environment where I could see many people who looked like me, and then finding myself in a military organization in which I was the only black officer among the eleven in the squadron, and about 10% were black in a group of 1500 enlisted men, the reality of "minoritism," a situation in which a relatively small group of people, especially one commonly discriminated against in a community, society, or nation, differed from others in race, religion, language, or political persuasion. Growing up in a racially segregated society had meant that the unknown yet acknowledged comfort of similarity was a key element of social comfort. My singularity was made even more acute when I was faced with the task of finding a roommate. Fortunately, there were two junior officers, Doug Smith from Purdue and Dave Rowe from Nebraska, seeking a person to occupy the third bedroom of their apartment. These young officers were easy to live with. When I joined them, their monthly rental costs were significantly reduced. We discussed social and political issues in a fashion which reflected a progressive view of life in America. For six months, I would travel to and from the base and frequently to the Strip and downtown Las Vegas for entertainment. Perhaps because I did not activate my worship services, I rarely came into contact with other African-Americans. Yet, I soon discovered that black people lived in Las Vegas; the near west side contained a variety of cottage industries that were similar to those which I had experienced in the South as a child. West Las Vegas bore the signs of Jim Crow and separate and unequal lifestyles. There were separate facilities for commercial activity, including hotels, motels, and restaurants, in the Las Vegas Valley. The Moulin Rouge Hotel had opened on May 24, 1955, built at a cost of $3.5 million. It was the first integrated hotel casino in the United States. Until that time, almost all the casinos on the Strip were totally segregated - off limits to blacks unless they were the entertainment or in the hired labor force.

The Moulin Rouge Hotel was in West Las Vegas, where the black population lived. West Las Vegas was bounded by Washington Avenue on the north, Bonanza Road on the south, H Street on the west, and A Street on the east. The establishment was the epitome of eye-catching, with 110 rooms, a gorgeous showroom, swimming pool, restaurant/coffee shop, dress-shop, and bar, which was constructed of highly polished and expensive hardwoods. However, in the early 1960s, Las Vegas began to make progress in the area of public accommodations and relaxation of segregation laws. Gradually, this signaled the end of the success of the Moulin Rouge, but other cottage industries such as barber and beauty, churches, soul food restaurants, funeral homes, etc., that catered to blacks continued to flourish.

After my daily duties at Nellis AFB, I would drive around the town of North Las Vegas; thus began my discovery of the "side," but the novelty of the discovery soon wore off. Growing up in the South and living in the Midwest had accustomed me to middle-class blacks and their social and political aspirations, but that same aspirational characteristic was not as evident in Las Vegas. In the midst of this epiphany, I was still a lonely bachelor spending hundreds of dollars each month for telephone calls to Nashville, TN. Each night, Joy and I talked; the internet did not exist, so texting was out. We did exchange long letters every week too. When she accepted my marriage proposal, we did not set a date. In our minds at that time, we both felt that she should complete her undergraduate work before getting married.

Placing our marriage in perspective, we considered her parents and their willingness to welcome a new son-in-law. Thus, during the 1968 Christmas holiday season, Joy invited me to visit her and meet her family. The trip back to the South began with a flight to Dayton, OH. The delay en route offered an opportunity to visit my family. While there, Plummer, Jr. agreed to lend me his car to drive from Dayton to Huntsville, AL. The road trip began as I was adjusting to the wears of the cross-country flight from Nevada. The drive to Huntsville was 12 hours. When I arrived in Huntsville, my body was stressed and fatigued. However, when one is young and in love, stress and fatigue could be quickly overcome. Thus, attired in my Air Force dress blue, I knocked on her door at about 6 PM. My heart was pounding with anxiety; it was just a few minutes, but it seemed a lifetime. But there she stood, and we melted in each other's arms. I was ushered to the living room, and her mother and father were introduced. My heart raced as I looked around the warm and inviting house. Inside my mind, I believed that a man, a strong man, should always look dignified and calm, that any expression of anxiety was an expression of weaknesses. Moreover, I believed that a strong man would not be nervous, but confident in who he was, calm, and balanced. But, reality as I interpreted it was that my travel across the country was, in effect, an "interview" to demonstrate to the Pulleys that I was sincere and capable of supporting their daughter. Fortunately, in February 2019, we celebrated fifty years of marriage.

Marriage decision

In one of our nightly phone calls after returning to Las Vegas from Christmas holiday, 1968, I suggested to Joy that we marry before her June graduation day. It was like she was reading my thoughts, and she readily agreed. I put into motion leave time for mid-February; we made arrangements for blood tests and settled on going to the Justice of Peace in Franklin, TN, a town outside of Davidson County (Nashville) about fifteen miles away.

Over the years, I would come to know that the traditional patriarchal model of families in the USA positioned the male as provider and the female as homemaker. Given the protests for gender equality, I knew the traditional model was in need of repair, or at least, was in need of adjustment regarding its place in the household of which we were dreaming. At the time when we were graduating from college, the country was in the midst of a cultural shift: egalitarianism was the new moniker. My childhood tapes featured the traditional model of male as material provider and female as homemaker. Egalitarianism or equalitarianism is that school of thought that prioritizes equality for all people. In our undergraduate social science studies coupled with the real-world impact of the Civil Rights Movement and the Women's Movement, it maintains that all humans either should "get the same or be treated the same" in some respect, such as social status and political, economic, and civil rights. Joy and I advocated removal of economic inequalities among people, economic egalitarianism, and decentralization. We signed our first Christmas card with the line "liberation in our time."

Yet, it would be years later before I fully embraced the reality of this philosophy. My epiphany was that food and shelter were not the only things needed in a household. Self-actualization and esteem, the commodities that are key to a healthy relationship, were not something that I consciously sought to develop in our household, nor was I observant enough to reflect on how to foster its development. During the days of my parents and Joy's parents, it was not expected that a woman would be just as prepared to support herself; men brought home the "bacon." Self-actualization and esteem did find a place in both households, but they came in spite of the absence of conscious concern for their evolution. In only a minority of black families prior to the 1960s were there demonstrations of the importance of the liberation of the woman. In the mid-1940s before either Joy or I were born, six in ten African-American women were household servants who often worked 12-hour days for substandard wages. Most blacks lived in the South and on land as laborers and sharecroppers (only one in eight owned the land on which he worked). Around 5% of black men were engaged in nonmanual, white collar jobs. Moreover, segregation in the South and discrimination in the North fostered creation of a sheltered market for some black businesses (cottage industries, funeral homes, beauty parlors, barbers, etc.,) that served the black community and simultaneously barred the black residents from having to patronize "white" establishments. But, the number was small, and that environment fostered the non-egalitarianism in the black community. I reflect on courses in undergraduate psychology that first introduced the importance and role of self-esteem in individual development; that experience proved to be significant as I managed to find a pathway to navigate through this epiphany. To be sure, I owe a lot to my undergraduate education.

From the time that Joy and I set up our household, she held a professional job, and we instantly became a two-car family since our work locations were in separate parts of the city of Las Vegas. Among most of my friends and colleagues, the traditional model was not elevated. We were revolting against custom. Yet, it was a challenge to return home between sophomore and junior years and have conversations about the importance of the elevation of black women in society. I was still growing, and in one conversation with my mother about the need for social change in the black community, I used the phrase "you people"; this was a mistake because my language suggested that, somehow, I was superior and looked down on my home training. Of course, that was not my intent. My mother and I discussed politics, social relations, religion, etc., and such polemical conversations did continue as she showed me how my use of language got in the way of my message. This was as important as Professor Pearl Dansby's psychology course.

Chapter XI

MEETING THE REST OF THE PULLEY FAMILY

In June 1969, Joy and I returned to Nashville. When she was awarded her undergraduate degree, her parents, aunts and uncles, siblings, family friends, and cousins were there. I had met her parents and some of her siblings when I visited them shortly after Joy and I were engaged. The gathering to celebrate Joy's bachelor's degree attainment was a stark contrast for me since my family seemed to gather in mass only for funerals.

That occasion brought together many of my wife's extended family relatives. Most of her nine siblings were joined by their uncle, Leander Patton, finance vice-president at Alabama A&M University, and his wife Eliza Patton (Joy's paternal aunt), who was a professor at the same university. Most of Joy's siblings had completed their undergraduate work at A&M. All in all, the Pulleys personified hard work and rewards of accomplishment. The head of the family was her father, John L. Pulley. His wife and my mother-in-law, Lula Butler, was an attractive woman who helped John raise their eight daughters and two sons that made up the family in 1969.

Early on in our marriage, I came to see what I thought were several significant similarities between our paternal backgrounds. My father was the undisputed head of our family while my mother was his attractive mate who assisted him in raising a group of seven sons and one daughter. Both men were skilled in agriculture and only a year or so separated in their birth years. Both families encouraged higher education, although the head of those households did not complete college. Both families were strong Christians, and the fathers were active as either a deacon in the Baptist Church (my father) or a trustee in the Methodist Church (my father-in-law). Both were married to the women who mothered their children and had lengthy marriages; my parents were married 65 years before the death of my mother, and the Pulleys celebrated 75 years of marriage before the death of the husband broke the circle. Even our placement in the chain of offspring was similar: we were both born in the fourth quartile of children. Joy's mother birthed children for twenty-five years, while my mother birthed children for twenty-one years. That is where the similarities come to a halt.

John L. Pulley was the autocrat of the breakfast, dinner, and supper tables at the farmhouse on Dan Crutcher Road. Most of his and Lula's children had been born on that farm that consisted of hundreds of acres of crops. During one of my visits to the Pulley family after Joy and I had been married for about 7 years, Father Pulley and I would go walking along Dan Crutcher Road that ran past the house. For about four miles or so on either side of the road, he pointed out the massive acreage that he and his older brother Issac had farmed for decades. Between the two, there was in excess of 500 acres. Decades later, the agriculture production would be replaced by creating a housing area, Pulley Acres.

Joy and her siblings would bring their families home yearly, and we would gather around the dining room table for meals fit for kings. The head of the table was the reserve of Mr. Pulley, and when there were other sons-in-law visiting, he would ensure the order of seating reflected seniority among his sons-in-law. The table was the place for discussing and solving the political and social affairs of the known world. As I observed the occasion, my mind would go back to college literature, where the class had discussed Oliver Wendel Homes. In Holmes' book "Autocrat of the Breakfast Table," the author is quoted as saying, "every now and then, a man's mind is stretched by a new idea or sensation and never shrinks back to its former dimensions." While the words of Holmes and Pulley were not the same, the nuance was similar. The days when family were seated around the dinner table were memorable and spirited. Truly, goodwill was the monarch of the house, and cordiality enabled civil discourse… this is not to suggest that there was unanimous agreement about the current-day concern, what with the social revolution in the streets, the Vietnam War, flower power, long hair, and the hippies. Opinions ranged from conservative right-winged debunking of the black power movement to declarations of, "I am not black, I am brown, hasn't anyone noticed?" Those of us left wingers in the group who celebrated bell bottom trousers and afro-style hair-dos knew that when the real revolution came, some of us would catch it on television with chicken hanging from our mouths, but we would know that it was revolution because there would be no commercials. Some of us loved Stokely Carmichael and Rap Brown, but expressions of support for the cause soon gave way to dessert. Discussion of the "impending revolution" would have to wait until the next holiday.

Christmas was the grandest holiday, and it was expected that an annual visit would be made to "home." On the grand holidays, uncles, aunts, cousins, and family friends brought mirth to the household. For some of Joy's sister's husbands, the trip to northern Alabama and the fact of its open-ended expectation were considered a bit of a burden, particularly when all of us had young children and since the sons-in-law also had parents and families that lived hundreds of miles away from northern Alabama. But, the unspoken edict was that the main place to visit during the holiday was that farmhouse on Dan Crutcher Road where the daughters had grown up. There were many redeeming values for the visits; at the top of the list was the grandparenting from John and Lula. My son and my daughter knew they were treasured; each visit brought their grandmother's breakfast with fried apples. There were always gifts on Christmas.

Through this experience, I developed an appreciation for family tradition of uniting whenever possible. Mr. Pulley was one of ten children born to middle-class parents, James and Odelia Issac. James had honed his skills in agriculture, and Odelia studied at Fisk University, earned an undergraduate degree, and became a teacher at a time when blacks (then referred to as coloreds) did not ordinarily gain higher education. Their social class was due in no small measure to the land they owned. Landownership meant they were not sharecroppers, as was the plight of most Southern coloreds of that day. Odelia Issac was known for her refinement, a characteristic that has been practiced by her many of her granddaughters. In 1978, John and Lula celebrated their 50th wedding anniversary. The daughters had orchestrated a joyous celebration. Among Joy's sisters, there was a special bond. They loved their parents and their own developing families. Over the years, I have grown to love Joy's sisters since each one has always treated me with the highest regard, even when I did not deserve such accord.

Following the deaths of John Pulley in 2003 and Lula Pulley in 2008, the children and their cousins continue to gather for family reunions. Plans for the occasion are usually taken with great care; committees that have the responsibility for site selection, tours, and entertainment are formed. A family directory was developed and updated annually. The reunions have become movable feasts, weekends of rekindling with relatives biannually in places such as Chicago, IL; Washington, DC; Nashville, TN; Louisville KY; Atlanta, GA; and Birmingham and Huntsville, AL. The guiding force behind the movable feasts was an effort to ensure that subsequent generations would know the family members that had passed on. The biannual event brings to life the lyrics of Kenneth Gamble and Leon Huff's song as recorded by the O'Jays in 1975, *Family Reunion*:

"It's so nice to see
All the folks you love together
Sitting and talking 'bout
All the things that's been goin' down
It's been a long, long time

Since we had a chance to get together
Nobody knows the next time we see each other
Maybe years and years from now
Family reunion (Got to have)
A family reunion
Family reunion
(It's so nice to come together) To come together
(To get together)
I wish grandma could see
The whole family
I sure miss her face
And her warm and tender embrace
And if grandpa was here
I know he'd be smiling for me a tear
To see what he has done
All the offspring from his daughters and sons..."

Chapter XII

POST-BACCALAUREATE LIFE, MARRIAGE, AND THE USAF

After returning from Joy's commencement celebration in June 1969, our homemaking efforts stepped up. We had seen older siblings establish their homes. However, we were situated at least 1,800 miles from Nashville or Dayton. Neither of us had a dowry. I had placed all my belongings in the trunk of my 1968 Malibu in October 1968. When Joy joined me, I was living in a furnished apartment at 2601 Stewart Street, and we remained there for about three months. Then, we moved to 5044 Turner Street. Because it was unfurnished, we had to establish credit, but we both had solid jobs. We purchased living room and bedroom furniture. Important to me was setting up a room that included a stereo phonic system. Shortly after my initial arrival in Las Vegas, I had become acquainted with DJ Bob Joyce, who had one of the best jazz radio shows since Danny Owens WVOL and Sunday jazz in Nashville. Both Owens and Joyce would feature in big bands such as Quincy Jones, Gerald Wilson, Count Basie, and Neal Hefti; the voices of Joe Williams; the quintets of Jazz

Crusaders, Cannonball Adderley, Miles Davis, Horace Silver, Les McCann, and Lee Morgan, and later, the group Chicago. Between my brother Ezell and college friends at TSU, I acquired a small collection. Infused with the jazz was a great deal of beautiful sounds such as the Delfonics, Blue Magi, ChiLites, the Stylistics, and the Dramatics. Thus, that meant I would "have" to have a studio where I could relax and listen. Our second bedroom became that studio. These sounds coupled with live music on the Strip, meaning we were living an extended honeymoon.

A typical day would see us leave home around 7 AM when I would drive toward Sunrise Mountain, which overshadowed the Las Vegas Valley, en route to Nellis AFB. Joy would drive herself to Clark County Social Services, where she was employed as a social worker. Clark County, Nevada's social service department provided a variety of services for needy residents of Clark County who are not assisted by other state, federal, or local programs. The end of the workday was the best time. I would tune in to Bob Joyce's jazz show for the twenty-minute travel time between our apartment and the Air Force base. There were few times when we did not have 12 hours of sunshine. The sun was always brighter on the West Coast, and the temperatures were far hotter than any we had ever experienced. Rain was rare. From time to time, we would have dust storms that would block visibility for hours. That was a time I had never previously imagined but in my senior adult years of reflection, and as such, I wish we had taken Paul Simon's suggestion:

> "Slow down, you move too fast
> You got to make the morning last
> Just kicking down the cobblestones
> Looking for fun and feeling groovy
> Ba da-da da-da da-da, feeling groovy

Hello lamppost, what'cha knowin'
I've come to watch your flowers growin'
Ain't you got no rhymes for me?
Doo-ait-n-doo-doo, feeling groovy
Ba da-da da-da da-da, feeling groovy
I got no deeds to do, no promises to keep
I'm dappled and drowsy and ready to sleep
Let the morning time drop all its petals on me
Life, I love you, all is groovy"

Our social life was binary; there were other recent college graduates we discovered, and there were a few military folks who would become lifetime friends. Upon moving to 5044 Turner Street from 2601 East Stewart Street, I learned that a childhood friend from the days of Sunday school at Friendship Church and classmate from Oak Park High School was also recently married, and he and his wife were residing in an adjoining apartment. Otis Perkins and I played in the streets of Laurel, completed Oak Park High School together, and went our separate ways, he to Grambling State University and I to Tennessee State University. But, four years after college, there we were. Otis is a friend I cherish. He and Dorothy Jean Dickerson met on the campus of Grambling. It was ironic that we lived in the same apartment complex for nearly a year before discovering our new similarities. Otis was everybody's friend; through him, we came to meet several other recent college graduates that had taken up residence in Las Vegas. They became the joyous, laughing people whose acquaintance generates wonderful memories decades later. When we grew bored of the routine in Las Vegas, we would travel to Los Angeles. I specifically recall a trip to Disneyland in the spring of 1971, listening to the West Coast group "War" on the eight-track tape.

"Music is what we like to play
Yeah, yeah
All day, all day, all day, all day, all day
To soothe your soul, yeah
Down at the beach or a party in town
Making love or just lying around
To soothe your mind, yeah
Music is what we like to play, yeah yeah
All day, all day, all day, all day, all day
To soothe your soul, yeah
Let's have a picnic, go to the park
Rolling in the grass till long after dark
To soothe your mind, yeah
Down at the beach y'all partying down
Making love or just lying around
Let's have a picnic, go to the park
Rolling in the grass till long after dark
Down at the beach y'all partying down
Making love or just lying around
Let's have a picnic, go to the park
Rolling in the grass till long after dark
Down at the beach y'all partying down"

War's recording of the album "All Day Music" was the epitome of funk, a music genre that originated in African-American communities in the mid-1960s when African-American musicians created a new rhythmic danceable form of music through a mixture of soul music, jazz, and rhythm and blues (R&B). Funk de-emphasizes melody and chord progressions and focuses on a strong rhythmic groove of a bass line played by an electric bassist and a drum part played by a drummer. Like much of African-inspired music, funk typically consists of a complex groove with rhythm instruments playing interlocking grooves. Funk uses the same richly colored extended chords found in bebop jazz.

During my introduction to Las Vegas and West Coast Jazz and R&B, I met Lowrey Warren. Lowrey was a few years my senior and had moved to Las Vegas after completing his undergraduate degree in Texas. He was a good companion, and an even better friend and jazz aficionado. Lowrey was a professional social worker employed at a facility in Clark County. I recall weekend evenings when he would correct my misapprehension about what artist had written what song or lyric. Most vivid in my recollection was his correction about who had written the hit single "Natural Woman." I argued strenuously that Aretha Franklin had to have written the song because of the way she performed the song. The next weekend, Lowrey brought to our dialogue the talent and artistry of Carole King. *Tapestry* is the second studio album by the American singer-songwriter Carole King, released in 1971 on Ode Records and produced by Lou Sadler. It is one of the best-selling albums of all time, with over 25 million copies sold worldwide. In the United States, it rose to diamond status in the Recording Industry Association of America, with more than 10 million copies sold. It was Lowrey had introduced me to the four Grammy Awards in 1972, when *Tapestry* was voted album of the year. The lead singles from the album - "It's too Late" and "I Feel the Earth Move" - spent five weeks at #1 on both the *Billboard Hot 100* and *Easy Listening* charts. In 2003, *Tapestry* was ranked #36 on *Rolling Stone* list of the 500 greatest albums of all time. King wrote or co-wrote all of the songs on the album, several of which had already been hits for other artists, such as The Shirelles' "Will You Love Me Tomorrow" (in 1960). Despite becoming aware of Carole King's accomplishments, I still thought (then and now) that Aretha Franklin, the Queen of Soul, had no equal despite having heard Nancy Wilson (How Glad I Am, Happy Talk, Guess Who I Saw Today), Dionne Warwick, (Walk On By, You'll Never Get to Heaven if You Break My Heart) and the Chantels (Maybe), and later on, Anita Baker (Fairy Tales, Coloring Book) and any recording by Chaka Khan, Mary Wells, etc. Of course, music tastes are personal; they reflect the culture to which one has become accustomed, as well as social class. Lowrey Warren and I would spend Saturday and Sunday evenings listening to and critiquing these and other recording artists.

Our social circle was not limited to Otis and Dorothy; Lowrey and his fiancee, Clonnie Gay, an aristocratic, polished young woman whose family had moved from Arkansas in 1946 and made Las Vegas their home, rounded out our social associates. Clonnie's dad, Jimmy Gay, was one of the few Las Vegas blacks that worked the floors of the gambling casino as a pit boss. In Fordyce, Arkansas, he was a mortician. In the early 1950s, Mr. Gay was a black hotel executive at a time when blacks - including his longtime friends Sammy Davis, Jr., Nat King Cole, and Billy Eckstine - were not allowed to stay in Las Vegas Strip hotels. Clonnie's dad was not just a pioneer black civic leader, but he had risen to the upper reaches of the social establishment well before I moved to Las Vegas. Clonnie and Lowrey were long-time residents of the Las Vegas Valley; they represented the black establishment, whereas our other social friends, Otis Perkins and his bride (Grambling State) and Thomas and Ouida Brown (Alcorn State), were immediately out of undergraduate school. There was also Richard and Amanda Wicker. Wicker was a bit older; he rose to the rank of chief master sergeant. In my active duty days at Nellis, he was the only black CMS I ever knew. He had come into the military prior to the Vietnam War as an enlistee from Detroit. I came to know that Wicker's rank, CMS for short, is the ninth and highest enlisted rank in the US Air Force, just above senior master sergeant (SMS), and is a senior non-commissioned officer rank. The official term is "Chief Master Sergeant" or "Chief." Attaining the rank of chief master sergeant is the pinnacle of an Air Force enlisted person's career. Some chief master sergeants manage the efforts of all enlisted personnel within their unit or major subsection, while others run major staff functions at higher headquarters levels. All chief master sergeants are expected to serve as mentors for non-commissioned officers and junior enlisted members and as advisors to unit commanders and senior officers. By federal law, roughly 1% of the Air Force enlisted force may hold the rank of chief master sergeant. CMS Wicker was respected by all members of the Field Maintenance Squadron, not just because he occupied a position that few in the service would ever obtain, but because he was gracious and approachable, and he never allowed his rank to be a barrier to friendship and mentorship. He always regarded me as an officer and worked behind the scene to ensure I, a young officer, would achieve the respect that a young lieutenant, soon to be captain, should be granted. Wicker was a surrogate big brother; he graduated high school about the same time as my older brothers did. After leaving the military, Joy and I would return to Las Vegas and, during those visits, hook up with Richard and Amanda. When Wicker retired from the military, he became a successful automobile salesman and sold us a new 1972 Chevy Vega.

In the meantime, active duty life in the US Air Force continued. Three years on active duty, along with strong Officer Efficiency Reports (OER), meant I was eligible for promotion to captain. At that point, Colonel Kephart was my commander, and he had no reservation or equivocation about my consideration for a promotion. I was proud to be Captain Sampson!

Separating from the USAF and moving across the country

In the early springtime of 1972, Joy and I got down to the nitty-gritty of separating from the US Armed Services. Life in the desert for us as newlyweds was fast coming to a close, and now, we turned the page. We considered applying for civilian jobs. The prospect of not having to endure the hot sun in the desert and returning to civilian life loomed large. I applied for the city management program in Phoenix, and much to my surprise three weeks later, I received an offer. Because of my federal experience as a US Air Force officer, I also considered work as a civil service employee and applied for a position at the China Lake, the Californian naval weapons center. I was offered GS-9 appointment; however, we would have to live in China Lake, which was much smaller than Las Vegas. It offered little opportunity for non-work life. That being said, LeRoy and Rebecca had made a life for themselves at the naval weapons center, Nevertheless, we continued to seek positions east of the desert.

LeRoy and Becky lived about three hours away from Las Vegas near Ridgecrest, California, a town in Kern County. It is located along US Route 395 in the Indian Wells Valley in northeastern Kern County, adjacent to the Naval Air Weapons Station *China Lake* (NAWS, or *China Lake*). People who lived in Ridgecrest would travel to Los Angeles, San Diego, and Las Vegas for an urban experience. Otherwise, they had to settle for bowling or racing in the desert three-wheeled vehicles known as dune buggies. The dune buggy is a recreational vehicle with large, wide tires that are typically designed for use on beaches or sand dunes. The design is usually a roofless vehicle with a rear-mounted engine. Whereas dune buggies usually have open chassis, they are often modified from an existing vehicle. Many desert residents developed the hobby of building them, and then racing across the desert. Those who were familiar with cooler weather were not enamored with dune buggy racing, so interest in other recreational pursuits took hold. LeRoy's work colleagues became aware of his Southern background, as well as his nonchalance about desert life. An acquaintance of LeRoy's told him that an oasis existed in the desert despite overwhelming contrary evidence. LeRoy told Joy and I about the claim of his work colleague and convinced us to join them on weekend travel to Inyokern, California to find that oasis in the desert. Consistent with my testosterone and my rough, yet-to-be-tamed youth, I considered myself to have a good sense of humor. My misdirected sense of my skill to be a stand-up comedian fantasized that upon hearing about the oasis in the desert, I would develop a funny story. I generated a fantasy that when we would have made our way across the desert terrain, we would unearth treasures including the discovery of a 3,000-year-old mummy who died of heart failure. We would then report our findings to a natural history museum, and the museum curator would eventually say "you were right about the mummy's age and cause of death; how did you guys know?" I then imagined that I would chime in in my juvenile fashion and say, "easy, there was a piece of paper in his hand that said 'Ten thousand shekels on Goliath.'" I quickly came to my senses because the reality of the heat was undeniable, and my story was not funny. The desolate, hot, dusty days were never a condition that we embraced, and the reality was that LeRoy's colleague's story about an oasis turned out to be a hoax! The "oasis" was an outdoor toilet covered by a tent. We felt foolish that we fell for the story of a place in the hot sun that would bring waterfalls, green grass, etc. During our stay in the Nevada desert, monsoon storms would bring a wicked combination of high winds, thunder, lightning, walls of dust, and sometimes, heavy rain and hail to the area. The dust storm, called a haboob, limited visibility in the area and disrupted travel conditions. Winds of up to 40 mph (64.37 kph) with gusts up to 50 mph (80 kph) would accompany a wall of dust. That was reality!

Nevertheless, during our visits to the Valley, we had experiences and memories of the challenge of living in the hot desert and travels to Los Angeles, San Diego, and San Francisco for non-gaming entertainment. We always enjoyed spending time with LeRoy and Becky, and the search for the "oasis" paled in comparison to the wonderful times when we traveled to the San Francisco, Disney Land, Hollywood, Beverley Hills, and football games at the Colosseum.

In the spring of 1972, I took advantage of an "early out" and began the process of designing my commission as an officer in the USAF. My separation date would have been in August 1972. However, since President Nixon's declaration of Vietnamizing the Vietnam war, I could separate from the services with an honorable discharge war. So, we prepared to move from Las Vegas to Pittsburgh, PA. Our lives would never be the same again. The four years in Vegas with steady jobs and income, trips to Southern California, Lake Tahoe, and the San Francisco Bay Area, and explorations of the southwest's desert would soon become a thing of the past.

We had accumulated household furniture and goods. When I moved to Las Vegas in the fall of 1968, I was able to place all my worldly belongings on the back seat and trunk of my 1968 Malibu. Joy's belongings consisted of a trunk of clothes and a few boxes. In the spring of 1972, we had to contact a moving company to transport our materials across the country. The fear of transitioning to lives as graduate students and an otherwise unknown future was contemplated, but we were bold enough and

(I think in retrospect) wise. Neither of us had the promise of a job; we had a few bills, and the cost of finding new lodging had to be acknowledged. Sometimes, I think we were foolish to take this chance. Several of our Las Vegas friends questioned why we would give up employment and related security to pursue graduate education. Our decision to leave the promise of a bright future in Las Vegas was our road not taken. We had come to a fork in the path in the woods of our life. Choices such as the choice in Frost's "The Road Not Taken" are linked to the future and would likely change our life. Leaving Las Vegas meant lost opportunities as our choice took us into a future that we had not a scintilla of what the outcome would be.

Chapter XIII

GRADUATE SCHOOL AND PARENTHOOD

My motivation for pursuing the PhD was due in no small part to the professors with whom I had become acquainted and whose influence fostered a new dream beginning with my undergraduate and continuing through my first graduate degree, and my doctoral education. When I left Laurel to attend Tennessee State University in pursuit of the baccalaureate, I had never heard of the PhD; the only doctor title that I was acquainted with was the medical degree. In Laurel, we had two black physicians, Dr. Nave and Dr. Barnes. Upon enrolling at TSU and pursuing a degree in political science, I became acquainted with Dr. George Davis, my major advisor who had studied and earned his degree at the University of Pittsburgh. Several of my other history and political science professors held the terminal degree, and those who did not were enrolled in programs where they pursued them on a part-time basis. Eventually, I became familiar with what a PhD meant, and upon enrolling at University of Nevada for the master's degree, all my professors had the earned doctorate. I became fascinated with their command of a body of knowledge and their place in the academic and professional community, as well as their lifestyle, their work dress, their travels to foreign countries, etc.

As I noted earlier in this memoir, when I was in undergraduate school, I had learned the worth of a strong study ethic, and in my final semester at TSU, due in part to encouragement from a variety of TSU professors, my brothers Plummer and Therman, Dr. Ray Murray, and a number of others, I made applications and subsequently began to receive offers of attending graduate school and law school. I was particularly fascinated with earning a law degree. Among the offers for post-baccalaureate study was the University of Mississippi Law School. However, that was not to be since I had an obligation to join the US Armed Forces as an officer after completing the undergraduate degree. Yet, the idea of studying at Ole Miss, where James Meredith had to be escorted by the National Guard to enter class, captured my fancy for several weeks. Six years earlier, on October 1, 1962, after federal troops took control, Meredith became the first African-American student to enroll at the University of Mississippi. Meredith's admission is regarded as a pivotal moment in the history of civil rights in the United States.

My motivation for pursuit of the Doctor of Philosophy degree was a general desire to equip myself for engagement in four enterprises normally engaged in by those in academia. Political scientist Charles S. Hyneman had stated them in in his book, *The Study of Politics* (University of Illinois Press, 1959). The enterprises are the freedom to:

Carry on scholarly study and pass on the fruits of that study in writings and teachings;

Give advice on current issues of public policy and participate in the formation and execution of public policy;

Train men and women for the public service; and

Carry on activities in foreign countries directed toward the education and training of people and improvement of government and political parties.

More specifically, I aimed to specialize in the area of urban affairs. At the time of my application in the early 1970s, I was becoming keenly aware of the fact that one of the greatest challenges facing America at that time was the plight of American cities. Cities, then and now, have been subject to continuous growth, at an ever increasing pace, of the poorer, lower social and economic classes, the underprivileged, and in the 1970s, a robust number of militant freedom fighters. 11 million people migrated from rural areas to urban areas between 1870 and 1920, and a majority of the 25 million immigrants who came to the US in these years moved into the nation's cities.

By 1920, more Americans lived in cities than in rural areas for the first time in US history.

My assumption in the 1970s, and now in the 2000s, is that our government and private enterprises can solve urban problems connected with education, employment, and housing. The essential ingredient for a massive concerted and energetic effort is creative leadership and a sense of seriousness and urgency in reordering our national priorities.

I felt, then and now, that the completion of rigorous intellectual exercises involved in pursuit of the doctorate is the surest attainment of an inalienable education. Education designates something one becomes; training designates something we put to use. It was this backdrop that contextualized my application to graduate schools at Pitt, Vanderbilt, and the University of California. Each of my applications was successful; however, the reply from Pitt revealed an offer of the R.K. Mellon fellowship and a graduate assistantship. Between the two and my GI bill benefits, we could have revenue streams that would keep us afloat.

One of the attractions to Pitt was the fact that I had been assigned to work there in the few weeks after my graduation from TSU, when Dr. Murray agreed to find work for me during the couple of months before I had to report to active duty. A more compelling attraction was the fact that Joy's oldest sister, Ann, and her family lived in Pittsburgh; thus, we thought we would have family in the vicinity. However, upon arriving in Pittsburgh in August, we learned that Ann's husband, who was a Methodist Church minister, had been assigned to a church in Phoenix, Arizona.

After a week or so of searching for an apartment, we found a housing facility named West Gate Village. West Gate was a federally subsidized housing facility located in the Fairywood neighborhood of the Pittsburgh West End, near McKees Rock, PA. The village was a working-class neighborhood and had rental rates that us two "dreamers" could afford. During our search for housing, we explored apartment complexes that were more in line with what we had had in Vegas. But, we had little choice and limited funds. The reality of living elementary, high school, and college in a village brought to meaning Frost's *Fork in the Road*. Our neighbors were very friendly; nearly all of the men boasted of the time they had been incarcerated, and they were proud to overcome the problems of being a black man in America. The style in which they expressed their blackness was foreign to me. As I learned to know them, I also came to see what street life had taught many young black men, such street teachings that were not in the textbooks used in elementary school, high school, undergraduate school, or my first graduate studies. W. Somerset Maugham reminds us there are two good things in life - freedom of thought and freedom of action. My thoughts and actions bolstered by the providence of God had led us to this living place in the West End of Pittsburgh. Our surrounding living conditions, i.e., life in a working-class black community above the Mason-Dixon line, was not what my dad had expected when he visited us in 1970, and upon seeing where we were living, he asked, "this is the projects, ain't it?" For a second, I was a bit embarrassed, but in the back of my mind, my eye was on the prize. The housing project is the place where several of my friends lived while in Laurel. My sister Mazie had lived in the project. Fortunately, I knew West Gate Village was a means to an end.

I know (in retrospect) that I was not wise enough to make most of the decisions that became investments in my life. My faith teaches me that believers have the Holy Spirit that resides within each of us. For the large majority of Christians, the Holy Spirit (or Holy Ghost, from Old English "gast," meaning "spirit") is a member of the Trinity: The "Triune God" manifested as Father, Son, and Holy Spirit, each Person being God.

Our trip to the university each day involved about a thirty-minute commute from the village to the Oakland community in Pittsburgh. Oakland is the academic and healthcare center of Pittsburgh and one of the city's major cultural centers. In addition to Pitt, there were Carnegie-Mellon University, Duquesne University, and Carlow University. The Oakland neighborhood is also home to museums, hospitals, and shopping stores, as well as recreational activities. The Oakland community is also home to the Schenley Farms National Historic District. To sum it all up, the Oakland community was a high-rent district that included two designated historic districts, Schenley Farms and the Oakland Civic Center, an area that graduate students, such as we, could not afford.

Cathedral of Learning at Pitt

Arriving on the campus of the University of Pittsburgh (Pitt), we were struck by the sight of the Cathedral of Learning, a Pittsburgh landmark listed in the National Register of Historic Places and the centerpiece of the University of Pittsburgh's main campus in the Oakland neighborhood of Pittsburgh, PA. Pitt was established in 1787, a decade after the USA was formed. The "cathedral" stands 535 feet with 42 floors; it is the second tallest university building in the world, after the main building of the Moscow State University in Russia. It is also the second tallest gothic-style building in the world. The Cathedral of Learning is a steel frame structure overlaid with Indiana limestone and contains more than 2,000 rooms and windows. It functions as a primary classroom and administrative center of the university and is home to many of the university's colleges and departments. The first class was held in the building in 1931, and its exterior finished in October 1934, prior to its formal dedication in June 1937. It houses many specialty spaces, including a studio theater, food court, study lounges, offices, computer and language labs, 31 nationality rooms, and a $\frac{1}{2}$-acre 4-story-high vaulted gothic study and event hall.

The sight of this facility began an epiphany of sorts; it began to acquaint me with how higher education in the various states are funded and, most importantly, the funding differences between historically white and historically black universities. I also became aware of the distinctions between research institutions as listed by the American Association of Universities (AAU). AAU member universities, including 60 in the United States and Canada, are on the leading edge of innovation, scholarship, and solutions that contribute to scientific progress, economic development, security, and well-being. Pitt is among the sixty institutions that award nearly one-half of all US doctoral degrees and 55% of those in science and engineering. There are about 5,300 universities in the USA, including 56 historically black colleges (HBCUs).

For a while, I did not know whether to celebrate my admission to such a prestigious institution or bemoan in anger the fact that HBCUs, like many of the black institutions in the US, were severely underfunded. HBCUs in the US were established before the Civil Rights Act of 1964 with the intent of primarily serving the minority communities. This was necessary because during the period of recognized segregation, the overwhelming majority of PWIs (predominantly white institutions) disqualified blacks from enrollment. For a century since the end of slavery in 1865, most colleges prohibited African-Americans from attending, and a number of other PWIs employed quotas to limit admissions to blacks. As was the case of so many issues that demonstrated injustice and unfairness, I chose to do my best to successfully complete my doctoral work, but I never forgot about the impact of what second-class citizenship had meant.

At that time of my entry to Pitt, however, the summer forest of my mind connected me to my childhood tapes, and I rationalized adoption of Maslow's hierarchy of needs. This was my escape valve. I could compartmentalize the rights, wrongs, good, and evil and decide I had no power to make a difference and keep moving. Thus, I enrolled in the doctoral program at Pitt. The years of being a research assistant and a teaching assistant had brought exposure and good fortune within GSPIA. Likewise, Joy's graduate experience in the School of Social Work was coming to a successful conclusion. Soon, that segment of our lives came to end.

Returning to civilian life in 1972 had challenged me to revisit one of the driving forces for my becoming a reserve officer in the USAF: the war in Vietnam. As I prepared to leave the Armed Forces, there was, not too far in the recess of my mind, the impact of the Gulf of Tonkin resolution, a bogus legislative initiative designed to justify the US involvement in the war pushed by the Johnson Administration. In 1972, Americans and Vietnamese were still being killed; however, in that same year, there was now a new president of the US in the person of Richard Nixon. Nixon was a skilled politician who eventually resigned in disgrace to avoid impeachment and conviction. Nixon was the focal point of the Watergate scandal. The scandal resulted from a burglary attempt of the Democratic National Committee (DNC). What would have been a routine criminal check turned out not to be since President Nixon attempted to cover up his administration's involvement, leading to a constitutional crisis.

The Vietnam conflict was one of the elephants in the room in 1968 that I talked about in the chapter on my undergraduate days. After four years of my service to the US military, I was still challenged as to what I should do about a policy I felt was wrong. All I had done, while in undergraduate school, to deal with a policy that sent young men and women to their deaths was to support the leadership of the US government. In 1995,

Vietnam released its official estimate of war dead: as many as 2 million civilians on both sides and some 1.1 million North Vietnamese and Viet Cong fighters. The US military has estimated that between 200,000 and 250,000 South Vietnamese soldiers died in the war. A total of 58,220 soldiers died from a range of causes, including death from wounds, getting killed in action, accidents, and even self-infliction. During the bloodiest month of 1968, over 2,000 soldiers were killed in May alone. Of course, my strength as an individual to confront the government was tepid. Yet, I was perturbed by my absence of consciousness and courage. If Harriet Tubman had not the courage of her consciousness, many slaves would not have found freedom; if Rosa Parks had not taken a seat on the bus, or if MLK had not acted on the courage of his consciousness, the Western world would likely be at a stage where Donald Trump would more unabashedly praise the absolute white supremacy that fortunately never successfully evolved.

As I embarked upon my doctoral study, I vowed to play my part in uplifting the less well-off individuals where I could, and my record as an academic demonstrates my commitment. During my faculty/administrative appointments, I sought and obtained more than $15 million from the National Science Foundation, the US Department of Education, and other agencies to support the matriculation of graduate and undergraduate program enrollment. Fortunately, I was able to compartmentalize past injustices as we were continuing to acquaint ourselves with our new environment. The daily trip to campus took us across the bridge that connected downtown and the Oakland community with West Gate Village.

Three rivers converging in Pittsburgh

Pittsburgh is famous for its Three Rivers, the militarily and commercially strategic point where the Allegheny and Monongahela rivers converge to form the Ohio river. It was also the sight where the NFL franchise Pittsburgh Steelers played their games.

Getting adjusted to the daily grind of studies was not at all difficult; just four years previous, Joy and I had been TSU undergraduates. Course work was stimulating. We had doctoral seminars that required written research papers every two weeks. Because my R.K. Mellon Fellowship required me to assist my major advisor as a teaching assistant, I assisted Dr. Joseph E. McLean, who became my dissertation advisor, and more importantly, my second white mentor. Midway through the semester, Dr. McLean was stricken with cancer and was not able to meet his teaching responsibility. I was able to prepare for my comprehensives examination during my preparation for conducting instruction to beginning graduate students. Back then, Professor McLean worked with the Dean of the Graduate School of Public and International Affairs (GSPIA) to assign the teaching responsibility to me when he would go in for treatment. This was a bittersweet opportunity for me. I was able to build on my previous experience of teaching US history to undergraduates at Clark County College upon completing my MA from the University of Nevada in 1971. During the term, Dr. McLean would come to his office and consult with me to assess how the experiment, i.e., my role as teacher of record, was fairing. I was plenty anxious; I had to spend hours in preparation for the teaching and to take my doctoral seminars. I can say without hesitation that the conversations we had in his office became unexpected learning opportunities. His desk would always be unkempt, I don't know how he found things, but his mind was sharp.

Professor McLean was a former New Jersey official whose experience and scholarship facilitated robust dialogue within the academy and the outside world. He was on the faculty of Princeton University from 1946 to 1954, when Gov. Robert E. Meyner of New Jersey appointed him State Commissioner of Conservation and Economic Development. He had managed Mr. Meyner's 1953 election campaign. He was an activist scholar. This professor coined the term "marble cake federalism," distinguishing between layer cake and picket federalism. Since one of the areas of my comprehensive examination would involve federalism and intergovernmental relations, this one-on-one time became precious. It is more than fair to say that Dr. McLean was my second white mentor. He was an avid Democrat and supported Adlai Stevenson's bid for president of the US. When he retired from Pitt, after I had completed my degree, he became a scholar in residence at the University of Virginia's Institute of Government in the early 1980s and prior to that time served on the staffs of the Brookings Institution and the East-West Center of the University of Hawaii. His work at Pitt began in 1967 when I was yet in undergraduate school. He served Pitt from that time until 1980. He followed my career and would keep in touch when health allowed. He passed away in 1986.

Although Dr. McLean became my second white mentor, he was not the only supportive white professor at GSPIA. Professors Ed Foster, Joe James, and Ray Richmond are added to the list, and although there were few black professors at Pitt, Clyde McDaniel and Earl Onque were also among those who lifted me up while correcting my misstatements and faulty assumptions about urban affairs and sound research. As I travel through the summer forest of my mind, I recall my research methods class which was anchored in Fred Kerlinger's book *Foundations of Behavioral Research*. This text examines the fundamentals of solving a scientific research problem, focusing on the relationship between the problem and the research design. I came to understand the fact that scientific research is a systematic, controlled, empirical, and critical investigation of hypothetical propositions about the presumed relations among phenomena. This edition included new information about computer statistical software, multivariate statistics, research ethics, and writing research reports in APA style. It was ideal for graduate students in that it covered statistics, research methodology, and measurement all in one volume. From this text and the instruction by Dr. Clyde McDaniel, I became aware of the independent variable paradigm, ways of knowing, etc. Dr. McDaniel was so concerned about my grasping the details of social research that he would extend his office hours, and on one occasion, he came to my house to tutor me. I have kept the Kerlinger text in my library ever since I left my studies at Pitt. There were many other significant papers and books, along with talented professors, that shaped me to become a member of academia. The other textbook that rises to the top of my list is Daniel P. Moynihan's *Maximum Feasible Misunderstanding*. The "maximum feasible misunderstanding" Daniel P. Moynihan had in mind was the morass of confusion stemming from a key phrase in the Economic Opportunity Act of 1964, the declaration that "community action" projects funded by the War on Poverty, which many observers interpreted to mean the "maximum feasible participation of the residents of the areas and the members of the groups involved in the local programs." But, the title of this fascinating book has a certain ironic resonance, for its author was well on the way toward becoming the most misunderstood figure in American public life. His famous 1965 Department of Labor report, *The Negro Family: The Case for National Action*, was distorted beyond all recognition in the controversy that followed its release. A document intended to point the way toward the most constructive innovation in American social policy in thirty years - employment guarantees and income redistribution measures which would eliminate the underclass of desperately poor people who lived in "the other America" - was branded as reactionary and racist. Caught in a withering crossfire between the Left and the Right, the Moynihan report disappeared into oblivion. The dominant thrust of the War on Poverty as it developed was in quite a different direction, away from a national employment and income redistribution strategy and toward the mobilization of poor people for social action at the local level. My revised critique of the Moynihan contribution is that the difference between original intent and unintended consequences generates a lifetime of ineffective policy practices. Mobilization of poor people for social action continues in 2019, and there is no indication of it going away. As a society of people, Liberals and Progressives still believe in national employment and removal of the economic gap between the haves and the have-nots. There are many varied stakeholders that participate in the dialogue, but unfortunately, few are willing to compromise. Nevertheless, these experiences were key to my writing a successful dissertation, "An Assessment of the Relationship between the Political Ethos and Types of Productivity Measures Used in Urban Government."

The spring of 1974 is a time I will always remember. During that time in my life, at the age of 28 years, ten years from the time

I graduated from OPHS, Joy and I acquired our first mortgage, the 518 Foltz Drive property in Verona, PA. Upon completion of my coursework, we decided to relocate to a suburb of Pittsburgh. During this time period, I had also completed the requirements for the doctoral degree in April, and at 9 PM on Wednesday, May 14, at Magee Women's Hospital, Joy delivered our firstborn, a 7 lb., 8 oz. baby boy! I seriously shared in the birth, but I was more a spectator than an assistant in the birthing process; in those days, the husband was not allowed to participate as I understand they do today. Yet, I was riding on cloud nine. All this was happening so fast! The exhilaration lasted literally for years! Sometimes, I think I believed that this was all my doing. It was not the first time I was guilty of hubris, but I did not have the wisdom and spiritual development to distinguish between grace and self-trust. Wisdom is considered the first and the greatest of the gifts. It acts upon both the intellect and the will. According to St. Bernard, it both illumines the mind and instills an attraction to the divine. Adolphe Tanquerey explained the difference between the gift of wisdom and that of understanding: "The latter is a view taken by the mind, while the former is an experience undergone by the heart; one is light, the other love, and so they unite and complete one another."

Parenthood, the most important task but no "how-to" manual

There is no guidebook that teaches how to be a parent. On a Wednesday morning, May 14, 1974, Joy told me she was ready to give birth to our son. She packed a bag, and we set out for Magee Women's Hospital, a unit of the University of Pittsburgh. Neither of us knew what to expect; I just knew that Joy was experiencing birth pains and that the birth pains meant that something was about to happen. After what seemed like a lifetime in the waiting room, around 8 PM, I assisted the hospital staff and wheeled her into the delivery room. The staff physician instructed me to stand behind a partition in sight of Joy, but my vision was blocked by the attending staff. At 9 PM on Wednesday, May 14, 1974, our firstborn, RaShad Abubakka Sampson, was born.

For five years previously, Joy and I had been accustomed to traveling across the country whenever we desired, entertaining ourselves as we saw fit. Now, that largesse was coming to a close. To be sure, parenting RaShad was not a burden; it was a gift! However, with my hubris in second gear, I thought we did not need assistance from her mother (about parenting and many other matters). I am now grateful that she came.

We brought RaShad from the hospital to our home on Foltz Drive in Verona, PA, our first residence in the suburbs. It was quite different from West End of Pittsburgh and the housing development called West Gate Village. A few days after our son's birth, I had transported the mother and son to our house. During the early stages of getting acquainted with life as graduate students, we had met a number of other graduate student couples, some of whom had already begun their families. Ann Bostic, wife of William Bostic, who was a graduate student in GSPIA, came to stay with Joy while I drove to Greater Pittsburgh International Airport to meet mom's plane. Upon greeting mom and collecting her bags, I drove the 40-minute journey home as we renewed our relationship; she had always been a kind and gentle woman. She and her husband, John, had been blessed with eight daughters and three sons. Thus, she knew something about caring for a newborn. Joy was the eighth offspring of John and Lula; her older siblings had already begun their families.

Soon, we had driven through the traffic of the big city and crossed through the Fort Pitt tunnel connecting to Verona via Penn Hills. Leaving the noise and crowds of the city, we made our way past Monroeville, PA, another Pittsburgh suburb. Suddenly, we were making our way through the lush greenery of Verona and pleasantness of Foltz Drive. There was unmeasured exuberance when my wife and her mother embraced. Mom then acquainted herself with her latest grandson. "What a fine boy," she said in a way in which only a grandmother could coo. It wasn't long before mom assigned me to the downstairs bedroom and directed me to move the baby's crib into our master bedroom with Joy; she took the adjoining bedroom.

Mom was gentle, loving, and secure in her ways; she was never the dreaded mother-in-law often fantasied in television, books, and movies. For all my life, I had been blessed with my own relationship with my mother, and now, I knew the blessing that Joy had with her mother. I fell in love with Lula Pulley during her stay. This was a week when my manhood transitioned to fatherhood, and I evolved in the view of two adoring women. So much was happening, and I admit I was not prepared for upcoming decisions Joy and I faced. We had not long been in our new home before I began to receive offers of employment in several different locations around the country.

To complicate the challenge of deciding whether we would accept a job offer outside of Western Pennsylvania, we had the responsibility of a newborn; that reality brought challenges we had never had before. The first five years of our marriage revolved around traveling and being entertained. When we began our married life, we were just out of college. While in college, we had no money; all we had was each other. Now, with an infant, we knew that the selfishness we had showered on each other had to be set aside. Coming to grips with parenthood, we knew that parents are responsible to provide their child with the necessary food, clothing, shelter, medical care, and love. We knew that we would eventually have the responsibility of providing sound education and a strong foundation of our religion and moral training. Joy and I were responsible for RaShad's social, emotional, cognitive, and physical well-being. We were not frightened by that onerous task. My mother had told me once that parents influence their child's social skills directly and indirectly, through management of the child's activities.

We were aware we would influence our children unintentionally through our own actions, such as conversing with other adults while in his presence. These responsibilities had been the gifts that our respective parents modeled for us. Now, in May 1974, there was no more rehearsal. RaShad was cooperative. He was a good baby; he rapidly learned the difference between night and day. Although we slept with one eye open during his first few months, he was never a burden. We were eager to attend to his whimpers through the night.

Time was fast approaching for us to decide whether to remain in the Pittsburgh area or to relocate. Thus, in the fall of 1974,

I accepted an appointment as chair of the newly designated Department of Political Science at Tennessee State University. My academic advisors and friends all cautioned against taking the job. They were wiser than I, and I was not prepared to seriously take on such a high undertaking when the ink on my dissertation had hardly had time to dry. So, hubris struck again. I focused on the significance of such a position at such a young age, not considering the reality of bureaucratic wars in the academy. By August 1974, we had sold the property in Verona and bought a house that was being completed in the Enchanted Hills area, a housing development where established professionals resided. The task of completing the house located at 128 Queens Lane became a time for Joy's ideas and imagination to flourish. Just as we had done so in Verona, we set up house in Nashville.

Somewhere in the back of my mind, I knew that the illusion of certainty in decision-making creates a *moral hazard*, a condition that exists when a party to a transaction has an incentive to take unusual risks because he or she is unlikely to suffer potential damage. The lessons from the research methods doctoral seminar taught that all decisions have a degree of uncertainty, regardless of experience-based skill in planning, approximating, and anticipating. This is caused by two factors, the limitation of the decision-making instrument (systematic error) and the skill of the decider in making meaningful assessments (random error). Exact measurements of the wrong things can drive out good judgments of the right things, imperiling the future. But the cult of calculation, perpetuated by the infamous McKinsey maxim - "What you can measure you can manage" - creates the same type of risk, offering the illusion of control and mastery of knowledge.

From my undergraduate days, I recall lectures given by Dr. Lawrence Simmons' philosophy course that introduced the philosopher Soren Kierkegaard, who wrote, "life is lived forward but understood backward." Lessons learned in the school of life have taught me that once a method of making a decision becomes entrenched as part of the conventional wisdom, it is usually impenetrable to logic, intuition, critical thinking, or better ways to do something. I wish that back then, I would have been wise instead of being educated.

In the meantime, my main responsibility was being a good husband and father. RaShad was continuing to grow, and I looked forward to time when the three of us could be alone. RaShad was 9 months old when he began to walk. I vividly recall the February morning in 1975 when he appeared in the sitting room where Joy and I relaxing after breakfast. We thought he was in the crib in his room. He had to have climbed over the thirty-inch rails of crib and walked twenty or so feet from his bedroom to the sitting room, where he astonished us. When he was a toddler, his exploration of his environment reminded me of the nightly news reports on US activity in Vietnam. There would be reports of American "search and destroy missions" in the jungles of Southeast Asia, a term popularized during the US involvement in Vietnam to describe American soldiers pillaging villages in that country. But, the activity Joy and I were witnessing occurred in our house on Queens Lane, in the Enchanted Hills subdivision in Nashville. I never considered what a positive connotation the term "search and destroy" could impart. We were admiring parents. Our young toddler was an active, physically robust child who was never afraid of what he would discover. Before his fifth birthday, he literally taught himself to ride a bicycle without training wheels.

We had, since his birth, been a happy family, and we were in 1977. I had the good fortune of having a wonderful family to return to when my days at the office would often be filled with administratively putting out fires and settling bureaucratic wars.

Residing in Nashville meant proximity to Joy's family. Her parents lived about eighty miles south, near Huntsville, AL. Most of her siblings were also nearby. This meant family time was abundant. Major holidays, minor holidays, reunions, and "just because" days found us in the central place of northern AL.

Bonding with my in-laws was easy. We had a social life like we have never had previously or since. While our social life in Las Vegas had been more than satisfying, life with family became a mutual admiration way of life. Our new home in Enchanted Hills was happy, and our fraternity and church life sprung into being. Our backyard was the location for cookouts and birthday celebrations. It was a joyous time for a while. Having lived in predominantly white communities and middle-class black neighborhoods, we could see the difference that race and class brought. In the Nashville black community, we benefited from the past days of racial segregation that resulted in blacks having their place in society, and most of the black professional class had developed institutions and facilitated a viable culture. Places where there was a critical mass of African-Americans reflected black contributions to American life. The distinct identity of African-American culture in Nashville reflected the fact of a culture that is rooted in the historical experience of the African-American people. "Separate but equal," which had been the guiding law since the 1896 Supreme Court decision for *Plessey v. Ferguson* in which the court declared that racially separate institutions did not violate the Fourteenth Amendment, echoed at the ruling on Dred Scott which affirmed that blacks had no rights that whites were obliged to acknowledge. The force of law and custom fostered black educational institutions, including colleges and professional schools that produced a class of people that became accustomed to "pulling themselves up by their own bootstraps."

Contrasted with life in white suburbia (and in my work life in the USAF, and my graduate study), I have experienced not resistance nor unfriendliness, but an absence of the recognition of my culture as a black Southerner. Geographical distinctions are also real. The South produces warmth in daily expression. From far and near, it is not uncommon for individuals to say, "hello, how are you doing," and otherwise engage in small talk. In fact, when I moved to the Midwest and upon approaching my white friends, there was not always the warmth that I had become accustomed. There was no knowledge of the impact that was fostered on a dark-complexioned male from the South. Often, I misread the body language of some of my white colleagues and felt they were cold and distant or had undeveloped social skills. Nevertheless, family life was always the refuge from the storm. During this time, RaShad grew into a delightful lad. From the time he was old enough to attend preschool, he was enrolled in the TSU early childhood educational center. Ten years would pass before we had the gift of another child.

Chapter XIV

THE PROFESSORIATE, ACADEMIA, AND BUREAUCRATIC POLITICS

For 40 years (1974-2014), I have had but one type of job since my honorable discharge from the US Air Force. That job was in academia, the worldwide group composed of professors and researchers at institutes of higher learning. The term "academia" can be traced to Plato's school of philosophy, founded approximately 385 BC at Academia, a sanctuary of Athena (the goddess of wisdom and skill) north of Athens, Greece. I have had three appointments to institutions of higher learning: Tennessee State University (TSU), the University of Illinois-Springfield (UIS), and the University of Missouri (MU). I have held administrative positions, including as department chair at TSU and UIS, dean in the graduate school at MU, associate to the president at UIS, and of course, member of the faculty.

My first appointment was effective in the fall of 1974. I was designated chair of the newly authorized Department of Political Science. There are more reasons why I should not have taken the assignment than reasons that I should have. Just about everyone with whom I spoke about the decision urged me to look at an alternative. The naysayers included family friends and University of Pittsburgh professors. They could see what I had not imagined. In retrospect, I fully agree that it was not in my best interest. It was at this juncture that I crossed the Rubicon River for the first time. From my undergraduate literature classes, I had read about Julius Caesar's crossing the Rubicon in January 49 BC that precipitated the Roman Civil War, which ultimately led to Caesar becoming dictator and the rise of the imperial era of Rome. Caesar had been appointed to a governorship over a region that ranged from southern Gaul to Illyricum (but not Italy). As his term of governorship ended, the Roman Senate ordered Caesar to disband his army and return to Rome. He was explicitly ordered not to bring his army across the Rubicon river, which was, at that time, a northern boundary of Italy. In January 49 BC, Caesar brought the 13th legion across the river, which the Roman government considered insurrection, treason, and a declaration of war on the Roman Senate. According to some authors, he is said to have uttered the phrase "*alea iacta est*," a term meaning "the die is cast," as his army marched across the shallow river. Today, the phrase "crossing the Rubicon" is a metaphor that means to pass a point of no return.

To be sure, my appointment as department chair was no equal to Caesar's governorship, and I certainly did not have an army of supporters. But, just as Caesar had been warned not to cross the Rubicon, several friends, graduate school professors, and family urged me to consider an alternative position. My "declaration of war" would be my fight to get established as a professor and administrator at my undergraduate alma mater amidst unknown jealousy and resentment from a number of individuals and groups that were antagonistic of each other and only joined in their interest to return to a state of control over undergraduate and graduate education of the University of Tennessee.

When I was an undergraduate at TSU, political science was a unit within the fiefdom of history, political science, and geography. Fiefdoms in academia are not unheard of, and they serve to protect the interests of an elite group of individuals. The history, political science, and geography fiefdom at TSU was headed by Dr. Alonzo Stephens. Students and faculty affiliated with political science had long pushed for separation during the entire time I was a student at the university. Dr. Stephens, knowing that the board of curators had authorized the stand-alone unit in 1973, was assigned the responsibility of creating the new department. The first major step was to establish a search for the positions. Normally, in such instances, search committees are authorized, and membership on the search committee would include faculty with legitimate interest in the new department. That was not the case. There was no search commit of record, no mission and vision statement that would have been presented to professors who would have an interest in the long-term future of the unit. There was no widespread publication of the employment opportunity. Dr. Stephens worked closely to his vest; he knew that interest in history and geography would not have the same number of interested students as political science would. All factors pointed to a diminution of the once proud history unit at the university. Word of mouth was the marketing method. I was not aware of this set of pithy circumstances. Thus, with the ink on my dissertation still wet, I was presented the offer, and I eagerly accepted the position. My first-time appointment out of graduate school was department chair. I would later come to know "all that glitters is not gold." When Dr. Stephens invited me to a faculty meeting of the holdovers who would be appointed, I came face-to-face with Dr. George S. Davis, who just six years earlier directed my senior project. Upon seeing me, Dr. Davis was astonished, and not in a gleeful fashion. Immediately, he left the room and declared that he did not want a faculty appointment in the new unit. Later in my career, I would know firsthand the burden of resisting faculty roles in academic governance.

The initial task for me was to recruit three faculty positions for the newly designated department. Two of the holdovers from the original History, Political Science, and Geography Department were Dr. James Dennis and Professor Ora Eads. When my appointment as department chair became official, these professors had not been granted tenure and had no choice but to move to the unit. Dr. Stephens had warned me that Dennis and Eads were up to no good and should be denied tenure, a decision that had to be made by the end of the current academic year. The task clouded the steps I would need to make to effectively recruit needed talent; denying tenure to individuals that had worked to earn their degrees, and moreover, were 20 years older than me, caused me to see the challenge of my recruiting new faculty unless they were graduate students that did not possess their doctorates. The history department under Dr. Stevens had a number of tenured professors, some of whom had instructed me during my undergraduate days. Thus, the newly authorized department would struggle, eventually succumb, and return to the established unit.

My first day on the job was a Monday in early September. As I approached the building where my office was to be located, there was a vehicle parked in front of the building containing a professor who wanted to be appointed in the new unit. He was an adjunct and sought a chance to acquire full-time tenure track. He was 20 years my senior, and more importantly, I thought after a brief discussion with him that his lack of a terminal degree along with his narrow perspective about what the new department should be caused me to seek "new blood." He was adamant in his persistence; daily, he would park in front of the building although I told him each time that I was not open to a tenure track appointment for him. These unexpected problems greeted me during the first days of my chairmanship.

When I began the task of setting offices, acquiring necessary office supplies, and establishing a telephone system, I was told that there was not a budget for the new unit. I had to make requests to the history and geography department. During my trek over to Dr. Stephens' office, I began to see the bind I was in. I was chair, yet this humbling experience generated hostility and resentment, but I knew it was not wise to show my feelings. Soon, I knew that some office senior to the chair of history had to intervene. This brought me to the acquaintance of Arts and Sciences Dean Robert Hudson. Dr. Hudson had been a long time English professor, and I knew of him from my undergraduate days. Dr. Hudson granted access for resources, sometimes at the annoyance of Dr. Stephens. I would have to finalize a fall teaching schedule, hire a secretary, and move furniture to offices where the new department was located. Dr. Stephens, Dr. Hudson, and Dr. George Davis had garnered social capital as a result of their long years at TSU. Social capital is the accumulation of resources and power built through relationships, trust, goodwill, and influence between individuals and other stakeholders, such as constituents. It refers to the resources available to people and entities because of their networks, the assets we possess by virtue of the social relations that we develop and maintain, and the shared values which arise from those networks. Social capital results from proximity, time, and quality of interpersonal investments. Suffice to say I had a scant amount of capital of any sort at that juncture. I would have to earn the trust of the established campus administrators.

In the meantime, the task of recruiting faculty and scheduling classes became front and center on my "to do" list. The first-year faculty appointments were largely adjunct, but we were able to bring the academic year to closure, though not before I acceded to Dr. Stephens' recommendation to deny tenure to Dr. Dennis and Professor Ora Eads. Deep within the confines of the summer forest that is my mind, I felt awful about going along with the tenure denial. To be sure, both Dennis and Eads knew most of the students and had cultivated social capital among them. The unit needed a new face and a mission consistent with what we were seeing on other campuses that offered political science amidst public affairs. I urged departmental faculty to adopt a new department name: Department of Government and Public Affairs. This administrative arrangement would allow master's level instruction in public administration and urban affairs at a time that the country was dealing with the urban crisis.

Absolutely none of these matters were the subject of the bureaucratic warfare in academia. Instead, I had to abandon my research agenda, urban management and its political underpinning. My Pitt advisors tried to install in my consciousness that research was the coin of the realm in the academy. In the first two years, my research productivity was nonexistent. Working at TSU caused me to recall the admonition my Pitt advisors has voiced, that research would give way to teaching and community service. At the onset of my third year, I was able to make connections with the National Aeronautics and Space Administration (NASA) when the agency was working to build bridges to historically black colleges and universities.

Lurking in the not-too-far distance was one of the two elephants in the room in 1968: one was the litigation of the *Geier v. University of Tennessee* case, which was introduced in the chapter on my undergraduate years at TSU. The lead plaintiff was Rita Geier, a former adjunct faculty member of the History, Political Science, and Geography Department, who was supported by *George Barrett*, a *Tennessee* civil rights *lawyer* known for handling the case that ultimately desegregated the state's public colleges and universities. The Tennessee desegregation case arose 14 years after the United States Supreme Court declared segregated public schools unconstitutional. The case, along with others on the state level, broadened desegregation to include higher education. Barrett's file on Geier's behalf had its basis in the fact that Tennessee maintained a dual system of higher education. "Our suit applied the principle that 'open doors' at all institutions were not enough if there was a system of education where barriers still existed," Barrett stated. In 1972, the federal judge, Frank T. Gray, Jr., allowed Sterling Adams and Raymond Richardson (two black professors of mathematics at TSU), and nearly 100 other black citizens from across Tennessee, to enter the Geier case as plaintiffs. Adams and Richardson led the formation of Tennesseans for Justice in Higher Education. Their complaint centered on the issue that the presence in Nashville of two state-supported universities, Tennessee State University, a historically black institution, and the predominately white University of Tennessee at Nashville, perpetuated a state of segregation in higher education in Nashville.

Subsequently, Judge Frank Gray, Jr. ruled that the state had to dismantle that system. In February 1977, Judge Gray ordered the merger of both institutions under the governance of Tennessee State University. This was the first time that a court in a higher education desegregation suit had ordered a historically black college to take over a predominately white one. In **1979,** the University of Tennessee at Nashville merged with Tennessee State University, creating an enlarged institution with two campuses and increased enrollment. The original TSU campus, located in North Nashville, is designated as the main campus, and the former UT-N campus was renamed in honor of an African-American civil rights icon of the Nashville area, Avon Williams, Jr. Boosted by a stipulation of settlement in 1984, there emerged a blueprint for "remedying" past wrongs and ensuring equal access. Upon careful reflection, the "blueprint" was the embodiment of Pharisees' yeast. The suit culminated in the court-approved Geier Consent Decree in 2001, which resulted in a $23 million windfall to TSU and a total of more than $41 million distributed among other state institutions. Despite spending enhancements for the Nashville campus, physical improvements ironically made the campus more inviting to white students. In the months and years leading up to *Geier*, there was no significant increase in white presence. Ten years after *Geier*, white student population rose to 2.4%. There was limited infrastructure for high-level research.

The actual process of combining the University of Tennessee, TSU, and other state-funded schools into a single system of higher education was an arduous task in the State of Tennessee that had historically legislated separation of races. The separate and unequal access to financial resources generated strong feelings on both sides (TSU and UT-N) and fostered distrust and antagonism in 1970. Eventually a truce surfaced. Two academic units, urban affairs and engineering, were set to initiate the new arrangement. For three years, I had worked alongside political science and public affairs department faculty from the Avon Williams and main campuses to report to the presidents of each campus. In the weeks and months leading up to July 1, 1979, the presidents of the two campuses agreed to appoint me as the initial director of the Center for Urban and Public Affairs (CUPA) and Dr. Edward Isobar, Dean of the TSU School of Engineering, to head the engineering program for the two campuses. This administrative decision would begin the process of formalizing matters that both sides had agreed upon and subsequently submitted to the US District Court from the basis of the state center of urban and public affairs. But, there was a price to pay for those who were designated to assume positions of leadership within the process of TSU subsuming control of UT-Nashville. I was to be appointed director of the Center of Urban Public Affairs effective July 1, 1979. My appointment came as no surprise to my colleagues, but some faculty at UT-N and other community members who lived outside of North Nashville felt that the position should have gone to someone more senior. In no uncertain way, some political science and public administration affairs faculty at UT-N expressed anger at what they saw as a "token appointment." These emotions surfaced, in part because there was only a thin layer of trust between the predominantly white UT-N and the HBCU, TSU. The war was raged in the press where TSU administrators and faculty were routinely maligned. Of course, a few safe blacks would not be dragged into the milieu along with the unworthy blacks who deigned to stand up for principles and human rights and were appointed to administrative leadership positions at the downtown facility. To many in North Nashville, those were token appointments, i.e., practices of making only a perfunctory or symbolic effort to do a particular thing, especially by recruiting a small number of people from underrepresented groups in order to give the appearance of sexual or racial equality within a workforce. But, as the saying goes, "he who has the gold makes the rules."

The Geier court case brought to mind what I had known about an earlier contest of policy direction when there was federal litigation in which the main plaintiffs were North Nashville (the black community) and greater Nashville, when the issue of planning the location of Tennessee's interstate system in the 1940s was under consideration. Planners had to figure out how to get the interstates in and out of the major cities without causing too much disruption in the city street system and existing buildings.

In Nashville, planners routed I-40 eastward through the middle of the predominantly African-American community in North Nashville. This caused concern among black residents, who felt the interstate would damage property values and the uniqueness of the black community. The proposed route ran near Tennessee State University, Fisk University, and Meharry Medical College, as well as pharmacies, restaurants, and the city's lone black bank. Citizens Savings in Nashville has been the lone black-owned bank in Nashville since 1904.

The struggle over the route of I-40 through Nashville is considered one of the most bitter in national highway history. While this series of events was not the first to demonstrate how the black community felt marginalized by the majority-white community, it formed a scab over an incurable sore. It was the epitome of amyotrophic sclerosis, the motor neuron disease known as Lou Gehrig's disease, an incurable prognosis. Two decades later, the matter of TSU and UT-N before the US District Court merely lifted the scab of distrust. The court's judicial ruling in favor of TSU did not have the impact of cultural change. Winning the court case meant time on the cross for those of us that had been designated to lead the effort to litigate for the end of a form of desegregation in 1979.

I was one of the first of a number of sacrificial lambs that signaled TSU's court determined dominance over UT-N, but the reward for my effort was to spend time on my cross. I did not become director of the Center for Urban and Public Affairs; instead, I found myself facing the full forces of the law. During that time, I quickly became aware that my arms were too short to box with the powers that supported University of Tennessee. In my humiliation, justice was denied. I was "countered among the transgressors." Ultimately, I resigned my position and went in search of a new appointment in academia.

After the resignation, I examined my brief career and felt wounded, but thankfully, not slain; it was time to lay down and bleed awhile, but I knew I would rise and fight again. Even in that moment, I sensed I had endured unjustified persecution, but I endured them all because the Lord delivered me. I took comfort from Paul's letter to the church at Corinth (2nd Corinthians 4:8-9). My wife and I were troubled on every side, yet not distressed; we were perplexed, but not in despair. We had been persecuted, but not forsaken; cast down, but not destroyed. In the summer forest of my mind, I remembered the 1970s movie *Tora, Tora, Tora* about the attack on Pearl Harbor. "Tora!" is a Japanese term meaning "tiger." *Tora* was the Japanese code word made famous when the Japanese attacked Pearl Harbor on December 7, 1941, propelling the United States into World War II. The expression was a code signal back to Tokyo, signifying that the stab-in-the-back mission was complete. I reasoned that the UT-N faculty had signaled to UT "mission accomplished," but in my mind, I knew that parting from TSU awakened the tiger in me. From that moment, I became absorbed, engrossed, focused, immersed, and preoccupied… I was determined that with God's guidance I would rebuild my career. Indeed, in retrospect decades later, I came to know that God had already cause me to be "fruitful in the land of affliction." I walked in the fear of the Lord and the comfort of the Holy Spirit. That was forty years ago, as I write these memories. It was forty years ago when I began to realize that failure is a better teacher than success.

My wife, my son, and I left Nashville in the summer of 1980 with my bruised ego and my nearly empty pockets. We placed our Enchanted Hills property on the market; my siblings and my wife's siblings continued to be supportive, as was the community of black and white public affairs faculty across the country. There were many lessons I learned from my fight with Goliath; chief among them was the fact that one knows who a true friend is based on their behavior when the chips are down.

In the spring of 1980, I was granted an untenured faculty position at University of Illinois-Springfield (UIS) beginning in the fall of that year. This began my second appointment in academia. It was at this point I crossed my Rubicon River for a second time. The difference between the first time and second time of my crossing the Rubicon was that at UIS, there was not the hoard of antagonistic erstwhile colleagues rooting for choppy waters that I would have to navigate.

Springfield, capital city of Illinois, was significantly different than Nashville, capital city of Tennessee. The campus at UIS was then known as Sangamon State University, but its growth and influence in the state capital caused it to be recognized as the public affairs upper division campus in Illinois. UIS also afforded me time for investment in my research productivity. It was at this institution that I began a 35-year contribution of more than 75 panel presentations, journal article publications, three books, and raising more than $15 million to support student matriculation. I resumed my membership in the American Society for Public Administration.

Beginning in fall, 1983, my colleagues requested that I serve as department chair. I was elected to this open-ended position by colleagues, but after one year, I resigned to accept duties as chair of the Faculty Senate. As chair, I was responsible for the usual variety of administrative details surrounding academic departments, e.g., budget development and management, class scheduling, recruiting, program meetings, interfacing with other academic and professional programs as well as university officials, interacting with external boards, and convening and chairing MPA advisory committees.

The mid-1980s was also a time when my research output unfolded. By this time, I was presenting research papers at national conferences including ASPA, the National Conference of Black Political Scientists (NCOBPS), and the Midwestern Political Association.

On the academic side, professorial branches were pruned, and the pruning made room for additional administrative opportunities. In 1986, I was asked by university president Durward Long to serve as a member of the University Administrative Council, where I assisted the direction of comprehensive university and academic affairs policy, assisted the coordination of Higher Education Cooperative Act grant program, participated in the formulation of administrative procedures to facilitate the policies of planning and budget committees, and served as liaison to the Office of the Vice President of Academic Affairs. I continued this work until I resigned from my position at UIS in 1988.

After about six years in Illinois, my colleagues who were members of the American Society for Public Administration (ASPA) asked and subsequently elected me to serve as national president for the Conference of Minorities in Public Affairs. ASPA is a membership association of almost 10,000 professionals in the United States sponsoring conferences and providing professional services, primarily to those who study the implementation of government policy, public administration, and to a lesser degree, programs of civil society. Its annual conference is an important meeting for those interested in bureaucracy, civic engagement, program evaluation, public management, budgeting and budget theory, government strategic planning, policy analysis, contract administration, personnel management, and other related topics.

ASPA is the "flagship organization" for the public affairs profession and academic interests. It was founded in 1939, following growing concerns about the management of the federal government and the report of the Brownlow Committee. It was formally incorporated on September 13, 1945. The Conference of Minority Public Administrators is the national entity devoted primarily to providing professional development opportunities for all of America's racial minority public administrators. COMPA works to eliminate the institutional and social barriers to the professional development and employment of minority public administrators. Specific goals are to provide leadership in the elimination of discriminatory practices in the public sector; promote recruitment of minorities for leadership positions at all levels of government; provide a forum to promote, upgrade, and refine skills of minority administrators; and develop and maintain a roster of skilled minority professionals in public administration. Having been voted by colleagues across the country to lead this prestigious organization was a strong contrast to 1980 when I left Tennessee State University.

I had been given a new life in academia, but my most cherished blessing was my time spent with my wife and my son. RaShad and I would ride our bicycles through the neighborhood and beautiful Washington Park, which is listed on the National Register of Historic Places. Located at 1400 Williams Boulevard, the park was in walking distance of our residence on Interlacken Drive in Country Club Estates. It featured walking trails, a botanical garden, large duck pond, rose garden, carillon, and carillon concerts. These days allowed me to enjoy meaningful time as father and husband. We, my son and I (and occasionally my wife), watched some outstanding football games at Illini, and perhaps the most enjoyable one was the Pitt v. Illinois game in November 1982. Of course, Pitt won, 20-3. I was elated because the Pitt victory provided an opportunity during the ride home to tell RaShad about his parents' days as graduate students before he was born. I am sure I embellished the details of our lives when Joy and I were graduate students at Pitt; nevertheless, two years after RaShad was born, Pitt won the NCAA national championship with a Sugar Bowl victory against Georgia which featured All-American running back Hershel Walker. Pitt also had Toney Dorsett, the running back who won the Heisman in 1976. In 1982, RaShad was just 8 years old; he took in just about everything we told him. Truth be told, Pitt's athletic kudos paled in comparison to academic achievements and alumni contributions, including advances in medicine, engineering, theoretical physics, as well as one of the founding fathers of television and Pulitzer and Nobel prize winners. Dr. Jonas Salk was a faculty member at Pitt when his research led to the creation of a vaccine that resulted in rapid deterioration of the polio virus. When my son was only a few months old, I took him to the Cathedral of Learning to show him off to my Pitt professors. On the elevator, one of them stated "I had forgotten what a young any looked like. You have a fine son!" It was always my desire to return to Pittsburgh when he could appreciate his beginnings, but that occasion never came to be.

Upon moving to Springfield, we began a search for a church home. Our first choice was to find a church like the one at which we worshipped in Nashville, Howard Congregational. But, that was not to be; Nashville had a large upper-middle-class black community and a much wider variety of worship places. The black community in Springfield is comparatively much smaller and home to an even smaller group of upper-middle-class blacks. Given what scriptures warn against regarding social class, my subconscious did yearn for an upwardly mobile black community and churches. Black churches have, for good or bad, marked the presence of politically and economically viable black communities.

Likewise, black-owned banks have also been lynchpins to black economic development. Black-owned banks have a human and historical connection to the Reconstruction, when newly freed slaves had nowhere to go but these banks, and the most available worship facility was the black church. It became clear to me that my Southern comfort zone did not exist in downstate Illinois. In short, Springfield was not the place where such worship place choices similar to those in Nashville could be found. It was at this time that I became a Methodist. Becoming a Methodist was not that much of a stretch; after all, my mother had grown up in St. Paul Methodist in Laurel, where my grandfather once served as Sunday school superintendent. Our searching led to St. John AME Church, a vibrant, spirit-filled place of worship under the guidance of Pastor Sammy Hooks. Joy and I became Sunday school teachers, and I became a member of the group that met with the pastor to discuss the panoply of matters that concern a church. As the weeks and months turned into years, we felt at home in Springfield and St. John.

Life in Springfield was what I came to know as typical Midwest culture. Midwestern living style is laid-back but not quite as friendly as Southern folks. When I was on campus, I would say "hello" to colleagues who were walking by. Sometimes, there would be no response; contrast that with the South wherein the greeting would be exchanged with exuberance. I soon learned that my new acquaintances were not shy or reticent, just reserved. In our neighborhood, we were one of a few African-American families. Country Club Estates was predominantly Republican and middle-class. Our neighbors were very friendly; RaShad could walk to his neighborhood school as he began first grade. The neighbors welcomed us when we moved in. During the 1992 presidential campaign, I was nominated as a delegate to the national convention.

Soon, we began to take note of the Lincoln sites; Springfield is the central point for historical sites devoted to the 16th President of the USA. It is in Springfield where the only house Lincoln ever owned is located; likewise, Lincoln's final resting place and the streets where the young lawyer made himself a national figure can be found here. The starting point is Lincoln Home National Historic Site, a preserved district of a dozen or so buildings including the home he and his wife, Mary, bought in 1844. Park rangers give free tours of the home, showing the room where his son Edward died, and there is also the Lincoln Presidential Library, a museum featuring films that freely admit how many of the features of his life have been blown out of proportion. Lincoln's New Salem in Menard was where the future president lived from 1831 to 1837. While in his twenties, the future president made his living in this village as a boatman, soldier in the Black Hawk War, general store owner, postmaster, surveyor, and rail splitter, and was first elected to the state general assembly.

Lincoln left New Salem for Springfield in 1837, and the village was generally abandoned by about 1840 as other towns developed. In the 1930s, the Civilian Conservation Corps built a historic recreation of New Salem, complete with the kinds of farm animals common in those days, based on its original foundations, establishing a state park commemorating Lincoln and the frontier history of Illinois. The village is located 15 miles northwest of Springfield and approximately 3 miles south of Petersburg. Its location allowed Joy and I to share this venue and its historical significance with visitors that traveled to Springfield.

Our social life, our professional lives, our role in our church, and our community renewed our adrenaline. However, as great as it was, that exhilaration paled in comparison to how I felt in the spring of 1987 when Joy told me she was again with child.

Chapter XV

MY EARTHLY RESURRECTION: RISING LIKE A PHOENIX FROM THE ASHES

To *rise like a phoenix from the ashes* means to emerge from a catastrophe stronger, smarter, and more powerful. An example of *rising like a phoenix from the ashes* is someone who opens a new, successful business after his previous business has failed. Another example is someone who builds a new house after his previous house has been destroyed in a tornado. The metaphor is appropriate in my 1989 experience when my professional career and ability to work in academia was challenged. The *phoenix* bird is a mythical bird from Greek mythology. It was a feathered creature of great size with talons and wings, its plumage radiant and beautiful. The *phoenix* lived for 500 years before it built its own funeral pyre, burst into flame, and died, consumed in its own fiery inferno. Soon after, the mythical creature rose out of the ashes in a transformation from death to life.

I consider the period beginning in the spring of 1986 and continuing through the spring of 1997 as the best time in my professional life and as the worst of time in terms of my personal life. Most important, in my estimation, is the grace I can witness to in my family life. Having said that, it is important for me to state that my experience as a husband and father was always intact. Joy and I had been married sixteen years; we had a handsome son, but something else could add to our mirth. Another child! The news of our daughter's impending birth coupled with my skyrocketing career placed me on a cloud of happiness. I held a seat on the council of the American Society for Public Administration and won a national election to the presidency of the Conference of Minority Affairs. These placements lifted me to a national limelight that produced several new employments as a variety of academic institutions. Among requests for me to consider new employment around the country, there were employment opportunities from Cleveland State, Nebraska, and MU. Joy, RaShad, and I traveled to each of these venues during the spring and summer months of 1986.

We were not unhappy with Springfield and UIS. In fact, we were beginning to feel the warmth of the city and the community. Our neighbors were friendly, and we came to know at least three families that had similar backgrounds and interest. Elbert Betts and his wife Pauline Gavin Betts, both public school teachers, had lived in the neighborhood ten years before Joy and I took up residence there. Becoming acquainted with Pauline did not take long for me to discover we had identical Gavin grandparents in Jasper County, MS. Lee and Velma Carey were among long-time members of the movers and shakers in the city. They spared no social or political capital as they focused on introducing us to life and people in the community. Mamie and Alex Sanders, Sr. were also neighbors that helped us get accustomed to our new place of residence. Their son, Alex, Jr., and RaShad played together as only boys could.

Our church, St. John AME, had Sunday school classes where both Joy and I were teachers, and where I had been elected to the trustee board. Leadership provided by Rev. Sammy Hooks proved most effective as a number of worshippers chose to join the pulpit ministry. Youth participation and grooming were a staple of St. John's. Geographically, we were only a few hours away from Chicago to the north and about 90 minutes from St. Louis to the west. Trips to Chicago brought us to some of my relatives and Joy's cousins. During those years, we would drive to Chicago's Soldier Field to see the Chicago Bears. On other occasions, we traveled by train to Chicago. We would always drive to St. Louis where the NFL Rams were playing then. Trips to both St. Louis and Chicago brought us into contact with African-Americans, the likes of which we had not experienced since living in Nashville. The trips meant a welcome culture change, choices in shopping, and variety in restaurant choices. Often, while in St. Louis, we would be met by family members, and we enjoyed weekends in the area.

During the spring of 1986, we were invited to the University of Nebraska School of Public Administration, a national leader in public service education, with five of its programs ranked in the nation's top 25. We were warmly received on that campus, which ranked in the top 10% of all public affairs programs in the country. The university was a member of AAU institutions, signaling its placement among one of the thirty-two most prestigious public institutions in the country. Nebraska college football was in its heyday, having won national football championships in 1970, 1971, 1994, 1995, and 1997. Joy's pregnancy was becoming more obvious; although I was offered a tenured position, we felt that the main disadvantage of Nebraska was that we would be further away from family. Sometimes, the challenge of turning down an offer of employment was challenging. I remember, among other reasons, the faculty and administrators wanted us to know that Nebraska is the state credited with the founding of Kool-Aid, the soft drink.

A month or so later, I was invited to fly to Cleveland, OH to consider a position at Cleveland State University. CSU is a public institution that was founded in 1964. It is located in downtown Cleveland where more than 12,000 students were enrolled, and it offered more than 200 undergraduate and graduate programs. Notable CSU alumni include the late Tim Russert, the longest-serving moderator of NBC's "Meet the Press" news program, and the late Carl Stokes, former mayor of Cleveland and the first African-American elected mayor of a major American city.

Off campus, the city of Cleveland offered city museums, good restaurants, professional sports teams, and a culture more similar to that which I became accustomed to in Dayton. It was not lost on us that black churches reflected the importance of religious institutions realizing that the Church has provided support and direction in the development and strengthening of African-Americans communities for centuries. There were many churches to investigate as home churches had we chosen to live in Cleveland.

The faculty and administrators at CSU were genuine and made me a generous financial offer, and most importantly, we would be about fours driving time from Dayton. The non-incentives included consideration of winter weather and blustery winds off Lake Erie, coupled with repeated requests to consider a campus-wide position at the University of Missouri in Columbia.

The summer and fall of 1986 were characterized by anticipation and unbridled excitement in anticipation of our new gift from God. Our treks to Chicago and St. Louis gradually slowed as fall turned to winter. The fall routine revolved around my treks to UIS. Initially, we traveled together, but in the waning months of her pregnancy, she took a leave from her job. By then, my job as assistant to the president left time for only one class per semester. I was not new to university administrative responsibilities. It seems all administrative chores revolve around putting out fires. Such was not the case when I served as administrative officer in the military. In that setting, there was less uncertainty about who was to do what and how to accomplish the task.

When I look back on "administrativity" within the academy, I draw upon experiences from previous institutions. It seems that there were always urgencies of putting out administrative fires. In retrospect, I can see that these weren't really crises at all. The truth is that the main problem wasn't office workload. And it wasn't my colleagues dropping the ball or doing shoddy work, though that was an issue from time to time. The problem was centered around my work style. Most "fires" I was putting out could've been prevented with a few changes to the way I did things, e.g., waiting until the last moment to do things, not paying attention when people gave information, taking on too much so that I could impress my colleagues, and beginning my workday rushing each morning. Being in crisis mode all the time, either as an individual or as an organization, isn't the norm, and it is not healthy since rushing and failure to plan and prioritize won't produce the best work. Fortunately, the months between April 1986 and December 1986 were not always "house on fire," although we did have a kitchen fire that brought emergency personnel and a resultant new kitchen.

Our habitat was a place of happy anticipation. Based on Joy's visits to her obstetrics and gynecology physician, we planned for a January 1987 delivery. Each scheduled visit to the obstetrics and gynecology office leading up to that date made for smiles on our faces. Eventually, in the month of December 1986, there was severe cold and snow. Daily temperatures decreased by 8°F, from 45°F to 37°F, rarely falling below 20°F or exceeding 60°F, while daily low temperatures decreased by 8°F, from 31°F to 23°F, rarely falling below 4°F or exceeding 45°F. There were howling winds ranging from 16 to 34 miles per hour, with blowing snow. It was in this weather challenge that Joy's sister Zola and her husband Mack planned to visit us so that they could assist in the time leading up to Melodi's birth. The drive from Nashville had always been challenging during the winter, and in December in particular, with black ice and stranded vehicles along the interstate. Nevertheless, the Jolleys had made a commitment, and they began their travel by car on the early morning on December 12. Meanwhile, at 2 Interlacken in Springfield, Joy told me that her water had broken. I was challenged to control my anxiety and keep a cool head. I called her physician to alert him and his support group. Then, I woke RaShad and told him what was going on and further stated that I would ask our neighbors Mamie and Alex Sanders to pick up him up while I transported his mom to the hospital. Everything was a blur as the snowfall continued without abatement. Nevertheless, we made that spirited trip to Memorial Medical Center in the early morning hours of Friday, December 12, 1986. I don't remember much about checking in at Memorial. What I remember was going into the place where traditional hospital births were still the most common option. I helped the attending staff to move her from the labor room to the delivery room, and then, after the birth, to a private room. The miracle of a new family member was at hand. After Melodi arrived and before she was fully dry, I reached my hand toward her and she grabbed my index finger. This was a signal of a covenant that remains in my heart forever. When my daughter was wrapped in swaddling clothes and laid upon her mother's breast, my heart leapt with exoneration. Melodi had come one month before her projected arrival date, a "preemie" at 5 pounds, four ounces. She would not be discharged that day. Before noon, I returned to the home of the Sanders, where I picked up RaShad. He was ecstatic to learn he had a sibling; in fact, there were few times, if any that I remember greater joy and satisfaction expressed by my firstborn. In mid-afternoon, the Jolleys arrived and were astonished to learn that they now had a new niece. All of us then retraced the route to Memorial Hospital through the snow-blowing wind. Inside, we took the elevator to the floor, and still chilled and shivering from the single-digit outdoor temperature, we saw the mother and our daughter. We were told that Melodi would not be allowed to go home until she gained sufficient weight. It was not an exciting proposition to have Joy return home to Country Club Estates without her newborn. We were the recipients of God's grace when, three days later, Melodi had gained enough weight to be able to go to the nursery that Joy had begun and Zola, Mack, RaShad, and I were able to complete. The Jolleys returned to Nashville, and there began a new life for us at 2 Interlacken. No amount of cold and blowing snow could dampen the spirits in our house. For an entire year, we experienced mirth and exuberance. It was the best of times; if I could control time, this experience would linger forever.

Christmas 1988, Mirth and Exuberance

To borrow the words of Mary Hopkin, "those were the days we thought they'd never end. We'd sing and dance forever for a day, we'd live the life we choose, we'd fight and never lose, for we were young and sure to have our way." For about ten years, that was the case, but subsequently, we would learn that Father Time had many other experiences that would occupy our paths. In the meantime, our family of four bonded, vacationed around the country, enjoyed amusement parks, and stayed in resort locations. It was also a time for sibling bonding. RaShad was big brother, protector, and admirer of his kid sister. Just as Melodi and I bonded on her birthday, she and RaShad bonded when she came home from the hospital for the first time.

He had longed wished for a sibling, and now that wish had come to pass. Thankfully, each of them grew fond of their sibling. The mutual admiration was evident in the earliest time. When Melodi began to walk and talk, she acted as though her appointed duty was to command that he perform certain tasks. I would often hear her as she commanded her big brother "sit." He would drop what he was doing as she would then command him to open either a drawer or a cabinet that she could not reach. Sometimes, he would say, "Mello, get it yourself," or, "I don't have time," or simply, "no." There was never any hostility or resentment between the two of them. As she grew up, she was becoming interested in participating in the Columbia Entertainment Company's community theater and becoming a member of a dance team. Both RaShad and I were her biggest boosters.

When Melodi was not yet 2 years old, I became aware of an employment opportunity at the University of Missouri in Columbia. During the time that I was active in the activities and projects of the American Society for Public Administration

(ASPA) and when I had been nationally elected to the ASPA national council, I met many "movers and shakers" in the profession. One of them was Bob Denhardt, who had been a council member, and then national president. At that time, Bob was vice provost at University of Missouri, and he told me of a campus-wide administrative position at MU. Two positions were being advertised, one as vice provost for minority affairs and the other as one of the deans in the graduate school. Over a period of months when we would be attending an ASPA conference or conducting council business, Bob would speak to me about the opportunity. One day, I decided to drive from Springfield, IL to Columbia, MO before I had decided to make a formal expression of interest. Upon arriving, I drove around the campus, which had a student body population in excess of 25,000 and a physical plant that "screamed" of its flagstaff status. The campus of the University of Missouri measures 1,262-acres (2.0 square miles), just south of Downtown Columbia, and the campus is maintained as a botanical garden. It was the first public university established in the US which was west of the Mississippi River. There were seventeen colleges on the MU campus where deans administered fiefdoms. My interest peaked. I returned to UIS and began talking about this to Joy. We decided that I should make a formal expression of interest. A few weeks later, I was invited to an interview, which went smoothly. MU offered a tenured faculty position and a substantial pay increase in addition to the administrative appointment. What I failed to grasp was the enormity of the challenge. Many graduate schools had been eliminated because of the turf battles between graduate administration and the other colleges or schools, particularly the College of Arts and Sciences. The graduate schools did not have their own faculty. The graduate faculty were assigned to their tenure homes across the campus. Yet, the graduate school was the only entity offering admission to graduate study and authorized to approve graduate degree conferral. Moreover, graduate deans at a research institution were almost always tenured in either the life or physical sciences, not social science as was my case. But, the most significant challenge had to do with legal skirmishes featuring the US Departments of Justice and Education on one side and MU on the other side. The issue was declining minority enrollment both at the undergraduate and the graduate level. The tool for resolution of the issue of under-representative enrollment of blacks and other minorities at MU turned out to be a consent decree. A consent decree is an agreement or settlement that resolves a dispute between two parties without admission of guilt in a criminal case, or liability in the case of MU. A consent order is governed by federal and state laws, which vary by jurisdiction, and generally has the same effect as a court order and can be enforced by the court if any party does not comply with the orders. In this case, the plaintiffs were the Legion of Black Collegians and the Columbia chapter of the NAACP while the defendant was University of Missouri-Columbia. The Community Relations Service, US DOJ, and USDOE finalized the language on May 22, 1988. The driving force behind the university's agreement was the threat of the Department of Justice to pull all federal funds from the institution unless an agreed-upon process to remedy the paucity of minority enrollment at the institution was executed.

So, there I was facing a challenge of administering a program to market, recruit, and enroll graduate students, and to manage and administer funds for law and medicine, as well as graduate studies. A huge responsibility, yet, I was undaunted, even thrilled, by the challenge. Beginning with the time I enrolled as a graduate student at Pitt, I felt that higher educational institutions needed to develop time-based programs with sufficient initiatives to bring about a better state of affairs. Thus, this was considered by to me to be an opportunity to make a meaningful contribution to society.

The challenges of adjusting to a new job were tempered by the reception we received when we moved into our house at 2904 Canterbury Drive. Each of the neighbors up and down the street stopped by to welcome us with either a dish of food, cookies, or just kind words. We had relocated to a college town, and much attention in the town had been focused on affairs at the University of Missouri. Among the neighbors was a new family, Karl and Becky Schenck. Karl had recently been appointed senior pastor at Missouri United Methodist Church, and their house served as parsonage for MUMC. Karl and Becky had six children. It was instant friendship between my son and the elder Schenck son, Rob. They were in the same age cohort, and both enjoyed basketball. Karl and Becky became instant friends, and in the more than thirty years, we have remained friends.

In the fall of 1988, the MU Graduate School began to develop recruitment strategies designed to increase minority enrollment in its 105 master's and 67 doctoral programs. The effort yielded significant increases in minority (largely African-American) graduate students. The path to successful recruitment in the middle of Columbia, Missouri occurred at a time when African-American residents of Missouri felt unwelcome on the Columbia campus. Distrust of the mid-Missouri culture was not misplaced. Missourians lynched 60 African-Americans between 1877 and 1950, which makes Missouri the state with the second highest number of lynchings outside of the South.

A news story published in the *Maneater* in 2016 documented 4,084 racial terror lynchings throughout the United States. The majority of the lynchings were carried out in 12 Southern states: Alabama, Arkansas, Florida, Georgia, Kentucky, Louisiana, Mississippi, North Carolina, South Carolina, Tennessee, Texas, and Virginia. The Maneater data reported 341 lynchings that occurred outside of those states. Oklahoma led the list with 76 lynchings. Just behind was Missouri with 60, then Illinois with 56, West Virginia with 35, Maryland with 28, Kansas with 19, Indiana with 18, and Ohio with 15.

As late as the late 1980s and early 1990s, Missouri was referred to as being "up South" by many black students that had come to study at the university. Ironically, the desire for "Dixie" in Missouri reflects the culture that aligns itself with the Southern Confederacy. This culture was manifested in the rivalry between the University of Kansas and the University of Missouri. The nuance is associated with open violence involving anti-slavery and pro-slavery elements that took place in the Kansas Territory and the western frontier towns of Missouri throughout the 1850s. These incidents were attempts by some Missourians (then a slave state) to influence whether Kansas would enter the Union as a free or slave state. The era of political turbulence and violence has been termed Bleeding Kansas. When the Civil War began, the animosity that developed during the Kansas territorial period erupted in particularly vicious fighting. In the opening year of the war, six Missouri towns were plundered and burned by various forces from Kansas, generically termed jayhawkers. These attacks led to what is called the Lawrence Massacre, a retaliatory raid on Lawrence, Kansas led by William Quantrill, a Confederate soldier.

During the 1850s, the Kansas-Nebraska Act of 1854 became the organic act that created the territories of Kansas and Nebraska. It was drafted by Democratic Senator Stephen A. Douglas, passed by the 33rd United States Congress, and signed into law by President Franklin Pierce. The bill mandated "popular sovereignty" - allowing settlers of a territory to decide whether slavery would be allowed within a new state's borders. The act also served to repeal the Missouri Compromise of 1820 which prohibited slavery north of latitude 36°30′. Missouri was granted statehood along with slave status. The compromise additionally admitted Maine as a free state, restoring the political balance. It also drew an imaginary line west of the Mississippi and north of the 36°30′ latitude past which slavery would not be allowed after 1820. The act failed to end the national conflict over slavery. Antislavery forces viewed the statute as a capitulation to the South, and many abandoned the Whig and Democratic parties to form the Republican party. Kansas soon became a battleground over slavery.

An analysis of the rivalry's history by a University of Kansas professor concludes that historical memories of the Civil War era were not introduced into the athletic rivalry until the 1970s, and the historical angle did not seep into the popular imagination until the 1990s. A rebuttal provided extensive evidence the rivalry, "from its start, was influenced by animosity dating to the Border War." Evidence cited included a newspaper article on the 1891 game opening with a reference to the Border War, and a University of Missouri professor stating in 1910, "the annual football game… is but a continuation of the border warfare of earlier times."

The incidents cited above reflected the environment in Missouri regarding race relations. Decades later came Columbia's lynching of James T. Scott in 1923. That lynching reverberated and impacted blacks' notions of how they would be "welcomed" for study at the Columbia campus. These incidents served to characterize Columbia as an unfriendly place for African-Americans well into the 1980s. Scott, a black man, was working as a janitor at MU's School of Medicine when he was accused of sexually assaulting 14-year-old Regina Almstedt. According to news accounts, there was questionable identification of a perpetrator. Reporters additionally determined identification steps to be unreliable. Nevertheless, James T. Scott was promised a fair trial and "swift justice," but he did not live long enough to receive either. On April 23, 1923, a mob made up of MU students and community members dragged him from his cell, threw a noose around his neck, and hanged him over the Stewart Street Bridge, which is now a section of the MU campus that houses the MU School of Journalism. All members of the lynch mob were acquitted. Scott's last known words were, "I know I am going to die, but I am innocent."

Leading up to this event, Missouri had partisan factions within the Confederate Congress and was part of the territory that the Confederacy claimed during the war. With a history and tradition as rich as that of the South, the prevalence of Confederate culture should be no surprise. It was common to see the Confederate flag flying the stadium and to hear "Dixie" played by the University of Missouri marching band whenever the team scored a touchdown. To many regular Missouri sports fans, there was no harm intended by playing a tune that revitalized nostalgia for the lost cause of the confederacy. The song originated as background music at minstrel shows where white men in blackface purported to show happy black people. It was in the early 1960s when Dan Devine, the famous Missouri football coach, asked for two changes during football games: 1) flying the Confederate battle flag in the stadium, and 2) the marching band playing Dixie.

The background of those past events foreshadowed many days of grey skies that impeded the task of recruiting and enrolling students of color on the MU campus. While the majority of faculty and administrators in 1988 supported increased diversity among both the student body and faculty, there were pockets of strong resistance to efforts to create inducements that would further integrate the campus. Upon assumption of my duties, I received strong support from Judson Sheridan, my supervisor, vice provost for research and graduate studies. One of the strongest initiatives was the placement of all graduate and professional fellowships and stipends across the entire campus on my desk. A viable staff was headed by then recent doctoral recipient, Curtis White, my right arm, along with student affairs staff, marketing support, fiscal assistance, and external grant support. By fall, 1989, we had fashioned strategies to create "critical masses" of black and minority students that would lead the way in developing a welcome environment on the campus. The initiative emanated from an admissions, marketing, and enrollment management plan wherein we determined the national population of prospective students and calculated what would be a market share for MU.

Ten decision arenas were investigated: 1) the Graduate Division as an institution, 2) the external environment, 3) graduate study as an industry, 4) students as consumers, 5) competing institutions, 6) graduate programs and support services at MU, 7) MU's geographic location, 8) communicating and marketing efforts, 9) personnel and staff required to implement the plan, and 10) financial support in the form of assistantships and stipends.

Application data to the graduate school for the period 1991-95 reveal average annual increases of 82.5%, while admissions data for that same period increased annually by 31%, and enrollment data for that period revealed annual increases of 40% over the same period. The key weapon in our arsenal was the Campus Visitation Program. After settling down in Jesse Hall on the MU campus, my staff and I were able to develop a list of 45 historically black colleges and universities (HBCUs) and send MU recruiters to these campuses in search of prospective graduate students. The visits to these campuses would begin immediately after Labor Day and continue through the first week in November. Our ambassadors were instructed to seek students that demonstrated promise based on their undergraduate transcripts, their interest in getting a degree beyond the bachelor's, and willingness to exploring a campus that may not be as friendly as that which they had become accustomed. Upon returning to the MU campus, we would examine the ambassadorial "harvest" and send promising applications to the departments across our campus. I would meet with directors of graduate studies in programs across the campus and encourage them to take a long look at the student interest. When departments showed an interest in the material that described the students, we would invite individuals to come to Columbia for a weekend and visit the graduate school staff and directors of graduate studies in programs that fitted the student backgrounds. We provided air transportation to the potential graduate students and lodged them either on campus or adjacent to campus for a two-night, three-day visit that culminated with Saturday brunch in the homes of blacks and other faculty before returning to their campus homes. Students who followed through and completed application were made aware that they would be considered for a substantial fellowship and teaching or research assistantship that would cover them in doctoral studies or master's degrees. This program "caught fire" around the country. There was more interest in our recruitment efforts than we could accommodate. Campus leadership had made an investment in my office when they placed, on my desk, funds to distribute to campus departments and to successful applicants so as to make the recruitment effort bear fruit.

A major outcome of the Campus Visitation Program was that among the graduate students who had no prior knowledge of each other, some became husband and wife! It was also rewarding when fellowship students would visit me and tell me of their future plans. All these events made known to me the rewards of helping people get their careers started. Years later, in my retirement, former students who are now professors, directors, and captains in their enterprise still tell me how much my efforts meant to them as they were graduate students. There is no price tag on the feeling their remarks give me.

The centerpiece attraction, aimed at getting our market share of black graduate students, was a fellowship that would be competitive with all the fellowships that the campus had never awarded to a minority student, such as the G. Ellsworth Huggins Scholarship for doctoral students. This was a program established in 1979 with a $3.5 million bequest from G. Ellsworth Huggins, the largest gift up to that date received by the University of Missouri. The award was to be made to doctoral students in any field, with special consideration given to students from Huggins' birthplace (Barton County, MO), especially graduates from schools in Lamar, MO. Nominees must have and maintain a 3.5 GPA. International students were not eligible for nomination for this fellowship. The Huggins was the most prestigious doctoral on the campus. It is important to note that the white racial makeup of Barton County has for decades hovered around 97%, 0.29% Black or African-American, 0.83% Native American, 0.28% Asian, 0.10% Pacific Islander, and 0.14% from other races. These data undoubtedly reflect the reality that the chances for an award to a black student was nonexistent. The award was $10,000 and brought with it its remission of tuition and fees and a graduate research or teaching assistantship.

The opportunity to launch a fellowship for underrepresented minority students allowed my discretion to award a fellowship for $12,000 that brought with it its remission of tuition and fees. The issue we had before us was what to call the fellowship. Staff and deans in the graduate school pondered many possibilities, and we agreed upon casting the honor upon the first black person to earn a graduate degree from the university. Gus T. Ridgel was Mizzou's first African-American graduate degree recipient when he earned a master's degree in economics in 1951; my staff was very enthusiastic about our office's opportunity to blaze a trail that would be attractive for future enrollment of underrepresented minority students. Ridgel had graduated magna cum laude the previous spring from Lincoln University with a bachelor's degree in business administration. I called Ridgel to ask if he would be willing to have a fellowship named for him. Ridgel replied, "this is quite an honor." I followed up with a written letter. Thus began a muscled campaign that would pay off in the years to come. Among the many options was to name the degree for the first doctoral award to a black student. Our research caused us to focus on Hazel Teabeau, a professor at Lincoln University. While on sabbatical from Lincoln University, Hazel Teabeau became the first black woman to enroll at the University of Missouri. She enrolled there at the age of 57 to seek a PhD in Speech and Dramatics, and in 1959, she became the first black woman to receive a doctorate from the University of Missouri. I learned a great deal about the history and culture that is the flagship institution in the state.

Other fellowships included the Professional and Graduate Degree Admissions (PGDA) Program that was aimed at master's degree students and first year law students and medical students. During my tenure in the MU Graduate School, I sought and obtained greater than $15 million in grants and contracts. The centerpiece in this initiative was an award from the National Science Foundation to enhance opportunities for underrepresented minorities in degree programs in fields related to science, technology, engineering, and mathematics. Our baseline data had demonstrated that Missouri students had a paucity of students that would seek education leading to careers in life sciences, accounting, civil engineering, psychology, statistics, electrical engineering and computer programming.

We were also successful in obtaining many other fellowships, including the Patricia Roberts Harris Program. The Patricia Roberts Harris Public Affairs Fellowship was a 1-year fellowship program designed to provide a dynamic professional development experience to students interested in public affairs. I was also able to garner funding for a fellowship named in the honor of Thurgood Marshall.

Another fellowship was the William Gregory Fellowship which had been endowed by St. Louis dry goods merchant, Charles R. Gregory, in memory of his brother, William. The Gregory Fellowship was established in 1914, and university records suggest that it furthered the academic careers of many of MU's most outstanding graduate students. Awards could be made to doctoral students in any discipline. It was a modest amount: $5000.00. Doubtlessly, its value in 1914 was significant, but in 1988, its value was not as competitive as those established in 1988 onwards. Nevertheless, nominees must have and maintain a 3.5 GPA. International students were eligible for nomination for this fellowship.

The final fellowship I was to administer was the David R. Francis Fellowship. It was an endowment from former Missouri Governor David R. Francis (1850-1927); this fellowship program was established in 1927. Awards were for graduate students newly admitted into master's or doctoral degree programs in either public affairs or creative literature. The nomination materials for this fellowship program from creative literature applicants must include an original composition. International students are eligible for nomination for this fellowship.

It was clear that none of the fellowships had been awarded to a member of an underrepresented minority group; after all,

African-American students were not admissible to the university prior to the 1950s.

Aside from the success of the graduate recruitment and admissions marketing program, another success of students who were choosing to pursue a graduate degree from MU was the commencement ceremony. MU commencement was truly pomp and circumstance of the highest order. In June of 1988, a few weeks after my appointment had been activated, Judson Sheridan, vice provost of research and graduate education, asked me to assist the hooding ceremony for doctoral students. The hooding ceremony is symbolic of passing the guard from one generation to the next generation. Candidates for the hooding ceremony will be full recipients of their doctorates at the graduation ceremonies. The hooding ceremony is a key feature of the graduation ceremony as faculty and doctoral students would be dressed in academic attire. During the ceremony, the name of each doctoral candidate is called, and the graduate goes on stage with his or her academic advisor. The advisor places the doctoral hood over the head of the graduate, signifying his/her success in completing the graduate program followed by congratulations from university officials. During the ceremony, a candidate presents themselves to their faculty advisor or another authorized member of the faculty with their hood placed over their left arm. The candidate hands the hood to the advisor and turns away from the him/her (often to face the crowd for photos) while he/she places the hood over the head of the graduate. As I stood on the platform, participating in the pomp of commencement, I remembered that neither Joy nor I waited to be hooded at the Pitt graduate ceremony. My academic advisor, Dr. Joseph E. McClean, mailed my hood and degree to our home in Nashville. Year after year, observing the significance of the event at MU made me remorseful.

In the meantime, I still had a life beyond campus administration. The year 1992 marked four years after arriving at MU. At that point, graduate school enrollment and graduation data began to positively demonstrate performance effectiveness associated with my 1988 appointment. During the spring of 1992, we purchased a time share at the Lake of the Ozarks, and over the years, we would trade our apartment for opportunities to vacation across the country.

Frequently, we visited Las Vegas, the Colorado Rockies, Gatlinburg in Tennessee, Disney World, the Mississippi Gulf Coast, and numerous locations in the Carolinas and Florida. After spring commencement of 1992, my family and I ventured to the Colorado Rockies. The reprieve for me and my wife and children was vacation trips and visits to family. Getting away from it all was what we longed for after work and school sessions were done. Seeing the Colorado Rockies, the mountain scenery of Gatlinburg, TN, and the Pacific coastline in Southern California always renewed us and energized us for life in Columbia. Even when it was only temporary, these visits filled in when we were being drawn to feelings of doom or simply hum drum times. Memories of beautiful sights that only God could create became the stuff I visited when I needed to travel through the summer forest that is my mind... remnants of my memory allowed certain events, certain people, and certain thoughts to be replayed on my tapes. Consequently, I have from time to time lived in a pastime paradise. I glorified days long gone because they helped me escape from the "nowness" that I would otherwise experience. I also would climb into the cockpit of my time machine and daydream of a future paradise.

The opportunity to see God's handiwork was and is inspiring and refreshing; over the years, I have come to view God's handiwork as a time for prayer and meditation. These family vacations also provided time for my children to continue sibling bonding. To be sure, the sibling bonding was not put on hold for vacations. Bonding between my children began the day Melodi was brought home from the hospital.

I experienced some sunshine when RaShad graduated from Rock Bridge High School in the spring of 1992. He was now entering manhood. During the second semester of his junior year and continuing through the second semester and summer of his senior year, RaShad and I had visited several prospective colleges and universities. Among them were UCLA, Jackson State, and Xavier and Dillard in New Orleans.

Meanwhile back in COMO, Melodi was busy with her dance classes and her participation in plays at the local Columbia Entertainment Club, a facility where local actors and play directors presented their work. RaShad and I would always attend Melodi's dance recitals until the time for RaShad to go to undergraduate school in the fall of 1992. As a proud father, I could not help but notice the different ways in which boys and girls related to each other. It was not unusual that a young lady would pull up in our driveway to pick up RaShad and drive him to school. Students in 1990s COMO were seemingly impervious to color and ethnicity.

RaShad had taken up the alto saxophone and performed in the Rock Bridge marching band and jazz band, and successful participation rarely allowed focus on school mates as "others" or being different. My high school experiences had been quite different. My childhood tapes contain numerous memories of a segregated society and culture.

Death of my mother in 1992

With the good comes the bad, or so it seems; the year 1992 also saw the beginning of more life-changing events, and the most significant in my memories was the passing of my mother. It was in the middle of a snowy morning in March when my brother Clarence called me from Dayton, OH to tell me of mother's passing. Clarence's voice was low and subdued as he told me of her slipping away. The message was not a surprise. Over the years, there was ample evidence of dementia that had been earlier diagnosed. This once witty and nurturing mother I remember as a youngster had battled Alzheimer's for more than three years previously. Nevertheless, the news was not welcome. My brothers and I relocated my parents from Laurel to Dayton in 1984, due to my dad's health. Amongst my brothers and I, we reasoned that our parents would be better off if we were not so far away. My mother had been the caregiver for my dad during his illness. Based on each of my brothers' traveling from either Ohio or Missouri to attend to matters at 115 Melon, we knew the drive from Dayton to Laurel was a little more than 15 hours, and the drive from Columbia, MO to Laurel was a little over twelve hours. Her demise came eight years after relocating from Laurel. When she passed away, she and my dad had been married for 65 years. She had birthed eight children, one daughter and seven sons, and was grandmother to 33 grandchildren, 29 great-grandchildren, and three great-great-grandchildren. To many nieces and nephews, she was "Aunt Leen" and was cherished for her smile, laughter, affection, and wit.

A funeral for a parent is an ominous experience. My mother was eulogized twice, once in Dayton on March 7, 1992 at New Zion Baptist Church, where my brother Therman was pastor, and again the following week in Laurel at Friendship Baptist. It was an emotional ordeal sprinkled with sadness and remembrance of happy days and occasions. I remembered the scripture (Psalm 30:5), "*weeping* may *last through the night*, *but joy comes* with the *morning." Yet, there were years that passed before the morning came in my life.*

Eight years earlier, in the summer of 1984, my brother Ezell had offered one of his houses, 241 Shoop Ave., a well-kept dwelling in a well-kept, friendly neighborhood, as a place for my parents. Most importantly, it was within short driving distance for the six brothers who lived in Dayton. Very shortly, 241 Shoop became the central place, as grandchildren, cousins, my dad's siblings, and my siblings could frequently be found there.

The transition from Laurel to Dayton had not been easy for my mother. Despite the new surroundings of her children, grandchildren, and dad's siblings, and their families, something was "missing." Therman and I observed a few months into the move that mother had physically relocated but figuratively "never unpacked her bags." At the time we moved her, she was 78 years old, living comfortably in her church community and enjoying her home and her neighbors; these activities garnered a sizable amount of social collateral. For longer than a half century, she was "Sister Sampson" at Friendship Baptist Church. She sang in the church choir and taught Sunday school.

The sadness of her passing lay with me for years. To this day, I miss her hugs. After she passed away, I was cleaning out my office and came upon the 1988 photo taken when we brought Melodi to Dayton to meet her Dayton family. While I always carried my camera when we traveled to visit family on our rest and recuperation vacations, I was not always in search of a momentous photo. In fact, I know that some of the "best" photos are accidents of light and the subject. Thus, I had long forgotten that the photo of my mother, my daughter, and Therman's daughter, Wanda, had ever been taken. Nevertheless, I was jubilant to find this photo taken at 241 Shoop in Dayton. I located it and first took notice of it after my mother had passed away. During our visit, my nephews and nieces and my brothers all came to welcome our daughter. In this photo, Wanda, my niece and daughter of Therman and Ethel, was fascinated by this new creature. It is of some note that about four years later, Wanda would marry Keith Dixon and Melodi was a flower girl at the wedding. It is also noteworthy that when Melodi went off to undergraduate school at the American University in Washington, DC in the fall of 2005, Keith and Wanda lived in Upper Marlboro, MD, about an hour or so driving time. My work responsibilities many times required meetings in the Washington, DC area; when I traveled to the DC area before Melodi's final years in high school, I would factor in time to visit Keith and Wanda in Upper Marlboro, as well as time with Cleophus and Dorothy Patton, Joy's sister and brother-in-law who resided in Washington, DC.

RaShad becomes "Joe College"

In the fall of 1992, RaShad was admitted to undergraduate study at Dillard University in New Orleans. We decided to drive him to the campus and take a delay en route to have a vacation in the Louisiana Bayou. The route along I-55 passed through Memphis, the Mississippi Delta, Jackson, and McComb. Once we reached Brookhaven, we were two hours away from our destination. The Mississippi towns we passed through were familiar to me as a result of high school football games, band trips, drama club, and Hi-Y activities. As we anticipated our car journey to New Orleans, we read that the lush Southern landscape, dubbed Bayou Country, would be teeming with seafood, wildlife, and passels of lively Cajuns. We envisioned dark swamps thick with cypress trees to sun-kissed marshes playing host to herons and egrets.

From television and movies, we came to expect the Mississippi River Delta to be a watery but photogenic wonderland. Much of southern Louisiana, where rivers empty their waters and sediment into the Gulf of Mexico, comprises the delta. From prior conference travel and professional meetings in the Big Easy, we had come to know about Dooky Chase Restaurant and staples such as red beans, rice, hot sausage, gumbo, Po Boys, Shrimp Clemenceau, and an assortment of Creole dishes. In addition to Dooky Chase, we knew about Antoine's, Galatoir's, Brennan's, Broussard's, Commander's Palace, Arnaud's, Tujague's, and Willie Mae's. Of course, it is impossible, it seems, to cite them all. Dish by dish, they won the city its reputation as a world-class dining destination - a title that is centuries old. There was also Bourbon Street and Dixieland jazz and the cafe where scantily clad women swing from the inside of a restaurant/bar onto the pavement where tourists traveled.

Of course, we had come to New Orleans to see our son begin his college career at Dillard University, a private, historically black liberal arts university. Dillard University had been founded in 1930 and was the product of the Straight College of New Orleans and New Orleans University. The important context was that in the Deep South of the United States, local black and white leaders felt there was a need to develop a larger, more notable African-American institution of higher learning in New Orleans and the greater South. While there was a general consensus on establishing institutions that would serve the black populations in that part of the USA, economic hardships and rounds of negotiations between the parent institutions, Straight College, a black college in the city, and the predominantly white New Orleans University, were obstacles to this. Finally, the "birth" of Dillard occurred on June 6, 1930 via charter. Suffice to state, Dillard's development was significantly impacted by the Jim Crow era. Many local whites took issue with the probability of a black president supervising white faculty members, and the compromise resulted in a white Southern preacher becoming the first acting president. The institution's rich heritage, associated with higher education for blacks, was the outstanding characteristic that attracted us and RaShad. As the institution developed, it had attracted prominent scholars such as Horace Mann, faculty member in psychology and education; St. Clair Drake, faculty member in sociology and anthropology; Frederick Douglas, for whom a building was named, etc. It was not lost on me that the institution favored blacks of a lighter hue, but I had also come to know that the color of a person's skin was not the only factor that measured his or her devotion to fairness.

So, we left New Orleans to return to Columbia, but not before RaShad had to ask his mother to leave the room layout to him and his roommate, who was yet to be assigned. New Orleans and Dillard University represented freedom from parental control, much like the independence Nashville and Tennessee offered me twenty-four years earlier as a college freshman away from home for the first time.

Joy and I had told RaShad, on many occasions since his high school years began, about the importance of earning a college degree. We urged him to enjoy that new journey even though there would be plenty of stress and even homesickness. We told him to attend all orientations, get to know his roommate and others in the residence hall, get better organized, go to class, get to know the professors and his academic advisor, find an ideal place to study, etc. Of course, since Joy and I had a combined 36 years as college professors, we knew that as parents, our advice would not be fully embraced. Nevertheless, the rest of the freshman year went on without fanfare. My MU work, which involved establishing relations with some select black colleges, would take me to the New Orleans area once or twice a year. Of course, he would either return to COMO for the holidays, and on one occasion (1993), the family motored to New Orleans for the Thanksgiving holiday.

We would call RaShad three or four times a week during his freshman year, although land lines were the medium and there were long-distance charges. In COMO, our routines went along as usual. Joy traveled to Jefferson City for professorial duties at Lincoln University, and I spent 10-hour days in the MU Graduate School. Melodi completed preschool and her first years in elementary school. Despite the age difference (or perhaps because of it), RaShad and Melodi maintained a close-knit relationship.

As I recalled earlier, the decade of the 1990s was the best of times and it was the worst of times. During those years, my mother passed away (1992), RaShad graduated high school in the spring of 1992, and about two years later, in a telephone conversation sometime during RaShad's junior year, he told me of a health concern of his. This turned out to be the most consequential news in my life (A consequent is the second half of a hypothetical proposition. In the standard form of such a proposition, it is the part that follows "then". In an implication, if P implies Q, then P is called the antecedent and Q is called the consequent. In some contexts, the consequent is called the apodosis. This neat psychological formula is too cute to describe the new journey we would travel from 1994 through 1997 and there forward. My son's physical condition (p) implied a fork in the road (q) and we could label "physical condition" as "p" and the outcome of consultations with physicians as "q".). In this instance, there was no "hypothetical proposition," there was only reality; I wish I could have inserted a hypothetical and altered our future pathways. Alteration was not the case. Not even when I travel through the summer forest of my mind and sum up the conversations, consultations with physicians, and religious influences in my life as simple as stated here, altering our new challenge never became the case. Instead, we became familiar with new medical vocabulary, e.g., "T-cell lymphoma," "blood transfusion," etc. In my effort to wrap my head around this unexpected and unwelcomed challenge to my family, I thought of the words of Thomas Paine (**Thomas Paine, The Crisis No. I written 19 December 1776, published 23 December 1776):** "These are the times that try men's souls. The summer soldier and the sunshine patriot will, in this crisis, shrink… but he that stands it now, deserves the love and thanks of all mankind. Tyranny, like hell is not easily conquered, yet we have this consolation with us that the harder the conflict, the more glorious the triumph." Although Paine's remarks were directed to a national governance crisis, the nuance was appropriate to my family's crisis. Our tyranny was Non-Hodgkin's Lymphoma, and we were not vying for accolades as we faced our tyranny. I will always remember RaShad's words as we were first told of his medical challenge. First, he said, "how are we going to tell Melodi?" and second, he said "I am going to complete my degree."

And yet, the band played on. Awareness of my son's illness foreshadowed the eve of destruction of the most valuable family unit I ever had; I cherished the fact of a son and a daughter and a beautiful wife. But, my wife and I had to attend to the challenges of maintaining home in COMO, parenting Melodi, and devoting attention to our roles as children of our parents who were transitioning into their senior years; sandwiched in between were the jobs we had that kept the mortgage paid and food on our table.

Our main task became a search for second and third opinions. We were assisted by RaShad's oncology physician, Michael Perry, a renowned hematologist and fellow church member who became a special friend. Dr. Perry made contact at University of Nebraska Hospital, and we subsequently flew to the University of Nebraska, but they were not able to handle the challenge. A few months later, we were directed to Duke University oncology center. At Duke, we found talented physicians who, in addition to their expertise, had great bedside manner. Thus, in the fall of 1994, based on the medical advice, we traveled to Durham, NC to admit RaShad to the Duke University Cancer Center, a state-of-the-art patient care facility that brought together almost all outpatient services in one convenient location. The programs and services included a patient resource center, retail pharmacy, self-image boutique, quiet room, cafe, and outdoor garden. For the admissions visit, we all traveled to Duke for a second time. Joy took a leave of absence from Lincoln University, and RaShad withdrew from Dillard. When RaShad returned to COMO, he enrolled at the University of Missouri.

Melodi was a second grader; upon returning from Durham to COMO, her elementary schooling continued. Now, I had the task of singularly caring for my daughter while her mom attended to the needs of our firstborn. During a family crisis, one finds out who his or her friends are. A plethora of blessings were manifested. Family; new neighbors, especially the Schenck's; my boss, Judd Sheridan, who traveled to Duke University for a meeting and took time to visit RaShad when he was hospitalized; and MU graduate students, including Tanzia McFarland, a doctoral student, made themselves available when I needed them as I struggled to get Melodi attired for school, etc. Each weekend, Melodi and I would fly to Durham and visit Joy and RaShad. Joy had acquired lodging at an apartment that was almost exclusively associated with housing families that did not live in the Raleigh-Durham area. During the fall stay at Duke, Mack and Zola, John and Belinda, and LeRoy and Rebecca on separate occasions stayed with RaShad for a week and thereby relieved Joy so she could then travel back to COMO.

After a couple of months, the treatment regimen began to demonstrate signs of significant improvement. However, the road to remission finished yet in the distance. This meant the split homes in COMO and Raleigh would be in operation as the holiday season rolled around. Christmas time at our house was always a time for celebrating. However, in the winter of 1994, we prepared to celebrate Christmas at the medical center. For the trip of 926 miles, Melodi and I had a memorable time as I drove the 15-hour trip. Without Melodi's knowledge, Santa had placed her Christmas gifts in the trunk of our car.

When we arrived in Durham, we went to the hospital where we were all together again. Later, Melodi, her mom, and I returned to our car to unload baggage so that we could take up holiday residence. All four of us were learning new lessons about life and the things that really mattered. I was not prepared to explain to Melodi the adult version of Santa Claus. I opened the trunk of the Cadillac to begin removing Melodi's gifts. I quickly moved in front of my daughter so that she could not see, but my timing was too late. My daughter had seen the luggage and the extra items in the trunk. She did not let on that she had seen the gifts; she asked no questions, even when on Christmas morning, the same items were under the Christmas tree. On Christmas Day, RaShad was still hospitalized, but the treatment demonstrated cell regeneration that caused celebration among the physicians. Of course, the celebration amongst the four of us was even more exuberant. We all acknowledged that Christmas of 1994 was the best that we had experienced. We had Christmas dinner in the hospital and gave thanks for the most meaningful signs of recuperation.

After a few days into 1995, Melodi and I returned to COMO via a flight and left the car for Joy so that she could have a means of transportation. Later in the spring, RaShad was discharged from Duke. Between Tanzia McFarland and Grandma Schenk, Melodi was able to have her grooming needs attended to (because I was a complete failure at the task of attending to my daughter's hair care). For the return to COMO, Joy and RaShad took a commercial flight, and I drove the return 926-mile, 15-hour drive. I was alone in my thoughts, and I thought of the popular soap opera "Days of Our Life," when the narrator would paraphrase Socrates, who stated, "our lives are but specks of dust falling through the fingers of time like sands through the hour glass, so are the days of our life." Daytime soap opera's first golden couple chronicled their love story on and off the screen, offering an intriguing look behind the scenes at the Golden Age of daytime drama during the 1970s and 1980s, their own success in the entertainment world, and their rise to stardom as Doug and Julie on *Days of Our Lives*. The poetic line suggests that our lives flow away swiftly and inexorably, just as the sand grains in an *hourglass* did in the premodern days, i.e., when the *hourglass* was used to calculate the passage of time. As the sands flowed through the hourglass, Father Time was boarding passengers to the next excursion to the land of milk and honey and gold-paved streets.

Death of my father in 1995

In July 1995, my father passed away three weeks short of his 91st birthday in Dayton, OH. Dad's passing meant my returning to Dayton for his homegoing celebration. As I reflect on these events, it is difficult not to revisit the stress of those days. Dad had survived the passing of my mother in 1992, and he never really adjusted to being a widower. During conversations with me, he often recalled the days of their early life as newlyweds and his challenge to be a good son-in-law. He was extremely proud of each of his children. I knew that he had no known favorites among his offspring, but that if there was such a category, I was equal to any of the favorites. His passing meant that at 39 years old, I had become an orphan. Each of my brothers and I experienced a void that would never be filled.

My brother, Therman, eulogized our dad at New Zion Baptist Church, where his siblings expressed their love and admiration for their oldest family member. As had been the case when mother passed, there was a Dayton service and a Laurel service at dad's beloved Friendship Baptist Church. The day following the Dayton service, we placed our dad's remains on an airplane, and my brothers and I set out to drive to Laurel for final funeral and burial arrangements. We had driven from Dayton to Nashville when we received a phone call from Joy stating that RaShad had yet another relapse. My brothers then drove me to the airport in Nashville, where I secured a ticket for St. Louis. I honestly felt at the time that I had been denied the opportunity to pay my final duty to my father. I was challenged to keep my wits about myself. My concern for my son's health and my grief at the loss of my father were burdens whose pain was difficult to mask. When such trials come upon one, there is no preparation, no "manual of procedure" for direction. This was a time when I had to, by whatever step necessary, live above my daily circumstance.

By autumn of 1995, a sense of "normalcy" reappeared at 2904 Canterbury in COMO. RaShad survived the hospitalization and was now enrolled full-time at MU, Joy returned to Lincoln U., and Melodi continued her third-grade studies and became active in dance classes, as well as becoming a participant in Columbia Entertainment Company, a local theater that provided opportunities for aspiring actors. However, just as we behaved as though our long nightmare was over, RaShad was rehospitalized in COMO after an interaction with a medication. He was discharged in a few days later; however, the sands through the hourglass continued to flow and the band played on.

Continuing life in MU Grad School

One visible means of living above my circumstance was my job at MU, but even there, on the administrative agenda was the issue of dissolution of the graduate school. The Graduate School had been a four-dean unit in 1988, and in 1995-96, I was the only dean in the unit. Ironically, the stress of my son's illness and the grief of losing my dad could temporarily be tempered by the bureaucratic wars at work.

Meetings that used to be humdrum became reprieve, an escape from the real concerns on my mind. The issue of healthcare for graduate students and increased stipends to become more attractive to new graduate students captured the campus' attention. Likewise, the challenge for making the campus friendlier to black graduate students was always at the center of my concerns. These issues were in no means simple; they had been confounding challenges for years, but in 1996, they allowed me to live above the reality of the issues that were in the back of my mind.

Avoidance of the dread was temporary; however, I am now convinced that although the load gets heavy, our Maker knows what we can bear. The holiday season of 1996 also brought a reprieve. In December, RaShad appeared to be seriously on the mend. Weeks earlier, he began driving Melodi to movies. They really enjoyed each other's company. Upon returning, they would tell us about the movie and encourage us to see what they had experienced. Melodi's birthday on December 12th also brought occasions for celebrating.

Around the time of Melodi's birthday in December 1996, RaShad wanted to share her celebration, and I surprised both of them with the photo I was able to capture. The photo remains one of my most cherished. During that same December, RaShad wanted to help me play Santa Claus. He was a master at assembling toys. After he checked on whether she was actually asleep on Christmas Eve, we worked to assemble and place the gifts. When dawn came, Melodi rushed downstairs and showed her gifts to her parents and her brother. That Christmas remains a wonderful memory.

After the holiday was past, Joy returned to Lincoln, I returned to MU Graduate School, RaShad began a full-time class load at MU, and Melodi continued at Mill Creek Elementary. The new year of 1997 again appeared to be normal at our abode. Since RaShad was on campus, he and I lunched together on his class days. Appropriate to describe the tenor in our house were the lyrics from a Linda Hopkins recording in the 1960s written by Gene Raskin: "Those were the days, my friend, we thought they'd never end; we'd sing and dance forever and a day; we'd live the life we choose; we'd fight and never lose... oh yes, those were the days."

But, the more appropriate lyrics were Nina Simone's recording, "everything must change, nothing stays the same, everyone will change, no one, no one stays the same. The young become the old, and mysteries do unfold, for that's the way of time; no one, and nothing goes unchanged. There are not many things in life one can be sure of, except rain comes from the clouds, sun lights up the sky, and hummingbirds fly, winter turns to spring, a wounded heart will heal, oh, but never much too soon. No one and nothing goes unchanged." I first paid attention to these lyrics while listening to the Quincy Jones rendition in 1978. They were haunting then, but I did not understand why. Twenty years later, the situations in my family life would make the meaning of these chilling lyrics come to life.

As the 1980s and 1990s transpired, my work in the GS, particularly presiding at the commencement ceremony, among other job-related responsibilities, allowed me to abandon my pent-up anxiety.

Recalling how I managed to cope with the anxiety of RaShad's illness and my attempt to compartmentalize and thereby ensure that I could meet my professional responsibilities causes me to enter the cockpit of the time machine in the summer forest of my mind. My challenge (and I did not always fulfill it) was to disallow the problems of the day that lead me to conclude that, for me, life was not fair... it did seem that the playing field was disproportionately stacked against me. Deep inside my mind, however, I knew every problem has an answer, and if I could not find that answer, I would go and have a talk with God. Many of us feel we walk alone without a friend, never communicating with the Holy Spirit that resides within. My desire was to escape impending reality, and my attention would turn to a song credited to Billy Joel as performed by Tony Clark. It was popular during my undergraduate years in the late 1960s. The song was entitled "The Entertainer."

When I would lead the platform party of faculty and campus leaders into a crowd of 7,000 parents and friends of the graduates in the Mizzou Hearn's Arena, I muted the sound of the live orchestra performing "Pomp and Circumstance"; on such an occasion, my mental sound system would turn up the volume to lyrics that said, "the curtain‘s up, and your audience is waiting out there.

Now walk on stage, boy, like you don‘t have a care, and don‘t let them know that you‘re feeling so low... you‘re a sad-hearted clown, but the show must go on, go on and on, cause, you‘re the entertainer, the entertainer, you‘re the entertainer, the entertainer, yeah."

"Now hear that applause, and you know you made the grade; you fooled them well, for the money they paid. Now, walk off in style, and don‘t forget to smile. Though your heart tells you, "frown," you can‘t let the people down... I had been taught to suffer in silence."

To be sure, we did have days of sunshine. During fall, 1995, I had been designated honorary football coach as Mizzou played North Texas. As soon as I was told of this fun honor, I wanted RaShad to accompany me, and on the night of the game, we sat on the bench (staying out of the coaching staff as they worked the game). We went into the locker room at half-time and saw how the defense squad and the offense team made strategic adjustments to win the game. This was a fun event! There were a number of father-son events that I cherish in my memories. The days and weeks morphed into the spring of 1997. We celebrated his 23rd birthday in May. My son was continuing to demonstrate his overcoming of the lymphoma that had been diagnosed a few years earlier. However, in early June, he began to act sluggishly. This change became acute as he was scheduled for a visit to his physician. Joy and I noticed his lethargy, and we lifted him between us and walked down the stairs. We got him in the car and sped off to the hospital. As we were getting him into the back seat of the car, I asked him, "how are you feeling?" He replied, "out of place." Arriving at the hospital on June 4th, the attending physician took a look and told us he was experiencing an infection, but he should be able to be fully revived. The doctor's response was what we had hoped and prayed for. At that juncture, the hospital staff arranged for us to stay overnight. None of us thought we would be there for two weeks; we were truly in the wilderness of despair. On Friday, June 20th, at the break of dawn on the first day of summer in 1997, we lost our firstborn. He slipped the surly bonds of earth and danced the skies of laughter-silvered wings. He chased the shouting wind and flung through footless halls of air and saw the face of God. He was no longer "out of place." There had been many ironies. One month before his passage, we had gone to our condominium at the Lake of the Ozarks. We did not anticipate this to be the last family photo. In fact, we were in a celebratory mood since we enjoyed a family meal on May 14th, a few weeks earlier. But now, in our lap was the effort to plan a final memorial service. Five days after the 1997 summer had begun, we laid his body to rest. Twenty-two years have gone by, and there is still a loneliness in our hearts. Our family, MU and LU colleagues, neighbors, and friends at Missouri United Methodist Church continue to rally us onward.

I have learned that there is no one way of grieving, but what is certain is that if you love someone who passes on, grieving is inevitable. This experience became acute when my mother passed away in 1992, and my dad in 1995. However, as much as I loved my parents, the experience of losing my firstborn had its experiences that eclipsed the pain of parental loss.

I don't think we think about the aftermath of a death until the situation is unmovably placed in our lap. I was aware of the work of Elizabeth Kubler-Ross, a psychiatrist and visionary death expert who wrote about the five stages of grief. From my own experiences, I know that grief is not easily intellectualized, and there was no pattern or process that I had known to be referred to as typical. The five stages, denial, anger, bargaining, depression, and acceptance, are a part of the framework that makes up our learning to live with the reality of our loss. Grievers don't progress through these stages in a lock-step fashion.

Consequently, when my mother passed away, I found that I experienced the stages pretty much the way that Kubler-Ross outlined. When my father passed away, I skipped both the denial and anger stages, or at least had become inured to the notion of having any power to change the inevitable. When my son passed on, I repeated the bargaining stage over and over again and added stages of regret that Kubler-Ross never dreamed of. However, neither of these events would become, for me, an ordinary pain. I read of many grieving experiences before, during, and after these events had come to pass, and I eventually came to understand that Kubler-Ross didn't originally develop these stages to explain what people go through when they lose a loved one. Instead, she developed them to describe the process *patients* go through as they come to terms with their terminal illnesses. Kubler-Ross managed to change how much of the world thought about death. She helped soften some of the stigma that had previously been present, making it a little more acceptable to talk about and get support for loss. In fact, the actual grief process looks a lot less like a neat set of stages and a lot more like a roller coaster of emotions. When I grappled with my feelings, I came to know that grief doesn't proceed in a linear and predictable fashion. When my son passed on, my brother Therman told me there would be long walks in the dark woods, but that eventually, I would come to terms with the loss and gain a sense of acceptance. I walked through the woods, and more than twenty years later, I have come to accept the things that I cannot change.

The summer of 1997 brought beautiful sun-filled days that in other times would be welcome, but for me, it was blues in the summertime. My work at the university continued to be a retreat during my grieving. The highlight was always presiding at the commencement ceremony. The MU Faculty Council had recommended and approved conferral of the honorary doctorate to Bill Cosby.

During the winter of 1999, MU conferred that honorary doctorate. This was easily my most memorable time as dean in the MU graduate school. When I led the platform party out of the tunnel of the Hearn's Center, the crowd erupted with cheers when Cosby was by my side. I knew the cheers were not for me, but we were just excited that a celebrity of his stature was a key feature of our commencement. As could be expected, many campus leaders volunteered to host functions during the Cosby visit. I chose the task of driving our honoree to the airport after the ceremony. When campus photographers hoarded behind stage before we lined up to move from the tunnel onto the floor of the Center, I had a chance for a few one-on-one minutes with Coz. During our talk, we acknowledged losing our only sons in 1997. In February 1997, Ennis Cosby, his only son, had been killed in Los Angeles. We continued our conversation when I drove him to the airport. As we reached the entrance to the facility, I was directed to drive to the runway, where we saw his private plane. Coz insisted that we come aboard to the plane; he handed Joy, Melodi, and me some of his personal items so that all of us would have to enter the aircraft. Once on board, we saw accommodations for sleeping, lounging, watching television, and eating during the four-hour flight back to the east coast. There were no flight attendants. Only Dr. Cosby and the pilot occupied the aircraft.

A posthumous degree ceremony and award

When RaShad first learned of his diagnosis, he declared to Joy and I, "I am going to finish my degree." He did not do so because his parents pressured him; degree completion was his legacy. RaShad's major advisor at Dillard University traveled to COMO to visit us after the funeral. She had come to tell us that the Dillard University Registrar had reviewed the transcript of courses he had taken at MU, and he had satisfied Dillard's degree requirement for the bachelor's in history. She noted that in the long history of Dillard, no student had been awarded a posthumously. We held back our tears as she told us that she represented the DU president who was inviting us to attend the commencement ceremony in the spring of 1998. Dorothy Patten, Joy's sister, asked if she could accompany us, and we immediately agreed.

A year after RaShad's passing, we found ourselves on the campus of Dillard as guests of the university president. Jesse Jackson was the invited speaker. The lawn of the campus was carefully manicured; a sprawling crowd had gathered on that Mother's Day as the wind blew through the tree-laden grounds. Rushing back in my memory was an occasion on which I had previously visited Dillard on business and stood in the doorway of RaShad's dormitory as I waited for him. On that day, the campus was beautiful, and its appearance reflected the contributions of the Julius Rosenwald Fund, an African-American educational philanthropist that was responsible for aiding in the construction of over 5,000 schools in fifteen states in the southern United States. The university also conferred an honorary degree to recognize Gordon Parks at that ceremony. Joy and I were seated next to Mr. Parks.

The occasion was simultaneously bitter and sweet. As we approached the dais, the commencement speaker, Jesse Jackson, was first to greet us. RaShad's declaration indeed had come to pass.

In the months and years that passed, our family grieved. In the process, we learned that travel and vacations helped us "walk through the dismal woods." Although our quartet became a trio, the three of us looked forward to California, Philadelphia, New York, and Massanutten vacations, and cruises to Alaska, Hawaii, France, the Mediterranean, Nova Scotia, Spain, and Italy. They became temporary distractions that blotted out the incurable summertime blues. A few months after we had memorialized RaShad, we escaped to Disney World and, a few weeks later, set out for a trip to the east coast where we visited sites in Philadelphia and New York City.

We were in search of gloom avoidance. We would find such an escape when we experienced sights and sounds that were not reminiscent of a few months prior. It was a time when I more fully came to know how our daughter was developing and how much delight she would bring to us. Our first trip to Disney in Orlando brought out the child in me. The trip also seemed to rekindle the joy her mom and I had when we journeyed to Disneyland to escape Lass Vegas long before either RaShad or Melodi were gifted to us. The Florida trip in the 1990s was a signal of wonderful times when we would later venture on cruises to Alaska and Hawaii. Our travels also opened my eyes to the gift of parenting, particularly parenting a daughter. There were many known and observed father-daughter relations in my memory. There was my father's relationship with my sister, Uncle Ted Alderman's relationship with his daughters, and my observation of the relationship that Joy and her seven sisters had with their father. Each of these father-daughter relationships could be seen through the lens of Shakespearean plays. Shakespeare destines most father-daughter relationships to fail. Usually, the father proves to be inept and incapable as he neither knew his own child's nature, nor was willing to get to know her. The father's parental authority does not allow him to descend to his daughter's level and make an attempt to understand her will and her needs (Romeo and Juliet in 1596 and the Tempest in 1611). I do not claim that such failures characterized my observations. There are also father-daughter relationships recorded in the Bible. Scriptures (Luke 12:53; Matthew 10:35; 2nd Corinthians 6:18; Jeremiah 29, and Numbers 30:16) tell us that a healthy father-daughter relationship is a mutually respectful, open and honest, communicative, honoring, and trusting relationship whereby the daughter is confident in her father's enduring love, acceptance, and belief in her ability to choose despite any mistakes made.

Research confirms again and again that a father plays a unique role in the development of his children's self-esteem, behavior, life choices, and relationships. I cannot assert that I have been the perfect father to either of my offspring, but I can attest to a wonderful father-daughter relationship with Melodi. Truth be told, it began with her mother. Now well into our senior years, I am thankful of the mother-daughter relationship Joy and Melodi enjoy. Although our daughter has now graduatedfrom the American University and Johns Hopkins University, the mother and daughter are in constant contact and Melodi seeks our guidance in multiple enterprises. "Higher levels of father involvement in activities with their children, such as eating meals together, going on outings, and helping with homework, are associated with fewer behavior problems, higher levels of sociability, and a higher level of school performance among children and adolescents," writes Dr. Suzanne Le Menestrel in the Child Trends Research Brief *"What Do Fathers Contribute to Children's Well-Being?"* Although I didn't have to read the scholarly publication to know the importance of viable parent child relations, absorbing its content served to confirm what I knew before I became a father.

When the time had come for a decision regarding a place for her undergraduate studies, Melodi possessed the courage to seek undergraduate education away from Columbia. Despite the outreach to her from the University of Missouri admissions office, where the director continuously and strongly tried to recruit her and pledged to provide substantive financial assistance, she instead chose the American University in Washington, DC. The bright and shining object that is AU distracted her from the comforts of her home in Columbia. Despite such comforts, she has always had an elephant-sized work ethic, the likes of which were prominent in her graduating magna cum laude from American with a degree in international studies. Even before her undergraduate enrollment at AU, she had been somewhat inspired at the challenges of an international experience. She would tell me of her experiences with international matters and had become more interested in my international travel to Africa when she was in high school. Her high school, Rock Bridge, usually educated children of prominent COMO residents, many of whom had international pedigree. Melodi and I always had wonderful discussions when I would return from my international travels. Her mom was also a college professor who would talk about international experiences among her students. So, this self-motivated daughter of mine took a look at the requirements for the foreign service program that is run out of the US State Department. I knew she was in serious consideration about a Foreign Service career when she would occasionally ask a question about the Foreign Service Test. The constancy of the subject communicated that she was earnestly serious about such an endeavor. I admit that I was and still am a helicopter father and would share with her the "costs" that a foreign service officer would have to pay. I would tell her about the US ambassadors I met during my international travels and the dearth of African-American ambassadors I had come across. These tidbits were not entirely momentous in her decision for pursuits after the baccalaureate, but my intent was, in part, selfishness. I had seen a number of foreign service officers who sacrificed their personal goals for a post in an extravagant country. I had seen bright, ambitious young women struggle to have a close relationship with their families because of their commitment to international work interests.

The atmosphere at the American University gave her an appreciation for the rewards of higher education; the campus is physically situated in the northwest quadrant of the District of Columbia. In close proximity is Embassy Row, the informal name for the section of Massachusetts Avenue, N.W. between Scott Circle and the north side of the United States Naval Observatory, where embassies, diplomatic missions, and other diplomatic representations are concentrated. On Embassy Row, one can visit more than 20 countries in a matter of hours. During her freshman year, a group of her classmates went trick-or-treating on Embassy Row, a tradition I learned is embraced by AU's global-minded students.

AU's student body numbers over 13,000 and represents all 50 US states, as well as 141 different countries; around a fifth of students are international. Its prominent alumni include numerous journalists, media personalities, ambassadors, and Congress members. The American University is one of the top five feeder schools to the U.S Foreign Service, Congressional staff, and other governmental agencies.

My mother would have called her institution and her educational pursuit "high cotton," not in a despairing manner, but one where effort and ability met with reward.

After undergraduate study, Melodi informed me and Joy that she was going to take up residence in the area. I admit this move was not exactly a pleasant surprise. Joy and I helped her purchase goods for her apartment in Bethesda, Maryland. Her roommate, an undergraduate acquaintance, was enrolling in a PhD program at AU. At that juncture, Melodi was interested in immediately jumping into graduate study, but I urged her to get some life and work experiences in her resume. I don't know if I had had sufficient foresight, and if so, I would not have discouraged her. Some of her classmates went into medicine and became MDs. However, I had been dwelling in a past, during which I came to know that the best graduate students were those who brought life and work experiences to the classroom. What I have come to appreciate is the role of privilege in preparing children for higher education and beyond. My childhood tapes centered exclusively on work ethic. Melodi was from a household where both parents had lofty goals, but our undergraduate experiences were remotely different from those our daughter would face thirty years hence.

For her first job out of undergraduate school, Melodi found a position at a DC public charter school where she directed recruitment and enrollment efforts. For a while, this was a challenging position, although it was similar to a job she held during the summers while living in COMO and working at MU. She did not see many opportunities for professional growth; thus, she viewed the canvas of opportunities in the nation's capital. She received information about the DC Public Charter School (DC PCSB), whose goal was to ensure that students and families in the District of Columbia have access to quality public charter education through rigorous academic standards using a comprehensive charter application. DCPSCB is an independent government agency and is the sole public charter school authorizer in the area. Melodi has led adult education oversight, managed the production of the annual School Quality Reports, assessed schools' growth plans, and facilitated schools' data management.

Melodi is our "trophy daughter." I choose to refer to her as a trophy daughter despite the reality that the term "trophy," when originally used, was not a term of endearment. Consider that a trophy daughter was born when the parents only saw her as an extension of themselves and when her accomplishments could be associated with a measure of good parenting. My daughter is a unique individual whose personality, dreams, and decisions are not so much reflective of her mother and father, but a gift from our Maker that personifies what grace means, i.e., unmerited rewards. We have not requested her to bring some semblance of credibility to our family, nor do we seek ambitious outcomes that reflect credit on us, her parents.

Road Trip to Southern California

As much as I celebrate her achievements, I equally treasure my memories of a thoughtful young lady and the enjoyable family cruises and vacation trips. In her infancy and toddlerhood, I was regularly involved in her day-to-day care, e.g., feeding her, putting her to bed at night, and attending to her cries in the wee hours of the morning. I spent time every day down on the floor at her level. I sang to her, showed her pictures and toys, and read her "Good Night Moon" a zillion times. Her brother, RaShad, was as enamored with her as her parents. When she was in elementary school, he would take her on outings like the movies; they would go on outings for just the two them. Affection was not a one-way lane, reciprocity was unmeasurable.

Our vacation travels and our family cruises to the Bahamas, Alaska, Hawaii, Nova Scotia, and Mediterranean in the south of France, Spain, and Italy will forever remain in my tapes. Moreover, our many travels to Las Vegas when we would carry her and her brother RaShad to the place where their parents first lived have brought unforgettable joy. These memories are the cornerstone of my personal and professional resurrection.

Fulbright Award and travel to Southeast Asia, Thailand

In the spring of 2001, I left my administrative position in the MU Graduate School to assume my tenured faculty position in the Harry S. Truman School of Public Affairs. My TSPA assignment was research and teaching. Graduate-level instruction was my exclusive assignment at UIS, and at MU. I imagined that my career was in midsummer, and I wanted a new challenge. Ever since my Pitt graduate student days, I have had a desire to travel to international destinations, and at that juncture, I had traveled to more than a dozen African countries and several European countries. I wanted experiences other than in Europe or Africa. Subsequently, I completed an application to become a Fulbright scholar at Khon Kaen University in Thailand in 2012. I committed to conducting research on municipal government and governance in the locale around Khon Kaen, Thailand. Governance is a relatively new term, and it is a commodity characterized by interaction between public, private, and nonprofit agencies. The intent of the interaction is to bring about needed improvement in the public delivery of services. It is a scare commodity (Peters, 1996), and the Thai government has devised institutions, programs, and practices to exercise collective control and influence over its citizens. Until the last few decades, there were discussions of "government," and "governance" focuses on the need to include Thai citizens in the discussion. Although the USA purports to be a democracy and Thailand a monarchy, there are still issues, particularly at the local level, that make for mutual interests between the two countries. Therefore, I proposed to use the municipal government experience and practices in the USA to contextualize local governance activity in Thailand. Both Thailand and the USA have legislated public policies that are committed to assuring that citizens can participate in the governance process. Both countries continue to experience challenges in meeting the ideal as expressed in their respective constitutions. Local governments and governance networks in both countries provide a laboratory to study service delivery, transparency, and accountability. Local governments in the USA and Thailand have experienced tensions and violence between ethnic groups and have developed programs and approaches to help resolve or prevent conflicts and build more cooperative relationships between these groups. Each of these governments used diverse approaches to address and diffuse tensions and specific conflicts, make short and long-term changes, and influence those who directly participate in the intervention as well as the larger conflict situation. In the United States, several factors, including social class, religious intolerance, primogeniture, and mercantilism, gave rise to the search for new life when the Europeans came to America. In Thailand, the seeds of democracy date back to 1932, when the Constitutional Revolution abolished absolute monarchy and introduced democracy. The Thesaban Act of 1933 gave rise to a process of modernization and administrative structural reform initiated by King Chulalongkorn (King Rama V). This western-style government bureaucracy introduced an administrative structure, comprising different ministries such as defense, finance, homeland or interior, foreign affairs, commerce, agriculture, education, and public health.

Local government came into existence in Thailand when King Chulalongkorn organized the *Sukhaphibaan*, or "sanitary district." With this innovation, he set up the sanitary committee as a governing body. In 1898, this "experiment" became Thailand's first form of local government. This innovation occurred in Tha Chalom, Samutsakorn Province (UN ESCAP, 1997). Thirty-five years later in 1933, King Prajatipok (King Rama

VII) expressed the view that Thai people in local areas required local administration in order to learn more about self-governing. This royal vision was considered to be the starting point for the development and movement for local government in the country (Chayabutr, 1996).

The political and administrative structure of Thailand saw a sweeping change in 1932, when absolute monarchy was abolished by coup d'etat led jointly by a group of military and civilian leaders. A European-style parliamentary system was installed, and the Public Administration Act was promulgated shortly after that coup. The act laid down the foundation of the country's administrative structure in three levels: central administration, provincial administration, and local administration. It should be noted here that "level" was the choice of word, instead of "type." This is clearly an indication that although local administration or local government has been recognized since the latter part of the last century, its administrative placement at the lowest echelon in the political structure of Thailand makes it easier to subject it to control and to ensure its subservience to the provincial administration. Constitutional arrangements authorize an appointed governor who serves as central administration's representative as well. Thus, despite differences in culture and other important aspects, local governments in both countries are connected to delivering services to the citizens.

I believe that programs which are aimed at the places where people live, within townships and local political jurisdictions, offer many success stories which detail transformations in citizen attitudes and behaviors, intergroup relationships, and social institutions and policies, yet few efforts have been made to recognize and compare the variety of theories of change that shape these interventions.

I also proposed to teach comparative local government to graduate students in the public administration program at Khon Kaen University. Such a course would introduce students to American local government not only in its traditional doctrinal and case-based dimensions, but also for its historical, cultural, political, and theoretical significance.

As I compiled the data for the application, I believed my extensive educational experience (at that juncture, thirty-five years) in the areas of the public management, intergovernmental relations, and local government would be of benefit to the students at KKU. It already has in place a variety of outstanding programs in the field, but my years of teaching, research, and professional activity should allow me to contribute to these programs. In turn, I was confident that my own understanding of the challenges of municipal government and governance networks, especially from a comparative perspective, would generate mutual profit from exposure to issues confronting mature and developing democracies and other constituencies represented in the KKU's programs in local government.

My Fulbright Thailand project began in the Thai year 2555. In 2012, I flew out of St. Paul Minneapolis International Airport en route to Southeast Asia via a 17-hour flight. Noticing the calendar differences served as vivid reminder that life in America began long after many long-lasting civilizations around the globe had been in existence. The Fulbright project was clearly about Thai citizens and KKU efforts to enhance and grow civil society in the locale, and as such, it was imperative to see and speak with Thai citizens and KKU faculty and researchers within the context in which they live and work. The Fulbright appointment took me to many historical cities and landmarks within Thailand, e.g., Khon Kaen, Chiang Mai, and Ubon Ratchathani and Champassak Provinces. The landmark referred to as the Kings'

Summer Palace in Bangkok was an architectural site that captured my unmatched fascination. The time spent in Bangkok began the completion of my stay in Thailand. Peerasit Kamnuansilpa, my Thai host, urged me to take some time to see more of their lovely country and I obliged.

The unique architecture spoke volumes about the differences between USA and Thailand.

The dazzling, spectacular Grand Palace is undoubtedly the most famous landmark in Bangkok. It's one must-see sight that no visit to the city would be complete without. It was built in 1782 and for 150 years was the home of the Thai king, the royal court, and the administrative seat of government. It continues to have visitors in awe of it from all over the world. Its beautiful architecture and intricate detail are a proud salute to the creativity and craftsmanship of the Thai people. Today, the complex remains the spiritual heart of the Kingdom of Thailand.

Thailand is a monarchy, one of the oldest in the world. As such, in Thailand, it is illegal to defame, insult, or threaten the king, queen, heir apparent, or regent. This is criminalized by Section 112 of the Thai Criminal Code. I came to know this after I was on the ground in Thailand and after having taught doctoral seminars wherein students were shy about verbally criticizing any Thai public policy. With such stark cultural differences, there were inevitable class discussions about which ideology best served the citizens.

The culture in Thailand is a mix of strong Indian influences, Chinese traditions, and elements that are uniquely Thai. With its diverse geography, friendly people, and stunning scenery, "the Land of a Thousand Smiles" is a must-see destination in Southeast Asia. Thailand lies between Cambodia, Myanmar, and Laos, with the Gulf of Thailand to its south. It is the 50th largest country in the world, with an area roughly equal to that of France. With rugged mountains in the north and world-famous tropical beaches in the south, it is a land of pristine beauty. I was privileged to see Thailand and some surrounding countries during the time when my classes were not in session. When these countryside excursions were underway, the main highway to other cities in Thailand was called Friendship Road. It was similar to an interstate road in the USA except that there was no posted speed limit. It was not unusual to travel at speeds in excess of 90 miles per hour when they would take me to see parts of the country outside of Khon Kaen. After class session during the week, my hosts would make arrangements to travel to many of the surrounding areas. My Thai friends said that the highway was developed by the US Armed Forces during the late 1960s conflict in Vietnam. The highway connected with arteries that would connect to Udorn Royal Thai Air Force Base (RTAFB). The Udorn RTAFB had been established in the 1950s when there was a civil war inside Laos, and fears of it spreading into Thailand led the Thai government to allow the United States to use Thai bases covertly beginning in 1961. When the conflict with North Vietnam expanded, USAF Pilots could conduct bombing raids from northern Thailand to sites in Cambodia to support the US during the war in Vietnam. The year 2019 marks 50 years since the American military embarked on the biggest bombing campaign in history, decimating the small Southeast Asian country of Laos by dropping more than 2 million tons of bombs on it at the height of the Vietnam War. Half a century later, innocent lives are still being lost as the country struggles with the leftovers of the conflict.

I also visited other neighboring countries in Southeast Asia, including Indonesia. Not far from the recesses of my mind was the knowledge of what my country had done while I was in high school and undergraduate school. Years later, when I was beyond draft age, I was awarded the Fulbright and taught, researched, and traveled in a land I had never dreamed of visiting.

Participants in the 3rd International Conference on Local Government included Khon Kaen University president, Chanchal Phanthongviriyakul, MD; Dean of the College of Local Administration (my host) Peerasit Kamnuansilpa; Charles Sampson, USA; Ando Hirofumi, United Nations Population Fund; Dick Pratt, University of Hawaii; Charlotte Gibbs, Australia; Gayle Ness, University of Michigan; and Alexis Amtaika, South Africa. More than two dozen nations were represented.

My local travels in Thailand and travels to bordering countries, such as Laos, the border near Cambodia, and Indonesia, taught me a lot about Southeast Asia. As an undergraduate, I remained acutely aware the possibility of being conscripted for service during the Vietnam War. Many of my high school friends and college classmates were drafted, and many were killed in Southeast Asia. I was curious about how I, an American, would be received in the land where so many atrocities had fallen on the brown folks in that land. I was pleasantly surprised at the reception I received. Everyone was warm and welcoming. When my hosts to drove me to the mall in Khon Kaen, I was amazed as the door to the sprawling six-story building that covered many city blocks swung open to the sounds of Aretha Franklin's and Michael Jackson's recordings.

When we traveled to the "hinterlands" which were not developed in the same fashion as I observed in Bangkok, Chiang Mai, and Khon Kaen, I anticipated the stuff of my imagination, i.e., disdain for a foreign traveler whose country (mine) was a signal force in killing so many of their family and friends. However, the indigenous residents were warm and friendly, whether we were in Bangkok, Chiang Mai, or in the fields where we would see people riding on elephants. I could not help but feel a sense of relief when I learned that I was welcomed. Once, a conversation ensued between me and my host about the fact that, in particular areas, it was common to see men riding on elephants as one would see in America about 100 years ago, with people riding on horses. The place where this occurred was a tambon, a local governmental unit in Thailand. Tambons can be found within cities or towns and are not subdivided into villages, but may have fewer formal communities called chum chon that may be formed into community associations.

In the deep recesses of my mind, I recalled US efforts to address Unexploded Ordinance (UXO) issues in the region, along with joint efforts regarding other war legacy issues such as POW/MIA identification and Agent Orange or dioxin remediation. These initiatives have been important steps in building relations with Southeast Asia in the post-war period. The efforts that have proceeded furthest are in Vietnam, where the bilateral relationship has expanded across a wide range of economic and security initiatives. In Cambodia and Laos, where bilateral relations are less developed, UXO clearance is one of the few issues on which working-level officials from the US and the affected countries have cooperated for years. Although some Cambodians and Laotians view US demining assistance as a moral obligation, and the US government has viewed its support for UXO clearance as an important positive aspect of its ties with the two countries, the issue of UXO has not been a major factor driving the relationships.

Despite the friendly faces and voices, I felt a sense of guilt about what had been done to places in Southeast Asia by my country. I remembered the 1979 Vietnam War movie *Apocalypse Now*, where an American pilot mused, "I love the smell of napalm in the morning."

The villagers were prepared for our entourage and welcomed us in song.

My 2012 visit to Thailand was in November, around the time of the second election of Barack Obama as USA president. I was fully committed to honoring my responsibility as a Fulbright scholar to travel to Thailand for a second time; thus, I cast an absentee ballot prior to my travel. Upon arrival, my colleagues at Khon Kaen University were eager for me to begin my work as visiting professor and Fulbright scholar, but they also desired to immerse me in their culture, food, and tradition. November was the onset of a fantastic festival called Loy Krathong, known as the Thai Festival of Lights. The celebration is one of the most enchanting and the second-best known festival after its New Year's festival Songkran. It is held annually all over the country, as well as parts of Laos and Myanmar.

Krathong is a Thai term which refers to a piece of banana trunk decorated with flowers, banana leaves, and incense sticks. The word Loy means to float in the Thai language. This occasion includes a Buddhist worship and a banquet of food. I wanted to remain in the background and observe rather than participate in the worship service (On a previous visit to Khon Kaen, I had been taken to a Buddhist temple and instructed how to properly bow and curtsy before the Buddhist image. I subsequently vowed never to betray my beliefs, as I was caught off guard by their directions.). After the worship portion of the celebration, the food was brought out, and the monks were the first to be served. After the delicious food was served, that portion of the celebration ended.

There are many stories regarding how the festival originated. One of the versions is that Thai people have long been closely involved in rivers for ages, as Thailand is an agriculture-based country. This means that rivers are like their own blood veins. To show respect to the goddess of the river, called Pra Mae Khongkha, Thai people decided to make Krathong an occasion to worship and ask for forgiveness. My Thai escort explained to me that Krathong is also a time to wave goodbye to misfortune, wash away sins of the past year, and make wishes for the coming year. Despite my desire to observe rather than participate, the head monk (who was not able to walk without assistance) came to me at the end of the service and, through an interpreter, blessed me and expressed his jubilation that the people of the United States reelected Barack Obama. They seemed to know much about life in America and the plight for racial and ethnic minorities. Throughout the country, the most important values that Thai people hold on to are respect, self-control, and a non-confrontational attitude. Losing face by showing anger or by telling a lie is a source of great shame for Thai people.

In general, displays of emotion in public are viewed in a very negative light. No matter how frustrated or upset a person might feel, he or she will always strive to maintain a positive and friendly attitude, a sense of humor, and a smile. Family is central to Thai life. Although many newly-married couples will set up their own households, it is not uncommon for extended family to live with them. Often, grandparents, cousins, aunts, and uncles will all live in the same household and help to raise children and provide for the family. Children are expected to show great respect for their parents, and they maintain close ties, even well into adulthood.

I also came to see day-to-day respect for elders and for those in higher social positions. Hierarchies of social status characterize nearly every interaction. Children are expected to respect their parents and teachers, and the young must show deference to the elderly. This cultural affect was evident in how the young people regarded their elders, including myself. During my teaching days, I would be chauffeured to the office, and immediately upon arriving, I would see my desk adorned with a beautiful floral bouquet. Staff brought fresh tea and food daily. Young students would step aside to acknowledge the presence of a senior.

Although Thailand's family life and society has been traditionally male-dominated, women are granted considerable respect. Recent laws and legislation have allowed women more freedom to move out of traditional roles and into professions such as politics, medicine, and business. Just as in many western societies, this evolution has been slow in its development. However, respect and equal rights for women has, in recent decades, become an important part of Thailand's law and values.

Another concept that is very important in Thai culture is *sanuk*. *Sanuk* is a wide-reaching idea that embodies the playfulness and sense of humor that is so central to life in Thailand.

It could refer to a spontaneous and joyful meeting with someone on the street or a humorous pun made at just the right moment. The sense of humor and *joie de vivre* captured in *sanuk* is central to the Thai way of life. Working in Thailand on three different occasions has endeared me to their people, food, culture, and customs. Like in my earlier work in Africa, I gained more professionalism than any amount of dollars associated with those experiences.

Chapter XVI

RECONSIDERING LIFE IN THE GAP

As I began to focus on the gap between *promise-stimulated expectation* and *reality*, I pondered the reality of that chasm and considered a book by Gerd Gigerenzer, *Gut Feelings* (2007). An interpretation of a passage in that publication inspired me to create two allegorical figures: Expectation and Reality. They are two well-dressed young women sitting on their chairs, calmly facing each other, yet neither takes notice of the other. Expectation, the fickle, wheel-toting goddess of chance, sits blindfolded on the left, while Reality, the calculating and vain deity of science, gazes into a hand mirror, lost in admiration of herself. These two allegorical figures depict a long-standing polarity; Expectation brings good or bad luck, depending on her mood, but Reality promises certainty. Both these allegorical figures are akin to my beliefs, but I more closely relate to Reality. In my estimation, Reality is most able to provide a pathway that allows us to transcend the places that hold us. Survival depends on rising above the certainty of life in the gap.

The space between *promise-stimulated expectation* and *reality* is the gap most of us live in while on this earth. I have often looked at my life and wondered, "is this really how life should be for a Christian?" God has made glorious promises to his people in scripture. It is sometimes when I experience day-to-day life in America that I muse in conversations with myself that He has failed us. When I have suffered through marginalization and unending attempts to be recognized as a real American, my confidence is checked. Yet, I am reminded of Emily Steele Elliott's work, *Expectation Corner*, in which the character Adam Slowman learned about the "Delayed Blessings Department" where God keeps certain things prayed for until the wise time to send them. Delays are not necessarily denials.

Those of us caught in painful, stagnant, or simply unglamorous circumstances can also find a sympathetic figure in Abraham, who spent years living in the gap between promise and reality. As might be expected, history has recorded many figures who struggled and lived above the circumstances of life in the gap.

I was growing up in the 1960s when I was indoctrinated to believe in the concept of meritocracy. When I was a teenager, I was not astute enough to see the connection between expectations of meritocracy and the reality of living in the gap. My admiration and support for meritocracy reflected our country's love for stories about people who started from meager means and rose to riches. My high school teachers taught us that despite our current circumstances, the United States is the land of opportunity, where anyone from any circumstance can succeed. They would draw upon local examples such as opera diva Leontyne Price, who was born on South Fifth Avenue in Laurel, went to Oak Park High School, and rose to stardom. Our more conservative teachers would argue that race, gender, and disability were characteristics that could hold us back only if we allowed them to do so. "A man's reach should exceed his grasp," as geometry teacher Sam Malone taught; Mrs. Idella Hodge, one of my elementary teachers, also inspired us to move beyond present-day circumstances. As I see it, the problem is that these ideas function on the presumption that the playing field is level for everyone. I rationalized that it would be just as detrimental to offer excuses for not achieving and becoming the best that we could be. Unfortunately, that is far from the truth.

Barbara Adams authored the book *Women, Minorities and Other Extraordinary People: The New Path to Workforce Diversity* in 2018. She argued, and I agree, that we buy into the concept of meritocracy because it supports the sense of can-do individualism that has shaped American mythology and gives hope to all. But in reality, unconscious and structural biases based on people's social class, immigration status, gender, ethnicity, and other factors impede a fair system for all. Clinging to a false narrative undermines opportunities for developing a more productive, better outcome. Merit is a beloved but misguided assumption about the way most US organizations operate.

Previous atrocities against minority groups, including the mass killing and displacement of Native Americans, the enslavement of Africans, and the internment of Japanese-Americans during World War II, are sad chapters in our shared history. While those events are in the past, their echoes reverberate throughout our society today. When we act as though the disproportionately small number of members of minorities in the middle to upper levels of businesses is due to individual failings or lack of availability in the market, we ignore the effects of hidden bias, subtle prejudice, and structural discrimination. Put another way, this is the basis for the gap that is real in our daily existence.

During my days in the gap, I have seen many storms. Most of these storms caught me by surprise, so I had to learn very quickly to look further and understand that I am not capable of controlling the weather, per se, nor (unfortunately) of exercising the art of patience, and yet, I respect the fury of nature. There are many good things in life, but chief among them are freedom of thought and freedom of action. I have seen something else under the sun: the race is not to the swift or the battle to the strong, nor does food come to the wise or wealthy, to the brilliant or to the learned, but time, chance, and death destroy all our best efforts. Thus, the wise among us know that we should invest in things that outlast work, wealth, and power, like these three R's, righteousness, religion, and relationships. Although I am not Catholic, I agree with their catechism that wisdom is the first and the greatest of the gifts. I pray for wisdom daily. Wisdom acts upon both the intellect and the will. According to St. Bernard, it both illumines the mind and instills an attraction to the divine. Father Adolphe Tanquerey explained the difference between the gift of wisdom and that of understanding: "The latter is a view taken by the mind, while the former is an experience undergone by the heart; one is light, the other is love, and so they unite and complete one another."

Time, chance, and death will destroy our best efforts. The challenge is to invest in something that outlasts our time on earth. The prevailing capitalistic paradigm is to find rewarding work that brings wealth and power, but we should seek another paradigm: gratefulness, humility, and presentness. Reading between the lines of Ecclesiastes 2:9-11, I understand that this alternative paradigm implies that it provides some kind of security.

And yet, I find agreement with Helen Keller, who offered that "security is mostly a superstition. It does not exist in nature, nor do the children of men as a whole experience it. Avoiding danger is no safer in the long run than outright exposure. Life is either a daring adventure or nothing." Despite the reality of these statements, I have never been fully satisfied with the many daring adventures I have experienced and risen above. Let me say, however, without equivocation, that I do not credit my rise to my intellect! My explanation is grace. The scriptures tell us that suffering breeds character and character breeds faith. And in the end, faith will not disappoint. Faith, hope, and dreams will prevail. It was these elements that lifted me to a level where I could rise above life's circumstances.

Nature of the current-day gap

In my lifetime, there have been various problems that I recognized as gaps between rightful expectations and reality. The nature of the current-day gap is unacknowledged racism by too many otherwise decent people. Racism is not new to the American experience; in the year 2020, the centerpiece of racism in the USA is the country's own president. The Trump symbol of nationalism is the mountain that stands between the free and fulfilled USA (where the country was headed after the end of the Obama Administration) and the racism, sexism, and misogyny Trump has subsequently championed (Grandin, 2019). During the 2016 campaign for the presidency, Candidate Trump vowed to build a wall on the border between the southern United States and Mexico. He promised that Mexico would pay for the wall, but he failed to let the Mexican government in on the secret. The promise became a failed effort to fool the US into thinking Trump could bully the Mexican government, and more importantly, it calls into question whether a physical structure is desirable, or even necessary.

The border wall has been the symbol that has unified a number of different Trump themes, e.g., white nationalism and white supremacy, etc. It's a kind of a rejection of the "old order", i.e., the notion of American exceptionalism which was nominally internationalist, what Trumpicans despairingly call "globalist." Trump seized on the idea of a wall, and that message was central to the opening of his announcement that he would seek the presidency. The world remembers when he called Mexicans rapists and murderers. Unfortunately, the symbol caught on for many reasons. Among the primary reasons is the increased schism within the Republican Party that goes back at least to Ronald Reagan and the 1970s, when undocumented migration became a policy problem.

In December 2014, then President Barack Obama warned that the United States needed to prepare for an upcoming pandemic. In a speech to members of the National Institutes of Health - which came only a short time after the Ebola outbreak had threatened to spread worldwide - Obama emphasized the importance of building public health infrastructure to combat the next pandemic. "There may and likely will come a time in which we have an airborne disease that is deadly," Obama said. "And in order for us to deal with that effectively, we have to put in place an infrastructure - not just here at home, but globally - that allows us to see it quickly, isolate it quickly, respond to it quickly, so that if and when a new strain of flu like the Spanish flu crops up five years from now or a decade from now, we've made the investment, and we're further along to be able to catch it." Obama's words now seem depressingly prescient as the novel coronavirus has spread rapidly across the United States, infecting nearly 2 million Americans and killing roughly 123,650 people. According to published reports, a number of current and former officials who led or shaped preparedness efforts during the Bush, Obama, and Trump administrations worked on a two-decade evolution in how government leaders learned to fight killer viruses. Unfortunately, America forgot those hard-won lessons as the COVID-19 outbreak loomed. Under President Trump, government agencies slowly abandoned their pandemic-planning efforts, with the Homeland Security department in 2017 shelving its decade-plus efforts to devise models of how outbreaks affect the economy. Rather than training government staff to respond to a pandemic as some high-level officials urged, FEMA instead coordinated a massive mock exercise in 2018 across nearly 100 federal departments focused on a hypothetical Washington, DC hurricane.

As the coronavirus ravaged the country, President Trump has refused to take responsibility for the way his administration has failed to adequately respond to the crisis and has instead blamed others for the severity of the pandemic. Unfortunately for the USA, Trump was so fixated with President Obama that, early on in the Trump administration, there was an attempt to discredit any and every policy embraced during the Obama presidency. The majority of Congressional Republicans joined Trump. Subsequently, Trump defunded and fired all members of the national security unit that was assigned to the task. But, no plan for a probable challenge was forthcoming. COVID-19 began to take a worldwide toll. What leadership spot that the USA would usually take was empty.

Then, in 2020, there was a reprisal of police brutality, characterized by the killing of African-American citizens by law enforcement officials. When our nation needs a strong leader, we, unfortunately are led by an incompetent racist whose vanity and arrogance has become his countenance. The timing of the triple challenges manifests in a wall deigned to make America whiter, yet devoid of support by the American people; the COVID-19 pandemic, which saw more than 2 million cases and 120,000 deaths of Americans; and citizen unrest over the mounting cases of police brutality across the country. These 2020 events have placed the Trump leadership style in full review by the world.

The plethora of current-day (spring/summer, 2020) murders and lynchings of African-Americans caused me to review the number of murders or lynchings of African-Americans at the hands of law enforcement officers in my lifetime. It does not escape me that many of the murders at the hand of law enforcers are connected to the reaction of a segment of the US populace that grieved the election of Barack Obama (about this matter, Trump was right). In 2016, after two elections of a black president, the Trump campaign anchored itself on the belief that a sufficient percentage of white Americans was disgusted with the election of Barack Obama. Trump opened his campaign with lies about the birthplace of Mr. Obama, claiming that he had not been born in the USA; he castigates Mexican-Americans; he disregards the history of American institutions and the means to maintain a democratic society. He appears not to accept that in a democratic society, power is shared between lawmakers, the executive branch (Office of the President), and the courts. Moreover, he has yet to display any behavior that would suggest his appreciation of the race-based struggles over the life of the country. He openly championed white nationalism and the confederacy, a race-based rebellion against the United States that characterized the Civil War that ended in 1865.

In 2020, race continues to play a central role in police brutality in the United States. In most American cities, ethno-racial minorities have alleged human rights violations by police more frequently than white residents, and far out of proportion to their representation in those cities. Police have subjected minorities to apparently discriminatory treatment and have physically abused minorities while using racial epithets. Mistreatment comes in many forms, e.g., non-violent harassment and humiliation, such as racial profiling in which drivers are temporarily detained, often for driving in certain areas or for driving certain types of cars. At worst, it includes many kinds of extreme violence. Each new incident involving police mistreatment of an African-American,

Hispanic-American, or other minority - and particularly those that receive media attention - reinforces a general belief that some residents are to be subjected to particularly harsh treatment and racial bias.

These facts captured my attention, and I turned my attention to lynchings that have occurred in my lifetime. I define these lynchings as extrajudicial killings either when police kill before any charges can be filed or when citizens invoke their white privilege and kill folks whom they think are deserving of elimination. This is frequently a form of violence in which a mob, under the pretext of administering justice without trial, executes a presumed offender, often after inflicting torture and corporal mutilation. The term "lynch law" refers to a self-constituted court that imposes sentence on a person without due process of law. Lynchings are carried out by law enforcement offices and non-law enforcement groups. However, I limit my observation to those acts that involve law enforcement, including the FBI, state highway patrols, sheriffs, and local police departments. Many white citizens have murdered blacks, and the courts simply responded with a wink and a nod.

I distinguish racial terror lynchings from hangings and mob violence that followed some criminal trial process or that were committed against non-minorities without the threat of terror. Those lynchings were a crude form of punishment that did not have the features of terror lynchings directed against racial minorities who were being threatened and menaced in multiple ways. I also distinguish terror lynchings from racial violence and hate crimes that were prosecuted as criminal acts, although hate crimes are not recognized in many states in America. The lynchings I studied were acts of terrorism because they were carried out with impunity, sometimes in broad daylight. They could not be defined as frontier justice because they took place in communities where there was a functioning criminal justice system. In the decades before I was born, some spectacle lynchings were attended by the entire white community and conducted as celebratory acts of racial control and domination.

As I was beginning my formal education in the Laurel public schools, there was the case of Willie McGee, an African-American man from Laurel, MS who was sentenced to death in 1945 and executed on Tuesday, May 8, 1951, for the capital crime of raping a young white married woman in the predawn hours of November 2, 1945. The word on the street was that no such assault had taken place. Instead, the alleged victim and McGee had carried on in the past, but the husband found out, thereby leaving the wife with only one defense, i.e., rape. Four years after the lynching of Willie McGee, in 1955 came the Emmitt Till case. Till was a 14-year-old African-American who was accused of teasing a white store clerk, Carolyn Bryant. Her husband, Roy Bryant, and brother-in-law, J.W. Milam, kidnapped and brutally murdered Till, dumping his body in the Tallahatchie River. The newspaper coverage and murder trial galvanized a generation of young African-Americans to join the Civil Rights Movement out of fear that such an incident could happen to friends, family, or even themselves. Bryant and Milam maintained their innocence and would eventually be acquitted of the murder by an all-white, all-male jury. They later sold their story for $4,000 to *Look magazine*, bragging about the murder as a form of Southern justice implemented to protect white womanhood.

For African-Americans, the murder of Till was evidence of the decades-old codes of violence exacted upon black men and women who broke the rules of white supremacy in the Deep South, particularly for black males, who found themselves under constant threat of attack or death for mostly imagined sexual advances towards white women. Consequently, Till's murder reverberated a need for immediate change. Carolyn Bryant testified in court that Till had grabbed her hand, and after she pulled away, he had followed her behind the counter, clasped her waist, and using vulgar language, told her that he had been with white women before. At age 82, some 60 years later, Bryant confessed to Duke University professor Timothy B. Tyson that she had lied about this entire event. I have appended to this memoir a list of individuals known to have been lynched by police action since I was in first grade. The listing speaks to an ongoing travesty.

The tool for the police: qualified immunity

The question of how and why police culture does not acknowledge the constitutional rights of minority Americans is demonstrated by the brazenness of law enforcement officials as they violate their legal rights. This behavior of police agents is due in no small part to "qualified immunity." The irony of history is bedeviling. Police agents in America were originally designed to function as slave patrols. There was no penalty for abuse of Africans because Africans had no constitutional recognition. However, in 1871, Section 1983 of Title 42 of the United States Code was enacted by Congress as Section 1 of the Ku Klux Klan Act. The Klan Act was intended to protect recently freed slaves from the terror of antagonism perpetrated by supporters of the confederacy. Specifically, its purpose was to enforce the provisions of the Fourteenth Amendment to the US Constitution. Some labeled it the Civil Rights Act of 1871. The irony continues, since litigation outcomes over time have eroded the original intent of the legislation. As currently interpreted, Section 1983 provides damages remedies against state and local government officials and local governments for violations of a citizen's constitutional rights. Under the doctrine of qualified immunity, public officials are held to a comparatively much lower standard. They can be held only insofar as they violate rights that are "clearly established" in light of existing case law; such a standard shields law enforcement from countless constitutional violations. In the Supreme Court's statement, it protects "all but the plainly incompetent or those who knowingly violate the law." Litigation over time has, for all practical purposes, changed qualified immunity to absolute immunity.

The tragic killing of African-American George Floyd by Minneapolis police officer Derek Chauvin placed in focus serious deficiencies in §1983 and excessive force law. The Supreme Court's jurisprudence is so heavily tilted in favor of police officers and municipalities sued under §1983 that excessive force claimants often do not have a realistic chance of recovery. A *N.Y. Times* editorial appearing shortly after the police killing of Mr. Floyd charged that the US Supreme Court "has enabled a culture of [police] violence and abuse by eviscerating [§1983] to provide police officers [with] nearly limitless immunity" for their official actions. The editorial explains how qualified immunity has been employed by the Supreme Court and lower courts to deprive victims of police use of excessive force of a meaningful civil rights damages remedy.

The George Floyd killing was not an isolated incident; there have been many other unjustified police uses of deadly force: Michael Brown in Ferguson, MO.; Freddie Gray in Baltimore, MD.; and Eric Garner and Amadou Diallo in New York City. A police officer choked Eric Garner to death even though he was suspected only of selling loose cigarettes. Four police officers fired 41 shots killing Amadou Diallo, a 23-year-old immigrant with no criminal record whom the police thought had a gun but, in fact, was unarmed.

My final narrative regarding gaps and how I live with them outlines the various gaps I have experienced and continue to experience. Tracing the nuance of my experience begins with a Bible story. There are two men named Mephibosheth in the Bible, both direct descendants of King Saul and both rather unfortunate. The lesser-known Mephibosheth was a son of Saul and his concubine, Rizpah. The better-known Mephibosheth was the son of Jonathan, son of Saul, whose name appears to have originally been Merib-Baal (and is used as such by the chronicler). Although he lived long before I was born, there are experiences in his life to which I can relate. This Mephibosheth was 5 years old when reports arrived that his father and grandfather had fallen in the battle of Mount Gilboa, according to the Biblical narrative. When the news about the deaths of Saul and Jonathan arrived from Jezreel, Mephibosheth's nurse took him and fled in panic. In her haste to escape potential assassins, the nurse picked him up and ran off, but dropped the boy, and as a result, he became lame in both feet for the rest of his life (2nd Samuel 4:4). I was not born into royalty or prominence, nor did I have any employed nurse, aside from my mother, who could not send anyone an invoice for her services. The similarity is the fact of Mephibosheth's physical condition that left him unable to walk. While I had no such physical condition, I believe the legal reality of my experiences in Jim Crow, second-class citizenship while growing up in what had been the Confederate South were obstinate factors that I had to overcome. Fortunately for me, I was born after there came a new attitude about civil rights in the country. As I was graduating high school, many doors opened and paved the way for me to rise above the circumstance of the time, place, and condition of my growing up.

Soon after David gave an audience to Mephiboseth, he granted him residency in his mansion. For some years beforehand, Mephibosheth lived in the house of Machir, the son of Ammiel, in Lo-debar in the land of Gilead. In order to fulfill his covenant with Jonathan, David wished to exercise loving kindness toward anyone "left over of the house of Saul." A former servant in Saul's house, a man named Ziba, told King David about Mephibosheth, who at that time was living in the house of Machir. During the introductions, Mephiboseth asked why the king should care about a "dead dog," referring to himself. David consoled him, made him a landlord, and invited him to dine with him and his sons frequently. Though lame and stripped of his honor, Mephibosheth appears to have managed to acquire himself a wife, because when David reinstated him, Mephibosheth had a young son named Mica. Mephibosheth's labeling himself as a "dead dog" implied that he had a low opinion of himself. He was born long before Maslow's hierarchy of needs had been added to the canon (the motivational theory in psychology comprising a five-tier model of human needs, often depicted as hierarchical levels within a pyramid - from the bottom of the hierarchy upwards, the needs are: physiological, safety, love and belonging, esteem, and self-actualization). It is clear, at least in my mind, that Mephiboseth experienced only limited physiological needs prior to his introduction to David. By bringing Mephiboseth into the king's palace, they introduced him to love and belonging, opportunities for self-esteem, and even the chance for self-actualization. In contrast, in my childhood and onward, I was blessed with the fostering of all of the needs in Maslow's hierarchy. Yet, I have not been able to, at all times, live above the circumstances of being black in America.

Notwithstanding the strength of this nuance, I fully disassociate myself from Mephibosheth's behavior when there was a time when he could acknowledge the thanks for David's generosity. Mephibosheth appears to have been not so grateful for all of his newly found amenities while living in the palace. When Absalom revolted against David and the latter chose to get out of his son‘s way, Ziba brought provisions to David and his men, and he also told him that Mephibosheth was back in Jerusalem, expecting that the kingdom of Saul would be returned to him (2nd Samuel 16:1). But, Absalom was killed and the peace reestablished, and Mephibosheth told David that Ziba had tricked all of them and that he had never been disloyal to David (2nd Samuel 19:24-30). Whether David believed him or Ziba, or both in equal degree, isn‘t clear, but it seems that either he deems the matter not to be important or the task was not insurmountable for Mephibosheth himself to handle (2nd Samuel 19:29). What is clear, however, is that when the Gibeonites demanded the execution of seven sons of Saul, David spared the life of Mephibosheth, son of Jonathan (2nd Samuel 21:7).

It is true, at least from my vantage point, that suffering breeds character and character breeds faith. These are the elements that cause one to live above life's circumstances, and it is my prescription for getting through the gap we live in on this earth. From contemporary individuals, I draw from Martha Mason in her memoir, *Breath: Life in the Rhythm of an Iron Lung.* She lived on her back, encased in an 800-pound iron lung in which she spent 61 years until she died in 2009 at age 71. The first 10 years of her life were full of typical childhood fun. She was energetic and smart, living a carefree, rural life during the 1940s. Then, in September 1948 - three days after her brother died of it - Mason contracted polio, which took away her ability to breathe on her own. After a year's recovery, her doctor told her: "You're basically an excellent mind and an exuberant spirit locked inside an inert body - a prison. Can you live with that?" She was 12 years old. She answered him, "no… but I can live above it." Her memoir describes how she kept that audacious promise, including graduating at the top of her Wake Forest class. Both Mephiboseth and Martha Mason experienced physical stress that I have not known, and I do not desire to replicate their experience.

There are also non-physical obstructs that we face in life. The non-physical obstructs are instances where social norms, or the status quo, are challenged. I have been inspired by two figures: Marcus Garvey and Eugene V. Debs. There were three decades between their birth dates, Debs' in 1855 and Garvey's in 1887. Debs was white, and Garvey was African-American. Both challenged the status quo, and both paid the price of losing their freedom due to imprisonment.

Eugene V. Debs was critical of traditional political and economic concepts, especially capitalism. He challenged the status quo; he saw the labor movement as a struggle between classes. After announcing his conversion to socialism in 1897, he led the establishment of the Socialist Party of America and was its candidate for US President five times between 1900 and 1920. Debs was president of the newly established American Railway Union when it won national prominence by conducting a successful strike against the Great Northern Railway Company in April 1894. He gained greater renown when he was sentenced to six months in jail in 1895 for his role in leading the Chicago Pullman Palace Car Company strike. He would later be imprisoned and sentenced to a 10-year prison term for having criticized the US government's prosecution of persons charged with violation of the 1917 Espionage Act in 1918. He was released from prison by presidential order in 1921; however, his US citizenship, which he had lost when he was convicted of sedition in 1918, was restored only posthumously in 1976, fifty years after his death.

Debs' offending speech is a study in socialist oration, with memorable lines like "the master class has always declared the wars; the subject class has always fought the battles" (These same sentiments could be heard at the dinner table at 115 Melon when I was growing up). Speaking from a gazebo in a city park, the Socialist Party leader denounced the "Junkers of Wall Street" for enslaving workers in industrial despotism, confidently heralded the coming of the cooperative commonwealth ("it is as vain to resist it as it would be to arrest the sunrise on the morrow"), and exhorted listeners to join the Socialist Party, "the builders of the beautiful world that is to be."

As one historian notes, Debs "said nothing he had not said many times before and had referred to the war but once." However, federal authorities, gripped by World War I hysteria, had heard enough. They arrested him for intending to "cause and incite insubordination, disloyalty, mutiny, and refusal of duty in the military," as well as for trying to "obstruct the recruiting and enlistment service of the United States." Debs' years of living in harsh prison conditions adversely affected his health, and he spent long periods of the remainder of his life in a sanatorium in suburban Chicago. He is quoted as saying "it does not matter what others may say, or think, or do, as long as I am sure that I am right with myself and the cause. There are so many who seek refuge in the popular side of a great question. As a socialist, I have long since learned how to stand alone."

For the record, I am not a socialist, but I admire those who have the courage for their convictions. Even those who are racist are honest in their beliefs, and their behavior alerts me to seek alternative routes rather than travel alongside them as I travel through life.

I also draw from the life experiences of Marcus Garvey. Marcus Garvey was a proponent of the Black Nationalism and Pan-Africanism movements, inspiring the Nation of Islam and the Rastafarian movement. Born in Jamaica in 1887, Marcus Garvey was an orator for the Black Nationalism and Pan-

Africanism movements, to which end he founded the Universal Negro Improvement Association and African Communities League. Garvey advanced a Pan-African philosophy which inspired a global mass movement, known as Garveyism. He wrote a paper called "Negro World" during the Harlem Renaissance, which highlighted the accomplishments of African-Americans and the ideas that African-Americans deserved respect for. He returned to Jamaica in 1912 and founded the Universal Negro Improvement Association (UNIA) with the goal of uniting all of African diaspora to "establish a country and absolute government of their own." After communicating with Booker T. Washington, the American educator who founded Tuskegee Institute, Garvey traveled to the United States in 1916 to raise funds for a similar venture in Jamaica. He settled in New York City and formed a UNIA chapter in Harlem to promote a separatist philosophy of social, political, and economic freedom for blacks. In 1918, Garvey began publishing the widely distributed newspaper *Negro World* to convey his message.

By 1919, Marcus Garvey and UNIA had launched the Black Star Line, a shipping company that would establish trade and commerce between Africans in the USA, the Caribbean, South and Central America, Canada, and Africa. At the same time, Garvey started the Negro Factories Association, a series of companies that would manufacture marketable commodities in every big industrial center in the Western Hemisphere and Africa.

In August 1920, UNIA claimed 4 million members and held its first international convention at Madison Square Garden in New York City. Before a crowd of 25,000 people from all over world, Marcus Garvey spoke of having pride in African history and culture. Many found his words inspiring, but not all. Some established black leaders found his separatist philosophy ill-conceived. W.E.B. DuBois, a prominent black leader and officer of the NAACP, called Garvey "the most dangerous enemy of the Negro race in America." Garvey felt DuBois was an agent of the white elite. But W.E.B DuBois wasn't the worst adversary of Garvey; history would soon reveal FBI Director J. Edgar Hoover 's fixation on ruining Garvey for his radical ideas. Hoover felt threatened by the black leader, fearing he was inciting blacks across the country to stand up in militant defiance.

Hoover referred to Garvey as a "notorious Negro agitator" and, for several years, desperately sought ways to find damning personal information on him, even going so far as to hire the first black FBI agent in 1919 in order to infiltrate Garvey's ranks and spy on him. "They placed spies in the UNIA," said historian Winston James. "They sabotaged the Black Star Line. The engines... of the ships were actually damaged by foreign matter being thrown into the fuel." Hoover would use the same methods decades later to obtain information on black leaders like MLK and Malcolm X.

In 1922, Marcus Garvey and three others (UNIA officials) were charged with mail fraud involving the Black Star Line. The trial records indicate several improprieties occurred in the prosecution of the case. It didn't help that the shipping line's books contained many accounting irregularities. On June 23, 1923, Garvey was convicted and sentenced to prison for five years. Claiming to be a victim of a politically motivated miscarriage of justice, he appealed his conviction, but was denied. In 1927, he was released from prison and deported to Jamaica.

He began serving his sentence at Atlanta Prison in 1925. It's from there that he authored his famous paper "First Message to the Negroes of the World from Atlanta Prison." In it, he wrote: "After my enemies are satisfied, in life or death I shall come back to you to serve even as I have served before. In life, I shall be the same; in death, I shall be a terror to the foes of Negro liberty. If death has power, then count on me in death to be the real Marcus

Garvey I would like to be. If I may come in an earthquake, or a cyclone, or plague, or pestilence, or as God would have me, then be assured that I shall never desert you and make your enemies triumph over you."

Clearly, Garvey was not without controversy; he collaborated with outspoken segregationist and white supremacist Mississippi Senator Theodore Bilbo to promote a reparations initiative. His collaboration generated mostly negative comments from "leaders" in the black American community. He supported Congressional passage of the Greater Liberia Act of 1939, which would deport 12 million African-Americans to Liberia at federal expense to relieve unemployment. The act failed in Congress, and Garvey lost even more support among the black population. Garvey's philosophy is perhaps best exemplified in the following quote: "We must canonize our own saints, create our own martyrs, and elevate to positions of fame and honor black men and women who have made their distinct contributions to our racial history… I am the equal of any white man; I want you to feel the same way."

Doubtlessly, hindsight is 20-20; Garvey's collaboration with a white supremacist to achieve a policy outcome based on racial segregation is hardly what I would consider to be a brilliant idea. Nevertheless, his message of pride and dignity inspired many in the early days of the Civil Rights Movement in the 1950s and 1960s. To be sure, he had the courage of his convictions, and in the end, the US government targeted him as an enemy of the state. Garvey laid the groundwork for Kwame Ture (a.k.a. Stokely Carmichael) and Imamu Amear Baraka (a.k.a. LeRoi Jones). Both had scrapes with the law. Baraka was frequently arrested and spent *time* in *jail.* Also, Kwame was sentenced to prison on a gun charge. I relate to Garvey and the unknown disciples he influenced because of what they endured in the fight for human rights. I did not see the insides of a prison, and I am remorseful that did not have the courage to fight as others did. My equivalent of the Garvey experience and the experience of Eugene V. Debs was the fact of being collateral in the *Geier v. Blanton* case in a US district court in Tennessee.

I have traveled to many places in my life and time; I've seen every state in the CONUS except the Dakotas, traveled to and worked in more than a dozen African countries and five Southeast Asian countries, and visited about a fourth of the countries in Europe, all the countries that border the United States, and the Caribbean. Beyond what I observed during those travels and experiences, I read of the trials of folk like Martha Mason, Eugene V. Debs, Harriet Tubman, Marcus Garvey, Martin Luther King, Jr., Rosa Parks, Barbara Jordan, Gwendolyn Zoharah Simmons, Diane Nash, Kwame Ture, Imamu Baraka, and other civil rights heroes of the 1960s. Yet, few human beings have so thoroughly captured my fascination as Nelson Rolihlahla Mandela.

On three separate occasions, my field research brought me to South Africa (2003, 2004, and 2007), and on each of these trips, during my personal time, I took the ferry to Robben Island, the prison where Mr. Mandela had been incarcerated for 25 years and 8 months on a charge of treason and conspiracy. At the time of my visit, the prison had been transformed into an historical museum. Former prisoners who had been incarcerated with Mr. Mandela served as tour guides. They told us their brutal inhuman conditions of imprisonment. One whom I acutely remember was the individual who identified himself as Tu Lani Mbosse. Upon his initial introduction, he calmly stated that he was once a prisoner at Robben Island because of his conviction as a terrorist. In his soft-spoken voice, he stated that his "crime" was fire-bombing a building. Quickly, he added that there were no casualties and that his action and the actions of his fellow prisoners came about because the government was not inclined at that time to hear the voices of the black South Africans.

There was one story that poignantly registered with me and remains today in my consciousness. In prison, the inmates were under constant surveillance; they had no privacy. However, one place the guards did not enter was the outhouse facility on the prison grounds. It was there that Mandela and his fellow prisoners kept each other abreast of developments outside the prison, most significantly, the activities of the African National Congress (ANC). As a resistance movement, the ANC was preceded by a number of black resistance movements, among them, Umkosi Wezintaba, which formed in South Africa between 1890 and 1920.

The organization was initially founded as the South African Native National Congress (SANNC) in Bloemfontein in January 1912 with the aim of fighting for the rights of black South Africans. The organization was renamed the ANC in 1923. The African National Congress is now South Africa's governing party and has been in power since the transition to democracy in April 1994. While the organization's early period was characterized by political inertia due to power struggles and lack of resources, increasing repression and the entrenchment of white minority rule galvanized the party. As a result of the establishment of apartheid, its aversion to dissent by black people, and brutal crackdown on political activists, the ANC, together with the South African Communist Party (SACP), formed a military wing, uMkhonto we Sizwe (Spear of the Nation/ MK) in 1961.

Through MK, the ANC waged the armed struggle and obtained support from some African countries and the Soviet bloc for its activities. With the increasing internal dissent, international pressure, and the collapse of the Soviet Union, the apartheid government was forced to enter into negotiations with the ANC. This saw the collapse of apartheid and the ushering in of democratic rule in 1994. The meetings in the outhouse contributed to strategies that would see the success of the organization despite the opposition

A retired CIA agent, Donald Rickard, confirmed the US government's role in Mandala's 1962 arrest. The US and Britain had labeled Mandela as a terrorist much in the same fashion that FBI Director J. Edgar Hoover had labeled Marcus Garvey as one a few decades earlier.

In 1961, he had been arrested for treason, and although acquitted, he was arrested again in 1962 for illegally leaving the country. The South African government convicted and sentenced him to five years at Robben Island Prison, but he was put on trial again in 1964 on charges of sabotage. Such burdens would have collapsed lesser men, but the prisoners at Robben Island would not be denied. In school, Mandela studied law and became one of South Africa's first black lawyers. In the 1950s, he had been elected leader of the youth wing of the ANC liberation movement. When the government prohibited the ANC for racial reasons, Mandela organized a secret military movement. He had previously been involved in peaceful protests, but when they were met with violence from the government, he went on to support an armed movement.

During these times in South Africa, there was the simultaneous and similar civil rights struggle in the USA for access to education, public accommodation, and the ballot. The culture of white racism in both places proved to be daunting; in both locations, black people were forced to live life in the gap between what was humanly right and the day-to-day reality of second-class citizenship.

Mandela was a transformational figure; to be a transformer requires planning and having the vision to chart the course, as well as the skills to execute it. To be transformational is to have the courage of one's convictions, to sacrifice, to risk life and limb, to lay it all on the line.

After his release from prison, the ANC orchestrated his election to president of South Africa from 1994 to 1999. He was the first black president of South Africa, and the first president to be elected in a fully representative election. His government focused on destroying the apartheid life and culture that had burdened the black South Africans. His efforts were recognized by the Norwegian Nobel Committee, a five-member committee appointed by the Parliament of Norway. Mandela received the Nobel Peace Prize in 1993 for peacefully destroying the apartheid regime and laying the foundation for democracy. In addition to the Nobel Peace Prize, he won over 250 other awards. After retirement from politics, Mandela started the Nelson Mandela Foundation that focused on combating HIV/AIDS and supported rural development and school construction.

We are all unavoidably products of our life circumstances. All of us were born into some kind of circumstance by our race, religion, country of origin, ethnic background, or some combination of other factors. It is the family/situation we are raised in, and most of us are trapped forever in the conditions of that circumstance. This is why the world struggles so much to rise above life's circumstances. Our past will not leave us alone, but it is important to move through and rise above the circumstances to which we are tethered.

Moreover, the circumstances of the present show up every day in some kind of way. It is the situation of our living. How we deal with that is a function of the circumstance of our early living. Past meets the present, and that past dominates our reaction to the current set of circumstances. It does not matter what the particulars of that are; this is what happens everywhere, all the time. If one grows up black in the US, poor, with one parent, and in a ghetto environment, then those circumstances shape life views forever. If one grows up white, in a middle upper-class home, with both parents, and in a safe neighborhood, then one's way of life will be characterized by a very different paradigm. The world is not the same to each of these individuals. However, that is the fact of life: our individual pasts bumping into the current present. Often, this causes stress and friction. Past colliding with present is the way of life. Each of us bringing our history into the mechanism of history-making, each of us distorting in some unique way, our interpretation of what is going on, we each face common circumstances in unique ways. That makes 'common' unique to each of us and simultaneously makes for great frustration and conflict. My life and work experiences on this planet have taught me some ways to live above life's circumstances. I conclude this discussion by offering my prescription for doing so.

1. **Be clear about what defines you and resist the bigotry of low expectations (even from well-meaning acquaintances).**

It is important to know who you are and thereby move from the shore of insecurity to find true intimacy in victory. Understand how grace elevates and that each of us was created with a purpose, and be crystal clear about what makes you tick. It is tempting to hear words of praise from half-hearted acquaintances; the travesty occurs when we succumb to those words, especially when the words are intended to lower expectations of ourselves. I still remember my high school geometry teacher, Sammy Malone, who would often quote Robert Browning: "A man's reach should exceed his grasp, or what's a heaven for?"

2. **Live according to values that stand independent of circumstance.**

Personal values allow one to stand on solid ground. These values may be aligned with culture, but personal values reside above culture, political ideology, and social class. Own the fact that each of us is part of something greater. Build a life around values such as service and love and compassion. I learned from my dad integrity, accountability, candor, commitment, dependability, honesty, and honor. I learned achievement, accomplishment, credibility, challenge, and determination from my mother. These values serve as the infrastructure for my moral compass. My parents did not prepare a syllabus and lesson plans for my education, but they modeled behavior that I study years after their physical demise. I have come to learn from the school of life that individuals experience greater fulfillment when they live by their values. I trust that when I shall no longer live on this earth, I will have left lessons of integrity and ethics, respect and innovation. I pray for wisdom, foresight, and discernment.

3. **Practice living above circumstances before things get difficult.**

The time to learn how to live above challenging circumstance is the time to survey matters that make us happy, i.e., analyze when things are going well. This simplistic statement is not so black and white. There is the ever-present possibility of overthinking, overanalyzing, etc., but nevertheless, we must avoid the moral hazard of certainty even (and especially) when things are still going well. I have found it instructive to avoid being swept up into a situation based on the wrong values, values or behaviors that run counter to my sense of right versus wrong. The lesson is to learn how to avoid putting my eggs in the wrong baskets. Learn the difference between values that last and things that will ultimately falter. I remember the guidance from the book of Micah: "Though I fall, I will *rise*; though I sit in the darkness [of distress], the Lord is a light for me." I also remember Maya Angelou's poem "Still I Rise," an empowering poem about the struggle to overcome prejudice and injustice. When these thoughts are ingested by victims of wrongdoing, the poem becomes an anthem, a beacon of hope for the oppressed and downtrodden straight from the book of Micah. There is no class or syllabus that teaches us how to arrive at that state. You know it when you arrive.

4. Understand that relationships count.

Make the choices that value relationships ahead of the bottom line. Spend time with family and friends. If you are married, engage your marriage as a priority, not an afterthought. Honor your parents and friends. Remember: in the end, it's relationships that matter most. The wise among us know to invest in things that are timeless while realizing that time, chance, and death destroy all our best efforts. The wise among us know that we should invest in something that outlasts work, wealth, and power, that being righteousness, religion, and relationships.

5. Invest fiscally (and non-fiscally) in things that are timeless.

In my monthly budget, charitable giving is important. Such (self-acknowledged) generosity involves self-sacrifice, not my leftovers. I learned from my first-grade teacher, Idella Washington, that if we are generous with what we have, we won't miss it so much when it's gone. And yet, I know that for households that live from paycheck to paycheck, charitable giving does not come easily. I struggle with that reality. Yet, I recall Luke 6:38: "Give, and it shall be given unto you; good measure, pressed down, and shaken together, and running over, shall men give into your bosom. For with the same measure that ye mete withal, it shall be measured to you again. I know this to be true." *Things* have a beginning, a middle, and an end. But, only in our hearts we *can* grasp the *timeless.*

6. Do not look to other people for validation.

This was difficult for me since I had, at one time, been like the protagonist John Oakhurst in *the Outcasts of Poker's Flat,* a short story written in 1869 that I studied in Bertha Marshall's high school English literature class. Redemption is an important theme in the story. As the title implies, the characters are outcasts, expelled from so-called respectable society by its self-appointed moral guardians. Yet, in the midst of extreme adversity, they show themselves to be more moral than those who banished them. The protagonist was Oakhurst, a character of noble qualities who was exiled not due to his unsavory nature, but out of revenge and spite when he successfully wins a large amount of money from the leaders of the town. I never won a large amount of money, but I did gain a goodly amount of social collateral in the early days of my role as administrator at TSU. In the final analysis, my social collateral was insufficient to save my position in 1979. Yet, as did John Oakhurst, I modeled a character of good moral values (at the expense of inviting charges of hyperbolic claims), moved beyond the negative judgements of others, and found true intimacy in victory, as my family life and my subsequent job placements attest to.

7. Develop a clear vision of your destination.

A successful destination brand articulates ambition, raises expectations, makes a promise of quality, and keeps it. Planning, development, operations, branding, and marketing must be managed for the destination, as well as for the individual attractors, services, and infrastructure elements. Such a vision can come only when one develops a purpose for his or her life, and develops clear goals that come directly from the heart. A vision is more enduring than the temporary ups and downs of circumstance. Successful leaders take the time to think through and develop a clear picture of how life will look in 1, 3, and 5-year increments. Only a leader can think about the future and plan for the future each day. Most people have a general idea about what they want for their lives. The capacity to relay that vision to others is the challenge. This is something that sets apart a leader from the rest. The main quality that all leaders share is that they have a clear and exciting vision for the future, and crucially, the ability to communicate that vision.

8. Learn to distinguish between the temporary and the eternal.

When we understand what parts of our life line up under "temporary" and what parts can be listed as "eternal," then it's not so hard to maintain perspective when the temporary stuff threatens to overwhelm. In 2nd Corinthians 4, we find these words: "So we fix our eyes not on what is seen, but on what is unseen, since what is seen is temporary, but what is unseen is eternal..." To allow the eternal to give us peace requires a measure of effort. It is easy to allow the temporary - the day in and day out - to consume all of our energy and effort. As we grow older and wiser, we choose our battles and learn to distinguish between folly and sagacity. When I was a younger man, the temporary was clothed in testosterone, and my vision was limited. Temporary satisfaction, temporary fulfillment, temporary meaning... all come to an end, but you must not succumb, or else life will leave you with a terrible emptiness.

Richard Simmons writes about a meeting at which a speaker stood in front of a large group of people with a roll of stickers in his hand. Behind him, on the platform, were tables filled with props that represented the stuff of our lives... a matchbox car, a dollhouse, and a tiny desk that stood for jobs. The speaker roamed the stage and placed a red sticker on each item. He explained to the crowd that they may not be able to see it from where they were sitting, but each sticker contained the same word: TEMPORARY. The speaker said: "Everything that I am putting a sticker on is temporary. It will not last. It will fade away. We invest our emotions in them because when we acquire it, it gives us a little thrill, and we think that it will last. But it does not. It fades. And eventually, so will what we acquire." Wise people build their lives around what is eternal and squeeze in what is temporary. There was once a poll in which the participants, all over 95 years old, were asked, "if you could live your lives over again, what would you do differently?" One of the top answers was, "I would invest my life in more endeavors that would live on after I am gone." They had this yearning for their lives to count for something permanent, something that will last over time. There was an unmistakable desire for the imperishable... a life of significance.

9. Be reasonable.

Keep a sense of balance. Ask for help from those around you. Don't think you have to be the strong and silent one. Remember to live in community. Let yourself be loved and cared for. Striking a perfect balance between career and family has always been a challenge in the modern-day USA. Our schedules are busier than ever, which causes our work or personal lives to suffer. The search for work-life balance is a process in which people seek to change things in accordance with changes in their own priorities, whether physical, psychological, or both, and these can be triggered in turn by factors such as age, changes in working conditions, the demands of new technology, and poor management. When one feels a greater sense of control and ownership over his/her own life, he/she is able to have better relationships with work colleagues and leave work issues at work and home issues at home.

10. If you are married, be the best spouse.

A healthy marriage involves a life of service, not selfishness. No one should get married unless they have found someone to whom they are willing to give their life in service. Love does not seek its own, but the good of the other. When two people go into a marriage with such an attitude, only good can come from the union. It's a lot easier to deal with a lost job or a financial challenge, or even a difficult child, when you are confident in your relationship with your spouse. The scriptures tell us in Ecclesiastes 4:9-12 that two are better than one. "Woe to them that are alone when they fall… for they have no one to lift them up."

In a previous chapter, I described the time I met my wife and, subsequently, her family, and when I introduced her to my family. At that point in time, I had no real idea of the blessing our marriage would yield. "Give me a pulley, a lever, and a place to stand," Archimedes is said to have promised, "and I will move the world." This apocryphal quote from the Greek mathematician, scientist, and inventor was referring to his work on buoyancy. I have come to relate the literal translation of the tool (pulley) as an expression of the gift of my marriage to Joy

Pulley. A pulley is a wheel with a groove along its edge that holds a rope or cable. Usually, two or more pulleys are used together. When pulleys are used together in this way, they reduce the amount of force needed to lift a load. Such has been the experience of 51 years of marriage. A crane uses pulleys to help lift heavy loads. Archimedes studied how things physically work, and during my life as Joy's husband, I have come to know firsthand what a spouse means to a relationship. I carry her heart with me; I am never without her... Anywhere I go, she goes; I fear no fate, for she is my fate; I want no world, for beautiful is she in my world; she is whatever a moon has always meant and whatever a sun will always sing.

Epilogue

Throughout much of this narrative, I may have inadvertently mused that gloomy clouds hang over the heads of the generations that follow mine (the fourth generation). If that nuance was conveyed, I want to immediately disabuse it. There is indeed a silver lining in the clouds over the heads of the subsequent generations. There is abundant evidence to suggest that the future of my nephews and nieces have begun to "walk right up to the sun." Since the end of the Civil War, we have leapfrogged over decades of policy neglect that fostered generations of negative experiences. When I researched the life and times of my great-grandparents, I saw low wages, menial occupations, and unfriendly governments. During the days, months, and years that immediately followed emancipation, it was illegal for Africans to learn in a formal or recognized school setting; these times ushered into existence the Black Codes, laws designed to govern the conduct of free blacks. The truth is that such a culture of white supremacy was not limited to the South; many northern states had them as well (Connecticut, Ohio, Illinois, Indiana, Michigan, and New York). In 1832, in most states, there was a distinction in respect to political privileges of whites and free blacks. The codes were essentially replacements for slave codes.

As with most of my narrative, I have connected my story to the prevailing culture through a popular song or album. In this instance, the recording popularized by the 1970s group War, *The World is a Ghetto*, comes to mind. The recording spoke of the years of the presidency of Richard Nixon. Music festivals captured the nuance of the proponents of racial equality, women's liberation, and egalitarianism. Woodstock, a musical festival held in August 1969, dominated the talk and television social commentary. Many of the soul artists, such as War, did not appear on the three-day musical festival on a New York farm that attracted an audience of 400,000. Jimi Hendrix was one of the few black artists who performed, although performances by Janis Joplin and Creedence Clearwater Revival were not out of line with the black experience. The nuance of that three-day event was in lockstep with the movement. The group *War* was a musical crossover band that fused elements of rock, funk, jazz, Latin, rhythm and blues, and reggae. *The World Is a Ghetto* is one of the few black rock recordings that became a classic within the pan-African community. The song highlighted the challenges of poverty among plenty. Other War recordings, like "Deliver the Word" and "Four Cornered Room," could have been background music for a movie about the majority of urban black families in the USA. For those of us who were "down for the revolution," these phrases captured the moment.

Although "Ghetto," "Four Cornered Room," and "Deliver the Word" were scintillating and mesmerizing, they were not the only catchy tunes that brought attention to our reality. Another set of artists characterized the spirit of upcoming generations of the Sampson family. I enjoyed the Fifth-Dimension recordings such as *Stone Soul Picnic*; Earth, Wind, and Fire's *That's the way of the World*; Stevie Wonder's *Songs in the Key of Life*; and Edwin Hawkins' *O Happy Day*. Aretha Franklin with the Southern California Youth Choir could also be the background music to characterize my generation. My tapes evoke memories and aspirations that embraced the sounds of the Temptations, Delphonics, Blue Magic, Marvin Gaye, the O'Jays, Nancy Wilson, Cannonball Adderley, Anita Baker, and Les McCann, etc. I admit these tunes that span over two decades would, from time to time, float in my head. I acknowledge that many of my treasured relatives may not have heard of them and may not even appreciate all my life experiences. After all, I am on the cusp of the Silent Generation and the Baby Boomer Generation. My nephews and nieces are products of Generation X, Millennials, and beyond. Each generation has its own culture, eyes, ears, and experiences. I know that at least a few members of the successive generation appreciate some of my sounds, but they also listen to Tupac Shakur and rap music. Among the fifth and sixth generations of Sampsons are museum curators, doctorates, purchasing officers for the US Department of Defense, private sector and public sector engineers, ministers, K-12 teachers, school principals, newspaper editors, military soldiers, truck drivers, search engine optimization consultants, web developers, attorneys, private sector buying agents, law enforcement agents, court officers (e.g., judges), military soldiers, logistics managers, emergency room nurses, medical technicians, maintenance superintendents, service occupations employers, chefs, entrepreneurs, small business owners, etc. Their lines of work are dramatically different than those occupations held by my ancestors in generations one through three. At the same time, I know that what one does for a living does not define his or her character. It does not matter who you are; your character will be defined by your actions. Many times, all we have is our character, and if our character is bad, people will have very little to do with us. I am proud that post-fourth generation members are homeowners; some routinely travel to international locations as part of their jobs, and they all vote! I know that I and my parents, grandparents, and great-grandparents are proud of how they have turned out. They are the epitome of being young, gifted, and black.

Traveling through the summer forest of my mind, I again enter the cockpit of my time machine as I soar to 35,000 feet. I hear the refrain of the O'Jays' *Family Reunion* harmonizing about familial gatherings and moveable feasts after long periods of separation.

My memoir is a product of travels through the summer forest of my mind. These excursions caused me to reflect on my life experiences and learned thoughts that sprang from my readings and discussions. Those journeys caused me to reflect on, so far, seven decades of life on this planet. I have stared disappointment, failure, success, and exhilaration in the face. In many of my journeys, I have soared to 35,000 feet and, thus, come to agree with B.F. Skinner: failure is not always a mistake; it may simply be the best one can do under the circumstances. The real mistake is to stop trying.

When I look back on all the perils through which I have passed, all the mighty foes that have fallen in battle, and all the dark, deadly, frustrating designs life has had me experience, I have come to affirm that there is no justification for me to fear the future. Despite the reality that the world is unfair and unjust, we have come safely through the worst. For most of mankind, imagination is more robust than knowledge; myth is more potent than history; dreams are more powerful than facts. As did Ricky Romain, I refuse to accept the view that, as a people, we are tragically bound to a starless midnight of racism and war. I believe, as did Martin Luther King, that unarmed truth and unconditional love will have the final word. I have become convinced that those who have felt the deepest grief are best able to experience supreme happiness. Unfortunately, we must come to know what it is to die so that we may appreciate the enjoyments of life.

Figure 6 February 1969

February 2019

Table 2. Partial listing of white citizen and police killings of blacks since my first grade				
Name	**Year of Death**	**Place**	**Sex**	**Circumstance**
Willie McGhee	1951	Laurel, MS	Male	alleged rape of a white woman
Emmitt Till	1955	Money, MS	Male	whistled at a white woman
Rev. George Lee	1955	Midnight, MS	Male	organizer of voting rights
Lamar Smith	1955	Brookhaven, MS	Male	civil rights activist
Mack Charles Parker	1959	Lumberton, MS	Male	charged with rape of a white woman
Herbert Lee	1961	Liberty, MS	Male	civil rights activist
Addie Mae Collins	1963	Birmingham, AL	Female	worshipping while black
Cynthia Wesley	1963	Birmingham, AL	Female	worshipping while black
Carole Robertson	1963	Birmingham, AL	Female	worshipping while black
Denise McNair	1963	Birmingham, AL	Female	worshipping while black

Table 2. Partial listing of white citizen and police killings of blacks since my first grade				
Name	**Year of Death**	**Place**	**Sex**	**Circumstance**
Medgar Evers	1963	Jackson, MS	Male	civil rights activist
James Chaney	1964	Liberty, MS	Male	SNCC involvement
Louis Allen	1964	Liberty, MS	Male	witnessed the murder of Herbert Lee by a white lawmaker
Andrew Goodman*	1964	Money, MS	Male	support of black rights while being white
Michael Schwerner*	1964	Money, MS	Male	support of black civil rights as a white man
Jimmie Lee Jackson	1965	Selma, AL	Male	civil rights activist
Vernon Dahmer	1966	Hattiesburg, MS	Male	civil rights organizer
Rebecca Brown	1967	Newark, NJ	Female	in proximity to protests
Martin Luther King, Jr	1968	Memphis, TN	Male	being MLK

Table 2. Partial listing of white citizen and police killings of blacks since my first grade				
Name	**Year of Death**	**Place**	**Sex**	**Circumstance**
Fred Hampton	1969	Chicago, IL	Male	civil rights leader
Michael Donald	1981	Mobile, AL	Male	first white officer convicted of murder
Amadou Diallo	1999	Bronx, NY	Male	mistaken identity
Roger Owensby	2000	Cincinnati, OH	Male	chokehold while in police custody
Sean Bell	2006	Queens, NY	Male	mistaken identity
Oscar Grant III	2009	Oakland, CA	Male	mistaken ID, officer convicted
Damroy Henry	2010	Pleasantville, NY	Male	shoot first, then investigate
Aiyana Jones	2010	Detroit, MI	Female	misdirected raid by Detroit police
Kendrec McDade	2012	Pasadena, CA	Male	extrajudicial killing by police
Ramarley Graham	2012	Bronx, NY	Male	police(wrongfully) thought he had a gun

Table 2. Partial listing of white citizen and police killings of blacks since my first grade				
Name	**Year of Death**	**Place**	**Sex**	**Circumstance**
Trayvon Martin	2012	Samford, FL	Male	living while black
Santel Davis	2012	New York City	Female	overzealous police action
Tamir Rice	2014	Cleveland, OH	Male	playing while black
Michael Brown	2014	Ferguson, MO	Male	extrajudicial killing
Eric Garner	2014	Staten Island, NY	Male	extrajudicial killing
Laquan McDonald	2014	Chicago, IL	Male	officer charged and convicted, 2nd degree murder
Walter Scott	2015	N. Charleston, SC	Male	Officer Slager pled guilty to a civil rights violation
Sandra Bland	2015	Houston, TX	Female	driving while black
Freddy Gray	2015	Baltimore, MD	Male	broken back resulting from arrest

Table 2. Partial listing of white citizen and police killings of blacks since my first grade				
Name	**Year of Death**	**Place**	**Sex**	**Circumstance**
Ricky Ball	2015	Columbus, MS	Male	running from the police
Philando Castile	2016	St. Paul, MN	Male	overzealous police action
Terrance Crutcher	2016	Tulsa, OK	Male	overzealous police action
Korryn Gaines	2016	Baltimore, MD	Male	overzealous police action
Pamela Turner	2019	Baytown, TX	Female	overzealous police action
Atatina Jefferson	2019	Ft Worth, TX	Female	overzealous police action
Javier Ambler	2019	Austin, TX	Male	failure to dim auto lights
Elijah McClain	2019	Aurora, CO	Male	extrajudicial killing
Ahmed Aubrey	2020	Brunswick, GA	Male	vigilante law enforcement
Derrick Scott	2019	Oklahoma City, OK	Male	asphyxia while in police custody